# TEACHER'S EDITION

## Progress™
### English Language Arts

**3**

**For additional online resources, go to www.SadlierConnect.com
and enter the Teacher's Access Code:**

| State | Access Code | State | Access Code |
|---|---|---|---|
| Alabama | SBPI01AL3G | Missouri | SBPI29MO3G |
| Arizona | SBPI04AZ3E | New Jersey | SBPI34NJ32 |
| Arkansas | SBPI05AR3P | New York | SBPI36NY3C |
| California | SBPI06CA32 | North Carolina | SBPI37NC31 |
| Colorado | SBPI08CO3I | Ohio | SBPI39OH39 |
| Connecticut | SBPI09CT32 | Oklahoma | SBPI40OK3X |
| Florida | SBPI12FL35 | Pennsylvania | SBPI42PA3L |
| Georgia | SBPI13GA39 | South Carolina | SBPI45SC3K |
| Illinois | SBPI17IL3L | Tennessee | SBPI47TN3N |
| Kentucky | SBPI21KY3F | Texas | SBPI48TX3M |
| Louisiana | SBPI22LA3P | Virginia | SBP51VIUY7 |
| Massachusetts | SBPI25MA3T | Wisconsin | SBPI55WI3P |
| Michigan | SBPI26MI3H | All Other States | SBPINA230Z |
| Mississippi | SBPI28MS3R | | |

## Sadlier School

D1279157

# TEACHER'S EDITION

**Progress**
*English Language Arts*

**Cover:** *Series Design:* Studio Montage; *Title design:* Quarasan, Inc. **Photo Credits:** *Cover:* Alamy/B.A.E. Inc.: *bottom left.* Getty Images/John Burcham: *center;* GK Hart/Vikki Hart: *right;* Stocktrek: *top left.* Used under license from Shutterstock.com/nikolarisim: *background. Interior:* Corbis/Rob Lewine: T12; Ocean: T17; Dann Tardiff: T09. Used under license from Shutterstock.com/wavebreakmedia: T03. age fotostock/Blend Images/Michael Poehlman: 40 *top;* Index Stock/Group Inc HMS: 151 *inset;* IndiaPicture/Gurpal Singh Datta: 54 *top;* JGI/Jamie Grill: 192 *top;* KidStock: 10 *top;* Michael S. Nolan: 8 *top right.* Alamy/Blend Images/Andersen Ross: 178 *top;* Danita Delimont/Kenneth Garrett: 63; Everett Collection: 69; Glowimages RM: 242; ITAR-YASS Photo Agency: 58 *bottom;* jvphoto: 8 *bottom right;* National Geographic Image Collection/Karel Havlicek: 57; Pictorial Press Ltd: 64; Picture Press/Detlev van Ravenswaay: 244; The Print Collector: 66; Adrian Sheratt: 152; Dave Watts: 218; A.T. Willett: 147, 149. AP Photo/Tannen Maury: 150–151 *bottom;* Museum of Antiquities, Basel/Andreas F. Voegelin: 88. Blend Images/Andersen Ross: 148 *top.* Corbis: 8 *bottom left;* AP: 170; Blend Images/KidStock: 216 *top;* National Geographic Society/Hiram Bingham: 68; Robert Harding World Imagery/Andrew McConnell: 164; Wave: 156. Dreamstime.com/Ralf Broskvar: 72; Vicki France: 236 *inset;* Mature:130 *bottom.* Fotolia.com/Paul Moore: 215, 217. Getty Images/AFP/Randy Johnson: 154 *inset;* AFP/Laurent Fievet: 60; Bloomberg: 162; Paula Bronstein: 177, 179; Gamma-Keystone: 76; Hulton Archive: 74, 75; IMAGEMORE Co, Ltd: 127, 129; Jupiterimages: 230 *top;* NASA/SPL: 158;Lori Adamski Peek: 132 *bottom;* PhotoQuest: 168; SCIENCE SOURCE: 239; Harald Sund: 229, 231; SuperStock: 160; TPG: 166. Francis Latreille: 56. Library of Congress/Prints and Photograph Division, LC-USF34-004052: 169. NASA: 238, 245. Punchstock/Digital Vision: 128 *top.* Science Source: 157; Friedrich Sauer: 8 *top left.* Used under license from Shutterstock.com/cecoffman: 220; Lim ChewHow: 265, 275, 277; denispro: 75 *inset;*M. Dykstra: 130 *top,* 132 *top;* Jana Guothova: 10 *bottom,* 40 *bottom,* 54 *bottom,* 84 *bottom,* 98 *bottom,* 128 *bottom,* 148 *bottom,* 178 *bottom,* 192 *bottom,* 216 *bottom,* 230 *bottom;* Eduard Kyslynskyy: 58 *top;* Erik Lam: 180; Pius Lee: 53, 55; Ye Liew: 83; Timothy Michael Morgan: 70; nikolarisim: 1; Nikita Olga: 163; Mahesh Patil: 265 *inset,* 275 *inset;* Santia: 236 *bottom;* Brad Sauter: 182; Sinelyov: 278; SueC: 86; wong sze yuen: 98 *top;* WitR: 62. SuperStock/Blend Images: 84 *top.* **Text Credit:** Common Core State Standards Copyright © 2010. National Governors Association Center for Best Practices and Council of Chief State School Officers. All rights reserved. **Illustration Credits:** Tim Beaumont: 41, 42, 44, 99. Peter Bull Art Studio: 18, 19, 20. Smiljana Coh: 200, 201, 202, 204. Sally Wren Comport: 100, 101, 102, 104. Christine Jenny: 16. Kristin Kest: 24, 25, 26, 28. Glen Mullaly: 22, 106, 108, 109. Michele Noiset: 194, 195, 196, 198. Piotr Parda: 11, 30, 31, 32. Rob Schuster: 232, 233, 234, 240, 246, 248, 250, 251, 252, 257. Jago Silver: 12, 13, 14. Penny Weber: 118, 119, 120. Jason Wolff: 112, 113, 114, 116, 193, 206, 207, 208. **Lexile Trademark and Copyright Statement:** LEXILE®, LEXILE® FRAMEWORK, LEXILE® ANALYZER and the LEXILE® logo are trademarks of MetaMetrics, Inc., and are registered in the United States and abroad. The trademarks and names of other companies and products mentioned herein are the property of their respective owners. Copyright © 2012 MetaMetrics, Inc. All rights reserved.

**For additional online resources, go to sadlierconnect.com.**

William H. Sadlier, Inc.
9 Pine Street
New York, NY 10005-4700

Printed in the United States of America.
ISBN: 978-1-4217-3063-9
1 2 3 4 5 6 7 8 9 WEBC 18 17 16 15 14

# Contents

## Access Your Digital Resources

### Get Started

**1. Go to www.SadlierConnect.com**

**2. Log in**

Don't have a username and password? Teachers click "Get Started!" in the Teacher Registration section.

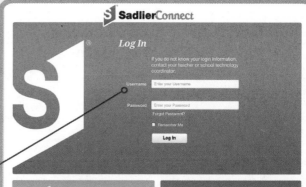

**3. Select your program to begin accessing content.**

With one username and password, you now have access to all your Sadlier Mathematics and English Language Arts content.

T3

# Contents

*continued next page*

# Contents

## Unit 4 | Text Types and Purposes: Write Informative/Explanatory Texts

## Unit 5 | Reading Literature: Craft and Structure

*continued next page*

# Contents

**Unit 6** | **Text Types and Purposes:**
**Write Nonfictional Narratives**

    *Establishing a Situation • Using Dialogue and Descriptions*
    *of Actions • Using Time-Order Words and Phrases • Providing*
    *a Strong Ending*

**Language**

**Unit 7** | **Reading Informational Text:**
**Craft and Structure**

*continued next page*

# Contents

**Unit 8** | **Text Types and Purposes:**
## Write Opinion Pieces

**Unit 9** | **Reading Literature:**
## Integration of Knowledge and Ideas

*continued next page*

# Contents

## Program Overview

Research indicates that high student performance results from alignment of curriculum, instruction, and assessment. *Progress English Language Arts* is a reading/language arts program that puts standards-based instruction into practice by aligning curriculum, instruction, and assessment in every unit, and at each grade level, K–8.

The foundation of *Progress English Language Arts* is the analysis and integration of state and national standards, curriculum guides and/or frameworks, current research on instruction and best classroom practices. Instruction in reading, writing, vocabulary, conventions of standard English, and speaking and listening is prioritized to create an instructional focus for each unit. Each element of the unit—including direct and guided instruction, and independent work—focuses on these critical skills, and provides students the range of encounters, varied practice opportunities, and levels of application necessary to gain the proficiencies required by the standards.

### In *Progress English Language Arts*, students will:

- Engage in close reading of high-quality, challenging informational and literary texts through a gradual-release of responsibility, leading to independent and proficient reading.

- Increase knowledge of history/social studies, science, and technical subjects by reading rich, content-area texts.

- Analyze student writing models and engage in constructing both informational and narrative essays with a focus on appropriate language usage.

- Cite evidence from complex texts to respond to text-dependent questions and support critical thinking.

- Acquire and use academic and domain-specific vocabulary accurately.

- Practice analytical and writing skills with rigorous Performance Tasks that reflect the structure of standardized test tasks.

### With the support of a comprehensive Teacher's Edition, teachers will be able to:

- Scaffold student learning with easy-to-use, comprehensive lesson plans.

- Use student assessment data, both observational and formal, to inform and redirect instruction.

- Understand the progression of English Langage Arts requirements across grade levels and tailor instruction to grade-level standards.

- Support diverse learners, including English language learners, struggling learners, and those needing extended learning opportunities.

- Access online and professional development resources to enhance their instruction.

## Founded on the Standards

*Progress English Language Arts* draws on a rich research base and aligns with the Standards for the English Language Arts jointly published by the National Council of Teachers of English (NCTE) and the International Reading Association (IRA) in 1996 and reaffirmed in 2012 by the NCTE Executive Committee, supports the Guiding Visions, and recognizes the central role of the learner in the standards and the four dimensions of language learning: **content, purpose, development,** and **context** that lead to the attainment of the standards. These dimensions are integrated throughout the program and are integral to *Progress English Language Arts* and the sound foundation it provides for student success.

| NCTE and IRA Guidance and Standards-Focus | | How Addressed in *Progress English Language Arts* |
| --- | --- | --- |
| **Content**<br><br>Addresses what students should know and be able to do in regards to English Language Arts | The development of literacy and the attainment of English Language Arts standards depend on experience with and systematic study of a wide array of texts. | *Progress* units expose students to a collection of rigorous texts, fifty percent of the texts are informational and fifty percent are literary and encompass a wide range of genres and topics.<br><br>Through *Progress*, students learn a range of processes and strategies for comprehending and producing texts. Program instruction is centered on texts and skills rather than on related activities that draw attention from texts. Repeated readings and analysis of complex, content-area texts expose all students to new information and ideas. Writing instruction builds on student models and supports students in responding to an array of texts and becoming skilled with writing narrative, informational, and opinion essays, as well as research papers.<br><br>In addition, *Progress* includes study of the systems and structures of language and of language conventions, including grammar, punctuation, and spelling. Students learn how to apply their knowledge of the systems and structures of language depending on the context. |
| **Purpose**<br><br>Addresses why students use language | English Language Arts instruction should focus on four purposes of language use: for obtaining and communicating information, for literary response and expression, for learning and reflection, and for problem solving and application. | *Progress* integrates reading, writing, language and speaking and listening instruction with the goal of developing students who are independent learners, critical thinkers with deep knowledge, effective communicators, skilled problem solvers, and therefore, prepared for success in college and careers. With *Progress*, students' knowledge of history/social studies, science, and technical subjects and their academic and domain-specific vocabulary increase through reading rich, content-area texts. |

| NCTE and IRA Guidance and Standards-Focus | | How Addressed in *Progress English Language Arts* |
|---|---|---|
| **Purpose** (continued) | | Relevant and meaningful opportunities for speaking and listening engage students in developing lifelong oral communication skills. Writing units ensure students develop effective written communication skills for a broad range of purposes. Integrated language instruction develops students' knowledge and use of conventions of standard English. Through a variety of carefully planned tasks that increase in their cognitive demand, students apply and extend the acquired knowledge and skills. |
| **Development**<br><br>Addresses how students develop competencies in English Language Arts | Students acquire knowledge and develop language competencies with practice over time. The quality of students' performance improves over time as students learn to use language clearly, strategically, critically, and creatively. | *Progress* is grounded in research-based learning progressions. Skill-based lessons reflect a gradual release of responsibility instructional model in which students assume increasing independence in reading and analyzing text, writing—including in response to text, developing and using vocabulary, employing the conventions of standard English, speaking, and listening. The program's scope and sequence balances instruction and practice so that students grow in their language competencies and effectively integrate all aspects of language development to learn, think and communicate effectively. For example, the readability of texts increases across units. Guided practice and independent practice are scaffolded and allow students to successfully engage with tasks that increase in cognitive demand. |
| **Context**<br><br>Influences all areas of learning and encompasses the three preceding dimensions | Language is by definition social. Reading, writing, speaking, and listening take place in a context which influences the learning process and the resulting knowledge, skills, and communication. Students' interests and motivations are integral to English Language Arts instruction, practice, and application. | *Progress* is designed to engage and motivate the students who use the program. The magazine-like format was developed with today's learners in mind. The diversity of content, characters, and topics represented is inclusive and the selection was intentional. Each passage, each writing text, each speaking and listening activity was developed with the audience in mind and was purposefully selected with relevance to the participants in mind. Similarly, instruction was developed to guide students to think of the purpose and audience when communicating. |

## Flexible Program Use

*Progress English Language Arts* serves as a flexible resource for supporting schools in meeting English Language Arts standards. Reading selections incorporate a variety of genres and reflect English Language Arts expectations regarding text complexity. Writing units reflect English Language Arts text types and language expectations.

### *Progress English Language Arts* can be used as:

- An alternative core English Language Arts program that provides standards-based instruction, which can be supplemented with independent reading materials for additional practice.

- Supplemental lessons to fill curriculum gaps in a current core English Language Arts program.

- Targeted preparation materials for state-standardized assessments.

## Linking Reading and Writing

Reading and writing units are linked by theme and, where appropriate, by reading genre/writing type. Students are first introduced to key concepts in reading selections based around a theme, usually a social studies or science topic based on grade-level standards. In the related writing unit, they encounter a Student Model, exemplifying excellent grade-level output in the same theme.

### Writing types in *Progress English Language Arts* include:

- Fictional narrative text reflecting the sequential narrative structure of text within the related reading unit.

- Informative/explanatory text with the idea-detail structure of related reading selections.

- Nonfictional narrative text that reflects the structure of an historical text in the related reading unit.

- Opinion piece modeled after a reading selection with a structure identifying an opinion and related supporting reasons.

- Research report whose research topic reflects the setting/theme of the selections within the reading unit.

## Diverse Grouping Models

The *Progress English Language Arts* program employs diverse grouping and instructional models to help teachers provide effective instruction in key English Language Arts skills/concepts.

**Guided Instruction** The program uses **whole-class** instruction to provide direct skill instruction and think-aloud modeling while students **read along** with the teacher. Discussion-based comprehension checks provide an opportunity for learners to ground skill instruction in collaborative academic discourse.

**Guided Practice** Lessons incorporate **partner reading in heterogeneous pairs** for scaffolded practice as the teacher circulates to provide targeted support as needed. Written comprehension checks offer multiple-choice and short-answer questions for pairs to work through together and then share their thinking with the class.

**Independent Practice** Lessons offer **independent reading application with callout support** as the teacher circulates to ensure that all readers are on task and effectively engaging with text. Written comprehension checks offer multiple-choice and short-answer questions as opportunities to demonstrate standard mastery.

➡ Alternative grouping models are suggested for struggling learners and English language learners, such as **heterogeneous pairing** with more proficient readers or **small group work with the teacher**.

## Foundational Skills Support

Foundational skills review and on-level instruction are provided in the following ways in *Progress English Language Arts:*

- Targeted spelling instruction/practice are featured on Language pages in both reading and writing units.

- Review skills featuring key Phonics and Word Recognition skills from earlier grades are integrated at point of use within reading selection instruction.

- A comprehensive Foundational Skills Handbook providing instruction on all grade-level Foundational Reading Skills, including Phonics, Word Recognition, and Fluency, is located in the back of this guide.

- Fluency instruction and practice are integrated at point-of-use within reading selection instruction. In addition, downloadable continuous-text reproductions of Student Worktext passages are provided for use in fluency practice and timed readings.

## Student Worktext

(in print and eBook formats)
Colorful, engaging standards-based instruction including complex, rigorous reading selections and structured writing models. ▶

**Grade 3 Pages 18–19**

## Teacher's Edition

(in print and eBook formats)
Teacher-friendly lesson plans with targeted standards instruction and supportive features suitable for both novice and experienced teachers.

**Grade 3 Teacher's Edition Pages 18–19**

## Progress Monitor* (Optional Purchase)

Four benchmark assessments to identify instructional needs as benchmarked against grade-level English Language Arts skills and concepts.

*Items are mapped to CCSS.

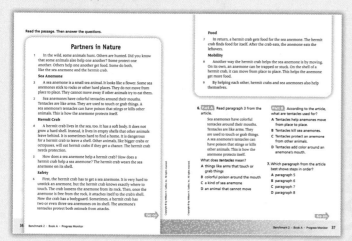

**Grade 3 Progress Monitor Pages 36–37**

## Online Resources

A rich array of online resources at **www.SadlierConnect.com** supports program implementation and extends learning opportunities.

- **Home Connect Activities** support family member involvement.
- **Unit Performance Tasks** provide a wealth of practice opportunities for standardized Performance Tasks related to the content of each unit.
- **Performance Task 1 and 2** enable students to use downloadable unseen text with in-book Performance Tasks and provide teachers with robust evaluation support. These tasks can be used for mid-year and end-of-year assessment purposes.
- **Additional Practice** offers opportunities to augment program practice.
- **Full-Length Reading Selections** provide continuous text passages for fluency practice.

## iProgress Monitor* (Optional Purchase)

This dynamic assessment component is available for enhancing grade-level English Language Arts skills and concepts. See page T17 for more information.

*Items are mapped to CCSS.

## eBooks (Optional Purchase)

**Student Worktext eBook** The eBook provides the same quality content as the print Student Worktext. Delivered via Sadlier's one-stop platform at **www.SadlierConnect.com**, the eBook format also provides access to robust tools that allow students to:

- Read Text
- Make notes and highlight important information
- Search for key words
- Zoom in on specific content

**Teacher's Edition eBook** The eBook provides the same quality content as the print Teacher's Edition. Delivered via Sadlier's one-stop platform at **www.SadlierConnect.com**, in addition the eBook format also provides access to robust tools that allow teachers to:

- Toggle between the Student and Teacher's Edition
- Use Full-screen Mode to project the Student Edition onto a whiteboard to focus on instruction
- Assign lessons to an entire class or a specific group of students to take offline (in PDF format)
- View digital resources at point of use
- Make notes and highlight important information
- Search for key words
- Zoom in on specific content

**Progress English Language Arts Grade 3 eBook**

*Progress English Language Arts* contains many formative and summative assessment opportunities to help teachers gather evidence of students' progress toward mastering grade-level skills and concepts and prepare for the new state-standardized assessments.

## Integrated, Ongoing Assessment Opportunities

**Lesson Observational Diagnostics** appear at point-of-use within lessons, reminding teachers to observe student response to instruction and offering a reteaching prescription. ▶

### Assess and Respond

**If** students have difficulty answering the questions in the Comprehension Check . . .

**Then** have pairs of students review the story and create a list of the inferences they made as they read. Students should identify the clues they used to make their inferences.

---

**UNIT 1 REVIEW**

Read the following passage, which you will use to draw inferences, determine theme and summarize, compare and contrast story elements, and identify synonym and antonym word relationships. Then answer the questions on pages 37 and 38.

### A Different Kind of Summer School
(Genre: Realistic Fiction)

1 Making some money in the summer by working with my cousin Eric in Oregon sounded like a fantastic idea, but I never guessed what I was in for.

2 Unlike me, Eric was an "early to bed, early to rise" person. Bedtime was right after dinner the day I arrived. At 4:00 AM we were delivering newspapers. By 5:30 AM Eric's aunt had dropped us off at the strawberry fields. For eight hours we hunched over, picking berries with the other workers. A truck took us home.

3 The day's work wasn't over. Eric had a contract to shear sheep—huge ones. I led them to where Eric did the shearing. By dinnertime I had never been so tired. This was real work!

4 By the end of summer, I'd made more money than I ever imagined. But what I really got from that summer—an understanding of what it means to "earn your living"—was worth far more than cash.

**Fill in the circle of the correct answer choice.**

1. Which sentence in the story comes the closest to stating its theme?
   ○ paragraph 1, sentence 1
   ○ paragraph 4, sentence 2
   ○ paragraph 2, sentence 5
   ○ paragraph 3, sentence 1

2. Which word is a synonym for *fantastic* in paragraph 1?
   ○ unrealistic
   ○ strange
   ○ wonderful
   ○ unusual

Unit 1 ▪ Reading Lit...

◀ **Unit Reviews** are provided with each unit and offer an opportunity for students to encounter standardized test practice for the skills that have been taught within the unit.

**Grade 5 Page 37**

---

Name _____

**Read the passage. Then answer the questions.**

### An Unbreakable Code

1 Ben struggled and slipped through the soft sand, his eyes scanning the beach for signs of movement. It looked deserted, but he knew that Japanese troops could be hiding out, waiting to launch their counterattack on the U.S. Marines. The wind whipped the sand around him, stinging his eyes and clouding his vision. Ben's fingers locked tightly around his radio, and his heart pounded in his chest. He had not been recruited to fight, although he was equipped and trained for combat. Ben was a messenger, a Navajo Code Talker. His most powerful weapon was the radio in his hand.

2 The United States was at war. A few years earlier, the Japanese had launched a surprise attack on Pearl Harbor. Ben was just a teenager then, living on the Navajo reservation where he had grown up. One day, a childhood friend came to the reservation, recruiting soldiers for an important mission. Ben still remembered his words: the Navajo language could be used as an "unbreakable code," a tool that the United States desperately needed.

3 Ben hadn't hesitated. He had never been away from the reservation, but he had been chosen to serve his country. Growing up, Ben begged his parents to let him speak English; the Navajo language

*Navajo U.S. Marine Code Talkers are sworn in.*

was too complicated, too unusual. But now, Ben's language had made him invaluable in the war. At a boot camp in California, he and other Navajo soldiers had devised a dictionary to keep track of their messages. They woke at sunrise and worked through the night, memorizing the codes. Even Ben's dreams became a jumble of code words and military jargon. He knew that when the day came to use his skill, he had to be prepared—in battle, there would be no room to make mistakes.

4 Here, on a tiny island in the Pacific, was Ben's first test as a Code Talker. Ever since he had left boot camp, Ben's fellow soldiers had mocked him,

 Go on

Benchmark 1 ▪ Book A ▪ Progress Monitor  **3**

**Grade 5 Progress Monitor**

◀ **Benchmark Assessments\*** in Progress Monitor (an optional purchase) provide comprehensive assessments that can be administered periodically throughout the school year to evaluate students' knowledge and skill level relative to grade-level English Language Arts skills and concepts.

\*Items are mapped to CCSS.

**Unit Performance Tasks** provide a wealth of practice opportunities for students to demonstrate their development of critical thinking and analysis skills and the ability to reason in response to text through writing and speaking.

**Performance Tasks 1 and 2** ▶ provide tasks that parallel those in standardized assessments. The tasks incorporate both text items and an extended response essay question—which assesses students' ability to think critically about text as well as write using supporting evidence. Performance Tasks 1 and 2 are also available online at **www.SadlierConnect.com**. These Performance Tasks can also be used for mid-year and end-of-year assessment purposes. These Performance Tasks play a vital role in helping you determine if students are able to integrate skills and concepts being taught and apply them in real-life.

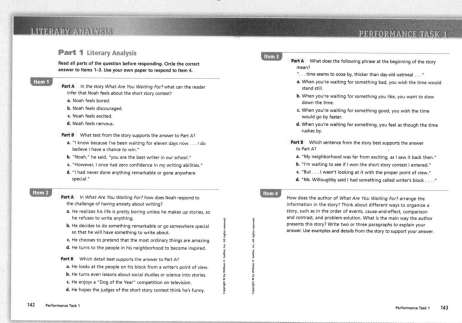

**Grade 5 Pages 142–143**

## iProgress Monitor* (Optional Purchase)

Augment your assesment resources with customized assignments and test-building power!

With the **iProgress Monitor**, teachers can:

- Assign, evaluate, and monitor student progress with preformatted program assessments in an interactive format.

- Build custom assessments with a built-in test generator.

- Track students' progress and guide instruction with real-time data.

*Items are mapped to CCSS.

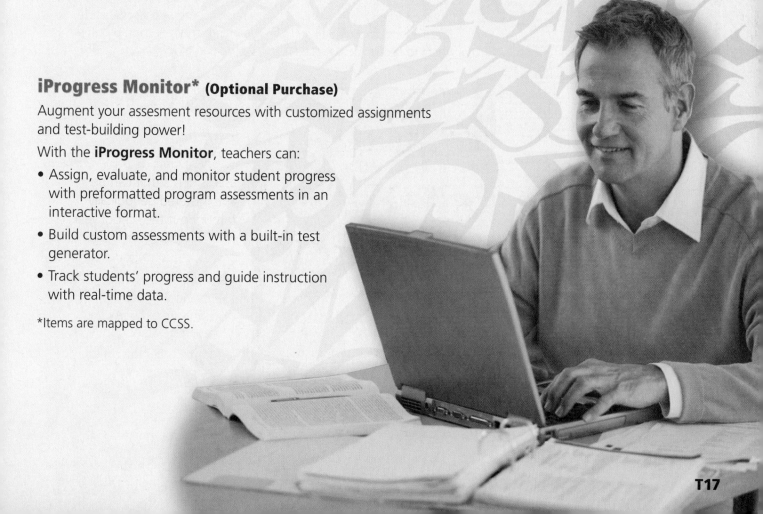

## Student Worktext

With a full-color, magazine-like design, the engaging Student Worktext gives students opportunities to:

- Read both informational and literary texts
- Build knowledge through comprehension of texts
- Encounter increasingly rigorous and complex texts
- Answer text-based questions and engage in academic discussions about text
- Write in a clear and coherent manner using the conventions of standard English
- Build academic vocabulary

Organized by English Language Arts standards, the reading and writing units are linked by theme and, where appropriate, genre. The reading units address a rich variety of genres while the writing units focus on the standards-supported writing types.

## A Unit Introduction That Focuses on Standards

**Grade 4 Page 97**

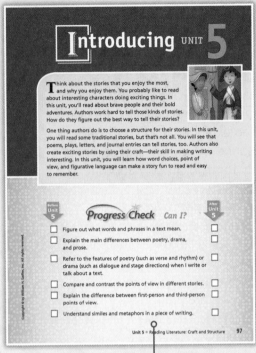

**Home Connect** activities for each unit provide families a window into their child's learning and encourage them to take an active role.

**Progress Check** at the beginning of each unit allows students to focus on the unit's key skills and concepts, self-assess before learning, and reflect on progress at the end of the unit.

**Grade 4 Page 98**

An **Essential Question** featured on the Unit Opener serves as a hook into the big idea of the unit and serves as a focal point of rigorous, academic discussion.

Four texts per thematic unit offer ample reading opportunities with complex texts.

**Grade 4 Page 99**

## Encountering Complex Reading Text: Gradual Release of Responsibility

Each standard is taught using one continuous text following a gradual release of responsibility instructional model. By gradually decreasing the level of support within each text, students are prepared for independent encounters with complex text and can best master complex standards.

**Guided Instruction:** Direct standard instruction and teacher modeling

Grade 4 Page 100

**Guided Practice:** Scaffolded standard practice in a partner-reading environment

Complex **informational texts** with a rich array of informational features comprise half of each grade's reading selections.

Embedded questions support rigorous, standards-based **conversations about text** in the context of selections.

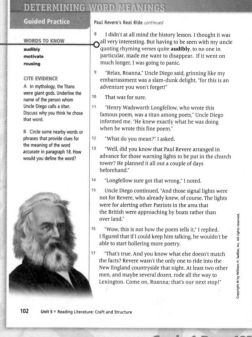

Grade 4 Page 102

**Academic** and **domain-specific vocabulary** is introduced in a text-based context with the appropriate standards-based instruction.

**Text-dependent questions** require students to respond with evidence from the text to support their answers.

Each unit contains multiple opportunities to **write to text sources**.

**Independent Practice:** Extensive independent practice on standards enables students to build mastery.

Grade 4 Page 104

# Close Reading for Critical Comprehension of Text

Close reading—careful, purposeful reading and rereading of text—requires students to integrate the unit's reading standards as they comprehend text and answer questions providing reasons and justifications for their responses. In the Close Reading and the related Unit Review assessment, students build reading stamina, analyze text, grow comfortable with increasing text complexity, and demonstrate an understanding of unit standards. A **language lesson** follows each Close Reading.

**Grade 4 Page 118**

Close Reading text reflects the unit's content-area theme and related academic vocabulary to **build knowledge through text comprehension**.

Rigorous **text-dependent questions** require application of the unit's standards, use of supporting evidence, and link to a critical understanding of the text.

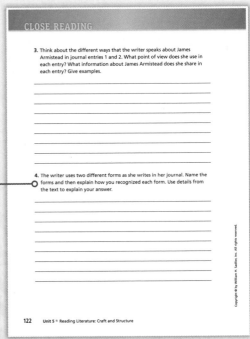

**Grade 4 Page 122**

Language page develops **language skills** and academic vocabulary taught in the context of unit texts.

Students engage in **rigorous academic discussion** as they talk about multiple texts and the unit's Essential Question.

**Grade 4 Page 123**

**Grade 4 Page 124**

## Writing Units with a Standards Focus

Writing units, along with the Writing Handbook, reflect the key writing types in English Language curriculum: opinion, informative/explanatory, narrative (both fictional and nonfictional), and research report. Language and Speaking and Listening pages are integrated to build students' accurate use of academic language in both written and spoken forms.

Each **writing model** is surrounded with support, including an introduction to the related writing standards, explanations of each component of the type of writing, and opportunities for students to analyze, organize, and write a passage of the same text type.

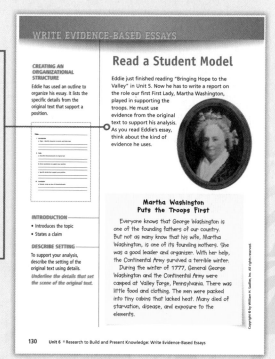

**Grade 4 Page 130**

Integrated **Language** pages focus on conventions of English and knowledge of language—grammar, usage, and mechanics—through a gradual release model.

**Grade 4 Page 134**

**Speaking and Listening** lessons support students as they engage in rigorous, academic discourse about the unit's Essential Question about the writing type. A graphic organizer helps to focus students on active participation and employing speaking and listening skills.

**Grade 4 Page 138**

## Built-In Assessment Practice

Both the reading and writing units conclude with Unit Review assessments that provide practice with items similar to those students will encounter on state-standardized assessments.

### Reading Unit Review

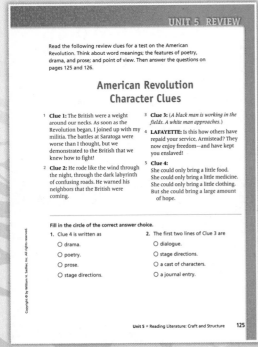

**Grade 4 Page 125**

Integrated assessment and standardized test practice feature new theme-related texts that reflect a genre introduced in unit selections. **Text-dependent questions** ask students to **write** and cite text evidence. A variety of question formats help teachers assess mastery of unit content, monitor progress, remediate, and prepare students for state assessments.

**UNIT 5 REVIEW**

3. In Clue 2, what is the most likely meaning of *labyrinth*, a word from an ancient myth?
   - ○ tunnel
   - ○ treasure
   - ○ battlefield
   - ○ maze

4. In Clue 1, what does *demonstrated to* mean?
   - ○ battled
   - ○ argued with
   - ○ showed
   - ○ acted out

5. Underline the simile in Clue 2.

6. Circle the clues that could help you figure out the meaning of *militia* in Clue 1.

7. Was the narrator of Clue 1 part of the battles at Saratoga? How do you know?

8. In Clue 3, how do you learn about Lafayette's feelings?

9. Rewrite Clue 2 so that it has a first-person point of view.

10. Find the metaphor in Clue 1. What two things does the writer compare? What does the metaphor help you to understand?

126    Unit 5 ▪ Reading Literature: Craft and Structure

**Grade 4 Page 126**

### Writing Unit Review

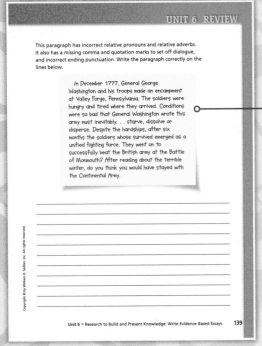

**Grade 4 Page 139**

**UNIT 6 REVIEW**

**Assignment:** Write an evidence-based essay on a character or event you've read about.

On the lines below, write your final copy of the evidence-based essay you created on page 133. Be sure to use specific evidence from the original text and descriptions of characters, events, or setting to support your position. Conclude your essay with a restatement of your position. See the Writing Handbook (pages 275–283) for ways to improve your writing as you revise.

140    Unit 6 ▪ Research to Build and Present Knowledge: Write Evidence-Based Essays

**Grade 4 Page 140**

Students apply unit Language skills by correcting the errors in a paragraph, similar to grammar, usage, and mechanics correction they will encounter on state-standardized assessments.

Students produce writing in the text types commonly found in English Language Arts standards using the writing process. This on-demand writing practice helps to build writing stamina. (Support for teaching the writing process appears in the Writing Handbook at the end of the Student Worktext.)

# Overview of a Teacher's Edition Unit

## Teacher's Edition

Teacher-friendly, easy-to-use lesson plans support teachers in providing systematic instruction, practice, and application of English Language Arts skills and concepts. The Teacher's Edition is also available in eBook format.

- Easy-to-use rubrics at point of use enable busy teachers to assess and modify instruction quickly.

## At-a-Glance Unit Introduction Pages

Unit introduction pages, featuring student self-assessment, a home connection, a planner for understanding key concepts at a glance, and learning progressions for comprehension standards, provide a quick reference for busy educators!

## Unit Planner

**Grade 3 Teacher's Edition Page 147 and 148**

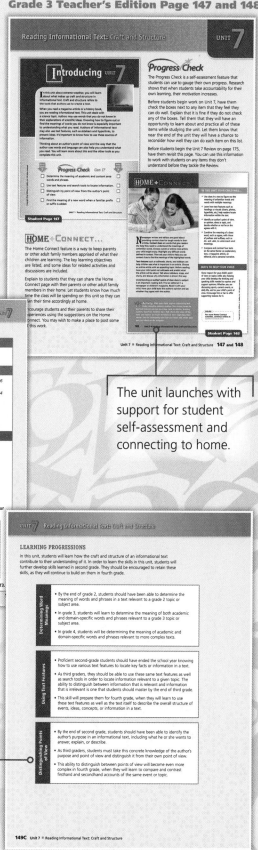

The unit launches with support for student self-assessment and connecting to home.

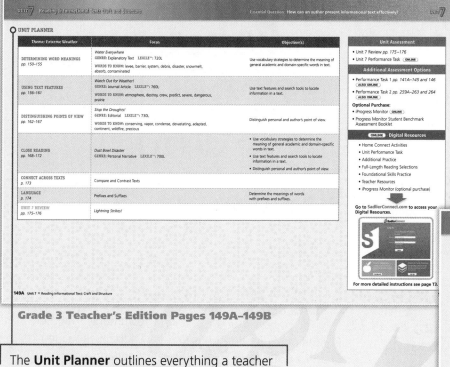

**Grade 3 Teacher's Edition Pages 149A–149B**

The **Unit Planner** outlines everything a teacher needs to know to gather unit resources and understand unit objectives and selections.

**Learning Progressions** provide context and background knowledge of the critical skills and skills progression across the years by showing what students learned in the previous grade and connections to what they will learn in the next grade, building coherence within and across the grade levels.

**Grade 3 Teacher's Edition Page 149C**

## On-the-Spot Lesson Support Makes Teachers English Language Arts Experts!

Teacher-friendly Lesson Plans provide targeted standards-based instruction and supportive features suitable for both novice and experienced teachers.

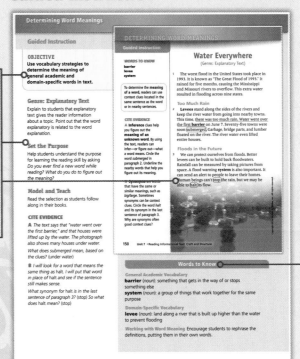

Each lesson segment has **student objectives** clearly noted.

Genre instruction supports close examination of the features of **text types**, which aids text comprehension.

On-page annotations help teachers monitor whether students are identifying text evidence during instruction.

**Academic vocabulary** is defined, and research-based vocabulary-building activities (e.g., Marzano's six vocabulary acquisition strategies) support acquisition.

**Grade 3 Teacher's Edition Page 150**

Teacher think-alouds model a good reader's approach to the standard, and an additional prompt **scaffolds skill application** for those who need additional support.

**Modifications** for English language learners, struggling learners, and students who need additional challenge embrace all learners.

# Successive Increase of Student Responsibility Leads to Success

**Answer explanations** support the teacher in helping students understand where they may still have gaps in applying the skill or concept effectively.

### Guided Practice

**Whole-class, partner, and individual instructional settings** build scaffolding for all students to be successful with English Language Arts skills and concepts.

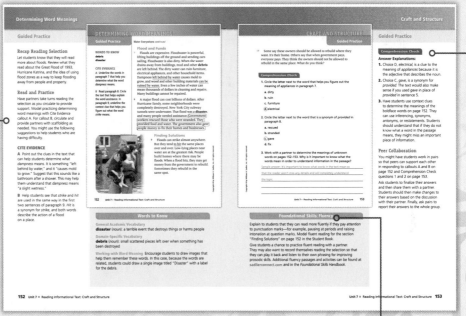

**Grade 3 Teacher's Edition Pages 152–153**

**Foundational Skill practice** is integrated at point-of-use in lessons.

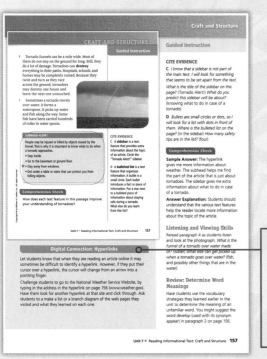

**Grade 3 Teacher's Edition Page 157**

Discussion Skills, based on key skills and concepts and Resnick's research-based Accountable Talk strategies, integrate speaking and listening instruction into every unit and support **academic discussion** of text.

**Digital Connections** support students in understanding digital text as a genre in line with the thinking of new standardized assessments.

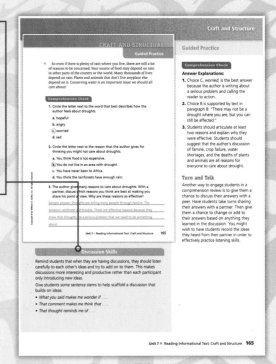

**Grade 3 Teacher's Edition Page 165**

## Scaffolded Practice Makes Independent Application of Skills Accessible

*Progress English Language Arts* provides ample opportunity for rigorous independent practice allowing students to develop English Language Arts skills with conceptual understanding.

### Independent Practice

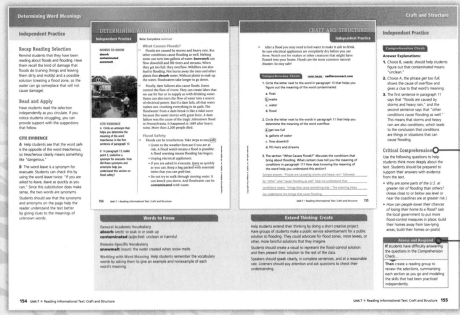

**Grade 3 Teacher's Edition Pages 154–155**

Critical Comprehension questions at the end of each Independent Practice and Close Reading require students to demonstrate a **deep understanding** of selections that comes from close reading of text.

**If-Then diagnostics** allow teachers to remediate immediately when students need additional support.

### Close Reading

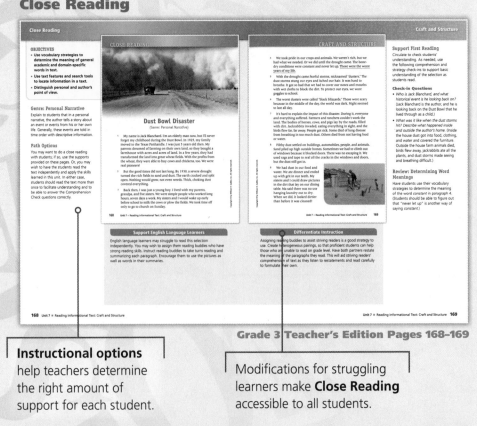

**Grade 3 Teacher's Edition Pages 168–169**

**Instructional options** help teachers determine the right amount of support for each student.

Modifications for struggling learners make **Close Reading** accessible to all students.

# Assessment Tools Make Grading Simple

*Progress English Language Arts* supports busy teachers by offering easy-to-use rubrics and results charts that outline next steps after grading or assessment.

## Grade 3 Teacher's Edition Page 173

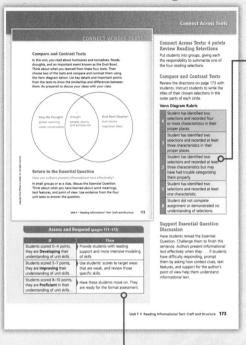

**Clear assignment rubrics** help teachers analyze student work products.

All assessment items are **aligned to an ELA standard** so that teachers can easily determine which standards are mastered.

**Assessment rubrics for short-answer questions** take the worry out of assigning grades to open-ended questions.

An If-Then chart links grading results to **next steps** after Close Reading activities.

## Grade 3 Teacher's Edition Page 176

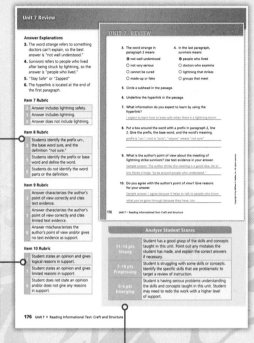

**Analyze Student Scores charts** detail next steps that teachers should take with students based on assessment results.

---

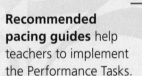

**Performance Task 1**

The Performance Tasks in *Progress English Language Arts* are designed to determine a student's ability to closely read and understand a complex text, locate textual evidence to support analysis of the text, and create an extended response that shows deep comprehension of the text. Writing prompts in each part of the Performance Task address requirements for creating opinion pieces, informative texts, and narratives. Each Performance Task has three main parts: a Literary Analysis Task, a Narrative Writing Task, and a Research Simulation Task.

Each Performance Task requires students to read multiple thematically related texts—literature, a nonfiction narrative, and a research-based informational text—and to respond to two types of assessment items:

- **Selected response items** require students to choose the correct answer from a number of options. Selected response items are divided into two parts: Part A requires students to answer a question related to the content or language of the text; Part B requires students to identify textual evidence that supports the answer to Part A.

- **Constructed response items** require students to create a brief written response—a literary analysis, a narrative, or an informational text—in response to a prompt.

You can help your students by introducing the overall topic of the Performance Task, orienting students to the requirements of each part of the task, and communicating helpful reminders that will enable students to approach each part successfully. Once students have completed each part, go over the items and correct responses with them, especially focusing on the connection between textual evidence and acceptable responses.

**Recommended pacing guides** help teachers to implement the Performance Tasks.

Detailed **Performance Task rubrics** provide clear and thorough guidance on how to evaluate written performance tasks.

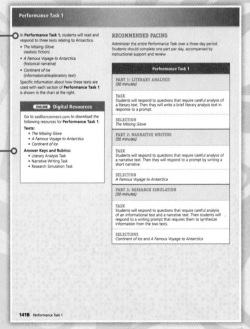

# Suggested Planning and Pacing Guide

| Weeks | Student Worktext | Online Resources to Enrich, Support, and Assess |
|---|---|---|
| 1–3 | Unit 1, pp. 9–38 | Unit 1 Performance Task; Additional Practice; Full-Length Reading Selection; Foundational Skills Practice; Teacher Resources<br>Optional purchase: iProgress Monitor |
| 4–5 | Unit 2, pp. 39–52 | Additional Practice; Teacher Resources<br>Optional purchase: iProgress Monitor |
| 6–8 | Unit 3, pp. 53–82 | Unit 3 Performance Task; Additional Practice; Full-Length Reading Selection; Foundational Skills Practice; Teacher Resources<br>Optional purchase: iProgress Monitor |
| 9–10 | Unit 4, pp. 83–96 | Additional Practice; Teacher Resources<br>Optional purchase: iProgress Monitor |
| 11–13 | Unit 5, pp. 97–126 | Unit 5 Performance Task; Additional Practice; Full-Length Reading Selection; Foundational Skills Practice; Teacher Resources<br>Optional purchase: iProgress Monitor |
| 14–15 | Unit 6, pp. 127–140 | Additional Practice; Teacher Resources<br>Optional purchase: iProgress Monitor |
| 16 | Performance Task 1 | Performance Task 1 Selections, Rubrics, and Answer Key |
| 17–19 | Unit 7, pp. 147–176 | Unit 7 Performance Task; Additional Practice; Full-Length Reading Selection; Foundational Skills Practice; Teacher Resources<br>Optional purchase: iProgress Monitor |
| 20–21 | Unit 8, pp. 177–190 | Additional Practice; Teacher Resources<br>Optional purchase: iProgress Monitor |
| 22–24 | Unit 9, pp. 191–214 | Unit 9 Performance Task; Additional Practice; Full-Length Reading Selection; Foundational Skills Practice; Teacher Resources<br>Optional purchase: iProgress Monitor |
| 25–26 | Unit 10, pp. 215–228 | Additional Practice; Teacher Resources<br>Optional purchase: iProgress Monitor |
| 27–29 | Unit 11, pp. 229–258 | Unit 11 Performance Task; Additional Practice; Full-Length Reading Selection; Foundational Skills Practice; Teacher Resources<br>Optional purchase: iProgress Monitor |
| 30 | Performance Task 2 | Performance Task 2 Selections, Rubrics, and Answer Key |

*Progress Monitor Student Assessments,* an optional purchase, contains four comprehensive assessments that you may administer throughout the school year to assess students' mastery of grade-level skills/concepts.

# Introducing UNIT 1

Since the earliest times, people have been telling each other stories. Many of the stories that have been passed down to us are fables, folktales, and myths. In this unit, you will read some of these stories about heroes from the past.

We don't know who first told these stories. Yet we still enjoy them. Each one has an important message for us. It might be a lesson on how to act toward other people, an inspiring tale that makes us stand up for what is right, or a way for people of former times to explain things in nature that they could not understand. As you read each story, you will pick out details that tell where and when things happen. You will learn who the characters are and what they are like. You will learn to ask and answer questions about the story's conflict and how it is solved.

Connecting details in stories will help you better understand the stories of long ago. Then you can pass them along to someone else!

**Before Unit 1** ⬇        **Progress Check** *Can I?*        **After Unit 1** ⬇

- [ ] Ask and answer questions to help me understand a story. [ ]
- [ ] Retell important details to help determine a story's message. [ ]
- [ ] Describe the characters and how their actions affect the story. [ ]
- [ ] Use context clues in a sentence to learn the exact meaning of unknown words. [ ]

Unit 1 ■ Reading Literature: Key Ideas and Details

**Student Page 9**

# Progress Check

The Progress Check is a self-assessment feature that students can use to gauge their own progress. Research shows that when students take accountability for their own learning, it increases their motivation.

Before students begin work on Unit 1, have them check the boxes next to any item that they feel they can do well. Explain that it is fine if they don't check any of the boxes. Tell them that they will have an opportunity to learn about and practice all of these items while studying the unit. Let them know that near the end of the unit they will have a chance to reconsider how well they can do each item on this list.

Before students begin the Unit 1 Review on page 37, have them revisit this page. You can use this information to work with students on any items they don't understand before they tackle the Review.

# HOME ◆ CONNECT...

Focused readers **ask and answer questions** as they read. What is the story about? Who are the characters? How does the story turn out? Finding important details to answer questions helps your child understand the meaning of a story. Choose a print or online text your child might enjoy. Read it together, asking each other questions such as "What's going to happen next?"

Knowing the author's **central message or lesson** in a story lets children relate the story to their own life. Choose a print or online folktale about a character you and your child admire. Take turns reading aloud to each other. Then ask questions such as "What can we learn from this character?" and "How would we act in a similar situation?"

Uncovering **characters' traits and motivations** helps young readers understand why things happen in a story. Why did the character do this? Watch a television drama with your child. During breaks, talk about what the characters said and did. Make predictions about the story's outcome based on your observations.

**Conversation Starter:** With your child, brainstorm what might occur if a hero from a myth or folktale were brought to life in the modern world. How would the character's powers or skills be used today? How would modern people react to the character? Sketch pictures of the original hero and how the character's appearance would change.

10      Unit 1 ■ Reading Literature: Key Ideas and Details

### IN THIS UNIT, YOUR CHILD WILL...

- Ask questions and answer them, using details from the text, to gain a better understanding of the text as a whole.
- Retell stories, including important details about characters, setting, and events.
- Determine the central message of a text and how the author conveys the message through details.
- Describe characters' traits and motives and explain how their actions move a story along.
- Use context clues to define words that are unknown or that have multiple meanings.
- Compare and contrast three texts with the same theme: a fable, a folktale, and a myth.

### WAYS TO HELP YOUR CHILD

Help your child enjoy reading. Encourage your child to find and share short texts about interesting topics, and read them aloud to each other. Ask questions about the texts that promote reasoning skills: Why do you think the person did that? What might have been a better thing to do? Challenge your child to offer supporting reasons for any opinions.

**ONLINE**
For more Home Connect activities, continue online at sadlierconnect.com

**Student Page 10**

# HOME ◆ CONNECT...

The Home Connect feature is a way to keep parents or other adult family members apprised of what their children are learning. The key learning objectives are listed, and some ideas for related activities and discussions are included.

Explain to students that they can share the Home Connect page with their parents or the adult family members in their home. Let students know how much time the class will be spending on this unit so they can plan their time accordingly at home.

Encourage students and their parents to share their experiences using the suggestions on the Home Connect page. You may wish to make a place to post any of this work.

# UNIT PLANNER

| Theme: It Takes a Hero | Focus |
|---|---|
| **ASKING AND ANSWERING QUESTIONS** <br> *pp. 12–17* | *The Dove and the Ant: A Retelling of an Aesop Fable* and *The Crow and the Pitcher: A Retelling of an Aesop Fable* <br> **GENRE:** Fable  **LEXILE®:** 540L, 540L <br><br> **WORDS TO KNOW:** condition, swooped, hatchling, stealthy, bait, commotion, grief, despair, invention |
| **DETERMINING A CENTRAL MESSAGE** <br> *pp. 18–23* | *John Henry: A Retelling of an American Folktale* and *Old Stormalong and the Octopus: A Retelling of an American Folktale* <br> **GENRE:** Folktale  **LEXILE®:** 570L, 610L <br><br> **WORDS TO KNOW:** lay claim, cave-in, steam-powered, onlooker, outdrilled, spirit, ultimate, hinge, massive |
| **DESCRIBING CHARACTERS** <br> *pp. 24–29* | *Atalanta the Huntress* <br> **GENRE:** Myth  **LEXILE®:** 630L <br><br> **WORDS TO KNOW:** offering, expert, approaching, murmur, focused, Centaur, outrage, bloodshot, enormous, intervened |
| **CLOSE READING** <br> *pp. 30–34* | *Heracles and Atlas* <br> **GENRE:** Myth  **LEXILE®:** 590L |
| **CONNECT ACROSS TEXTS** <br> *p. 35* | Compare and Contrast Texts |
| **LANGUAGE** <br> *p. 36* | Context Clues |
| **UNIT 1 REVIEW** <br> *pp. 37–38* | *The Daydreamer* <br> **GENRE:** Folktale  **LEXILE®:** 500L |

## Objective(s)

Show an understanding of the text by asking questions and citing evidence from the text to answer questions.

Determine and explain the central message, lesson, or moral of a story, using key details from the text.

Describe characters in a story, including how their actions contribute to the sequence of events.

- Show an understanding of the text by asking questions and citing evidence from the text to answer questions.
- Determine and explain the central message, lesson, or moral of a story, using key details from the text.
- Describe characters in a story, including how their actions contribute to the sequence of events.

Use context to determine the meaning of unfamiliar words and phrases.

## Unit Assessment

- Unit 1 Review *pp. 37–38*
- Unit 1 Performance Task ( ONLINE )

## Additional Assessment Options

- Performance Task 1 *pp. 141A–145 and 146*
  ( ALSO ONLINE )
- Performance Task 2 *pp. 259A–263 and 264*
  ( ALSO ONLINE )

**Optional Purchase:**

- iProgress Monitor ( ONLINE )
- Progress Monitor Student Benchmark Assessment Booklet

## ( ONLINE ) Digital Resources

- Home Connect Activities
- Unit Performance Task
- Additional Practice
- Full-Length Reading Selections
- Foundational Skills Practice
- Teacher Resources
- iProgress Monitor (optional purchase)

**Go to SadlierConnect.com to access your Digital Resources.**

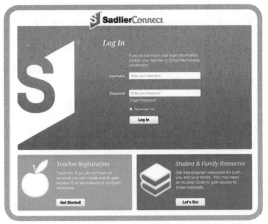

**For more detailed instructions see page T3.**

## LEARNING PROGRESSIONS

In this unit, students will learn how an author of a fictional text conveys a central message or lesson through key ideas and details. In order to learn the skills in this unit, students will further develop skills learned in second grade. They should be encouraged to retain these skills, as they will continue to build on them in fourth grade.

**Asking and Answering Questions**

- Proficient second-grade students should have ended the school year with an ability to ask and answer such questions as *who, what, where, when, why,* and *how* to show understanding of a text.

- As third graders, students should be able to refer explicitly to the text as the basis for their answers to these same types of questions to show understanding of a text.

- This skill will prepare them for fourth grade, when they will be expected to refer to details and examples in the text when explaining what the text says explicitly and when drawing inferences from the text.

**Determining a Central Message**

- By the end of grade 2, students should be able to recount stories, including fables and folktales, from diverse cultures, and determine their central message, lesson, or moral.

- In grade 3, students will build on this skill by explaining how the central message, lesson, or moral is conveyed through key details in stories, including fables, folktales, and myths from diverse cultures.

- When students move on to grade 4, they will expand on the use of this skill to determine the theme of a story, drama, or poem from details in the text and to summarize the text.

**Describing Characters**

- Grade 2 students should have completed the year able to describe how characters in a story respond to major events and challenges.

- In the third grade, students will widen their application of this skill to describe characters in a story (e.g., their traits, motivations, or feelings) and explain how their actions contribute to the sequence of events.

- Students will be expected to build on this skill in grade 4 and describe in depth a character, setting, or event in a story or drama, drawing on specific details in the text (e.g., a character's thoughts, words, or actions).

# Reading Literature: Key Ideas and Details

**Essential Question:**
How do authors convey a central message or lesson?

**Essential Question:**
How do authors convey a central message or lesson?

In this unit, students will focus on key ideas and details in stories to help them ask and answer questions to clarify understanding, determine the message in a story, and describe characters.

## Theme: It Takes a Hero

Students will read literature selections related to the theme of the need for heroes. They will read about heroes in two fables, two folktales, and two myths.

## Curriculum Connection: English/Language Arts

Students will read about two types of heroic characters—characters who are heroes because they save others or themselves, and characters who are heroes because they set a good example.

## Vocabulary Overview

**General Academic Vocabulary**

approaching 25, bloodshot 28, commotion 15, condition 12, despair 17, enormous 28, expert 25, focused 26, grief 16, intervened 28, invention 17, lay claim 18, massive 22, murmur 25, offering 24, onlooker 20, outrage 27, spirit 21, stealthy 14, swooped 12, ultimate 22

**Domain-Specific Vocabulary**

bait 14, cave-in 19, Centaur 26, hatchling 13, hinge 22, outdrilled 20, steam-powered 19

# Asking and Answering Questions

## Guided Instruction

### OBJECTIVE
**Show an understanding of the text by asking questions and citing evidence from the text to answer questions.**

### Genre: Fable

Explain to students that a fable is a type of short story, often first told many years ago. Point out that it usually includes at least one animal as a character and teaches a lesson.

### Set the Purpose

Help students understand the purpose for learning the reading skill by asking *Do you ever not understand what is happening in a story? What do you do to better understand the story?*

### Model and Teach

Read the selection as students follow along in their books.

### CITE EVIDENCE

**A** *I know that a problem is something that causes trouble for a character.*

*Which character is mentioned in paragraph 2?* (Ant) *What trouble is Ant having?* (She can't get back to land.)

**B** *The last two sentences in paragraph 3 explain what Dove does. Why does Dove pity Ant's condition?* (She knows that Ant can't get out of the water and feels bad for her.)

---

## ASKING AND ANSWERING QUESTIONS
### Guided Instruction

**WORDS TO KNOW**
condition
hatchling
swooped

To understand a text, **find details** in the text to help you **answer questions.**

#### CITE EVIDENCE

**A** To understand a story, it helps to **ask and answer questions**, such as, *What characters are in the story?* Underline details in the title that answer this question. It also helps to ask, *What is the main problem?* Circle the part of paragraph 2 that answers this.

**B** Questioning why characters do things is also important. Underline the sentences in paragraph 4 that explain why the Dove does what she does. What other fables or folktales have you read in which one character helps another?

## The <u>Dove</u> and the <u>Ant</u>:
### A Retelling of an Aesop Fable
(Genre: Fable)

1    The weather in the spring had been very hot and dry. An Ant dragged herself to the river, hoping to get a drink of water. However, weak from thirst, she fell into the water. As she struggled to get back to land, the current carried her away from shore.

2    Try as she might, the Ant could not get closer to shore. There was nothing else floating in the river for her to hold on to. "I am lost!" she thought. "Nobody saw me fall in. There is nobody to help me." Getting more and more tired, the Ant started to sink beneath the water.

3    High in a tree near the bank of the river sat a sharp-eyed Dove. Her strong eyes let her see the Ant splashing, and she knew the Ant was in trouble. She thought to herself, "What can I do?"

4    The Dove pitied the Ant's **condition**. She wanted to help. Spotting a small branch on the ground, she **swooped** down and grabbed it in her beak. She took a hop and flew out over the river.

**12**    Unit 1 ■ Reading Literature: Key Ideas and Details

---

### Words to Know

**General Academic Vocabulary**
**condition** (*noun*): the state of being, or the situation someone or something is in
**swooped** (*verb*): moved suddenly in a sweeping motion

**Domain-Specific Vocabulary**
**hatchling** (*noun*): bird, fish, or reptile that has just hatched, or come out of its egg

**Working with Word Meaning** Encourage students to draw a picture of each moment in the story that is described with the words.

## KEY IDEAS AND DETAILS

5    Where was the Ant? The Dove saw the weakest of splashes. Zooming out of the sky, she dropped the branch right by the Ant.

6    The Ant felt the branch. She got one leg up on it, then another, and finally scrambled on top. She shook the water from her eyes. Seeing that the Ant was safe, the Dove flew away.

7    The branch floated to shore, and the Ant stepped off onto land. "I have to thank the Dove," she thought to herself. "I don't know how I will, but I have to."

8    Spring turned to summer. The Dove's **hatchlings** grew, and the young birds left the nest. The Dove forgot all about saving the Ant.

9    The Ant also had work to do. With her mates, she tunneled underground. She also searched for food above ground and brought it back to the nest.

### Comprehension Check

1. Why does the Ant think she is in big trouble?
2. What in the text says that the Ant feels grateful?

### CITE EVIDENCE

**C**  Ask yourself, "What words does the author use that help me see the action?" Circle the words in paragraph 5 that help you see what is happening.

**D**  The story's setting includes *when* it happens. Underline details that tell you when this story happens. How much time passes in this story?

## Guided Instruction

### CITE EVIDENCE

**C**  *I know that "action" is what characters do. So, I will look for words that describe—or allow me to see—what the characters are doing.*

*Dove sees Ant splashing. What word helps you see that the splashes Ant makes are not very big or strong?* (weakest) *What word helps you see how Dove moves in the sky?* (zooming) *What phrase helps you see where Dove dropped the branch?* (right by the Ant)

**D**  *Many authors establish the setting at the beginning of the story. So, I will look at the first paragraph for a word that relates to time—or when the story happens.*

*What word in the first paragraph tells you when the story begins?* (spring) *When do you see the word spring again?* (paragraph 8) *What does the author say about "spring"?* (It "turned to summer.") *How much time has passed by this point in the story?* (one season)

### Comprehension Check

**Sample Answer:** The Ant thinks that she is lost because the current carried her away from the shore. She thinks no one saw her fall into the river, so no one will know to save her. The Ant wants to thank the Dove after being saved.

**Answer Explanation:** Students should recognize that the current is the way the water in the river flows. A current can be very strong and difficult to swim against. It can move you quickly from your starting point in a river, and soon you have no idea where you are. The Ant wants to thank the Dove because the Dove is the one who saved her.

### Support English Language Learners

Students who are learning English may have a difficult time making sense of idiomatic language that is more familiar to native speakers. Explain that an idiom is a phrase that means something other than the meaning of the individual words put together. Then point out these idiomatic phrases: *weak from thirst* (page 12, paragraph 1), *sharp-eyed* (page 12, paragraph 3), and *spring turned to summer* (page 13, paragraph 8).

Guide students to use context clues in nearby sentences and paragraphs to figure out the meaning of the idioms.

## Guided Practice

### Recap Reading Selection

Let students know that they will continue reading the fable about the Ant and the Dove. Review what they read about the Dove saving the Ant after she fell into the river, and how the Ant wants to thank the Dove but does not know how to find her.

### Read and Practice

Have partners take turns reading the selection as you circulate to provide support. Model practicing asking and answering questions with Cite Evidence callout A. For callout B, circulate and provide partners with scaffolding as needed. You might use the following suggestions to help students who are having difficulty.

### CITE EVIDENCE

**A** Prompt students to recall that in the last scene, time had passed from spring to summer. Ask students to name other words, based on the use of *spring* and *summer,* that the author is likely to use to show the passing of time. (autumn, fall, winter) Then have students look for the use of one of those words in paragraph 11.

**B** Help students identify that the Dove "hopped to safety" and "flew away" after she heard the man yell and slap his hand—which could have killed the ant. Have students identify what two actions the Ant had to take to cause the man to create the commotion.

---

**WORDS TO KNOW**
**bait**
**commotion**
**stealthy**

**CITE EVIDENCE**

**A** Ask yourself if the setting has changed. Underline the words in paragraph 11 that show that one part of the setting, the season, has changed.

**B** On page 15, circle two sentences where the Ant boldly helps the Dove. Think of a time when you took action to help a friend.

10 The Ant sometimes talked to her friends about the Dove. "Why worry about that? You will never be able to thank her," they said. "Now help me lift this blade of grass."

11 By the fall, hunters started coming into the woods. Some were noisy and would crash through the trees, wearing bright red and yellow coats. The animals had an easy time avoiding loud hunters.

12 Other hunters were **stealthy**. They walked quietly, and wore green and brown clothes. The bushes did not rustle as the quiet hunters went past. The animals had to be on the lookout for these hunters.

13 One day, the Ant was alone near a clearing in the woods. A young man was lying on his stomach at the edge of the opening, looking as if he was enjoying the fine weather. But the Ant did not like something about him. It wasn't just that he looked out of place there.

14 He had covered himself with leafy branches. He was holding two ropes in his hands, but he was not moving at all. And he was looking up into the branches of the tree above him.

15 The Ant understood. The ropes were a net, and the man had put **bait** in the net! The Ant looked up into the tree. Sitting on a branch eyeing the food on the ground was the Dove!

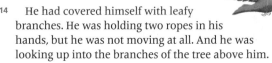

---

### Words to Know

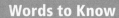

**General Academic Vocabulary**
**commotion** (*noun*): great activity, usually noisy
**stealthy** (*adjective*): quiet and secret to prevent anyone from noticing you

**Domain-Specific Vocabulary**
**bait** (*noun*): food put in a trap to attract and catch animals

**Working with Word Meaning** Have partners take turns acting out each phrase (using bait, creating commotion, and moving in a stealthy way) for each other.

Guided Practice

## KEY IDEAS AND DETAILS
### Guided Practice

16  (The Ant scrambled onto the man's hand.) As she did, the Dove fluttered to the ground. The Ant had to hurry.

17  (The Ant bit the man hard on the hand.) The man yelled and slapped his hand. The Dove heard the **commotion** and hopped to safety. As the Dove flew away, the Ant thought, "I did it. I saved my friend!"

18  *Moral: Little friends may prove to be great friends.*

### Comprehension Check

1. What is the young man in the story trying to do?

   a. get closer to the Dove to take her picture

   b. make friends with the Dove by giving her food

   c. rescue the Dove because it is injured

   (d.) trap the Dove, using food as bait

2. Why is the Ant so excited at the end of the fable?

   a. She defeated a much bigger enemy.

   (b.) She was able to save the Dove from danger.

   c. She can go back to her life without the Dove.

   d. She was able to drive the hunters out of the woods.

3. A moral tells the reader an important message of a fable. Think of questions you might ask and answer to prove that the moral given is correct. Use details from the story in your answers.

   Sample answer: Does it seem like the Ant will ever be able to thank

   the Dove? No, even her ant friends tell her she will never be able to.

   How does the Ant finally thank the Dove? The Ant thanks the Dove by

   biting the hunter and saving the Dove's life.

Unit 1 ■ Reading Literature: Key Ideas and Details   **15**

## Foundational Skill: Fluency

Tell students that they can read more fluently if they read with expression. Explain that to read with expression, they should change the pitch and pace of their voice to reflect the mood when reading narration, and to convey how a character may be feeling, when reading dialogue. Model reading paragraph 2 on page 12 with expression. Try to convey a sense of urgency when reading the narration and of despair when reading the Ant's dialogue. After students practice reading another paragraph with expression with a partner, have them record themselves reading the paragraph and then listen to their recording to improve prosodic skills. Additional fluency passages and activities can be found at **sadlierconnect.com** and in the *Foundational Skills Handbook*.

### Guided Practice

### Comprehension Check

**Answer Explanations:**

1. Choice D, *trap the Dove, using food as bait*, is what the young man is doing in paragraph 15. The text tells how the young man is holding a net and looking up, as if looking for the Dove, and how the Dove was eyeing the food in the net.

2. Choice B, *She was able to save the Dove from danger*, is why the Ant was so excited at the end of the fable. The Ant says, "I did it" as the Dove flew away because of the commotion she caused by biting the man's hand.

3. The questions and answers students note may vary but should reflect that the Ant is *little* and does not have an obvious way to thank the Dove, yet ends up thanking the Dove in a powerful way.

## Peer Collaboration

Follow this procedure for each item: Ask students to think independently about each Comprehension Check question and form their own ideas for answering them. Then have students discuss their responses to the questions with a partner. Encourage students to adjust their ideas about how to answer the questions based on their discussion with their partner. Finally, ask pairs to share their responses to the questions with another pair.

## Independent Practice

### Recap Reading Selection

Remind students that they read a fable. Have them recall the two main characters in the fable (the Ant and the Dove), the moral of the story (little friends can prove to be great friends), and what the author had the Ant do to convey the moral (the Ant saved the Dove's life).

### Read and Apply

Have students read the selection independently as you circulate. If you notice students struggling, you can provide support with the suggestions below.

### CITE EVIDENCE

**A** Explain that a story's setting includes where the story takes place, or the location of the events in the story. Help students identify that the country road, the small farmhouse, and the front porch are all places or locations.

**B** Help students see that the Crow is feeling faint, or weak, because of his thirst. Have them identify what the dust does to the Crow's level of thirst and why. Help students see that the water in the pitcher rises when the Crow drops *pebbles* into it.

---

## ASKING AND ANSWERING QUESTIONS

### Independent Practice

**WORDS TO KNOW**
despair
grief
invention

**CITE EVIDENCE**

**A** Circle words in paragraphs 1 and 2 that tell where this fable happens.

**B** Why was it difficult to get water from the pitcher? Underline evidence from the text in your answer.

# The Crow and the Pitcher:
## A Retelling of an Aesop Fable
(Genre: Fable)

1  A Crow was faint with thirst. He was so thirsty that he was too weak to fly. The (country road) was so dusty that his beautiful black feathers turned gray. The dust got in his throat, making his need for water even greater.

2  As he passed a (small farmhouse), the Crow could not believe what he saw. On the (front porch) stood a tall clay pitcher. It was the kind used to hold water. The Crow ran to it with delight. But when he reached it, his joy turned to **grief**. The pitcher contained only a little water.

3  He could not reach the water with his beak. If he turned the pitcher over, the water would run out. If he broke the pitcher, he would also lose the water. He had to have that water! He thought and thought until his head hurt.

**16**  Unit 1 ■ Reading Literature: Key Ideas and Details

---

## Words to Know

**General Academic Vocabulary**
**despair** (*noun*): the state of having no hope
**grief** (*noun*): deep sadness
**invention** (*noun*): a new way of doing something or a new machine to do something

**Working with Word Meaning** Reinforce the meaning of each word by having students use each word in a sentence unrelated to the fable.

4     In **despair**, he looked around at the pebbly ground. Pebbles! He picked up a few in his beak and dropped them in the pitcher. Again and again he did this. Soon the water level started to rise. At last the water was high enough that the Crow could reach it.

5     The pebbles and his own brainpower had saved the Crow's life.

6     *Moral: Necessity is the mother of **invention**. In other words, having a problem gives you a good reason to work hard toward a solution.*

### Comprehension Check

    ( MORE ONLINE ) **sadlierconnect.com**

**1.** Why is it so important for the Crow to get water?

    **a.** He is dying of thirst.

    **b.** He has to wash his feathers.

    **c.** He needs to rinse his throat to talk.

    **d.** He likes the pitcher.

**2.** According to the text, how does the Crow finally get the water?

    **a.** by finding a nearby stream

    **b.** by knocking over the pitcher

    **c.** by dropping pebbles in the pitcher

    **d.** by asking the owner of the farmhouse

**3.** Reread the moral at the end of this fable. Why do you think the author wrote this fable? Use information from the text in your answer.

Students should note that the Crow solves his problem in an unusual

way. He invented an original way to get the water. The author

probably wanted the reader to understand that there are often

many ways to solve a problem.

Unit 1 ■ Reading Literature: Key Ideas and Details    **17**

## Extend Thinking: Create

Help students extend their thinking by writing a one- or two-paragraph fable on paper or on a computer. Remind students to include an animal as one of the main characters, convey a moral or lesson, and illustrate their story.

Before writing, have partners brainstorm morals (bad friends lose friends; a bird in the hand is better than two in the bush; honesty is the best policy) that they could convey in their stories.

Have students present their fables to the class. Listeners should pay attention and ask questions to check their understanding. Speakers should speak clearly, in complete sentences, and at a reasonable rate.

### Comprehension Check

**Answer Explanations:**

**1.** Choice A, *He is dying of thirst,* tells why it is so important for the Crow to get water.

**2.** Choice C, *by dropping pebbles in the pitcher*, explains how the water rose in the pitcher, allowing the Crow to finally get the water.

**3.** Students' answers may vary but should reflect that the Crow solved his problem by inventing a new way of doing something, and that the author probably wants readers not to give up when faced with a problem.

## Critical Comprehension

Use the following questions to help students think more deeply about the text. Students should be prepared to support their answers with evidence from the text.

- *What are three details that show that the Crow is clever?* (The Crow knew not to turn the pitcher over; knew not to break the pitcher; figured out to add pebbles to it.)

- *What do you think would have happened if Crow had not thought to put pebbles in the pitcher?* (He would have died. He would have come up with another solution.)

### Assess and Respond

**If** students have difficulty answering the questions in the Comprehension Check…

**Then** work individually with them, providing sentence frames to guide them to the answers. Point to details in the text and ask how they help answer the questions.

# Determining a Central Message

## Guided Instruction

### OBJECTIVE

**Determine and explain the central message, lesson, or moral of a story, using key details from the text.**

### Genre: Folktale

Explain to students that a folktale is a short story first told long ago. It is often based on the life of a real person. It may tell, in an exaggerated way, about an amazing feat the person did.

### Set the Purpose

Help students understand the purpose for learning the reading skill by asking *Why do you think people tell folktales?*

### Model and Teach

Read the selection as students follow along in their books.

### CITE EVIDENCE

**A** *I will look for details that help me understand John Henry's life.*

*What details help us understand that he had the ability to do something amazing?* ("giant of a man," "most powerful")

**B** *The text tells me that John Henry worked for the C&O Railroad. When and where was the C&O Railroad being built?* (in 1870; through West Virginia)

---

## DETERMINING A CENTRAL MESSAGE

### Guided Instruction

**WORDS TO KNOW**

cave-in
lay claim
steam-powered

To explain how a folktale **conveys its central message**, you can **retell the key details** of the story.

**CITE EVIDENCE**

**A** To understand the **central message** of the folktale, look for how the author uses **key details** to communicate the central message. In paragraphs 1–2, circle the details that tell whom the folktale is about.

**B** In paragraph 4, underline the key details that provide this folktale's setting—its time and place. Many stories take place long ago or in faraway places. What is the setting of one of your favorite stories?

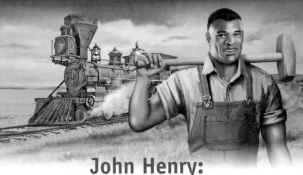

# John Henry:
## A Retelling of an American Folktale
### (Genre: Folktale)

1  John Henry was a giant of a man. Some say he was born in Virginia. Some say Carolina or Alabama. It seems like every state wants to **lay claim** to John Henry.

2  It seems pretty certain that John Henry was a real steel-driving man. He was born into slavery in the 1840s but was freed after the Civil War. He found work as a steel-driver for the Chesapeake & Ohio Railroad. He was known as the most powerful man working the rails.

3  The work was dangerous and back-breaking. The men drilled holes in solid rock. It might take all day to drill holes deep enough for blasting. And the tunnel might advance only 10 feet a day!

4  In 1870, the C&O Railroad was being built through West Virginia. But right in its path was Big Bend Mountain. It was more than a mile through that mountain. The men of the C&O were going to drill right through the heart of it by hand.

**18**    Unit 1 ■ Reading Literature: Key Ideas and Details

---

## Words to Know

**General Academic Vocabulary**

**lay claim** (*verb*): to say something belongs to you or is because of you

**Domain-Specific Vocabulary**

**cave-in** (*noun*): the collapsing or crumbling in of a cave or tunnel
**steam-powered** (*adjective*): powered by steam (as opposed to electricity or gas)

**Working with Word Meaning** Broaden students' understanding of the words by having them create a word web for each word, completing it with synonyms and examples.

## KEY IDEAS AND DETAILS

5    It took three long years to get through Big Bend. As many as a thousand workers lost their lives. If the **cave-ins** didn't get them, the smoke and dust did. Through it all, John Henry worked tirelessly. Some say he swung a 9-pound hammer. Some say it was 14 pounds or even 20 pounds! No other steel-driving man could match him for drilling holes.

6    The story is told that one day a salesman showed up at John Henry's camp. He had with him a **steam-powered** drill. He said it could outdrill any man. Those were fighting words to John Henry. They set up a contest: John Henry against the machine!

### CITE EVIDENCE

**C** Folktales often include larger-than-life characters whose special abilities move the story toward its central message. In paragraph 5, circle John Henry's special abilities.

**D** A folktale's central message is often reached by way of a dramatic event or contest. Underline the event or contest agreed upon in paragraph 6.

**Comprehension Check**

How is John Henry different from the other workers on the C&O Railroad?

Unit 1 ■ Reading Literature: Key Ideas and Details    **19**

## Guided Instruction

### CITE EVIDENCE

**C** *I'll look for details that show that John Henry can do things that other people can't—or that show he is "larger-than-life."*

*Drilling through a mountain seems like hard work that would wear people out. How did John Henry work through it all?* (tirelessly) *What details tell you he was incredibly strong?* (He swung a hammer that was 9, 14, or even 20 pounds.) *What could other steel-driving men not match him at?* (drilling holes)

**D** *I'll look for words that relate to a contest.*

*What word in paragraph 6 helps you understand who or what John Henry will be in a contest against?* (the machine)

**Comprehension Check**

**Sample Answer:** John Henry is stronger and works harder and faster than other workers on the C&O railroad.

**Answer Explanation:** Students should recognize that being able to swing a 20-pound hammer requires great strength. They should also understand that no one else could match Henry drilling, and he was willing to compete against a machine. These details show how John Henry was different from the other workers.

### Review: Ask and Answer Questions

Have students come up with questions about the upcoming contest described in paragraph 6 on page 19. Prompt students by asking what they are curious about at this point in the story.

## Support English Language Learners

Help Mandarin native speakers and other English language learners who speak languages that do not rely heavily on pronouns to make sense of sentences with pronoun references.

Explain that a pronoun is a word that takes the place of a noun. List common pronouns: *I, me, he, him, she, her, they, them, we, us*. Read the first two sentences of the story. Explain that "he" in the second sentence refers back to, or is taking the place of "John Henry," who is mentioned in the first sentence. Have students read the second sentence aloud, replacing "he" with "John Henry" to reinforce their understanding of how pronouns relate to nouns. Repeat as you continue reading the story with students, providing a gradual release to allow them to identify the noun.

## Guided Practice

### Recap Reading Selection

Have students recall what they have read so far about John Henry. They should mention that John Henry is a steel-driving man who helps build railroads. He is very strong and fast. He has just agreed to compete with a machine to see which one of them can drill through the mountain faster.

### Read and Practice

Have partners take turns reading the selection as you circulate to provide support. Model determining a central message with Cite Evidence callout A. For callout B, circulate and provide partners with scaffolding as needed. You might use the following suggestions to help students who are having difficulty.

### CITE EVIDENCE

**A** Ask students to look for a detail that relates to a possible outcome to the contest. ("die with this hammer in my hand") Ask them what that outcome might have to do with the central message of the story.

**B** Help students identify that John Henry "fell to the ground." Then help them recognize that "the greatest driller" in the last sentence refers to John Henry. This may help them understand that he dies. Then ask students if John Henry's victory was worth dying for. Prompt them to cite evidence to support their opinions.

---

# DETERMINING A CENTRAL MESSAGE

## Guided Practice

**John Henry:** A Retelling of an American Folktale *continued*

**WORDS TO KNOW**
onlooker
outdrilled
spirit

**CITE EVIDENCE**

**A** A story sometimes gives clues about what might happen later in the story. Circle a clue in paragraph 7 about what might happen later.

**B** Underline the key detail in paragraph 10 that shows what happened to the hero. Was the price the hero paid worth what he had won?

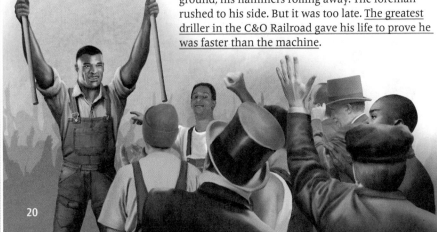

7    Some men said John Henry couldn't beat the machine. Some said he was holding back the future. But according to one of the songs sung about him:
"John Henry said to the Captain,
'A man ain't nothing but a man
But before I let that steam drill drive me down
I'll die with this hammer in my hand.'"

8    The contest began. Pretty soon, the smoke and steam started to choke the **onlookers**. The noise of the drilling matched the noise of the cheering. John Henry drilled deeper into the mountain. The machine did the same.

9    Some say man and machine fought it out from sunup to sundown. Others say it took less than an hour. Some say John Henry swung two 20-pound hammers, one in each hand. But everyone agrees on the result. John Henry **outdrilled** that steam drill!

10   John Henry held up his hammers in triumph! The men shouted and cheered. But folks tell different stories about what happened next. John Henry was exhausted, and some say the great man fell to the ground, his hammers rolling away. The foreman rushed to his side. But it was too late. The greatest driller in the C&O Railroad gave his life to prove he was faster than the machine.

20

---

## Words to Know

**General Academic Vocabulary**
**onlooker** (*noun*): a person watching something
**spirit** (*noun*): the way someone is; the qualities that make someone who they are

**Domain-Specific Vocabulary**
**outdrilled** (*verb*): drilled faster than anyone else

**Working with Word Meaning** Pair students and have one partner give the definition and the other partner then name the word. Then have partners switch roles. You may want to create flashcards for students.

## KEY IDEAS AND DETAILS

11    John Henry lives on in song and story. New tunnels are being dug every year. Workers risk their lives to go into the darkness to do their jobs. And with them goes the **spirit** of John Henry: a man who was nothing but a man.

### Comprehension Check

1. According to the text, why is it hard to say how John Henry died?

   a. No one thought it was important.

   b. No one remembers how he died.

   c. People tell different stories about John Henry.

   d. He disappeared and no one ever saw him again.

2. What superhuman feat does John Henry do in the story?

   a. He lives for a very long time.

   b. He works as a steel-driving man.

   c. He outdrills a machine in a contest.

   d. He drills deeper holes than any other worker.

3. Almost 150 years have passed since John Henry's feat. Machines have taken over most drilling work. Why is the story of John Henry still retold? Cite information from the text to support your answer.

   Students should mention that John Henry's feat is more than just a physical one. It is an inspiring story about fighting against impossible odds and winning through skill and determination. The text supports this by describing how John Henry lives on in song and story.

Unit 1 ■ Reading Literature: Key Ideas and Details    21

### Digital Connection: Post to a Website

Point out that John Henry's story has been told orally and in print since the late 1800s. Explain that today we can use the Internet to share information, such as a story.

Have students write one or two paragraphs to retell a fable or folktale of their choosing or one that you have assigned to them. Then help them post their retellings to the school or class website.

To challenge students, you may wish to have them create a screenplay of their retelling, acting it out with a partner or small group. If possible they can make a video recording of their retelling, and then post it to the website.

### Comprehension Check

**Answer Explanations:**

1. Students should have noticed the use of the phrase *some say* throughout the story, and recognize that choice C, *People tell different stories about John Henry,* shows why it is hard to say how he died.

2. Choice C, *He outdrills a machine in a contest,* is the superhuman feat John Henry does. The text emphasizes how much stronger and powerful John Henry is than any other driller to set up the idea that only he could have won the contest against the machine.

3. Students' responses may vary, but students should note that John Henry's story is inspiring, and people probably retell it to encourage others to not back down from challenges or contests that seem impossible to win.

## Writearound

Organize students in groups of four. Tell them they are going to summarize the story. Have all students write down this sentence starter on a piece of paper: *John Henry worked as a _____.* Ask students to complete the sentence individually. Then have them pass their papers to the right, read the sentence they receive, and add a sentence to build the summary. Repeat two more times. Then give each group time to review their four summaries, pick their favorite, and revise it.

## Independent Practice

### Recap Reading Selection

Have a short class discussion about the folktale "John Henry." Prompt students to recall John Henry's superhuman skills (very strong and very fast), the amazing feat he accomplished with those skills (He outdrilled a machine.), and the central message of the story. (You can win under impossible odds.)

### Read and Apply

Have students read the selection independently as you circulate to provide support. If you notice students struggling, you can provide support with the suggestions below.

### CITE EVIDENCE

**A** Students should recognize that no real human is "30 feet tall" or "12 feet tall when born," and that no real boat is ever in danger of "scraping" the moon.

**B** The words *wrestled*, *beat*, and *tied* should signal to students that this part of the paragraph describes the battle Stormalong had with the giant octopus.

Students should explain that Stormalong and John Henry both have superhuman strength and both won a battle despite impossible odds of winning it.

---

## DETERMINING A CENTRAL MESSAGE

### Independent Practice

**WORDS TO KNOW**
**hinge**
**massive**
**ultimate**

**CITE EVIDENCE**

**A** Underline the sentences in paragraph 1 that tell you unusual details about the main character in the story and his boat.

**B** In paragraph 5, circle a detail about Stormalong's battle with the giant octopus. Use this detail to tell how Stormalong and John Henry are alike.

22

# Old Stormalong and the Octopus:
## A Retelling of an American Folktale
### (Genre: Folktale)

1   Old Stormalong was the **ultimate** sailor. He stood 30 feet tall, although he was only 12 feet tall when he was born. His sailing boat, the *Courser*, was built to his size. Its masts were on **hinges** so it could sail past the Moon without scraping it.

2   One day Stormalong told his crew to lift anchor. But the anchor was stuck on something! Try as they might, the crew could not get it unstuck. Even Stormalong couldn't pull it loose. So Stormalong decided to go down to the depths of the ocean to see what was tangling the anchor.

3   Taking only a knife, Stormalong dove into the water. Soon the waters below the **massive** ship began to bubble. The waves grew higher and higher until the ship was tossed around like a rubber duck. Finally the sea grew calm. But there was still no sign of the captain! As the crew was about to give up hope, Stormalong popped up on deck. "All's clear, boys. Hoist the anchor!" he shouted.

4   The crew gathered around Stormalong, shouting questions. "What was holding us? How did you get us loose? How did you save us and the ship?"

---

## Words to Know

**General Academic Vocabulary**
**massive** (*adjective*): very large; huge
**ultimate** (*adjective*): the best; a perfect example of

**Domain-Specific Vocabulary**
**hinge** (*noun*): a device that bends and holds two pieces together so that one of them can fold or swing back and forth

**Working with Word Meaning** Have students share an example and a non-example for each word with a partner.

## KEY IDEAS AND DETAILS

5    "It was a giant octopus, twice as big as me," Stormalong explained. "It had grabbed the anchor with four legs. It was holding on to the seafloor with the other four legs. So I arm-wrestled the beast, one arm at a time. After I beat the last arm, I tied all of them into knots." Stormalong shrugged. "It will take him a week to get himself undone." And off Old Stormalong sailed!

### Comprehension Check

(MORE ONLINE) sadlierconnect.com

1. Folktales use exaggeration to tell about the characters. What do the exaggerated details in the story tell you about Stormalong?

   a. He is able to sail anywhere he wants.

   **b.** He is unusually strong, brave, and determined.

   c. He has a strange sense of humor.

   d. He needs a crew of people to help him.

2. Exaggerated details in a folktale are often based on a real problem. What is MOST LIKELY real in the story?

   a. A sailor wrestling an octopus

   **b.** An anchor stuck on the sea bottom

   c. A sailor diving to the bottom of the ocean

   d. An octopus holding on to an anchor

3. In a few sentences, retell the story of how Stormalong freed the *Courser*. Then cite evidence to support the folktale's message.

Sample answer: When the crew couldn't get the anchor loose,

Stormalong dove into the water. He fought a giant octopus that was

holding the anchor. He tied its legs into knots and freed the anchor.

This supports the message that a single act of bravery can save the day.

---

### Comprehension Check

**Answer Explanations:**

1. Students should understand that the exaggerations about Stormalong's battle with the octopus show that choice B, *He is unusually strong, brave, and determined*, is correct.

2. Choice B, *An anchor stuck on the sea bottom*, is something that could happen in real life. An octopus holding onto an anchor is an exaggeration of this problem.

3. Students' responses may vary but should retell the folktale and explain the message that a single act of bravery can save the day.

## Critical Comprehension

Use the following questions to help students think more deeply about the text. Students should be prepared to support their answers with evidence from the text.

- *What do the crew members do—or not do—to show they are not as brave as Stormalong?* (They do not dive into the water. They almost give up hope.)

- *Why do you think the crew almost gives up hope?* (They think Stormalong has drowned. The sea grows calm, and there is no sign of him.)

| **Assess and Respond** |
| --- |
| **If** students have trouble answering the questions in the Comprehension Check… |
| **Then** make sure students understand the questions before rereading the story. Have them paraphrase each story paragraph to check comprehension. |

---

## Foundational Skill Review: Inflectional Endings

Review reading words with the inflectional ending -*ed*, reminding students that the -*ed* ending can be pronounced in three different ways—/t/, /d/, and /ed/. Model these three pronunciations using words such as: *dressed* (/t/), *played* (/d/), and *boasted* (/ed/). Then have students identify the inflectional ending sound for these words from the text: *decided* (/ed/), *tossed* (/t/), *popped* (/t/), *shouted* (/ed/), *gathered* (/d/), *explained* (/d/), *grabbed* (/d/), *wrestled* (/d/).

Additional phonics activities can be found in the *Foundational Skills Handbook* at the end of this guide.

## Guided Instruction

### OBJECTIVE
**Describe characters in a story, including how their actions contribute to the sequence of events.**

### Genre: Myth

Explain that a myth is a story that was first told long ago. Myths often explain the natural world, tell a cultural tradition, or show good or heroic behavior. Greek myths feature humans, fantastical creatures, and gods and goddesses.

### Set the Purpose

Activate students' thinking about the reading skill by asking *What words would you use to describe yourself?*

### Model and Teach

Read the selection as students follow along in their books.

### CITE EVIDENCE

**A** *The first sentence tells me that the days are troubled. I will look for words that show how the king is feeling.*

*What words show that he felt troubled?* (heavy heart, full of worries)

**B** *From the first paragraph, I know that the king forgets to make an offering to Artemis.*

*How does Artemis feel about that?* (The goddess is offended and angry, so she sends the boar.)

---

## DESCRIBING CHARACTERS

### Guided Instruction

**WORDS TO KNOW**
approaching
expert
murmur
offering

> Think about details that help you **understand characters** and why they do what they do.

#### CITE EVIDENCE

**A** Each **character** has **feelings, qualities,** or **motivations** that help explain how he or she acts. Underline the words in paragraph 1 that tell how the king is feeling.

**B** In paragraph 2, circle the sentence that explains why Artemis sent the boar. Folktales and myths often have fantastical creatures in them. Which other story in this unit features a giant creature?

# Atalanta the Huntress
(Genre: Myth)

1   In troubled days, when the tribes were on the edge of war, King Oineus made **offerings** to the gods with a <u>heavy heart</u>. To the goddess of the harvest, he gave the first fruits of the field. To the god of grapes, he poured fine wine. To the goddess of wisdom, he offered shimmering oil from her sacred trees. To each god who dwells on Mount Olympus, the king gave what was fitting—except one. <u>Full of worries</u>, he forgot to offer flowers to Artemis, goddess of the hunt.

2   (The goddess was offended.) In anger, she sent a giant boar to the land around the city. The great boar ran wild. It tore up crops and farms. It chased the dogs and ruined the herds. It attacked farmers and travelers alike. Brave men did their best to put an end to the terror. They failed, one after another. The king was too old to go after the beast. And his good son, Meleager, was away on another adventure. Now the people were afraid. What was the king to do?

**24**    Unit 1 ■ Reading Literature: Key Ideas and Details

---

## Words to Know

**General Academic Vocabulary**

**approaching** (*verb*): coming closer

**expert** (*adjective*): very good at something

**murmur** (*noun*): a low sound, like many whispers happening at the same time

**offering** (*noun*): something given as thanks or out of respect

**Working with Word Meaning** Have students write a sentence for each word, leaving a blank for the word. Then have them trade papers with a partner and write the correct word to complete their partner's sentences.

---

## KEY IDEAS AND DETAILS

3  The ⟨aged⟩ king did his best to comfort the people. He sent word for help across all of Greece. ⟨**Expert**⟩ hunters and ⟨grim⟩ soldiers answered the call. The king, however, waited for his son, Meleager, to return. At last, the watchmen at the city walls saw Meleager and his friends **approaching**. On his way to the city, the king's son had seen the ruined farms and empty homes. From ⟨tough⟩ farmers who wouldn't leave their places, he learned about the curse of Artemis upon the land. Now the king's ⟨brave⟩ son entered the city with his friends. The citizens cheered as the group of twenty men marched into town. Then a **murmur** broke through the crowd. The people saw among those ⟨hard⟩ fighters a ⟨beautiful⟩ ⟨young⟩ woman. It was the huntress, Atalanta.

### CITE EVIDENCE

**C** Descriptive words, such as adjectives, help readers understand characters. Circle each adjective in paragraph 3 that describes a character.

**D** A story can only move forward through characters' actions. Underline the action of the new characters in the story. How do you think the arrival of Meleager and his friends will change the story?

### Comprehension Check

Why did the king forget Artemis and what was the result of his forgetfulness? Cite text evidence in your answer.

## Support English Language Learners

English language learners who are speakers of Arabic or another language that does not have an equivalent to the verb "to be" may have difficulty unpacking the meaning of sentences that contain *am, is, are, was, were,* and other forms of the verb. For these students, the meaning of "The goddess offended" is easier to determine than the meaning of "The goddess was offended."

Explain that "to be" is a verb that shows a state of existence. Create lists of the present and past tense forms of the verb. Read through the story with students, stopping at each "to be" word. Discuss whether the verb is in the present or past tense and how it affects the meaning of the sentence.

### CITE EVIDENCE

**C** *As I read, I'll look for a character name. Then I'll look for an adjective that describes him or her. The first character mentioned is the king. What adjective describes him?* (aged) *What does this tell you about the king?* (He is having a difficult time.)

**D** *I'll do the same thing for actions. What action does the king take?* (to comfort the people) *What does this tell you about the mood in the town?* (The mood is troubled; grim.)

### Comprehension Check

**Sample Answer:** King Oineus was "full of worries" because the tribes were on the edge of war.

**Answer Explanation:** Students should understand that King Oineus is the king of one of the tribes on the edge of war, and he is likely worried that his tribe would be hurt or killed in a war.

## Listening and Viewing Skills

Reread the last five sentences of paragraph 3 as students listen and look at the illustration on page 25. *Why do Meleager and his friends cause the crowd to cheer?* (They have weapons and armor.) *Why doesn't the crowd notice Atalanta at first?* (She is dressed like the men.)

## Review: Determining a Central Message

Remind students to identify key details in the text that will help them determine the central message of the story. Ask them to think about how Atalanta might relate to the central message.

### Guided Practice

#### Recap Reading Selection

Have students recall what they have read so far in the myth. They should be able to say that the king's son, Meleager, has just arrived in the town with his friends and Atalanta, the huntress, to battle the giant boar sent by Artemis.

#### Read and Practice

Have partners take turns reading the selection as you circulate to provide support. Model how to describe characters with Cite Evidence callout A. For callout B, circulate and provide partners with scaffolding as needed. You might use the following suggestions to help students who are having difficulty.

#### CITE EVIDENCE

**A** Point out the sentence "Atalanta grew up fit and strong" in paragraph 4. Then guide students to identify the sentences with evidence of her strength and ability to fight and hunt. (the sentences about her encounters with the Centaurs and Peleus)

**B** Direct students to the phrase "among them" and ask students to name who the "them" are. Then ask students to find the word that shows how Atalanta carried herself, or walked, among the warriors. (proudly)

---

## DESCRIBING CHARACTERS

### Guided Practice

**WORDS TO KNOW**

**Centaur**
**focused**
**outrage**

**CITE EVIDENCE**

**A** Circle evidence in paragraph 4 that provides information about Atalanta's traits.

**B** Underline the sentences in paragraphs 5 and 6 that describe how Atalanta's arrival affects the events that follow.

**Atalanta the Huntress** *continued*

4    People said a bear found Atalanta in the forest when she was a baby. The animal cared for Atalanta until a family of hunters found her. They raised her as their own in a wild mountain home. Atalanta grew up fit and strong. She learned to hunt and fight. She was as fine an archer as any man. She had a focused, steady eye. Everyone told stories about Atalanta. Two **Centaurs** once attacked the girl while she hunted in the forest. She heard them coming. She laid them low with two shafts from her bow. She once defeated the great wrestler Peleus in a fair match. She fought beside Meleager in far-off lands and didn't complain when she was injured.

5    Now here she was, traveling with the fierce friends of Meleager. Atalanta walked proudly among them. She was taller than many of the men. Her long hair was pulled back in a single braid. She carried a bow and a quiver of arrows over her shoulders. Whoever dared to meet her gaze saw a light that burned like fire in her eyes. The heroes got ready to hunt. The king came to meet them. People strained their necks for a glimpse of Atalanta.

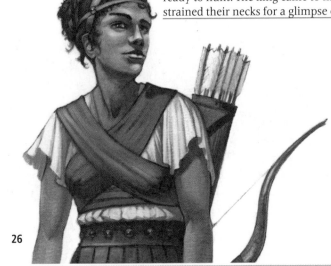

26

### Words to Know

**General Academic Vocabulary**

**focused** (*adjective*): deeply concentrated on or absorbed by something

**outrage** (*noun*): a feeling of great anger at an injustice

**Domain-Specific Vocabulary**

**Centaur** (*noun*): a beast in Greek mythology that has the head, torso, and arms of a man, but the body and legs of a horse

**Working with Word Meaning** Challenge students to write a one-paragraph short story about a Centaur by using the words in the selection.

## KEY IDEAS AND DETAILS

6    In those dark, ancient days, it was strange to see a woman standing equal with such men. Women didn't hunt, or fight, or wrestle champions. <u>When they realized Atalanta was joining the hunt, some of Greece's bravest heroes grew red in the face. A few reacted with **outrage**. They said they wouldn't hunt beside a woman.</u> But Meleager asked, "Are you afraid you won't match up?" Since no one would admit this, the hunt was on.

### Comprehension Check

**1.** According to the text, most of the people in the crowd probably want to see Atalanta because they are

- **a.** angry
- **(b.)** curious
- **c.** jealous
- **d.** hopeful

**2.** Which is a trait that is NOT supported by the text's description of Atalanta?

- **a.** brave
- **b.** unusual
- **c.** talented
- **(d.)** enthusiastic

**3.** Why were some of the heroes offended when they discovered Atalanta would be joining the hunt? Use evidence from the text to show the effects her actions had on following events.

Sample answer: It was unusual and improper for women to hunt in their

culture. The king then asks the warriors if they are afraid Atalanta will be

better and braver than they will be. They will not admit it.

### Comprehension Check

**Answer Explanations:**

**1.** Choice B, *curious*, is correct because paragraphs 6 and 7 state that people in the crowd "strained" to see Atalanta; they thought "it was strange to see a woman standing equal with such men."

**2.** Choice D, *enthusiastic*, is the only trait not supported by the text, which describes Atalanta as a brave and talented hunter and an unusual sight among the male heroes.

**3.** Students' responses should note how in ancient Greek culture, women were not accepted as hunters. Students should also note that some of the heroes might have worried that Atalanta would prove to be a better warrior and thus embarrass them.

## Grouping Options

Support striving readers in answering these questions, which require a fair amount of inferencing, by pairing them with proficient or advanced readers. Have partners discuss the questions and work together to answer them. Tell partners to be sure that both members of the pair understand each question before attempting to answer it.

## Discussion Skills

Explain to students that when they share ideas during a class discussion, it is important to follow certain rules, such as speaking one at a time, listening to others with respect and without interrupting, asking questions without being insulting, and not over-talking or monopolizing.

After explaining the rules for respectful discussion, present a series of scenarios to students and then ask whether a scenario reflects the rules. For example: *Ben shares an idea for a creative project. Gina says, "That's boring!"* (does not follow the rules) *Ben shares an idea for a creative project. Gina says, "That could be fun. But what if we did this other idea instead?"* (follows the rules)

## Independent Practice

### Recap Reading Selection

Remind students that they have been reading a Greek myth called "Atalanta the Huntress." Ask students what they remember about what they have read so far. Students should recall that the king has upset the goddess Artemis by failing to make an offering to her, so she sends a giant boar to destroy crops and attack people. The king's son, Meleager, and his friends, including Atalanta, show up at the king's town, ready to hunt the boar. However, some of the heroes do not like the idea of hunting with Atalanta because she is a woman.

### Read and Apply

Have students read the selection independently as you circulate. If you notice students struggling, you can provide support with the suggestions below.

### CITE EVIDENCE

**A** Students should recognize that no real boar is as big as a bull or has tusks that release sparks.

**B** Have students identify why the men are outraged. (Meleager gives the trophy to Atalanta.) Then have them identify why Meleager's uncles want to leave the city. This should help them recognize that Meleager stands up to the other men in support of Atalanta.

---

Atalanta the Huntress *continued*

**WORDS TO KNOW**
bloodshot
enormous
intervened

**CITE EVIDENCE**

**A** Circle evidence in paragraph 7 that suggests the boar is a supernatural, mythical creature.

**B** Underline where Meleager stands up to the men in support of Atalanta. This shows Meleager's loyalty to his friend. Is loyalty important to you and your friends?

7    The heroes set out to find the trail. They found marks of hooves and tusks. They unleashed their dogs to track the beast by its scent. A long time passed before the trail led to a deep, rocky valley. Now the hunters heard the dogs' wild barking ahead. They sprang into action. Atalanta was the first to see the boar. Big as a bull, it stomped and charged to keep the dogs at bay. Its **bloodshot** eyes burned like red coals. Its long tusks were as sharp as spears. Sparks flew from its tusks and set the grass on fire.

8    Atalanta stood still as stone, waiting for a clear shot. Two running hunters cast a net to catch the **enormous** boar between them. The monster charged, taking both men to the ground. It ran off, dragging the net behind. The dogs blocked its path. Now thirty hunters took their places. Each spear thrown missed its mark, as if Artemis herself had **intervened**. The boar snorted fiercely. Men and dogs lay wounded on the ground, or limped away from danger. Atalanta took one shot and missed her target. Her second arrow struck the beast behind its ear. When the boar went wild, it was Meleager who brought it down with his long spear.

28

---

## Words to Know

**General Academic Vocabulary**
**bloodshot** (*adjective*): very red and irritated
**enormous** (*noun*): very big; huge
**intervened** (*verb*): stepped into or got involved in a situation to stop something from happening

**Working with Word Meaning** Have students use a thesaurus to find one synonym and one antonym for each word. Then have them share their synonyms and antonyms with a partner, who will state which word each synonym and antonym relates to.

## KEY IDEAS AND DETAILS
### Independent Practice

9   Back in the city, the old king offered the monster's hide to his son. Meleager said the trophy wasn't his. He gave it to the huntress, the first to hit the mark. Some of the men were outraged to see the honor go to a woman. When Meleager wouldn't budge, his own uncles stood to leave the city. They left with a promise: "You haven't heard the last from us."

**Comprehension Check**    ( MORE ONLINE )  sadlierconnect.com

1. Which is a reason Meleager probably did NOT have for giving the trophy to Atalanta?

   (a.) He did not think she deserved it.

   **b.** He was grateful for Atalanta's help.

   **c.** He wanted to prove a point.

   **d.** Atalanta hit the boar first.

2. What character's (or characters') actions seem to protect the boar from the hunters?

   **a.** King Oineus

   **b.** the gods on Mount Olympus

   (c.) Artemis

   **d.** Meleager's uncles

3. What does the anger of Meleager's uncles make them promise, and what do they mean? Use details to support your answer.

   Sample answer: The uncles promise to return to take revenge because

   of Meleager's actions. The honor won by  Atalanta has made the

   uncles angry.

Unit 1 ▪ Reading Literature: Key Ideas and Details   **29**

## Speaking and Listening Presentation

Ask students to create presentations on fables, folktales, or myths. Have students from diverse backgrounds interview each other about stories from their cultures. After gathering information, students should take turns presenting to the class. Presenters should:

• state their topic and present appropriate facts with descriptive details.

• use formal language suitable for an academic presentation, including precise words for effect.

• speak clearly, in complete sentences, and at a reasonable rate.

• answer questions in complete sentences.

Students should listen attentively and ask questions.

### Independent Practice

**Comprehension Check**

**Answer Explanations:**

1. Students should recognize that all options other than choice A, *He did not think she deserved it,* are supported by details in the text.

2. Students should recall that paragraph 8 says the arrows missed their mark "as if Artemis herself had intervened," so choice C, *Artemis,* is correct.

3. Students' responses should explain that the "promise" means that the uncles will return to take revenge against Meleager.

## Critical Comprehension

Use the following questions to help students think more deeply about the text. Students should be prepared to support their answers with evidence from the text.

• *What details signal that Meleager was likely to be loyal to Atalanta?* (He travels with her. He fights by her side.)

• *How do you think the townspeople feel after learning that the boar has been brought down?* (They no longer need to be comforted. They are happy.)

**Assess and Respond**

**If** students have trouble answering the questions in the Comprehension Check…

**Then** model scanning the text, looking for details that relate to the first question. Guide students to use the details to answer the question. Repeat for the remaining questions.

### OBJECTIVES

- Show an understanding of the text by asking questions and citing evidence from the text to answer questions.
- Determine and explain the central message, lesson, or moral of a story, using key details from the text.
- Describe characters in a story, including how their actions contribute to the sequence of events.

## Genre: Myth

Remind students that a myth, like a fable and a folktale, is a short story that was first told long ago. Myths often explain something about the natural world, tell about a cultural tradition, provide an example of how people should treat each other, or show heroic behavior. Myths are a part of many different cultures. Greek myths usually feature humans, supernatural creatures, and gods and goddesses.

## Path Options

You may want to do a close reading with students; if so, use the supports provided on these pages. Or, you may wish to have the students read the text independently and apply the skills learned in this unit. In either case, students should read the text more than once to facilitate understanding and to be able to answer the Comprehension Check questions correctly.

---

# Heracles and Atlas
### (Genre: Myth)

1     When Zeus, king of gods, married Hera, the couple received a gift from Mother Earth. She gave them beautiful golden apples. These apples sparkled like the setting sun and brought joy to anyone who ate them. Hera planted them in the home of the Hesperides, three nymphs who were daughters of the Titan, Atlas. A garden of apple trees sprang up there. Hera asked the nymphs to protect the enchanted garden. She asked them to care for her fruit. But the nymphs couldn't help themselves from eating the apples—such sweet joy it was to eat them! So Hera brought a fierce dragon, Ladon, into the garden. The dragon would help the nymphs protect the garden from intruders. And it would help protect the apples from the nymphs.

2     Now the old Titan, Atlas, once made war against the king of gods. When he lost, Zeus banished him to the garden of the Hesperides. Then he lifted the dome of the Sky and put it on Atlas's shoulders. Now the Titan would stand forever, carrying the weight of the Sky in his daughters' garden.

---

## Support English Language Learners

English language learners may have difficulty making sense of some of the archaic language and phrasing that gives the myth an authentic feel. Pair English language learners with reading buddies who have strong reading skills, and have them work together to underline these phrases and sentences in the story: "brought joy to," "once made war against," "When the king commanded, Heracles obeyed," "Across the garden stood old Atlas," "He was quick to agree," "Too long I've suffered." Then have pairs discuss what each phrase or sentence means and to restate it in clearer, more familiar language. Encourage them to reread sentences and paragraphs for context clues that can help them unpack the meaning of the unfamiliar phrases and sentences. Circulate around the room, making sure that the stronger reader is not dominating the conversation.

## KEY IDEAS AND DETAILS

3    Many years later, a king ordered Heracles to bring him apples from that garden. When the king commanded, Heracles obeyed. But there was one small problem. Nobody seemed to know how to find the garden of the Hesperides.

4    Heracles, a son of Zeus himself, set out to find it. He scoured the world, searching high and low. But he couldn't find the garden. Eventually, he decided to ask Atlas's brother, Prometheus. Maybe he would know where it was hidden. Prometheus was easy to track down. He was chained to a mountain. Zeus had bound him there years ago, to punish him for stealing fire from the gods. Heracles went to Prometheus and made him an offer. "You've suffered long enough for your crime. I'll break these chains and set you free. But first, promise to tell me where to find the garden of the Hesperides. I'm bound to get some apples there."

5    Prometheus agreed. Heracles took one heavy chain in each hand. His whole body straining, he broke the chains with one tug. In return, Prometheus told him where he could find the garden. It was hidden in the mountains at the western edge of the world. He gave the hero a warning. The dragon that guarded the apples was too powerful to defeat, even for a son of Zeus.

6    Following Prometheus's directions, Heracles found the mountain at the edge of the world. He climbed the rocky mountain until he reached a moss-covered ridge. On the other side he saw the garden of the Hesperides, full of trees. Green and yellow leaves whispered in the breeze. Apples shone like little setting suns. The whole garden glowed with their golden light. Under the trees, Heracles saw three nymphs singing. He could barely hear their voices, sweet as the apples they loved. Curled around them, at their feet, was the dragon, Ladon. The creature was blue, like a deep river. Its long tail encircled the garden. Steam hissed from its nostrils when it breathed.

Unit 1 ■ Reading Literature: Key Ideas and Details    **31**

---

## Support First Reading

Circulate to check students' understanding. As needed, use the following comprehension and strategy check-ins to support basic understanding of the selection as students read.

### Check-in Questions

- *What gifts do Zeus and Hera receive? How does Hera protect them?* (They receive golden apples from Mother Earth. Hera puts them in a garden and has three nymphs and a dragon protect them.)

- *Who sets out to find the garden? Why? What challenges does he face as he tries to find the garden?* (Heracles, a son of Zeus, sets out to find the garden because a king orders him to bring back apples from the garden. At first, Heracles can't find the garden. Then he must break Prometheus's chains to free him so that Prometheus will tell him where the garden is. Finally, he must climb a rocky mountain and get past a powerful dragon.)

## Review: Asking and Answering Questions

Review with students that asking and answering questions can help them better understand the story. *What is Atlas's problem?* (He has to hold up the sky.) *Why does he have this problem?* (Zeus made him hold the sky after Atlas lost a war against him.)

---

## Differentiate Instruction

Striving readers may have difficulty keeping track of the many characters and settings. Pair them with reading buddies with stronger reading skills, and have each partner make their own illustrated character and setting list. Encourage partners to ask each other questions (e.g., *Is _____ a setting? Did you remember to include _____?* ). Have partners trade their illustrated lists and discuss any differences. Then give them time to update their illustrated lists based on their discussion. Students can then use their illustrated lists to help them keep track of characters and setting changes when they reread the text on their own.

## Check-in Question

- *How does Atlas betray Heracles? How does Heracles save himself from Atlas's betrayal?* (Atlas betrays Heracles by deciding to stay free and not take the sky back. Heracles saves himself by tricking Atlas into taking it back.)

## Review: Determining a Central Message

Review how to determine the central message of a story by looking for important details about the problems the characters face and how they solve them. *How does Heracles solve his problems? What central message does this help reveal? Cite evidence from the text to support your conclusions.*

## Review: Describing Characters

Ask students to cite evidence to explain why it is heroic of Heracles to give Atlas a break from holding up the sky. (Heracles went to the garden to get apples, not to help Atlas. Yet, he notices that Atlas "must be tired" and that the "load" is heavy, and wants to give him some "relief." He did something he did not have to do just to be nice.)

## CLOSE READING

7   Across the garden stood old Atlas, with his back to a rocky peak, holding up the Sky. How strong he was! How still he stood under his load! Quietly Heracles crept down to the spot where Atlas stood. He told Atlas how he was sent by a king to fetch the apples. And the hero made an offer. "You must be tired, old man, from carrying that load. I'll take it from you for a little while and give you some relief. But you must promise to bring me apples from your daughters' garden." Atlas had suffered so long under the heavy Sky. He was quick to agree.

8   Mighty Atlas grunted. Gently, he raised up the dome of the Sky. Heracles eased the burden off the Titan's shoulders. The hero groaned as the heavens pressed down on him. And for the first time in centuries, Atlas was free. The Titan heaved a massive sigh that shook the trees. He stretched himself. He kneeled to the ground. He laughed so hard he almost cried. Then, without a word, he bounded off to fetch the apples. Heracles strained under the weight of the Sky. He wondered how long he could hold it. He wondered if Atlas would ever return. For a moment he began to despair.

9   Soon Atlas returned with the apples. There was a crafty look in his eye as he spoke. "Too long I've suffered with that burden. I'm happy to be free. You're strong enough to hold it. In exchange, I'll do your duty. I'll bring these apples to your king." Heracles shuddered at these words. But he didn't lose his wits.

32

## Strategic Reading

You can support all readers by offering them a strategic reading tip: Look at the illustrations. Explain that authors use illustrations to visually show something that is happening in the story. Tell students that by looking at the pictures they can gain a better understanding of the action, the setting, the characters, and the key ideas and details. Explain that looking at the illustrations may even provide a clue to challenging vocabulary in the story. Point to the word *strained* in paragraph 8. Have partners discuss how the illustration on the same page gives a clue to the meaning of the word. Have students act out the way Heracles is *straining* to reinforce the word's meaning. Challenge students to identify other ways the illustrations for this myth help them better understand the story.

## KEY IDEAS AND DETAILS

10    "You're right, old man. You've suffered long enough. But before you go, hold up this Sky one last time. I'm not as tough as you. I want to get some rags to cushion my poor shoulders." Atlas shrugged and laid the apples down. Once more he took his place beneath the Sky. Now it was Heracles's turn to laugh. "I'm sorry, friend, but I won't trade my fate for yours." He grabbed the golden apples and departed.

11    Heracles couldn't blame Atlas. The hero had shared the Titan's burden. He knew how Atlas felt. Years later, he returned to the garden of the Hesperides. There he built two enormous pillars, strong enough to support the heavens. Now the pillars did the work old Atlas had done for too long. So Atlas lived in peace in the garden. He guarded the pillars that Heracles built. And he no longer bore the weight of the Sky.

### Comprehension Check

1. Which detail helps you answer the question: What is the main problem Heracles faces in the story?

   a. The three nymphs eat the golden apples.

   b. Heracles returns to rescue Atlas.

   (c.) Precious golden apples are protected in a secret garden.

   d. The garden glows with the light of the apples.

2. Why is Prometheus chained to a mountain, and why does Atlas hold up the sky?

   a. They stole apples from the garden of the Hesperides.

   (b.) They were being punished by Zeus, the king of gods.

   c. They wanted to prove they were strong.

   d. They wanted to trick Heracles.

Unit 1 ■ Reading Literature: Key Ideas and Details    **33**

### Research to Build Knowledge

Tell students that this myth tells about just one of the twelve labors that Heracles performed. Challenge students to use the Internet to find out what the other labors were and why Heracles performed them. You may wish to assign partners or small groups a labor to research. Extend this activity by asking students to make a drawing of Heracles performing the labor. Then have students present their drawings to the class and explain the labor. Compile the drawings in a book and distribute a copy to each student.

## Multiple Readings for Critical Comprehension

Have students reread this selection and pose questions that focus on critical comprehension. Remind them to annotate text in a way that will support their comprehension.

- *Does Heracles display heroic behavior once or more than once?* (More than once: when he faces the dragon, frees Prometheus, gives Atlas a break, and then later returns to help Atlas.)

- *What makes Heracles's decision to return to the garden to help Atlas heroic?* (Heracles saw things from Atlas's point of view and helped him.)

## Self-Select Text

As preparation for Connect Across Texts, have students select one of the four selections in this unit and reread it independently. Students can access full pdf versions of the selections at **sadlierconnect.com**.

### Comprehension Check

Begin scoring students' understanding of unit skills and texts from Comprehension Check on this page through Connect Across Texts on page 35. Use students' total score to determine their readiness for the Unit 1 Review on page 37.

## Multiple-Choice Questions: *1 point each*

1. Students should recall that all of Heracles's challenges relate to getting the apples, which are protected in a secret garden, so choice C is correct.

2. Students should understand from reading the text that Prometheus and Atlas were both being punished by Zeus, so choice B is correct.

# Short-Answer Questions: *2 points each*

### Item 3 Rubric

| | |
|---|---|
| 2 | Students are able to use their own words, citing three details from the text, to describe and explain Atlas's behavior. |
| 1 | Students are able to cite three details from the text to describe and explain Atlas's behavior. |
| 0 | Students cite only one or two details to either describe Atlas's behavior or explain it. |

### Item 4 Rubric

| | |
|---|---|
| 2 | Students are able to explain why Heracles rescued Atlas, citing several details from the text to support their answer. |
| 1 | Students are able to explain why Heracles rescued Atlas, but have trouble citing evidence from the text to support their answer. |
| 0 | Students cannot explain why Heracles rescued Atlas or support their answers with evidence that relates to Heracles's actions. |

## Theme Wrap-Up

Lead students in a group discussion on the theme of heroism. *Why does it sometimes "take a hero" to change a situation?* Talk about the different types of heroes featured in this unit. (Students should understand that sometimes people need heroes to help them, and other times people can work hard or be clever to help themselves and become the hero. Students should also understand that heroic behavior can come in the form of setting a good example for others.)

**3.** In paragraph 8, Heracles takes the Sky off Atlas's shoulders. Provide at least three details from the text to describe how Atlas behaved once he was free. How does Heracles's action lead to the next event in the myth?

Sample answer: The Titan sighed, stretched, kneeled, and laughed. He was relieved and happy to be set free and couldn't believe his luck. Because he no longer has to carry the sky, he can get the golden apples for Heracles.

**4.** Why did Heracles return to the garden to build pillars for Atlas? Use evidence from the text to support your answer.

Sample answer: Heracles felt sorry for Atlas. He felt how heavy the Sky was and knew that Atlas didn't want to be stuck holding it up forever. Heracles didn't even blame Atlas for trying to leave him holding up the Sky. He probably admired Atlas for being so strong, as suggested in paragraph 7, and felt they had something in common.

## Extend Thinking: Debate

Partner students and assign each pair a hero from the unit. (Make sure all heroes have been assigned.) Tell students that they will debate with another pair about which hero was more heroic. Have partners review the texts for details about both heroes to support their arguments. Encourage students to think about the argument the other team will make and to come up with a way to counter it.

Give each team one minute to argue, and 30 seconds to make closing comments. Then have the class vote on which team made the better argument. Call on volunteers to explain their vote respectfully.

## CONNECT ACROSS TEXTS

### Compare and Contrast Texts

In this unit, you read about the Dove and the Ant, the Crow, John Henry, Stormalong, Atalanta, and Heracles and Atlas. Think about the characters in these stories. Then choose any two characters and compare and contrast them, using the T-chart below. List key details and other evidence from the texts to show similarities and differences. Be prepared to discuss your ideas with the class.

| Similarities | Differences |
| --- | --- |
| Atalanta and Heracles: strong; brave; heroic; characters in myths | Atalanta: female; uses bow and arrow; not related to a god |
| | Heracles: male, uses strength and cunning; related to a god (son of Zeus) |

### Return to the Essential Question

*How do authors convey a central message or lesson?*

In small groups or as a class, discuss the Essential Question. Think about what you have learned about asking and answering questions, identifying details and determining the central message of a text, and describing characters. Use evidence from the six unit texts to answer the question.

Unit 1 ■ Reading Literature: Key Ideas and Details **35**

### Connect Across Texts: *4 points* Review Reading Selections

Lead the class in summarizing each of the four reading selections by providing summary sentence starters.

### Compare and Contrast Texts

Review the directions on page 35 with students. Have them write characters' names in each column of the T-chart.

**T-chart Rubric**

| | |
| --- | --- |
| 4 | Student identifies two characters and records four or more common and unique characteristics in their proper places. |
| 3 | Student identifies two characters and records at least three common and unique characteristics in their proper places. |
| 2 | Student identifies two characters and records at least three characteristics but may have trouble categorizing them. |
| 1 | Student identifies two selections and records at least one common or unique characteristic. |
| 0 | Student did not complete assignment or demonstrate understanding of selections. |

### Support Essential Question Discussion

Have students reread the Essential Question. Challenge them to finish this sentence:

*One way an author can convey a central message or lesson is to . . .*

If students have difficulty, prompt them to think about how characters' actions can reveal a central message.

| **Assess and Respond** (pages 33–35) | |
| --- | --- |
| **If** | **Then** |
| Students scored 0–4 points, they are **Developing** their understanding of unit skills. | ▶ Provide students with reading support and more intensive modeling of skills. |
| Students scored 5–7 points, they are **Improving** their understanding of unit skills. | ▶ Use students' scores to target areas that are weak and review those specific skills. |
| Students scored 8–10 points, they are **Proficient** in their understanding of unit skills. | ▶ Have these students move on. They are ready for more formal assessment. |

## OBJECTIVES
**Use context to determine the meaning of unfamiliar words and phrases.**

### Guided Instruction

Review the Guided Instruction section on page 36 with students. Be sure they understand that a context clue is a word or phrase that appears in the same sentence or a nearby sentence and that provides a clue to the meaning of the unknown or multiple-meaning word. By recognizing context clues, they can clarify meaning on their own and develop their vocabulary.

### Guided Practice

If students are having difficulty, have them say each sentence aloud, replacing the word from the chart with the first definition, and then repeating with the second definition to identify the correct meaning. You might also have them do this exercise with a partner.

### Independent Practice

If students are having trouble determining the correct meaning of the words in italics, have them say each sentence aloud, replacing the word with each definition until they identify the correct one. Have them underline clues in the sentence that confirm this meaning.

### Apply to Reading

Have students return to "The Dove and the Ant" to circle multiple-meaning words and underline their context clues. Students may find *spring* (page 12, paragraph 1), *fall* (page 12, paragraph 2; page 14, paragraph 11), and *sink* (page 12, paragraph 2).

---

# LANGUAGE

## Context Clues

> **bound 1.** *(adj.)* going or ready to go: She is **bound** for home. **2.** *(n.)* a leap or jump: They crossed the field in leaps and **bounds**.

**Guided Instruction**  **Context clues** can help you understand the meanings of unknown and multiple-meaning words. After using context clues, you can check the meanings in a dictionary.

Read this sentence from "Heracles and Atlas": *I'm bound to get some apples there*. Context clues in the text indicate that this sentence uses meaning 1 of *bound*.

Look at the chart to find other examples of multiple-meaning words.

| track | 1. *(n.)* a course for running |
| | 2. *(v.)* to follow the tracks of |
| scour | 1. *(v.)* to clean by rubbing |
| | 2. *(v.)* to move quickly while searching |

**Guided Practice**  Write the number of the meaning of the word from the chart above that appears in each sentence.

___2___ **1.** The hunter learned to *track* animals in the forest.

___1___ **2.** Bring your sneakers if you're going to the *track*.

___1___ **3.** Will you *scour* this sticky pot with this kitchen sponge?

___2___ **4.** I'll *scour* the city until I find her.

**Independent Practice**  Write the correct meanings of the word in italics. Use context clues and a dictionary to help you.

How long do you think the game will *last*?

_____

The shoemaker used his tools to *bore* a hole in leather.

_____

---

## Support English Language Learners

Recognizing a multiple-meaning word requires prior knowledge. Students who are learning English may not recognize that a word has more than one meaning. Help students develop a strong bank of multiple-meaning words by providing definitions for several multiple-meaning words in "The Dove and the Ant." Then have students work with partners to identify context clues to the meaning of each word as it is used in the text. For example: *bank* (page 12, paragraph 3); definition 1: a place to keep money; definition 2: land next to a body of water; context clues: "near" and "of the river."

## UNIT 1 REVIEW

Read the following passage in which you can apply skills for asking and answering questions, identifying details and determining the central message, and understanding characters. Then answer the questions on pages 37 and 38.

# The Daydreamer

(Genre: Folktale)

1    A poor farmer was walking through his fields, when he saw a rabbit hopping a few feet ahead.

2    "What a <u>stroke of luck</u>!" he shouted. "I'll catch that rabbit. I'll sell it at the market for ten dollars. With the money I earn, I'll buy a fat pig. The pig will have piglets. The piglets will grow to be big as their mother. Soon I'll be rich!

3    "I'll hire a housekeeper and cook. I'll get married. My wife will have two sons, Ilya and Ivan. The boys will plow the fields when they're able. I'll sit on the porch and <u>supervise</u>.

4    "'Hey boys,' I'll holler. 'Ilya and Ivan! Don't work yourselves too hard! You know you were born stinking rich!'"

5    The farmer bellowed these last words so loud that the rabbit was frightened and fled. So his riches, his wife, and his children were lost.

**Fill in the circle of the correct answer choice.**

1. Because the farmer is daydreaming, the rabbit
   ○ is caught
   ○ is sold
   ● escapes
   ○ bellows

2. *Bellowed* is closest in meaning to
   ○ daydreamed
   ○ whispered
   ○ listened
   ● shouted

Unit 1 ■ Reading Literature: Key Ideas and Details    **37**

## Unit Summary

At this point, students have had instruction and practice in reading fables, folktales, and myths, with a focus on heroism. Students have also learned different strategies for asking and answering questions, determining the central message of a text, and describing characters. Students have done an independent close reading of text, practiced working with concepts across texts, and practiced using context clues to determine the meaning of unknown and multiple-meaning words. They should be well-prepared for the review section.

## Introduce the Review

Explain to students that they will read a new passage that is related to the unit's theme and the selections they have already read. Instruct students to read the passage carefully and then answer the questions on pages 37 and 38.

### Answer Explanations

Scoring: Items 1–4 on pages 37–38 are worth 1 point each. See the rubrics on the next page for guidance scoring the short-answer questions on page 38.

1. The text describes how the farmer wastes time daydreaming, rather than acting quickly to catch the rabbit. So, the answer is the third choice, *escapes*.

2. The text states that the way the farmer "bellowed" so loudly that "the rabbit was frightened and fled." So, *bellowed* is closest in meaning to the fourth choice, *shouted*.

## Self-Assessment: Progress Check

Have students revisit the Progress Check on page 9 and respond to the questions again. Ask them to compare their Before and After responses.

You may wish to have students rate their own answers on a scale of 0–2 rather than simply checking (or not checking) the box. Instruct them to write a 0 if they feel they don't understand the given skill at all, a 1 if they feel they have some understanding, and a 2 if they feel they have a solid grasp of the skill.

# Unit 1 Review

## Answer Explanations

**3.** The text describes how the farmer dreams about getting married, so the farmer's wife *does not exist*. The third choice is correct.

**4.** It was *foolish* of the farmer to waste time rather than acting quickly to catch the rabbit. The fourth choice is correct.

## Items 5 and 6 Rubric

| | |
|---|---|
| **2** | Underlines the word and provides a meaning. |
| **1** | Underlines the word or provides a meaning. |
| **0** | Does neither. |

## Items 7 and 9 Rubric

| | |
|---|---|
| **2** | Describes the farmer, citing evidence. |
| **1** | Describes the farmer, but does not cite evidence. |
| **0** | Does not describe the farmer. |

## Items 8 and 10 Rubric

| | |
|---|---|
| **2** | Determines the central message/lesson, and explains how it is conveyed through key details in the text. |
| **1** | Determines the central message/lesson, but does not explain how it is conveyed through key details in the text. |
| **0** | Does not determine the central message/lesson. |

# UNIT 1 REVIEW

**3.** The farmer's wife
- ○ cooks and cleans
- ○ has two sons
- ● does not exist
- ○ scolds him

**4.** The farmer is best described as
- ○ hard-working
- ○ capable
- ○ angry
- ● foolish

**5.** Underline the phrase *stroke of luck* in paragraph 2, sentence 1. Explain the meaning of this phrase in your own words.

something good that happens by chance

**6.** Underline the word *supervise* at the end of paragraph 3. Provide the meaning of this word below.

to be in charge of

**7.** What did the farmer think the rabbit would bring him?

riches, a family, and a life of leisure

**8.** What is the central message of this story?

Sample answer: Only hard work will get you the things you want.

The farmer proves this by daydreaming and scaring the rabbit away.

**9.** How do the farmer's actions show what he was like?

Sample answer: They show us that he was not a serious person—

that he was lazy and imagined things instead of doing them.

**10.** What lesson should the farmer learn based on story events?

Sample answer: He should learn that if he worked as hard as he

dreamed, he might get the things he wants.

## Analyze Student Scores

| | |
|---|---|
| **12–16 pts Strong** | Student has a good grasp of the skills and concepts taught in this unit. Point out any mistakes the student has made and explain the correct answers if necessary. |
| **6–11 pts Progressing** | Student is struggling with some skills or concepts. Identify the specific skills that are problematic to target a review of instruction. |
| **0–5 pts Emerging** | Student is having serious problems understanding the skills and concepts taught in this unit. Student may need to redo the work with a higher level of support. |

# Introducing UNIT 2

I n this unit about animals, you will learn how to write a fictional narrative. A fictional narrative is a story about imaginary characters and events.

When you write a fictional narrative, you want to think carefully about the event sequence. The story should have a beginning, a middle, and an end. As a writer, you should help the reader by using words such as *first* and *then* to make the order clear.

To be effective, a fictional narrative should have carefully chosen words. The writer should use descriptive details and dialogue to help the reader understand the characters and events.

## Progress Check    *Can I?*

| Before Unit 2 | | After Unit 2 |
|---|---|---|
| ☐ | Write a story with imaginary characters and events. | ☐ |
| ☐ | Write the story with a beginning, middle, and end. | ☐ |
| ☐ | Use dialogue and descriptive details. | ☐ |
| ☐ | Use words to make the order of events clear. | ☐ |
| ☐ | Choose words and phrases for effect. | ☐ |
| ☐ | Write using nouns, including abstract nouns. | ☐ |
| ☐ | Write using regular and irregular plural nouns. | ☐ |
| ☐ | Write using possessives. | ☐ |
| ☐ | Write using correct punctuation in dialogue. | ☐ |

Unit 2 ■ Text Types and Purposes: Write Fictional Narratives

**Student Page 39**

## Progress Check

The Progress Check is a self-assessment feature that students can use to gauge their own progress. Research shows that when students take accountability for their own learning, their motivation increases.

Before students begin work on Unit 2, have them check the boxes next to any item that they feel they can do well. Explain that it is fine if they don't check any of the boxes. Tell them that they will have an opportunity to learn about and practice all of these items while studying the unit. Let them know that near the end of the unit they will have a chance to reconsider how well they can do each item on this list.

Before students begin the Unit 2 Review on page 51, have them revisit this page. You can use this information to work with students on any items they don't understand before they tackle the Review.

# HOME ◆ CONNECT...

The Home Connect feature is a way to keep parents or other adult family members apprised of what their children are learning. The key learning objectives are listed, and some ideas for related activities and discussions are included.

Explain to students that they can share the Home Connect page with their parents or other adult family members in their home. Let students know how much time the class will be spending on this unit so they can plan their time accordingly at home.

Encourage students and their parents to share their experiences using the suggestions on the Home Connect page. You may wish to make a place to post some of this work.

## HOME ◆ CONNECT...

I n this unit, children will learn about writing **fictional narratives**. A fictional narrative tells about an imagined experience or events. After reading a fictional narrative with your child, ask him or her to retell the story. Point out that the story is told in **sequence** with a beginning, a middle, and an end. Encourage your child's writing imagination by asking what he or she might have changed about a story's events.

Invite your child to share the story that he or she writes for this unit. Ask questions about the **characters** and **narrators**, and decide together what you learn about the characters through what they say and do.

When writing narratives, writers choose precise words to **describe events** and show **how the characters think, feel, or act**. Encourage your child to concentrate on finding the best, most appropriate words and phrases in his or her writing. Ask your child what different words he or she might use in a passage of **description** or **dialogue** that the two of you read together.

 **Activity:** Brainstorm about a character with your child. The character should be fictional but might be based on a real person you both know. Create a time and place for the character. With your child, describe how the character feels about something at a certain point (for example, lonely or excited). Then have your child write a few sentences of dialogue or description to show how the character feels.

**40**    Unit 2 ■ Text Types and Purposes: Write Fictional Narratives

### IN THIS UNIT, YOUR CHILD WILL...

■ Learn to write a story with imaginary characters and events, using dialogue, descriptive details, and a clear sequence of events.

■ Learn to use linking words, such as *first, then,* and *finally* to signal the order of events.

■ Learn language skills to use in writing a fictional narrative.

- Recognize abstract nouns and use them in sentences.

- Use the correct forms of regular and irregular plural nouns, such as *children* and *women*.

- Use a possessive to show ownership, such as *Katie's skate*.

- Write dialogue and use correct punctuation to show who is speaking.

### WAYS TO HELP YOUR CHILD

Help your child to read like a writer. As your child reads, ask questions about the characters, such as *How does the writer show how the character feels?* or *Why do you think the writer included that event?* Emphasize that the writer thinks carefully about his or her word choice to help the reader understand the characters, actions, and settings.

---

ONLINE

**For more Home Connect activities, continue online at** sadlierconnect.com

**Student Page 40**

## UNIT PLANNER

| Theme: It Takes a Hero<br>Curriculum Connection: Language Arts | Focus |
|---|---|
| **WRITING MODEL**<br>*pp. 42–44* | *What a Mess!* |
| **WRITING PRACTICE**<br>*p. 45* | **ORGANIZATIONAL STRUCTURE:** Outline |
| **LANGUAGE MINI-LESSONS**<br>*pp. 46–49* | • Nouns<br>• Regular and Irregular Plural Nouns<br>• Possessives<br>• Commas and Quotation Marks in Dialogue |
| **SPEAKING AND LISTENING**<br>*p. 50* | Discuss the Essential Question |
| **UNIT 2 REVIEW**<br>*pp. 51–52* | • Language Skills Summary<br>• Writing Process Summary |

## Objective(s)

Write a fictional narrative that includes an event sequence, dialogue and descriptions, sequence words and phrases, and that provides a sense of closure.

Plan a fictional narrative that includes an event sequence, dialogue and descriptions, sequence words and phrases, and that provides a sense of closure.

- Use nouns, including abstract nouns, in writing.
- Use regular and irregular plural nouns in writing.
- Use possessives in writing.
- Use commas and quotation marks in dialogue.

- Come to discussion prepared, and draw on that preparation to explore ideas.
- Ask questions to check understanding.

## Unit Assessment

- Unit 2 Review *pp. 51–52*

## Additional Assessment Options

- Performance Task 1 *pp. 141A–145 and 146*
  ( ALSO ONLINE )
- Performance Task 2 *pp. 259A–263 and 264*
  ( ALSO ONLINE )

**Optional Purchase:**

- iProgress Monitor ( ONLINE )
- Progress Monitor Student Benchmark Assessment Booklet

## ( ONLINE ) Digital Resources

- Home Connect Activities
- Additional Practice
- Teacher Resources
- iProgress Monitor (optional purchase)

**Go to SadlierConnect.com to access your Digital Resources.**

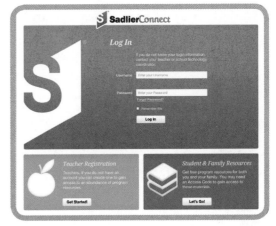

**For more detailed instructions see page T3.**

## LEARNING PROGRESSIONS

In this unit, students will learn how to develop a fictional narrative with character dialogue. In order to learn the skills necessary to craft a fictional narrative, students will further develop skills learned in second grade. They should be encouraged to retain these skills, as they will continue to build on them in fourth grade.

**Writing Narratives**

- By the end of grade 2, students should have been able to write narratives in which they recount a well-elaborated event or short sequence of events.

- In grade 3, students will build on this skill by establishing a situation and introducing a narrator and/or characters, and they will be able to organize an events sequence that unfolds naturally.

- When students move on to grade 4, they will orient the reader as they establish a situation and introduce a narrator and characters. They will continue to organize an event sequence that unfolds naturally.

**Including Details**

- By the end of grade 2, students should have been able to include details to describe actions, thoughts, and feelings.

- Throughout grades 3 and 4, students will build on this skill by using dialogue and descriptions of actions, thoughts, and feelings to develop experiences and events or show the response of characters to situations.

**Using Temporal Words and Phrases**

- By the end of grade 2, students should have been able to use temporal words to signal event order.

- In grade 3, students will use not only temporal words, but also phrases, to signal event order.

- Throughout grades 3 and 4, students will build on this skill by using a variety of transitional words and phrases to manage the sequence of events.

**Writing Conclusions**

- By the end of grade 2 and throughout grade 3, students should have been able to provide a sense of closure.

- This skill prepares students for grade 4, when they will provide a conclusion that follows a narrated experience or event.

# Text Types and Purposes: Write Fictional Narratives

UNIT 2

**Essential Question:**
How do writers develop fictional narratives?

**Essential Question:**
How do writers develop fictional narratives?

In this unit, students will learn that fictional narratives can include dialogue and should have a beginning, middle, and end.

## Theme: It Takes a Hero
Students will continue to explore different types of heroes as they read and analyze a fictional narrative writing model.

## Curriculum Connection: Language Arts
Students will use what they have learned from reading folktales and myths about heroes as they work on their own fictional narrative.

## Connect Reading to Writing
Remind students that they read a fictional narrative entitled "Heracles and Atlas" in Unit 1 (Student Book pages 30–33). Review the dialogue and details as well as the series of events in that fictional narrative. Tell students they will be reading and writing a fictional narrative in this unit.

## Writing Handbook

If students need extra practice with writing a fictional narrative, refer them to the *Writing Handbook* on pages 275–283. The Writing Handbook gives students detailed instruction on planning, drafting, revising, and editing their writing. They will also find tips on producing, publishing, and presenting their writing.

## OBJECTIVE
Write a fictional narrative that includes an event sequence, dialogue and descriptions, sequence words and phrases, and that provides a sense of closure.

## Introduce: Organizational Structure

Draw students' attention to the fictional narrative outline in the left margin and point out the key elements. Ask students to look for these key elements as you read and analyze the student model together.

## Analyze a Student Model

**EVENT SEQUENCE:** Explain to students that at the beginning of a story, readers find the basic situation and are introduced to the story's characters. Help students find the character names. *I don't find any people's names here, but I know that in some stories, animals are the main characters. The animals must be the main characters here.* (Owl, Rabbit) Assist students in finding the event that sets up the story's situation. *In the first paragraph, Owl signals that "all was safe." I read that trees have fallen. I know that I should look for an event that put the animals in danger. In the second paragraph, I find the event.* (a terrible storm)

### CREATING AN ORGANIZATIONAL STRUCTURE

Drew used an outline to organize his **fictional narrative**. It is divided into three sections: beginning, middle, and end.

```
Title: _____
Setting: _____
Characters: _____

I. Beginning
          Story Events
          _____
          _____

II. Middle
          Story Events
          _____
          _____

III. End
          Conclusion
          _____
```

### EVENT SEQUENCE

- The beginning of the story gives information about the events and introduces the characters.

*Underline the names of the characters on this page. Circle the event that happened last night.*

# Read a Student Model

Drew is a student in Mr. Tran's 3rd-grade class. He is writing a fictional narrative. He has been asked to use a clear event sequence and to use dialogue and descriptive details. As you read his story, think about how you will organize your fictional narrative.

### What a Mess!

"Hoo–hoo, hoo–hoo!" Owl's voice was the signal that all was safe. Rabbit peeked from under the brush and hopped out into the opening. She jumped over a couple of fallen trees. As she looked around, other animals gathered.

Everyone was talking about the terrible storm that blew through last night. As Rabbit waited for the meeting to begin, she looked at the playground. It was covered with large branches, and trash was scattered everywhere. The broken swings hung limply. Just yesterday, the playground had been filled with laughter and joy. Now, it was a mess.

## Genre: Fictional Narrative

Tell students that a writer writes a fictional narrative for a purpose: to entertain the reader. To entertain readers, the writer sets up characters and a series of events that unfold naturally. He or she also includes details and descriptions that tell about events and characters, as well as dialogue that brings characters to life. By the time the story ends, the writer has provided a sense of closure.

(Soon), Tabby Cat's soft meow got everyone's attention. "Last night was a scary night." Some of the animals shivered thinking about the powerful winds that knocked down many trees. "Luckily," she continued, "we're all safe."

(Then) why did you bring us here?" wondered Mouse.

"I've been thinking of the children," Tabby Cat responded. "They will be so sad not to be able to play tomorrow."

The animals enjoyed watching the children run outside each day, eager to climb the monkey bars, swing with their friends, and race down the slides. The animals' bodies sagged with disappointment.

(At first), no one said anything. (Then), Rabbit softly sighed. "We have to do something to help them."

(Next) Mouse looked around. "But what can we do? We are all so small, and the job is so big."

Everyone was quiet after that.

(Finally), Brown Dog raised his head. "Well, I can fetch sticks!" He ran and picked up a few sticks, carrying them back.

Tabby Cat purred, "Well that's a start!" Rabbit looked at Tabby Cat and Brown Dog [curiously]. (Then) she [excitedly] hopped away. She picked up a piece of trash and put it with the sticks. (Soon), the other animals began to cheer up. (Now), they had a plan!

— **DIALOGUE**

Dialogue shows thoughts and feelings of characters. Dialogue is surrounded by quotation marks.

*Underline what Tabby Cat says that tells what she thinks about the children.*

— **SEQUENCE WORDS**

Use words and phrases to signal event order and make the event sequence clear.

*Circle words that show the sequence of events.*

— **DESCRIPTIONS OF ACTIONS, THOUGHTS, FEELINGS**

Use descriptions to show how characters respond to events. Words such as *shivered* and *softly* help show characters' responses.

*Box words in the last paragraph that show how Rabbit responds to Brown Dog's actions.*

## Analyze a Student Model

**DIALOGUE:** Point out that Tabby Cat expresses more than one feeling in her dialogue—fear, gratitude—as she tells about her reaction to the storm. Model identifying Tabby Cat's thoughts about how she believes the children will feel. *In the first and second paragraphs, Tabby Cat mentions her feelings, but she does not mention the children. I will continue reading until I find where she mentions the children specifically.* (They will be so sad not to play tomorrow.)

**SEQUENCE WORDS:** Explain to students that Drew uses sequence words such as *soon* and *then* to show when and in what order the events took place. Have students identify other sequence words in the story. (*At first, Then, Next, Finally, Soon, Now*)

**DESCRIPTIONS OF ACTIONS, THOUGHTS, FEELINGS:** Point out that when Drew writes that Rabbit "softly sighed" in the fifth paragraph, this is describing how Rabbit is responding to Tabby Cat's statement. Ask students to use their own words to tell how they think Rabbit reacts. Then draw students' attention to the last paragraph and ask them to box words that show Rabbit's responses to Brown Dog's actions. (*curiously, excitedly*) If students are struggling, model finding the first word.

## Support English Language Learners

English language learners might have trouble recognizing English sequence words, or words that indicate when and in what order events took place. Review sequence words, such as *soon, later, first, next, then,* and *finally.*

Encourage students to work with a partner to name other sequence words. Then have them take turns using a few of the words to describe a sequence of the day's events.

# Write Fictional Narratives

## Analyze a Student Model

**EVENT SEQUENCE:** Review the ending of the story with students. Point out that the ending should provide a sense of closure. Explain that sometimes in a story, the characters learn a lesson. Ask students to underline the lesson that the animals learn. (Even the biggest jobs can be done when we all work together.)

## Evaluate a Writer's Work

Discuss Drew's fictional narrative with students. Remind them that a story should have a beginning, a middle, and an ending. Ask students to recall the situation at the beginning of the story. (A big storm has damaged the forest.) Discuss what problem the animals are trying to solve in the middle of the story. (The children will be sad because they will not be able to play in the forest.) Review how the characters try to solve the problem. (They work together to clean up the forest.) Ask students whether they found the conclusion of the story satisfying, and have them explain their thinking.

## Model: Organizational Structure

Ask students to think about how Drew might have outlined the story. On a board or projector, post the outline on page 45. Have students help you fill in the outline based on the story. Review the margin notes. Fill in the beginning, middle, and ending. Point out that well-written stories have strong organization, which requires planning and prewriting.

Students will next use the blank outline found in their books to plan their own stories, and then they will draft the story based on their outline.

### WRITE FICTIONAL NARRATIVES

**EVENT SEQUENCE**

The ending completes the story for the reader. It shows how the problem is solved.

*Underline the lesson the animals learn in the end.*

Throughout the night, they worked. Mouse ran back and forth carrying bits of trash to the trash can. Owl and Hawk used their beaks to hang the swing back up. All the animals did what they could.

As the sun rose in the morning, Rabbit looked around once again. "I can't believe it!" she cheered. "The children will be so happy."

Mouse patted Rabbit on the back. "I thought the job was too big, but we did it!"

Tabby Cat smiled. "It's just like I always tell my kittens. <u>Even the biggest jobs can be done when we all work together.</u>"

44

### Review: Asking and Answering Questions

Remind students that when they read the fables "The Dove and the Ant" and "The Crow and the Pitcher," they asked basic questions about the text and then found answers to their questions within the text.

Encourage students to ask questions about Drew's story (*How do Mouse's feelings change in the story?*), and have them find the answers to the questions within the text. (On page 43, Mouse says, "We are all so small, and the job is so big." This indicates that he thinks the animals cannot clean up the mess. On page 44, Mouse says, "I thought the job was too big, but we did it." This indicates he is proud of their work.)

Use an outline like the one below to organize your own fictional narrative about animal characters. Then write a first draft of your story on a separate sheet of paper. In your draft, be sure to use dialogue and descriptions of characters' thoughts, feelings, and actions to develop your story. Also, use words and phrases that clearly show your story's order of events. Finally, be sure to provide a clear ending. You will use this draft to write your final story draft in the Unit 2 Review section on page 52.

**Title:** _____

**Setting:** _____

**Characters:** _____

_____

I.  **Beginning**
    Story Events

    _____

    _____

II. **Middle**
    Story Events

    _____

    _____

III. **End**
     Conclusion

     _____

     _____

## Differentiate Instruction

Some students might have difficulty following the steps for completing the outline. Have students work in pairs to complete their work.

Encourage partners to work together to complete each step of the outline. Have them decide on the characters and the setting for their story. Then ask them to work out what will occur at the beginning and the middle of the story. Remind them that characters in stories usually face a problem that they try to overcome. Review with students that the ending of the story should make the story feel complete. Point out that one way to do this is to have the characters solve the problem that they have faced. Provide support as necessary.

## Create: Organizational Structure

### Brainstorming

Tell students that authors write stories about fictional characters and events that interest them. As a class, brainstorm characters and situations that students find interesting. List these ideas on the board so that students can build on them.

### Planning

Students will use the outline on page 45 to plan their fictional narrative. They should begin by filling in their setting and characters.

- Students should plan and write events for the beginning and middle of the story.
- Remind students that Drew included a lesson at the end of "What a Mess," and that the lesson helped make the story feel complete. Ask students how they will make their story feel complete.

### Drafting a Fictional Narrative

Students should refer to their outline as they draft their fictional narrative on a separate sheet of paper. Be sure students have a title, setting, characters, and a beginning, middle, and end. Remind them to use sequence words.

## Introduce the Writing Process

Remind students that in order to do a good job on a story, they must plan, draft, revise, and edit. These are all steps of the writing process. For more on the writing process, see the *Writing Handbook* on page 275 of this guide.

| Assess and Respond |
|---|
| **If** students have difficulty turning their outline into a story, |
| **Then** remind students to use dialogue and details to show how characters respond to events. |

## OBJECTIVE
**Use nouns, including abstract nouns, in writing.**

## Guided Instruction

Ensure that students understand what a noun is. Have them point to examples of persons, places, and things in the classroom and name the nouns. Then explain that abstract nouns name things that cannot be pointed out, such as childhood or feelings. Next have students study the boldface nouns in the examples. Ask them to find the abstract noun in the examples. (*joy*)

## Guided Practice

Have students begin by identifying the underlined noun in the first sentence. (*puppy*) Model how to determine what the noun names. *The underlined noun is* puppy. *A puppy is not a person or a place. It must be a thing.* Then have students write what the noun *store* in the second sentence names (place) and *vet* in the third sentence. (person) Ask students whether any of the underlined nouns is abstract. (no)

## Independent Practice

Have students write a sentence for each of the three abstract nouns. Provide sample sentences as needed.

### Assess and Respond

**If** students have difficulty using the abstract nouns in sentences,

**Then** provide them with sentence starters. *The best part of my childhood so far is . . .; Friendship is important because . . .; It takes courage to . . .*

---

LANGUAGE

### Nouns

**Guided Instruction**  A **noun** is a word that names a person, a place, or a thing. An **abstract noun** names something we cannot see or hold, such as *peace* or *talent*.

> I took my **dog** to the **park**.
> My **brother** brought a **leash** and **water**.
> A **pet** brings us great **joy**.

**Guided Practice**  Write *person*, *place*, or *thing* to tell what the underlined noun names. If it is an abstract noun, write *abstract*.

1. Drew got a new <u>puppy</u> yesterday. _____ thing _____
2. He went to the <u>store</u> to get dog food and a leash. _____ place _____
3. Mom and Drew took the puppy to see a <u>vet</u>. _____ person _____
4. She needed treatment for one small <u>problem</u>. _____ abstract _____
5. After the visit, they took the puppy <u>home</u> to rest. _____ place _____

**Independent Practice**  Use each abstract noun in a sentence.

1. childhood

   Sample answer: My dog was my best friend during my childhood.

   _____

2. friendship

   Sample answer: I formed a friendship with my neighbor.

   _____

3. courage

   Sample answer: My dog showed courage when it scared away the fox.

   _____

**46**  Unit 2 ■ Text Types and Purposes: Write Fictional Narratives

---

### Differentiate Instruction

Some students may have difficulty in understanding the concept of abstract nouns. Others may not be sure when a noun names a person, place, or thing.

Help these students better understand different types of nouns by having them review *all* of the nouns in the Guided Practice sentences. Instruct them to work in a group to name the nouns that are persons (*Drew, He, Mom, Dad, vet*), places (*store*), and things (*dog food, leash, puppy*). Then ask them to identify any abstract nouns. (*yesterday*)

## Regular and Irregular Plural Nouns

**Guided Instruction** A **plural noun** names more than one person, place, or thing.

| For most nouns, add the letter *s* to the end of the word. | For words ending in *s, ch, sh,* or *x,* add an *es* to the end of the word. | For some nouns that end in a consonant and *y,* change the *y* to an *i* and add *es.* |
|---|---|---|
| *rabbit    rabbits* | *grass    grasses*<br>*lunch    lunches*<br>*box    boxes* | *bunny    bunnies* |

Some nouns are irregular plurals. They do not end with the letter *s.* Instead, the spelling of the word is changed, or the word stays the same.

*singular:*    man    mouse    deer
*plural:*      men    mice     deer

**Guided Practice** Write the plural form of each word.

1. puppy _____ puppies _____
2. fox _____ foxes _____
3. hamster _____ hamsters _____
4. goose _____ geese _____

**Independent Practice** Write the plural form of each word in parentheses to complete each sentence.

1. The _____ children _____ learned how animals change. (child)
2. Caterpillars change into _____ butterflies _____. (butterfly)
3. _____ Birds _____ hatch from eggs. (Bird)

Unit 2 ■ Text Types and Purposes: Write Fictional Narratives    47

## OBJECTIVE
Use regular and irregular plural nouns in writing.

### Guided Instruction
Make sure that students understand that a plural noun names more than one person, place, or thing. Review the examples of the different ways to form plurals shown in the chart. Explain that when *-es* is added to nouns that end in *-s, -ch, -sh,* or *-x,* another syllable is added. Then point out the irregular plural nouns. Tell students that these words do not follow the usual rules and the plurals must be memorized.

### Guided Practice
Instruct students to write the plural for each of the words. Have students refer to the chart to check the different ways to form plurals. You may wish to tell students that one of the nouns has an irregular plural form that is not listed above. (*geese*)

### Independent Practice
Have students review the different ways to form plural nouns. Then ask them to write the plural form of each noun in parentheses.

| Assess and Respond |
|---|
| **If** students have difficulty forming plural nouns correctly, |
| **Then** give students extra practice by repeating the activity in Guided Practice with more examples. |

## Support English Language Learners

Forming plural nouns correctly can be difficult for English language learners. Students need to remember not only to add *-s* to form most plural nouns, but also the rule to add *-es* to words ending in *-s, -ch, -sh,* or *-x,* as well as the rule that for words ending in consonant *-y,* they change the *-y* to an *-i* and add *-es.* Along with these rules, English language learners need to learn which nouns have irregular plurals and don't follow any of these rules.

Write four column heads on the board: + *-s,* + *-es,* Change *-y* to an *-i* and add *-es,* and Irregular. Have students list common singular nouns and discuss under which column the noun belongs. Then demonstrate forming the plural. Make sure to provide other examples of irregular plural nouns, such as *women, teeth, fish,* and *feet.*

## OBJECTIVE
**Use possessives in writing.**

## Guided Instruction

Be sure students understand that a possessive noun shows when someone or something has or owns something and that most possessives are formed by adding apostrophe -s. Remind students that most plural nouns end in -s and that for these, possessives are formed by adding only an apostrophe.

## Guided Practice

Have students begin by recognizing who or what has something. (Tran) Then ask students if the noun is a plural that ends in -s. (no) Ask students how the possessive should be formed, and tell them to circle the correct response.

## Independent Practice

Have students review how to form a singular possessive and how to form a plural possessive for a word that ends in -s. Then instruct students to complete the activity, writing the correct possessive form for each noun in parentheses.

| **Assess and Respond** |
| --- |
| **If** students have difficulty forming possessives correctly, |
| **Then** have them review examples of possessives in the student model. (Owl's, Cat's, animals') Discuss with them how each possessive is formed. |

---

**LANGUAGE**

## Possessives

**Guided Instruction** **Possessive** nouns show ownership. They show who has or owns something.

> The **horse that Sandeep owns** is at the fair.
> Possessive: **Sandeep's horse** is at the fair.

To form a singular possessive, add an apostrophe and the letter s to the end of the noun. To form a plural possessive to a word that ends with the letter s, add only an apostrophe at the end of the word.

> The **horse's** coat needs brushing. (singular possessive)
> The **horses'** gate was left open, and they ran out.
> (plural possessive)

**Guided Practice** Circle the phrase that is the correct possessive form.

1. the saddle that Tran has — (Tran's saddle) — Trans' saddle
2. the colts who have a mother — the colt's mother — (the colts' mother)
3. the stable of the horse — (the horse's stable) — the horses' stable
4. the spurs the riders have — (the riders' spurs) — the riders spurs'

**Independent Practice** Write the correct possessive form of the noun in parentheses to complete each sentence.

1. The horses ran in the ____farmer's____ field each day. (farmer)
2. They ate the ____meadow's____ grass. (meadow)
3. They listened for the ____boys'____ call to return to the barn. (boys)
4. The ____horses'____ lives were safe and enjoyable. (horses)

---

## Differentiate Instruction

Some students may have difficulty understanding how to form possessives and when possessives should be used.

Help students by providing them with more examples of phrases that can be shortened by forming a possessive. Then have them form the possessive for each underlined word.

- The <u>cows</u> have a barn.    The _____ barn. (cows')
- The <u>cow</u> has a sore leg.    The _____ sore leg. (cow's)
- The <u>barn</u> has a red roof.    The _____ red roof. (barn's)

## Commas and Quotation Marks in Dialogue

**Guided Instruction** **Dialogue** is a conversation written as part of a story.

*Abbey said, "I would like a pet hamster."*

**Quotation marks** are used to show the person's words. A **comma** is used to separate the other words in the sentence from what the speaker says.

*Mom asked, "Would you take care of the pet?"*

**Guided Practice** Add quotation marks to show each speaker's words.

1. Ryan asked, Do you have any guinea pigs?

   Ryan asked, "Do you have any guinea pigs?"

2. The owner answered, Yes. We have three.

   The owner answered, "Yes. We have three."

3. That brown one sure is cute, Ryan whispered to his mom.

   "That brown one sure is cute," Ryan whispered to his mom.

**Independent Practice** Write the sentence using quotation marks and commas to separate the speaker's words from the rest of the sentence.

1. Ben exclaimed The guinea pig doesn't look like a pig at all!

   Ben exclaimed, "The guinea pig doesn't look like a pig at all!"

2. How big do guinea pigs get? asked Katie.

   "How big do guinea pigs get?" asked Katie.

3. Mrs. Volpe answered Adults are about two pounds.

   Mrs. Volpe answered, "Adults are about two pounds."

Unit 2 ■ Text Types and Purposes: Write Fictional Narratives   **49**

## OBJECTIVE
**Use commas and quotation marks in dialogue.**

## Guided Instruction
Make sure that students understand that in a story, quotation marks are used around the words that someone says.

## Guided Practice
Begin by asking students to identify the speaker's words. (Do you have any guinea pigs?) Then ask them to write those words and place quotation marks around them to identify the words as a quotation. Help students realize that in the third example, quotation marks should be placed *after* the comma, which sets the quotation apart from the rest of the sentence.

## Independent Practice
Instruct students to write the sentences, placing the quotation marks and commas where they belong to set off the quotations. Remind students that some quotations end with exclamation marks or question marks, and that quotation marks should be placed after.

### Assess and Respond

**If** students are having difficulty placing quotation marks correctly,

**Then** give students more practice by writing five more sentences like those shown in Independent Practice and having students place the commas and quotation marks where they belong.

## Grouping Options

Pair students having difficulty with a more proficient learner to gain more practice with quotations.

Write statements (for example, *Go to bed.*) on index cards and place them in a pile. Then make another pile of index cards with sentence parts that identify a speaker, such as *Maria says*, or *said Jonah*. Ask the partner with developing skills to choose a statement and rewrite it, placing quotation marks at the beginning and end. Then ask the more proficient partner to choose an index card from the sentence part pile, and have him or her write the sentence part at the beginning or end of the quotation, placing a comma where it belongs.

## OBJECTIVES

- Come to discussion prepared, and draw on that preparation to explore ideas.
- Ask questions to check understanding.

## Discuss the Essential Question

Before beginning a group discussion, copy and distribute the "Did I?" checklist, available on **sadlierconnect.com**.

### Leading the Class Discussion

Give students time to think about the questions before the class discussion.

1. Have students review events in the student model.
2. Instruct students to skim paragraphs for descriptions.

---

## SPEAKING AND LISTENING

### Discuss the Essential Question

How do writers develop fictional narratives?

Think about the Essential Question by responding to the questions below. Support your point of view with reasons and experience.

**1.** How does the writer sequence the story?

First, the animals gather at the messy playground. They decide to clean it up.

They work through the night. In the morning, they have a clean playground.

**2.** What are some words or phrases the author uses to describe events?

broken swings hung limply; powerful winds; race down the slides;

sagged with disappointment; fetch sticks; ran back and forth

Use your notes above to discuss the Essential Question in small groups or as a class. Remember to use the rules for being a good speaker and a good listener in the checklist below. When you speak, be sure to explain your ideas fully. As a listener, ask questions and make connections among everyone's comments in order to fully understand the conversation.

### *Did I:*

- ☐ Come to the discussion prepared?
- ☐ Follow agreed-upon rules for discussion?
- ☐ Ask questions to check my understanding?
- ☐ Stay on topic?
- ☐ Avoid interrupting others?
- ☐ Listen carefully to others and answer questions?
- ☐ Speak in complete sentences?

**50** Unit 2 ■ Text Types and Purposes: Write Fictional Narratives

---

## Discussion Skills

Introduce students to sentence starters for building on ideas of others:

- *What you said makes me wonder . . .*
- *What you said reminds me of . . .*

Then give students some sentence starters they can use when asking for clarification:

- *Could you repeat what you said about . . . ?*
- *I'm not sure what you meant by . . .*
- *What evidence do you have for . . . ?*

# UNIT 2 REVIEW

This paragraph has mistakes in sentences and agreement. There are incorrect plural nouns and possessive forms, as well as incorrect punctuation of dialogue. Write the paragraph correctly on the lines below.

Lauren has two bunnys, Patches and Hopper. They were in a terrible flood. When the flood came, Lauren put them in boxs and carried them to safety. Lauren whispered You will be okay. Hearing her voice made them feel calm. Patches and Hopper didn't have their favorite grassies, but they did have plenty of water and food. After the flood, Laurens mom suggested that she teach other peoples how to help animals in emergencys.

Lauren has two bunnies, Patches and Hopper. They were in a terrible flood.

When the flood came, Lauren put them in boxes and carried them to safety.

Lauren whispered, "You will be okay." Hearing her voice made them feel

calm. Patches and Hopper didn't have their favorite grasses, but they did

have plenty of water and food. After the flood, Lauren's mom suggested

that she teach other people how to help animals in emergencies.

_____

_____

_____

_____

_____

_____

Unit 2 ■ Text Types and Purposes: Write Fictional Narratives    **51**

## Introduce the Review

Explain to students that this review will give them an opportunity to apply the language and writing skills that they have studied and practiced in this unit.

### Language Skills Summary

Explain to students that they are going to use what they learned about all kinds of nouns, including plural nouns, irregular plural nouns, and possessives. Additionally, they will use what they learned about commas and quotation marks in dialogue to make their writing better. Good writers know the rules of grammar and punctuation.

- Have students explain what an abstract noun is. (It is a noun that names something that cannot be seen or held, such as peace or childhood.)

- Ask students to explain how to form plurals for nouns ending in -x, -ch, -sh, and how to form plurals for nouns ending in consonant -y. (For nouns ending in -x, -ch, -sh, add -es. For nouns ending in -y, change the -y to an -i and add -es.)

- Prompt students to name how forming a possessive of a plural noun ending in -s is different from forming a possessive of a singular noun. (For plural nouns ending in -s, add only an apostrophe. For singular nouns, add apostrophe -s.)

- Ask students to explain where to place quotation marks in a sentence in which someone's words are quoted directly. (Place quotation marks at the beginning and end of the words the speaker said.)

## Test-Taking Tips

Give students the following tips to help with taking assessments focused on editing skills.

- Tell students to make a list of the things that they should check for, such as correct spelling of plural nouns, correct form of possessives, and correct placement of commas and quotation marks in sentences that include quotations.

- Encourage students to read slowly. Suggest that they put a pencil under each word as they read to help them focus on one word at a time.

## Writing Process Summary

Remind students that planning helps them organize their ideas before drafting, and revising and editing make a draft better.

### Planning and Drafting

Have students look at the outline and draft they created earlier (page 45). They should check that the draft covers all the important points in the outline.

### Fictional Narrative Rubric

| | |
|---|---|
| 4 | The narrative includes: an introduction that sets up the situation, a sequence of events that unfolds naturally, description and dialogue; sequence words; a conclusion that provides closure. There are few or no editing errors. |
| 3 | The narrative has the elements listed under "4" above, though they are executed less successfully. Minor editing errors do not detract greatly from the overall essay. |
| 2 | The piece is missing one or more of the elements required. There are many editing errors, some of which are serious. |
| 1 | The narrative is unfinished or shows a minimal understanding of required elements. Serious editing errors make it difficult to read. |
| 0 | The narrative was not attempted. |

### Self-Assessment: Progress Check

Have students revisit the Progress Check on page 39 and compare their answers now with the answers they gave before they started Unit 2.

## UNIT 2 REVIEW

**Assignment:** Write a fictional narrative about animal characters.

On the lines below, write your final copy of the fictional narrative draft you created on page 45. Be sure to include dialogue and description to show thoughts, feelings, and actions. Make sure to choose your words carefully and use words to signal the order of events. Include a conclusion that wraps up events in your story. See the Writing Handbook (pages 275–283) for ways to improve your writing as you revise.

Students should write a fictional narrative that includes animal characters, uses effective technique, includes descriptive details, shows clear event sequences, includes dialogue and descriptions of actions, thoughts, and feelings to show the response of characters to situations, uses temporal words and phrases to signal event order, and provides a sense of closure.

### Digital Connection: Storybooks

Once students have finished writing their stories, they can make storybooks. If computers are available, encourage students to use a computer to write and edit their stories. Then have them choose public domain images they find on the Internet to illustrate their stories. Alternatively, they could use a drawing or painting application to create their own artwork.

## Introducing UNIT 3

**H**uman history, whether it is 50 years or 50,000 years ago, fascinates many people. Human beings are naturally social. They want to be connected to others—even others from our ancient past. This connectedness can help people of today in many ways.

In this unit, you will read about long-ago events. The echoes of these events still reach us today. The readings will show you people's desire to know the facts about our world. And they will explore how people use those facts to improve the present and the future. You will learn how authors craft informational texts to give readers a clear understanding of events and ideas. And you will also look at how authors use different words to express their exact meaning.

Being able to find and connect main ideas and details in texts will help you understand informational writing. This skill will help you understand your world.

### Progress Check  Can I?

**Before Unit 3** / **After Unit 3**

- ☐ Ask and answer questions about a text to better understand it. ☐
- ☐ Retell a text's important details to show understanding. ☐
- ☐ Summarize the main idea of a text. ☐
- ☐ Describe how events or ideas in a text are related. ☐
- ☐ Explain how certain words are used to describe real life. ☐

Unit 3 ■ Reading Informational Text: Key Ideas and Details

**Student Page 53**

## Progress Check

The Progress Check is a self-assessment feature that students can use to gauge their own progress. Research shows that when students take accountability for their own learning, their motivation increases.

Before students begin work on Unit 3, have them check the boxes next to any item that they feel they can do well. Explain that it is fine if they don't check any of the boxes. Tell them that they will have an opportunity to learn about and practice all of these items while studying the unit. Let them know that near the end of the unit they will have a chance to reconsider how well they can do each item on this list.

Before students begin the Unit 3 Review on page 81, have them revisit this page. You can use this information to work with students on any items they don't understand before they tackle the Review.

### HOME ◆ CONNECT...

**I**t is easy to **ask and answer questions** about a nonfiction text because it is full of details. Sometimes, asking yourself about what you have read is the only way to keep the information straight in your head. Choose a print or online news report on a topic of interest to your child. Use the article's title and subheadings to preview the subject and **main idea**. Read it together, asking and answering questions about **interesting details**. Pause at certain points to have your child summarize the information. Discuss the main idea of the text when you are done reading.

Authors of nonfiction texts use wording that **describes how a series of historical events or ideas are related**. In this unit, your child will learn about several important archaeological discoveries. Have your child describe events in his or her life that led to some kind of understanding or discovery. How did he or she come to play a certain sport, learn a new skill, or meet someone new? Talk together using language that connects different events.

⬥ **On the Go:** The texts in this unit focus on scientific research on ancient objects. With your child, think of ways that research skills might be used closer to your time and place. You might try to find out more about your ancestors, for example. Or, perhaps there is an old monument or landmark near your home. Finding out who built it and why can open up your town's history. A visit to a local historical society can add a hands-on element to any Internet research that you do.

#### IN THIS UNIT, YOUR CHILD WILL...

- Ask questions and answer them to gain a better understanding of an informational text.
- Determine the main idea of a text, and explain how details in the text support the main idea.
- Describe relationships between events or ideas in a text using words and phrases that show time order, sequence, and cause and effect.
- Connect the meaning of words to real-life situations.
- Compare and contrast four texts on the same theme: a magazine article, an historical text, a scientific text, and a biography.

#### WAYS TO HELP YOUR CHILD

Help your child connect "school" reading with everyday reading. Pick a topic from your child's schoolwork as a jumping off point. Use keywords from the topic to fuel an Internet search for similar, age-appropriate articles. Ask your child to tell you the most interesting facts from the articles. Follow up with your own search for additional information, either online or in print. Suggest that your child find out more about the subject and then teach you something new.

**ONLINE**
For more Home Connect activities, continue online at sadlierconnect.com

54     Unit 3 ■ Reading Informational Text: Key Ideas and Details

### HOME ◆ CONNECT...

The Home Connect feature is a way to keep parents or other adult family members apprised of what their children are learning. The key learning objectives are listed, and some ideas for related activities and discussions are included.

Explain to students that they can share the Home Connect page with their parents or other adult family members in their home. Let students know how much time the class will be spending on this unit so they can plan their time accordingly at home.

Encourage students and their parents to share their experiences using the suggestions on the Home Connect page. You may wish to make a place to post some of this work.

**Student Page 54**

## UNIT PLANNER

| Theme: Echoes of the Past | Focus |
|---|---|
| **ASKING AND ANSWERING QUESTIONS**<br>*pp. 56–61* | *The 40,000-Year-Old Baby*<br>**GENRE:** Magazine Article   **LEXILE®:** 610L<br><br>**WORDS TO KNOW:** extinct, sandbar, mammoth, prehistoric, skeleton, biology, digestive system, exhibit, cloning, DNA, protein |
| **DETERMINING MAIN IDEA AND KEY DETAILS**<br>*pp. 62–67* | *The Amazing Tomb of Tut*<br>**GENRE:** Historical Text   **LEXILE®:** 650L<br><br>**WORDS TO KNOW:** ruins, culture, tomb, royal,  chamber, sarcophagus, mummy, preserved, log book, original |
| **DESCRIBING RELATIONSHIPS BETWEEN IDEAS**<br>*pp. 68–73* | *Finding Machu Picchu*<br>**GENRE:** Science Magazine Article<br>**LEXILE®:** 630L<br><br>**WORDS TO KNOW:** expedition, university, civilization, dominated, constructed, precise,  demonstration, labor, irrigation, theory, excavate |
| **CLOSE READING**<br>*pp. 74–78* | *Howard Carter's Last Chance*<br>**GENRE:** Biography   **LEXILE®:** 620L |
| **CONNECT ACROSS TEXTS**<br>*p. 79* | Compare and Contrast Texts |
| **LANGUAGE**<br>*p. 80* | Real-Life Word Connections |
| **UNIT 3 REVIEW**<br>*pp. 81–82* | *Vikings in America* |

Essential Question: How do authors convey a main idea and use details to support it?

UNIT 3

## Objective(s)

Show an understanding of an informational text by asking questions and citing evidence from the text to answer questions.

Determine and explain the main idea of a text, using key details from the text.

Describe the relationship between ideas, using language related to time, sequence, and cause/effect.

- Show an understanding of an informational text by asking questions and citing evidence from the text to answer questions.

- Determine and explain the main idea of a text, using key details from the text.

- Describe the relationship between ideas, using language related to time, sequence, and cause/effect.

Understand how word in texts connect to real life.

## Unit Assessment

- Unit 3 Review *pp. 81–82*
- Unit 3 Performance Task  ONLINE

## Additional Assessment Options

- Performance Task 1 *pp. 141A–145 and 146*
  ALSO ONLINE
- Performance Task 2 *pp. 259A–263 and 264*
  ALSO ONLINE

**Optional Purchase:**
- iProgress Monitor  ONLINE
- Progress Monitor Student Benchmark Assessment Booklet

## ONLINE  Digital Resources

- Home Connect Activities
- Unit Performance Task
- Additional Practice
- Full-Length Reading Selections
- Foundational Skills Practice
- Teacher Resources
- iProgress Monitor (optional purchase)

**Go to SadlierConnect.com to access your Digital Resources.**

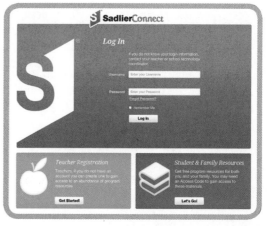

**For more detailed instructions see page T3.**

## LEARNING PROGRESSIONS

In this unit, students will learn how an author of an informational text conveys a main idea and supports it with details. In order to learn the skills in this unit, students will further develop skills learned in second grade. They should be encouraged to retain these skills, as they will continue to build on them in fourth grade.

**Asking and Answering Questions**

- Grade 2 students should have completed the school year able to ask and answer questions such as *who*, *what*, *where*, *when*, *why*, and *how* to demonstrate understanding of key details in the text.

- As third graders, students will build on this skill by referring explicitly to the text as the basis for their answers to these same kinds of questions in order to demonstrate understanding of the text.

- In grade 4, students will be expected to refer to details and examples in the text when explaining what the text says explicitly and when drawing inferences.

**Determining Main Idea and Key Details**

- By the end of grade 2, students should be able to identify the main topic of a multi-paragraph text as well as the focus of specific paragraphs within the text.

- In grade 3, students will widen their application of this skill to determine the main idea of a text and recount the key details and explain how they support the main idea.

- When students move on to grade 4, they will continue to practice determining the main idea and explaining how it is supported by key details, as well as learn to summarize the text.

**Describing Relationships Between Ideas**

- Proficient second-grade students should have ended the school year able to describe the connection between a series of historical events, scientific ideas or concepts, or steps in technical procedures in a text.

- Throughout grade 3, students' use of this skill will become more sophisticated as they learn to describe these same connections, or relationships, using language that pertains to time, sequence, and cause/effect.

- Students will be expected to apply this skill at a more complex level in grade 4 by explaining events, procedures, ideas, or concepts in a historical, scientific, or technical text, including what happened and why, based on specific information in the text.

# Reading Informational Text: Key Ideas and Details

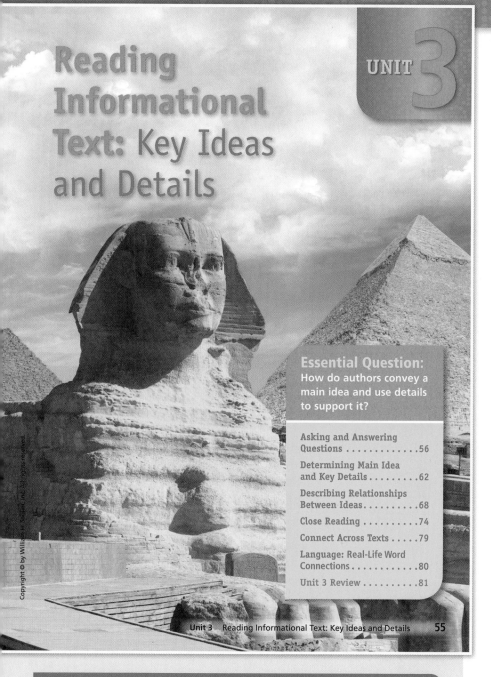

**UNIT 3**

In this unit, students will learn about how to identify and make connections between the main idea and key details of an informational text, specifically by asking and answering questions and describing relationships between ideas.

## Theme: Echoes of the Past

Students will read informational texts related to the theme of human history, or our collective past. They will read about the discoveries of a 40,000-year-old mammoth mummy, King Tut's tomb, and the lost city of Machu Picchu, as well as a biography of Howard Carter, the archaeologist who discovered King Tut's tomb.

## Curriculum Connection: Social Studies

Students will learn about the history of mammoths, ancient Egypt, and the Inca, as well as how scientists, archaeologists, and explorers study the past.

## Vocabulary Overview

**General Academic Vocabulary**

chamber 65, civilization 69, constructed 70, culture 62, demonstration 71, dominated 69, excavate 73, exhibit 60, expedition 68, extinct 56, labor 71, original 66, precise 70, prehistoric 57, preserved 66, royal 64, ruins 62, theory 72, university 69

**Domain-Specific Vocabulary**

biology 58, cloning 60, digestive system 59, DNA 60, irrigation 72, log book 66, mammoth 56, mummy 65, protein 60, sandbar 56, sarcophagus 65, skeleton 58, tomb 62

## Guided Instruction

### OBJECTIVE
**Show an understanding of an informational text by asking questions and citing evidence from the text to answer questions.**

### Genre: Magazine Article

Explain to students that a magazine article is a type of informational text that appears in a print or digital magazine.

### Set the Purpose

Help students understand the purpose for learning the reading skill by asking *What text have you read recently that you did not understand? What did you do to better understand it?*

### Model and Teach

Read the selection as students follow along in their books.

### CITE EVIDENCE

**A** *I know that* who *refers to people and* what *refers to things or creatures.*

*What is discussed in paragraph 1?* (long-extinct animals) *Who is discussed in paragraph 2?* (Yuri Khudi)

**B** *I know that something that "happens" is an event. I see that Yuri Khudi was tending his reindeer.*

*When was Yuri tending the reindeer?* (May 2007) *What did Yuri and his sons see?* (They saw the body of a small animal lying on a sandbar.)

---

**WORDS TO KNOW**
extinct
mammoth
prehistoric
sandbar

To **understand a text,** use details from the text **to ask and answer questions.**

**CITE EVIDENCE**

**A** To **understand a text,** it helps **to ask and answer questions,** such as *Who and what is the text about?* Underline details in paragraphs 1 and 2 that answer this question.

**B** It also helps to ask *What happened?* and *When did it happen?* Circle details in paragraph 2 that answer these questions. What other details give an idea of what happened next?

# The 40,000-Year-Old Baby
### by Hong Lee-Hyun
(Genre: Magazine Article)

1 Can long-**extinct** animals be brought back to life? The idea sounds like something out of a comic book. But a discovery in 2007 may have changed that.

2 In May 2007 Yuri Khudi was tending his herd of reindeer. He and his sons were near the Yuribey River. This river is in Siberia, in northeast Russia. They saw the body of a small animal lying on a sandbar. They could tell it was an animal they had never seen before.

3 They had heard of it, however. Their elders told many stories about the *mamonts*, or **mammoths**. These were giant beasts, like elephants. They were said to wander the frozen underworld. Yuri himself had seen many giant tusks. They came out of the frozen ground when spring arrived.

**56** Unit 3 ▪ Reading Informational Text: Key Ideas and Details

---

## Words to Know

**General Academic Vocabulary**
**extinct** (*adjective*): no longer living or existing
**prehistoric** (*adjective*): taking place before the time of recorded history

**Domain-Specific Vocabulary**
**mammoth** (*noun*): huge, hairy animal that is now extinct
**sandbar** (*noun*): a mound of sand built up near a shoreline

**Working with Word Meaning** Have partners make flashcards for the words—with the word on one side and the definition on the other side—and then take turns using the flashcards to quiz each other.

## KEY IDEAS AND DETAILS

4    Yuri did not touch the body. According to his people, mammoths were bad luck. Instead, he traveled 150 miles south to the nearest museum. His story interested the museum director. He sent officials to recover the body.

5    When scientists looked at the body, they agreed with Yuri. It was a baby female mammoth. She was about three feet tall. She weighed 110 pounds. Being buried in the frozen soil of northern Russia had preserved her. They decided to name her Lyuba, after Yuri's wife.

6    Mammoths were **prehistoric** relatives of elephants. They were about the same size as elephants. They grew huge tusks and had long snouts, too. And they ate the same kinds of foods. But mammoths were able to live in very cold places. Their bodies were covered with a dense coat of long hair. They had small, fur-lined ears.

7    About 14,000 years ago, the mammoths started dying off quickly. Researchers argue about why. Most think a number of things combined to make them extinct. One cause was a general warming of Earth. Another may have been a disease. A third may have been overhunting by humans.

### CITE EVIDENCE

**C** In most informational texts, it helps to ask *where* events happened. Box the words in paragraph 5 that answer this question.

**D** Texts that tell facts will also explain *why* something happened. Underline the details in paragraph 7 that tell why the mammoths died off. How can studying the reasons something in the past happened help scientists today?

**Adult and baby mammoth**

### Comprehension Check

What animal that is alive today is like the mammoth? How are they alike and different? Use details from the text as a basis for your answer.

Unit 3 ■ Reading Informational Text: Key Ideas and Details    **57**

### CITE EVIDENCE

**C** *I know that* where *refers to a place or location. This paragraph says that the baby mammoth had been preserved in frozen soil.*

*Which words tell you the location, or* where, *she was preserved?* (northern Russia)

**D** *Why* is the cause in a cause-and-effect relationship. The effect is the mammoths dying off. So I'll look for a word that signals the cause for this event.

*What word signals why they died off?* (cause) *How many causes does the text list?* (three) *How might knowing about these causes help scientists protect other animals?* (They can watch to see if these same events threaten to make other animals extinct today.)

### Comprehension Check

**Sample Answer:** An elephant is like the mammoth. The text says that mammoths were like elephants in that they were about the same size, grew tusks, had long snouts, and ate the same kinds of foods. The text says that mammoths were different from elephants because they were able to live in cold places, were covered with long hair, and had small, fur-lined ears.

**Answer Explanation:** Students should notice that the text explains that mammoths were prehistoric relatives of elephants, or in the same animal family as elephants. Students should recognize that this is why these two animals have some similarities.

### Support English Language Learners

Students who are learning English may have a difficult time understanding the rhetorical nature of the first sentence of the text, which takes the form of a question. Explain that the author does not expect the reader to answer the question before continuing to read; rather, the author poses this question to prompt the reader to think about the topic and to set up the ideas in the text. Discuss how posing it as a question captures the reader's imagination. Then rephrase the sentence to help students see the purpose it serves: *This text is about whether long-extinct animals can be brought back to life.*

Challenge students to identify and explain another rhetorical question in paragraph 17 on page 61. ("How is that possible?")

## Guided Practice

### Recap Reading Selection

Let students know that they will continue reading the article about the mammoth mummy. Review what they read about how the mummy was discovered and what might have caused mammoths to become extinct.

### Read and Practice

Have partners take turns reading the selection as you circulate to provide support. Model practicing asking and answering questions with Cite Evidence callout A. For callout B, circulate and provide partners with scaffolding as needed. You might use the following suggestions to help students who are having difficulty.

### CITE EVIDENCE

**A** Explain to students that keeping track of the different scientists mentioned in the text will help them better understand the events described. Help students identify that Alexei Tikhonov and Dan Fisher are introduced in paragraph 8. Help them see that a third scientist, Naoki Suzuki, is introduced in paragraph 10.

**B** Help students recognize that Lyuba was the first "fully formed mammoth" to be studied by scientists. Help students see that this allowed them to study mammoth teeth, tusks, and stomach contents for the first time, which would reveal new facts about mammoths.

---

## ASKING AND ANSWERING QUESTIONS

### Guided Practice

**WORDS TO KNOW**
biology
digestive system
skeleton

**CITE EVIDENCE**

**A** Check understanding by asking yourself *Who are the key people in this article?* Underline the name of each scientist on this page.

**B** Lyuba was an important discovery. In paragraph 9, circle the sentences that explain why. As you read, ask, *Why would the animal's stomach contents be important?*

**The 40,000-Year-Old Baby** *continued*

8 One of the first scientists to see Lyuba was <u>Alexei Tikhonov</u>. He was director of the St. Petersburg Zoological Museum in Russia. In July 2007, he called <u>Dan Fisher</u> at the University of Michigan. Fisher is an expert on prehistoric animals such as mammoths. When Fisher saw Lyuba, he was surprised and happy. This was the first time a prehistoric animal had been found in perfect shape!

9 Fisher knew what this find meant. Before, scientists could only imagine what the mammoths looked like. They only had **skeletons** or small body parts to look at. Now they had a fully formed mammoth! She looked as if she had been in good health when she died. Researchers could study her teeth and tusks. They could check her stomach contents and other features. These would reveal new facts on mammoth **biology** and habits.

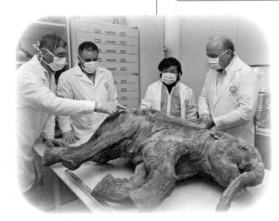

10 To do these studies, Lyuba had to travel around the world. First, samples of her skin were sent to the Netherlands. There, they were tested to find out how long ago Lyuba lived. The tests showed that she had lived about 40,000 years ago. Next, in December 2007, Lyuba traveled to Japan. There, <u>Naoki Suzuki</u> performed detailed X-ray scans on her.

**58** Unit 3 ■ Reading Informational Text: Key Ideas and Details

---

## Words to Know

**Domain-Specific Vocabulary**
**biology** (*noun*): the study of living things
**digestive system** (*noun*): the path of internal organs that food passes through to allow a body to absorb nutrients from it
**skeleton** (*noun*): internal structure of bones that support a body

**Working with Word Meaning** Guide students as they make a simple diagram of the human body, labeling the digestive system and the skeleton. Show references as needed. Encourage students to use the word "biology" and present their diagram to a partner.

11    In June 2008, Fisher, Suzuki, and other scientists performed surgery on Lyuba. Some of them removed the contents of her **digestive system**. This finding told them about Lyuba's diet. Others drilled into a hump on her back. They took out fat to study. Suzuki inserted a tube into her body. He checked an area he had seen in the X-ray. Fisher took out some teeth and a tusk that was forming. Other samples of body parts were taken for further study.

## Comprehension Check

1. Who is the main subject of this text?

   (a.) Lyuba, a baby mammoth

   b. Dan Fisher, an American scientist

   c. Alexei Tikhonov, a Russian scientist

   d. Yuri Khudi, a Russian reindeer herder

2. What happens to Lyuba after she is discovered?

   a. She is sent to a museum in Michigan.

   b. She is put on display in St. Petersburg, Russia.

   c. She is sold to a collector of prehistoric animals.

   (d.) She is studied by scientists from around the world.

3. Why is Lyuba so important to scientists who study extinct, prehistoric animals? Cite information from the text in your answer.

   Sample answer: Paragraph 9 says the scientists never had a complete

   mammoth before. Instead of guessing about the mammoth, they could

   study her. They could learn what she ate and how she lived.

## Guided Practice

### Comprehension Check

**Answer Explanations:**

1. Choice A is correct because the article explains how the baby mammoth mummy was discovered and studied. Lyuba is the subject, not the men who found and studied her.

2. Choice D is correct. The text discusses how scientists from Russia, Michigan, the Netherlands, and Japan studied Lyuba after her discovery.

3. Students' responses may vary, but they should note that Lyuba is important because she provided scientists with the first opportunity to study a fully formed mammoth. Students should cite evidence from the text in their answers.

## Peer Collaboration

Have students confirm their answer choices for Comprehension Check 1 and 2 on page 59 by turning to a partner and discussing why each answer option they did not select can be ruled out. For Comprehension Check 2, suggest that students discuss how the wording in the incorrect choices differs from the wording in the text. Encourage students to revise their answer choices based on their discussion with their partner. Then ask pairs to report their answers to the whole group.

## Foundational Skills: Fluency

Explain that students can read more fluently if they read with proper phrasing, which means they pause after appropriately grouped words, sometimes signaled by a comma. Demonstrate this concept by reading paragraph 1 with poor phrasing (*Can long / extinct / animals be / brought / back to / life?*) or by running all the words together. Then reread paragraph 1 with proper phrasing: *Can long-extinct animals / be brought back to life?* Allow students to practice reading another paragraph with proper phrasing. Next, have them record themselves reading the same paragraph and then listen to the recording to improve prosodic skills. Additional fluency passages and activities can be found at **sadlierconnect.com** and in the *Foundational Skills Handbook*.

## Independent Practice

### Recap Reading Selection

Remind students that they have been reading a magazine article. Have them recall the topic of the article (a baby mammoth mummy), why Lyuba was an important discovery (She was the first fully formed mammoth scientists could study; they would no longer have to make guesses about mammoth biology and habits.), and details about the surgery performed on her (removed contents from digestive system; inserted a tube to check an area; took out fat, teeth, a tusk, and other samples).

### Read and Apply

Have students read the selection independently as you circulate to provide support. If you notice students struggling, you can provide support with the suggestions below.

### CITE EVIDENCE

**A** Help students recall that Lyuba was so well preserved because she had been buried in frozen soil. Help students identify that the scientists had "kept Lyuba frozen" but would have to "warm her up" to perform the surgery. Help them connect that warming her up might destroy how well preserved she was.

**B** Help students identify that Lyuba became part of an exhibit that will travel around the world. Prompt students to pose a question about cloning.

---

**WORDS TO KNOW**

cloning
DNA
exhibit
protein

**CITE EVIDENCE**

**A** Ask yourself *Why would surgery on a mammoth that was already dead need to be done quickly?* Circle details in paragraph 12 that answers this question.

**B** Underline details that tell about Lyuba's future. What questions about cloning Lyuba would you ask a scientist?

12 All the work had to be done in only three days. Before then, scientists kept Lyuba frozen. But for the surgery to happen, they had to warm her up. The scientists could not stop to figure out what their findings meant. They had to cut fast and think later.

13 When asked about those days, Fisher remembered the whirl of activity. There were things he noticed about Lyuba that did not make sense. It wasn't until later that he could reflect on what he had seen.

14 Since her surgery, Lyuba's travels have continued. In 2010, she became part of an **exhibit** at Chicago's Field Museum. The director of the exhibit was Professor Fisher. He was still studying Lyuba. He wanted to better understand how mammoths lived. The exhibit will continue traveling to museums around the world. Its final stop will be London in 2014.

15 Fisher was asked about **cloning** Lyuba. This process would mean using **DNA proteins** from Lyuba to create a new mammoth. He explains that DNA could be taken from Lyuba. However, he thought scientists were not close to being able to create a mammoth.

16 Other researchers think cloning Lyuba is possible sooner. In 2012, Russian and South Korean scientists agreed to work together on cloning. The South Koreans have already cloned a cat, dogs, a pig, a cow, and a wolf. They say they can produce a mammoth by 2015.

---

### Words to Know

**General Academic Vocabulary**
**exhibit** (*noun*): a show or display

**Domain-Specific Vocabulary**
**cloning** (*verb*): copying or reproducing, using genetic material
**DNA** (*noun*): stands for deoxyribonucleic acid; contains all the genetic information (eye color, hair color, etc.) about a human, animal, or plant
**protein** (*noun*): a compound found in every cell in animals and humans

**Working with Word Meaning** Show pictures that relate to each word and have partners discuss which word goes with which picture.

## KEY IDEAS AND DETAILS

17 How is that possible? We already have elephants, which are distant relatives of mammoths. The scientists hope an elephant will be the cloned mammoth's mother. If they succeed, it would be one of the great moments in the history of science.

### Comprehension Check

MORE ONLINE  sadlierconnect.com

**1. What did scientists have to do to perform surgery on Lyuba?**

    **a.** take her to Chicago's Field Museum

    **b.** let her warm up

    **c.** create a new mammoth through cloning

    **d.** examine Lyuba's DNA proteins

**2. In 2010, three years after her discovery, why was Professor Fisher still studying Lyuba?**

    **a.** He wanted to better understand how mammoths lived.

    **b.** He wanted to extract DNA from Lyuba.

    **c.** He was the director of an exhibit in London.

    **d.** He had agreed to work on a project to clone Lyuba.

**3. How would scientists clone Lyuba? Why are some scientists sure they can do this? By what date? Use information directly from the text in your answer.**

Sample answer: Scientists would clone her by "using DNA proteins from

Lyuba to create a new mammoth." They "hope an elephant will be the

cloned mammoth's mother." Russian and South Korean scientists think

they can do this because they "have already cloned a cat, dogs, a pig, a

cow, and a wolf." They think they can do it by 2015.

## Foundational Skill Review: Consonant Digraphs

Review words with the consonant digraphs *ch*, *sh*, and *th*. Display <u>ch</u>ain, <u>sh</u>ake, and <u>th</u>em, and underline the digraph as you say each word. Point out that the two letters in each digraph combine to form a new sound. Explain that the digraph can appear at the beginning, middle, or end of a word. Then have students identify *ch* words in paragraph 1 (*changed*) and paragraph 4 (*touch*) on page 56, *sh* words in paragraph 9 (*Fisher; she*) on page 58, and *th* words in paragraph 1 (*the, something, that*) and paragraph 3 (*they, their; mammoths, these*) on page 56.

---

## Independent Practice

### Comprehension Check

**Answer Explanations:**

**1.** Choice B, *let her warm up*, tells what scientists had to do to perform surgery on Lyuba.

**2.** Professor Fisher was still studying Lyuba because *he wanted to better understand how mammoths lived*, so choice A is correct.

**3.** Student answers should reflect that scientists would use DNA proteins to clone Lyuba, that some scientists are sure they can do this because other animals have been cloned, and that they think they can do it by 2015.

## Critical Comprehension

Use the following questions to help students think more deeply about the text. Students should be prepared to support their answers with evidence from the text.

- *Why do you think Fisher, and not Tikhonov, became director of the Lyuba exhibit?* (Fisher's specialty is prehistoric animals.)

- *What details help you understand that the discovery of Lyuba was exciting to the science community?* (Scientists from around the world studied her; they put her in an exhibit; some want to clone her.)

### Assess and Respond

**If** students have difficulty answering the questions in the Comprehension Check,

**Then** work individually with them, helping them check each answer option against the text to help them rule out wrong options before selecting the correct choice.

## Guided Instruction

### OBJECTIVE
**Determine and explain the main idea of a text, using key details from the text.**

### Genre: Historical Text

Explain to students that an historical text is a type of informational text that tells about an event from the past, or something related to history.

### Set the Purpose

Help students understand the purpose for learning the reading skill by asking *Why do you think authors write about events that took place in the past?*

### Model and Teach

Read the selection as students follow along in their books.

### CITE EVIDENCE

**A** *I know that headings appear above sections or chunks of text and are often in larger letters.*

*Which word in the first heading helps you understand whom the text is about?* (Tut)

**B** *The title tells me that the text will be about the amazing tomb of Tut, so I look for a statement about it.*

*Which sentence in paragraph 2 contains some of the same details as the title?* (He would soon find an amazing and important tomb.) *What might scientists learn from studying this tomb?* (how Egyptian kings and queens lived)

---

### DETERMINING MAIN IDEA AND KEY DETAILS
**Guided Instruction**

**WORDS TO KNOW**
culture
ruins
tomb

Look for the **main idea** of a text. Find **key details** and explain how they **support the main idea.**

**CITE EVIDENCE**

**A** In an informational text, **details** in the title can point toward the **main idea.** In the title, draw a circle around three words that tell the main focus of this text.

**B** The author usually tells the reader the main idea early in the text. In paragraph 2, underline the sentence that tells the main idea. Why do scientists study things from long ago?

# The Amazing (Tomb of Tut)
(Genre: Historical Text)

1    Howard Carter was a British scientist. He studied old cultures by digging up their **ruins**. He was very interested in Egypt. Its **culture** was thousands of years old. Ancient Egyptians made the pyramids and the Sphinx.

2    In 1922, Carter was digging in a part of Egypt called the Valley of the Kings. He had been working there for five years. Many Egyptian kings and queens were buried there thousands of years ago. Carter was searching for undiscovered **tombs**. <u>He would soon find an amazing and important tomb.</u>

**Who Was King Tut?**

3    Tutankhamun became pharaoh, or king, about 3,300 years ago. His name means "living image of the god Amun." We often call him "King Tut." During the time of his rule, Egyptians believed their kings were gods.

---

### Words to Know

**General Academic Vocabulary**

**culture** (*noun*): the beliefs, traditions, arts, and behavior of a group of people who have formed a society or civilization

**ruins** (*noun*): parts of a building or other structure that remain after a destructive event

**Domain-Specific Vocabulary**

**tomb** (*noun*): a room, usually underground, that is used as a grave

**Working with Word Meaning** Ask students to write one sentence, unrelated to the information in the text, for each word.

## KEY IDEAS AND DETAILS

4  Tut started his rule when he was nine years old. This was a difficult time in Egypt. Tut's father had made many changes in Egypt. He changed how the empire was run. He had forced Egyptians to change their religion. Many Egyptians were unhappy with what he did.

5  When Tut took the throne, he turned back his father's changes. After that, we know almost nothing about his rule. He was in poor health and died at the age of 19. Most of the facts about his rule were wiped out by the next rulers. Tut and his tomb were forgotten.

### Life After Death

6  Egyptians believed in life after death. They built huge tombs for their rulers. The tombs took a long time to build. Sometimes work went on for the ruler's entire life.

7  Rulers and their subjects filled the tombs with things they thought the dead needed. These items included gold, jewelry, and furniture. People also thought the dead needed supplies for daily living. So they included spices, grains, and clothing.

8  Because Tut ruled for only 10 years, his tomb was not ready. He was buried in a tomb meant for another person. The entryway was covered by stones and dirt from other buildings.

> **Comprehension Check**
>
> What details from the text help the reader understand why King Tut and his tomb were most likely forgotten?

A wall painting inside Tut's tomb

**CITE EVIDENCE**

**C** Authors include details that support the main idea of the text. In paragraph 5, underline important details about King Tut.

**D** Authors also explain things so readers can understand the main idea. In paragraphs 6 and 7, circle details about Egyptian life that readers need to know. How do these details help you understand Tut's world?

## Guided Instruction

### CITE EVIDENCE

**C** *As I read, I'll look for sentences that tell me important information about King Tut.*

*What does the first sentence in paragraph 5 tell about him?* (At the beginning of Tut's rule, rules his father had made as king were changed.) *What does the third sentence in paragraph 5 tell about him?* (He died as a young man after being king for 10 years.)

**D** *Now, I'll look for sentences that tell me about Egyptian life.*

*What do we learn in paragraph 7 about Egyptian rulers and their subjects?* (They filled the tombs with things they thought the dead needed.) *What do these details tell us about ancient Egyptians?* (They wanted their rulers to have good afterlives.)

> **Comprehension Check**

**Sample Answer:** "Most of the facts about his rule were wiped out by the next rulers."

**Answer Explanation:** Students should recall that King Tut ruled "about 3,300 years ago," and recognize that this was before books and videos, so people could not easily record and save information for future generations.

### Review: Asking and Answering Questions

Remind students to ask and answer questions to better understand the text. Prompt them to look for details in the text that help them understand why we know so much about King Tut now, even though he was forgotten after his rule.

---

## Support English Language Learners

Help English language learners build and connect to background knowledge before they read this text so that they can focus their energy on comprehending the ideas the author presents rather than on trying to make sense of unfamiliar ideas and references.

Be sure English language learners recognize this text is about a discovery of something that has been buried for a long time, just like the mammoth mummy they read about on pages 56–61. Show pictures of archaeological digs to help students understand what Howard Carter was doing. Show pictures of entrances to tombs in the Valley of the Kings, as well as of the elaborate interiors of tombs. Use language from the text to talk about the images you show, pointing to words in the text as you say them.

## Guided Practice

### Recap Reading Selection

Have students recall what they have read so far about King Tut and his tomb. They should mention that King Tut ruled Ancient Egypt about 3,300 years ago, and that he and his tomb were long forgotten after his rule.

### Read and Practice

Have partners take turns reading the selection as you circulate to provide support. Model determining the main idea and key details with Cite Evidence callout A. For callout B, circulate and provide partners with scaffolding as needed. You might use the following suggestions to help students who are having difficulty.

### CITE EVIDENCE

**A** Help students recognize that *First* in paragraph 10 is a time order word the author uses to tell a sequence of details. Ask students to identify the details in the sequence. (Carter made a hole; then he used a flashlight to see inside; three weeks later, the crew entered the tomb; by the next day they got to a second door.)

**B** Help students identify the "wonderful things" that Carter saw through the hole in the door, such as paintings, carved chairs, a gold chariot, and giant statues. Prompt them to recognize that these details help support the idea that the tomb was "wonderful."

---

# DETERMINING MAIN IDEA AND KEY DETAILS

### Guided Practice

**The Amazing Tomb of Tut** *continued*

**WORDS TO KNOW**
chamber
mummy
royal
sarcophagus

**CITE EVIDENCE**

**A** In this section, the author uses time order to provide details about finding the tomb. In paragraphs 10 and 11, circle words that show time passing as the details unfold.

**B** The author gives a step-by-step account of the discovery of the tomb. In paragraphs 11 and 12, underline the details that tell about this. How do these details support the main idea?

9   Over the years, robbers broke into most of the Egyptian pharaohs' tombs. They stole the treasures. Untold thousands of valuable pieces were lost. However, nobody touched the rich Tut tomb, until Howard Carter was able to find it on November 5, 1922.

**The Discovery**

10   Carter stumbled upon Tut's tomb while checking other ruins. He uncovered a rock stairway going down into the ground. First, workers cleared it step by step. At the bottom, they found a sealed doorway. The door had **royal** signs with Tut's name. Carter made a small hole at the top of the door. He then used a flashlight to look inside. Behind the door was a passage filled with rocks. Carter was sure he had found a major tomb.

11   Three weeks later, Carter and his crew entered the tomb. They opened the first door and started clearing the rocks. By the next day, they got to a second door. This was sealed like the first door. Again, Carter dug a hole to look inside. "Can you see anything?" someone asked. "Yes, wonderful things," Carter answered.

**64**    Unit 3 ■ Reading Informational Text: Key Ideas and Details

---

## Words to Know

**General Academic Vocabulary**
**chamber** (*noun*): a room
**royal** (*adjective*): relating to a king or queen

**Domain-Specific Vocabulary**
**mummy** (*noun*): a dead body that has been preserved, often through a special process, such as wrapping it in cloth
**sarcophagus** (*noun*): a stone coffin

**Working with Word Meaning** Challenge students to draw a picture that includes items they can label with each vocabulary word.

12    It was wonderful! The walls were covered with paintings about the king's life. There were beautiful couches and carved chairs. There were flowers and vases and a gold chariot. There were giant statues of gods. And between the statues was another doorway. This led to the burial **chamber**.

13    Inside the chamber was the **sarcophagus**. This was the human-shaped coffin that held Tut's **mummy**. Carter opened the top. Inside was another sarcophagus. Inside that one was a third. This final one was made of solid gold! Here was the final resting place of King Tut.

### Comprehension Check

**1.** What details told Carter he had found an important tomb?

   **a.** The passage was filled with rocks.

   **b.** The tomb had more than one door.

   **c.** Ancient writings said Tut's tomb was important.

   **(d.)** The tomb's doors were sealed and had royal signs.

**2.** What was the room outside the burial chamber filled with?

   **a.** mummies

   **b.** rocks and dirt

   **c.** traps for robbers

   **(d.)** valuable treasures

**3.** Working with a partner, read the text to find details about what happened to most Egyptian kings' tombs. How do these details help explain the importance of Tut's tomb?

Sample answer: Over the years, robbers had broken into most of the

pharaohs' tombs and stolen the treasures. Finding a tomb like King Tut's,

with all of its treasures, was unusual and important.

Unit 3 ■ Reading Informational Text: Key Ideas and Details    **65**

### Comprehension Check

**Answer Explanations:**

**1.** Choice D is correct because it is supported by evidence in paragraph 10.

**2.** Choice D is correct. Paragraph 12 provides details about the *valuable treasures* in the room outside the burial chamber.

**3.** Partners' responses will vary, but students should note that most Egyptian kings' tombs had been robbed. As a result, King's Tut tomb was important because robbers had not stolen its many treasures.

## Numbered Heads Together

Organize students in groups of four, and have them number off from one to four. Then say *At what point after uncovering a rock stairway did Carter know that he was digging up King Tut's tomb? You have two minutes to find and discuss the answer.* (when they found the door that had royal signs with Tut's name) After the time is up, have students with the number three stand up and share the answer their group decided on. Affirm correct responses and guide students who give incorrect responses as they reexamine the text. Ask follow-up questions such as *Do you think Carter would have kept digging if there were no signs on the door?*

## Digital Connection: Online Research

Help students add to the knowledge they have gained from reading this text by reading an online article about King Tut or Ancient Egypt on a reliable site. Then display a search engine on the whiteboard and model how to use keywords to find a text online. (You should preselect a text.) Then read the online text together. Guide students as they use the lesson skills to identify the main idea and key details of the text. Discuss with students how the information in the online article confirms and adds to what they already know. Point out that the Internet is a good resource for learning more about a topic provided that the sites they read from are credible. Discuss what makes a site credible.

## Independent Practice

### Recap Reading Selection

Have a short class discussion about the last section of "The Amazing Tomb of Tut" that students read. Students should mention that King Tut's tomb was an important discovery because it had not been robbed, and thus contained its original treasures.

### Read and Apply

Have students read the selection independently as you circulate to provide support. If you notice students struggling, you can provide support with the suggestions below.

### CITE EVIDENCE

**A** Students should recognize that using "hand brooms and rags" allowed workers to clean in a careful way so as not to break the objects. They should also recognize that preserving objects in place, figuring out new ways of working, and wrapping pieces carefully also show that the workers took great care.

**B** Help students recognize that the first two sentences of paragraph 18 connect to the idea expressed in the title. The tomb was amazing because of the items in it and what scientists learned from them.

Students should explain that Carter's discovery of King Tut's tomb helped other scientists learn much about the ancient Egyptians, and allowed other scientists to perform tests on Tut's mummy to confirm the existence of a royal family that had been forgotten.

---

## DETERMINING MAIN IDEA AND KEY DETAILS

### Independent Practice

The Amazing Tomb of Tut *continued*

**WORDS TO KNOW**

**log book**
**original**
**preserved**

**CITE EVIDENCE**

**A** The author describes the care the workers took with Tut's treasures. In paragraphs 15 and 16, underline details that show this.

**B** In the article's final section, the author restates the main idea. Circle the two sentences in paragraph 18 that do this. How did Carter's find help other scientists?

#### Why Did It Take So Long?

14    It took three years for Carter to go from finding the stairway to seeing Tut's mummy. It took another five years for the whole tomb to be studied. Why did it take so long?

15    All of the work was done by hand. Outside the tomb, digging was done with shovels and rakes. Workers had to pick up rocks and carry them away. Inside the tomb, special care had to be taken so that objects were not broken. Small <u>hand brooms and rags were used to clean objects</u>. Because of their age, many <u>objects had to be **preserved** in place</u>. If not, they could crumble to dust.

16    Special machines had to be built inside the tomb. These machines helped remove the golden coffin from the outer coffins. <u>New ways of working had to be figured out</u> so nothing was destroyed. Each piece in the tomb had to be photographed and described in a **log book**. Then the pieces were <u>wrapped carefully</u> and shipped to a museum.

#### Why Was It So Important?

17    Before Tut's, no Egyptian tombs had been found in their **original** condition. Scientists knew about ancient Egypt from writings and paintings, but they had found very few actual objects from that period.

18    The items found with Tut were beautiful and valuable. More importantly, they taught scientists much about ancient Egyptian life. The statues and artwork told about the religion. The jewelry and crafts told about the work Egyptians did. The seeds and grains told about the foods they grew and ate. The woods and metals told about other peoples the Egyptians traded with.

---

## Words to Know

**General Academic Vocabulary**

**original** (*adjective*): untouched or unaltered, as when something is first created

**preserved** (*verb*): saved; purposefully kept in the same condition

**Domain-Specific Vocabulary**

**log book** (*noun*): a book for writing down facts and observations to keep track of something

**Working with Word Meaning**  Ask students to write a paragraph, using the vocabulary words. Have partners share their writing.

---

## KEY IDEAS AND DETAILS

19    Tut's mummy itself revealed details about Egyptian royalty. Eighty years later, scientists used modern tests on the mummy. They learned about Tut's parents and sisters. They learned about his health and possible reasons for his death. And they confirmed the existence of a royal family that had been erased from Egyptian memory.

### Comprehension Check     MORE ONLINE  sadlierconnect.com

**1.** What is the most important thing that researchers got from the items in Tut's tomb?

  **a.** the value of gold in ancient Egypt

  **b.** information about ancient Egyptian life

  **c.** the honor of being the first to see them

  **d.** details about Tut's illness and treatment

**2.** What is the purpose of each section of the text?

  **a.** to explain the death of King Tut

  **b.** to tell the story of Howard Carter

  **c.** to support the main idea about Tut's tomb

  **d.** to tell what happened during King Tut's rule

**3.** What is the main idea of the section "Why Did It Take So Long?" List the facts that the article uses to support the main idea.

Sample answer: It took so long because everything had to be done by hand and special care had to be used. Digging was done with rakes and shovels. Rocks were carried away by hand. Hand brooms and rags were used to clean objects, which were then wrapped and photographed.

Unit 3 ■ Reading Informational Text: Key Ideas and Details    **67**

### Extend Thinking: Develop a Logical Argument

Help students extend their thinking by having them compare the discovery of the mammoth baby (pages 56–61) to the discovery of King Tut's tomb, and then develop a logical argument about which discovery was more important.

Ask students to consider as they develop their argument why each discovery was amazing and what each discovery helped scientists learn.

Have students present their argument to the class. Listeners should pay attention and ask questions to check their understanding. Speakers should speak clearly, in complete sentences, and at a reasonable rate.

## Independent Practice

### Comprehension Check

**Answer Explanations:**

**1.** Choice B, *information about ancient Egyptian life*, is the most important thing researchers got from the tomb.

**2.** Students should recognize that each section of the text tells how King Tut's tomb was amazing, so choice C is correct.

**3.** Students' responses may vary, but should convey that the main idea of the section is that it took so long because everything was done very carefully.

## Critical Comprehension

Use the following questions to help students think more deeply about the text. Students should be prepared to support their answers with evidence from the text.

• *What detail, other than that King Tut was forgotten, helps you understand why robbers did not break into Tut's tomb?* (The entryway was covered by stones and dirt.)

• *What can you infer about Howard Carter from the detail that it took him three years to get to Tut's mummy?* (Possible answer: He had great passion for archaeology. He was a careful— and patient—archaeologist.)

### Assess and Respond

**If** students have trouble answering the questions in the Comprehension Check…

**Then** reread the text with students. Have them paraphrase each section to check comprehension.

# Describing Relationships Between Ideas

**OBJECTIVE**

Describe the relationship between ideas, using language related to time, sequence, and cause/effect.

## Genre: Science Magazine Article

Tell students that a science magazine article is a type of informational text about a scientific topic that appears in a print or digital magazine.

## Set the Purpose

Activate students' thinking about the reading skill by asking *What words would you use to tell someone about what you did this past week?*

## Model and Teach

Read the selection as students follow along in their books.

### CITE EVIDENCE

**A** *I know a date can include a month, day, and year.*

*What date is given in the first sentence?* (July 24, 1911) *When did a member of the expedition drown?* (a week earlier than July 24, 1911)

**B** *I'll look for words or phrases that signal when other events happened— before or after July 24, 1911.*

*What words or phrases tell you when other events took place?* (not the first time; only days earlier)

---

## DESCRIBING RELATIONSHIPS BETWEEN IDEAS

**Guided Instruction**

**WORDS TO KNOW**

civilization
dominated
expedition
university

Look for **language** that helps you **recognize the sequence of historical events.**

**CITE EVIDENCE**

**A** Authors use dates and other **time-related words** to let the reader know the **order of events**. Circle the date in paragraph 1. In the same paragraph, underline text describing events that happened before this date.

**B** Draw a box around other words in both paragraphs that indicate the time of events. Why are these words so important to the reader?

## Finding Machu Picchu

(Genre: Science Magazine Article)

1    It was the morning of July 24, 1911. Hiram Bingham found himself crossing a bridge on his hands and knees. He crawled over slippery logs joined with vines. The Urubamba River roared below. Bingham went slowly. His guide waited on the other side. Melchor Arteaga had crossed the bridge in bare feet, carefully. It was not the first time Bingham's **expedition** had faced danger. The mountains were steep. The jungle was full of snakes. The river was hard to cross. A week earlier, one member of the expedition had drowned in the rapids.

2    Arteaga was a local farmer. He had joined the expedition only days earlier, when the explorers camped near his home. Back at camp, Arteaga learned they were searching for ancient ruins. The farmer told Bingham there were some nearby. He said they were up the mountain, Machu Picchu. Now Arteaga led the way. They crossed the bridge and struggled through dense jungle. It was terribly hot. Arteaga brought them to the bottom of a steep slope. They climbed hard for over an hour.

---

## Words to Know

**General Academic Vocabulary**

**civilization** (*noun*): a group of people living in an organized, advanced way marked by their times; a society of a specific time period

**dominated** (*verb*): controlled; governed over

**expedition** (*noun*): a trip with a goal, often to search for something

**university** (*noun*): a place of higher education for after high school

**Working with Word Meaning** Have students write a sentence for each word, leaving a blank where the word should be. Then have them trade sentences with a partner and complete their partner's sentences.

## KEY IDEAS AND DETAILS

**A Daring Professor**

3    This was not Bingham's first time in Peru. He taught South American history at Yale **University**, but he had a taste for adventure. He had traveled throughout South America. He had written a book about his journeys. Now he was leading his third expedition on the continent. He had carefully planned every detail. The group aimed to explore Peru from the Urubamba River to the Pacific Ocean. They made detailed maps along the way. They collected insects, plants, and fossils. They explored ruins left behind by the Inca **civilization**.

4    The Inca had **dominated** the area centuries earlier. The remains of their buildings were found throughout Peru. In some places, roads they created were still in use. Bingham was fascinated with the Inca culture. He longed to discover a lost Incan city.

### Comprehension Check

List the sequence of events in paragraph 2 (involving Melchor Arteaga) that led to the dramatic scene described in paragraph 1.

### CITE EVIDENCE

**C** Authors often include text that helps connect the reader to a person's past. In paragraph 3, draw a box around text that tells about Bingham's life before the 1911 expedition.

**D** Language showing cause and effect can help the reader understand a sequence of events. Underline the effects of Bingham's third expedition to South America. What caused him to travel all over South America to begin with?

---

## Support English Language Learners

Students who are learning English may not recognize some of the proper nouns and will likely have trouble keeping track of what they signify.

Say and define these proper nouns for students, pointing to the words as they appear in the text, asking students to repeat them after you: *Hiram Bingham, Urubamba River, Melchor Arteaga, Machu Picchu, Peru, South America, Yale University, Pacific Ocean, Inca.* Then guide students as they draw a simple map of South America, marking Peru, the Urubamba River, Machu Picchu, and the Pacific Ocean. Next to the map, have students make an illustrated character list featuring Bingham and Arteaga. Tell students to refer to their map and character list, as needed, to help them clarify information as they read.

---

### CITE EVIDENCE

**C** *The text says that Bingham "had written a book about his journeys."*

*What does the phrase "had written" help you understand about the book?* (He wrote it before going on this journey.)

*What does "leading his third expedition" help you understand?* (He led two expeditions before this one.)

**D** *I know that the effect is what happens because of something else.*

*What did the group do because they were on the trip?* (They made maps; collected insects, plants, and fossils; and explored ruins.)

### Comprehension Check

**Sample Answer:** Arteaga learned what the explorers were looking for. Then he joined their expedition. He led the explorers through the difficult terrain in search of ancient ruins in the area.

**Answer Explanation:** Students should use the time-related words in the paragraph to figure out the sequence of events.

## Listening and Viewing Skills

Reread the first five sentences of paragraph 3 as students listen and look at the photograph on page 69. *How does the photograph help you understand that Bingham is an experienced adventurer?* (He is dressed for exploring rugged terrain; he has a tent and supplies.)

## Review: Determining Main Idea and Key Details

Remind students that the title of a text can hint at the main idea of the text. Have students think about the title and ask them to look for details that relate to the title.

## Guided Practice

### Recap Reading Selection

Discuss with students details from the previous section of the article, including that Hiram Bingham was leading a group exploring Peru and Arteaga, a local farmer, was leading them to ancient ruins on the mountain Machu Picchu.

### Read and Practice

Have partners take turns reading the selection as you circulate to provide support. Model practicing describing relationships between ideas with Cite Evidence callout A. For callout B, circulate and provide partners with scaffolding as needed. You might use the following suggestions to help students who are having difficulty.

**CITE EVIDENCE**

**A** Remind students that a cause is why something happens. Explain that the cause is usually stated right before or right after the statement that describes the effect. This should help students identify that the cause is "Arteaga did not seem eager to leave the shade."

**B** Tell students to picture an old parking lot. Discuss how grass grows through cracks in the pavement. Have students identify that the houses are ancient or built long ago. Help them see that this is why moss had grown and covered the houses the way grass grows through an old parking lot. Students should recall that the Inca had dominated the area centuries earlier and infer from these details that the Inca had built the houses.

---

## DESCRIBING RELATIONSHIPS BETWEEN IDEAS

### Guided Practice

**WORDS TO KNOW**
constructed
demonstration
labor
precise

**CITE EVIDENCE**

**A** Underline the cause that led to the following effect: "So, a young boy showed Bingham the way instead."

**B** Circle the words in paragraph 6 that hint at why the houses are "covered with moss." Who built these houses?

**Finding Machu Picchu** *continued*

#### A Child Leads the Way

5  The explorers reached the end of their long climb. There was a grass hut ahead. Native farmers greeted them. Bingham and his men rested in the shade. They enjoyed the view of the canyon. There were several terraces, flat steps of stone and earth. Bingham saw that the locals used the terraces for farming, just as the Inca had centuries before.

6  Local men told Bingham about ruins nearby. Bingham had heard tall tales before. He did not expect to find much. <u>Arteaga did not seem eager to leave the shade of the huts.</u> So, a young boy showed Bingham the way instead. The child led the explorer around a mountain ridge. As they walked, Bingham noticed the quality of stonework was improving. He crossed magnificently **constructed** terraces. He entered a forest. Suddenly, he found himself in a maze of (ancient) houses. The houses were made of granite, the same kind of rock as the mountain. They were covered with moss and vegetation. Still, Bingham could see the **precise** craftsmanship with which they had been built (so long ago).

70   Unit 3 ▪ Reading Informational Text: Key Ideas and Details

---

### Words to Know

**General Academic Vocabulary**

**constructed** (*verb*): built
**demonstration** (*noun*): a display or showing of something
**labor** (*noun*): work; the mental or physical activity exerted to create something
**precise** (*adjective*): specific; exact

**Working with Word Meaning**  Ask students to create a word web for each vocabulary word, noting an example, a synonym, an antonym, or other association for each word.

## KEY IDEAS AND DETAILS

### Guided Practice

7  Bingham's young guide led him to a cave. The cave was lined with hand-carved stone. Above the cave there was a beautiful, rounded building. Nearby was a stone stairway. Climbing the stairs, Bingham found magnificent ruins. The walls of these ancient buildings were made of perfect, white, ten-foot-tall stone blocks. The site was a remarkable **demonstration** of the Inca's skill, **labor**, and art.

### Comprehension Check

**1.** Who or what contributed most to Bingham's discovery of the ruins?

   **a.** Melchor Arteaga

   **b.** careful planning

   **(c.)** the young boy

   **d.** scientific instruments

**2.** Based on the text, it is most certain that

   **a.** the local farmers lived in stone houses built centuries earlier

   **(b.)** the local farmers knew of the ruins before Bingham did

   **c.** the Inca builders used metal tools after trading with explorers

   **d.** the Pacific Ocean climate preserved the Aztec stone work

**3.** The stone terraces were used for farming by both the Inca and the local people in 1911. Did the local people in Bingham's day build their own terraces? Cite evidence.

Sample response: No, the local people did not build their own terraces.

The text does not provide enough clues to be sure. However, the terraces

were made of stone, and the local people lived in grass huts.

Unit 3 ■ Reading Informational Text: Key Ideas and Details    **71**

### Guided Practice

### Comprehension Check

**Answer Explanations:**

**1.** Students should recall that *Melchor Arteaga* did not want to leave the shade, so a young boy showed Bingham the way to the ruins. Choice C is correct.

**2.** Choice B is correct because Melchor Arteaga was a local farmer. Other locals knew of the ruins and told Bingham about them or led him to them.

**3.** Students should express an opinion about whether the local people in Bingham's day built their own terraces and support it with text evidence.

### Team Jigsaw

Put students in groups of three. Assign paragraphs 1–2 to one student in each group, paragraphs 3–4 to another student in each group, and paragraphs 5–7 to the third student in each group. Ask students to independently reread their assigned sections and draw a map of Bingham's journey. Encourage students to be creative with their maps, such as including snakes in the jungle on the map for paragraphs 1–2. Then have students put their maps together and discuss the details they used to make their maps.

### Discussion Skills: Building on Ideas

Explain to students that in class discussion it is important to be respectful. Give examples of ways to be respectful, such as not interrupting others, making positive comments, and giving credit to other people when you get an idea from something they say. At the same time, they should feel confident to add to another student's ideas.

Provide students with these sentence starters:

*I think you make a good point, but I'd like to add that ….*

*I agree, but I also think that …*

*I see where you are coming from, but I think ….*

## Independent Practice

### Recap Reading Selection

Prompt students to share what they have learned from reading the article. Students should mention that a young boy took over leading Bingham and his group after they had climbed much of the mountain, and brought them to the ruins.

### Read and Apply

Have students read the selection independently as you circulate to provide support. If you notice students struggling, you can provide support with the suggestions below.

### CITE EVIDENCE

**A** Students should look for dates and years, such as "around AD 1450" and "about 100 years after building it." Point out that the losing battle against Spanish soldiers is what helped end the Inca civilization.

**B** Remind students that time-related words often, but do not always, include a date (since Bingham's day, more recently, from 2008). Have students recall that Bingham explored Machu Picchu in 1911. Help them understand that his idea that the site was the birthplace of Inca civilization is now outdated, as recent scholarship suggests it was a religious site or a royal summer palace.

---

DESCRIBING RELATIONSHIPS BETWEEN IDEAS

Independent Practice

Finding Machu Picchu *continued*

**WORDS TO KNOW**
excavate
irrigation
theory

**CITE EVIDENCE**

**A** In paragraphs 8 and 9, underline the phrases that point to the passage of time.

**B** Circle information in paragraphs 10 and 11 that helps you figure out how long the Inca lived in Machu Picchu. What helped end the Inca civilization?

### Palace of the Earth Shaker

8    Much has been learned about the Inca civilization at Machu Picchu <u>since Bingham's day</u>. People lived there and farmed. An **irrigation** system carried water through the area. About 200 buildings are set on terraces surrounding a central square. The Inca used the buildings as temples, warehouses, or homes. Their walls were designed to stand up to powerful earthquakes.

9    There is disagreement about why the Inca built Machu Picchu. Scholars have suggested several **theories**. Hiram Bingham thought that the site was the birthplace of Inca civilization. <u>More recently</u>, others have claimed that Machu Picchu was a religious site. A popular theory <u>from 2008</u> says that Machu Picchu was a royal summer palace for the great Pachacuti.

10    Machu Picchu was built (around A.D. 1450.) The Inca Empire was near the height of its power. Pachacuti was its ruler. His name, which means "earth shaker," was well deserved. Through warfare, Pachacuti turned his small chiefdom into a mighty empire.

11    The Incas deserted the site (about 100 years after building it.) At the time, they were fighting a losing battle against Spanish soldiers. There is no evidence that the Spaniards ever discovered Machu Picchu. The site was mostly forgotten over the next few centuries. Only the local people knew of it until Bingham's arrival.

---

## Words to Know

**General Academic Vocabulary**
**excavate** (*verb*): to dig and remove dirt and ground away from an area in order to find something buried there
**theory** (*noun*): unproven ideas

**Domain-Specific Vocabulary**
**irrigation** (*noun*): a system to deliver water through pipes or ditches to a specific area; often to water crops

**Working with Word Meaning** Challenge students to make a map of an irrigation system and discuss it with a partner using all three words.

## KEY IDEAS AND DETAILS

**Finding Machu Picchu**

12    After Bingham's discovery, other travelers claimed to have discovered the ruins before him. There is some evidence that Bingham was not the first foreigner to find the site. But he was the first to **excavate** the ruins. He photographed Machu Picchu and wrote about it in detail. It was Bingham who brought these wondrous ruins to the attention of the whole world.

**Comprehension Check**    (MORE ONLINE)  sadlierconnect.com

1. According to the text, until Bingham found Machu Picchu

   a. he had never seen Incan ruins

   b. he thought it was only a legend

   c. the site was completely hidden underground

   (d.) the site was known to only a few local people

2. What was an effect of Bingham's having found Machu Picchu?

   a. Archaeologists no longer study Machu Picchu.

   b. Scholars learned how the Inca Empire died.

   (c.) Machu Picchu was brought to the attention of the whole world.

   d. There is agreement about why Machu Picchu was built.

3. What caused the emperor of the Inca who built Machu Picchu to be known as "earth shaker"? Use text from the article in your answer.

   Sample response: He was known as Pachacuti, or "earth shaker," because

   by using warfare, he "turned his small chiefdom into a mighty empire."

   _____

   _____

---

## Independent Practice

**Comprehension Check**

**Answer Explanations:**

1. Choice D, *the site was known to only a few local people,* is the only option supported by details in the text.

2. According to the text, the site was unknown to outsiders until Bingham found it. Therefore, choice C, *Machu Picchu was brought to the attention of the whole world,* is correct.

3. Students' responses may vary, but should explain that the emperor was known as the "earth shaker" because he used warfare to turn "his small chiefdom into a mighty empire."

## Critical Comprehension

Use the following questions to help students think more deeply about the text. Students should be prepared to support their answers with evidence from the text.

- *Did the local people think it was good or bad that Bingham was exploring their lands? How do you know?* (Good; they helped him explore it.)

- *Was the Inca civilization advanced? How do you know?* (Yes. They built a complex city with walls that could stand up to earthquakes.)

### Assess and Respond

**If** students have trouble answering the questions in the Comprehension Check…

**Then** review how to eliminate incorrect answers by checking them against the text.

---

## Speaking and Listening Presentation

Have students create a presentation on one of the texts in this unit. If you have students from diverse geographic or cultural backgrounds, have students interview each other about whether any of the stories in the unit are from countries they are familiar with. After gathering information, students should take turns presenting to the class. Presenters should:

- state their topic; choose words for effect.

- present appropriate facts elaborated with relevant descriptive details.

- use formal language suitable for an academic presentation.

- speak clearly, in complete sentences, and at a reasonable rate.

## OBJECTIVES

- Show an understanding of an informational text by asking questions and citing evidence from the text to answer questions.
- Determine and explain the main idea of a text, using key details from the text.
- Describe the relationship between ideas, using language related to time, sequence, and cause/effect.

## Genre: Biography

Explain to students that a biography is an informational text about someone's life. A biography is written by someone other than its subject. Point out the word's root *–bio-*, and explain that it is Greek for "life." Then point out the root *-graph-* and explain that it is Greek for "to write." Deepen students' understanding of this genre by explaining that a biography differs from an autobiography, which is written by the subject.

## Path Options

You may want to do a close reading with students; if so, use the supports provided on these pages. Or, you may wish to have the students read the text independently and apply the skills learned in this unit. In either case, students should read the text more than once to facilitate understanding and to be able to answer the Comprehension Check questions correctly.

# Howard Carter's Last Chance
### (Genre: Biography)

1     Howard Carter was born in London on May 9, 1874. He was a sickly child. His parents sent him to live with his aunts in the countryside. They hoped it would improve his health, but he remained too weak for sports and exercise at school. The young Carter displayed great artistic ability, however. His father, Samuel Carter, was a successful illustrator and painter. He helped Howard learn these crafts.

2     Howard's early training paid off. Through his father's influence, he was hired by an archaeologist to draw sketches. In 1891, at age 17, Carter traveled to Egypt to join in the excavation of ancient tombs. He showed great enthusiasm for his work. His original approach to depicting tomb decorations was greatly admired. With the success of his first assignment, Carter easily found more work in Egypt. He spent the next eight years at archaeological sites around the country. He worked with some of the best archaeologists of the day. He learned everything he could.

Howard Carter

## Support English Language Learners

Help English language learners become familiar with *r*-controlled vowels. Explain that when *r* follows a vowel in a word, the *r* changes the way the vowel sounds. Display an example: *cat, cape, car.* Discuss how the *a* keeps its normal short or long sound in the first two words, but the *r* in the third word changes it. Explain that *a* only makes this sound when followed by *r*. Model pronunciation for the following *r*-controlled words in paragraph 1 and then ask students to repeat each word after you: *Howard, Carter, born, parents, sports, exercise, artistic, however, father, illustrator, painter.* Discuss how the *r* changes the vowel sound in each word. Have students find and pronounce *r*-controlled words in the second paragraph.

## KEY IDEAS AND DETAILS

3    Carter had come to Egypt as a gifted young artist. Through years of hard work, he had gained new skills. He was a good planner and manager. He was a careful excavator. He became an experienced engineer. In 1899, he was appointed chief inspector of the Egyptian Antiquities Service. As part of this job, Carter protected ancient ruins from decay. He protected ancient artifacts from tomb robbers. He approved plans for new digs. And he led many excavations himself. Carter left this job in 1905. But it was not long before his work in Egypt would continue.

**Lord Carnarvon**

4    His next opportunity arrived when he met George Herbert, the 5th Earl of Carnarvon. Lord Carnarvon was an English aristocrat. He was born to a very rich family. He went to the best schools in England. In an age when most people still rode horse-drawn carriages, he drove automobiles. In 1901, he was injured in a driving accident. Due to his injuries, he suffered in cold weather. To escape the cold, Lord Carnarvon began spending his winters in Egypt in 1903. In Egypt, he became interested in archaeology. He used his own money to fund expeditions. He searched the deserts for lost tombs.

5    Carnarvon's first attempts did not work out. So in 1907, he hired Howard Carter. Carter introduced Lord Carnarvon to modern techniques of excavation. He made sure that every detail of his work was recorded. Sure enough, with Carter in the lead, Carnarvon's team had some success. But all their discoveries would pale in comparison to the great find that lay ahead of them.

## Support First Reading

Circulate to check students' understanding. As needed, use the following comprehension and strategy check-ins to support basic understanding of the selection as students read.

### Check-in Questions

- *What was Carter too weak for as a youth? What talent did he display?* (He was too weak for sports and exercise at school. He displayed great artistic ability.)

- *What were Carter's job responsibilities as chief inspector of the Egyptian Antiquities Service?* (He protected ancient ruins from decay and ancient artifacts from tomb robbers; he approved plans for new digs, and led many excavations.)

## Review: Asking and Answering Questions

Review with students that asking and answering questions can help them better understand an informational text. *Who is this text about? How do you know?* (This text is about Howard Carter. The title identifies the topic of the text. Also, every paragraph tells something about Carter.) *Where did Carter do his excavation—or archaeology—work?* (He did his work in Egypt.)

## Differentiate Instruction

Striving readers may have difficulty keeping track of the sequence of events described in the text. Help students make a sequence of events graphic organizer. Encourage them to fill in the boxes on their organizer with dates and events as they read the text.

After completing their graphic organizers, students should meet with partners to compare them and discuss similarities and differences. Then have students revise their organizers based on their discussion with their partner. Encourage students to refer to their organizers when they reread the text to help them keep track of events.

# Close Reading

## Check-in Question

- *Where did Lord Carnarvon get approval to dig in 1914? What did he hope to find? Whom did he hire to lead the dig? Why was it risky to spend time and money digging in that location?* (Lord Carnarvon got approval to dig in the Valley of the Kings. He hoped to find a lost tomb. He hired Carter to lead the dig. It was risky to spend time and money digging in that location because most other archaeologists thought there were no more tombs to find in that area of Egypt.)

## Review: Determining Main Idea and Key Details

Ask students to cite details that help support the idea that Lord Carnarvon began to lose hope in Carter. (Years passed without a major discovery, and Carter's workers had moved 200,000 tons of rock, sand, and earth, but found nothing.)

## Review: Describing Relationships Between Ideas

Review how to look for time-related words that indicate a sequence of events. *What words help you understand how much time passed between when Lord Carnarvon got approval to dig in the Valley of the Kings, when Carter began his last dig there, and how quickly he found something after beginning his last dig?* (in 1914; on November 1, 1922; on the morning of November 4) Be sure students understand that eight years passed after getting permission to the start of the last dig, but only three days passed before Carter found something during that last dig.

6   In 1914, Carnarvon received approval for a new dig. He hoped to find a lost tomb in the Valley of the Kings. He hired Howard Carter to lead the job. Archaeologists had assumed there were no more tombs to be found in the Valley of the Kings. Carter aimed to prove them wrong. He organized a team and set to work. Years passed without a major discovery. Carter's workers moved 200,000 tons of rock, sand, and earth. They achieved next to nothing. It began to seem that Carter had been mistaken. Lord Carnarvon began to lose hope. He gave Carter one last chance.

7   On November 1, 1922, Carter led his team on one last dig. At first things went no better than before. But Carter's bad luck changed on the morning of November 4. A young Egyptian boy, hired to bring water to the workers, was using a stick to dig in the ground. He was making a hole to hold a water jar. Instead, he found a stone step! Carter's crew started digging in this area immediately. They found stairs leading down to a sealed door. Could this be the entrance to Tutankhamun's tomb?

8   Carter ordered the workers to refill the hole and guard it. He made preparations to return to the site. Carnarvon was out of the country. Carter sent word to him about the find. Weeks later, Carnarvon arrived in Egypt. At last, work at the site resumed. This time, the workers cleared the stairs completely. At the bottom of the door, Carter found the seal of Tutankhamun.

**76**   Unit 3 ■ Reading Informational Text: Key Ideas and Details

## Strategic Reading

You can support all readers by offering them a strategic reading tip: Set a purpose for reading. Explain that setting a purpose will help them think about the information in a text as they read. *If your purpose is to find out why a certain event happened, then as you read, you will know to look for possible explanations.* Point out that readers typically set a purpose for reading before beginning a text, but they can set a new purpose later. *For example, at first our purpose for reading this biography is to learn about Howard Carter's life. But after we start reading, we might change our purpose to learning about how Carter found King Tut's tomb.*

## KEY IDEAS AND DETAILS

9   The door was opened. Carter and Carnarvon found themselves in a dark passage full of rubble. The workers cleared the passage. They found another sealed door with the mark of Tutankhamun. Carter's hands shook as he made a small opening in the door. He saw only darkness beyond. Carter held a candle through the opening. He looked inside. The candle flickered as hot air rushed out of the chamber. Carter's eyes soon adjusted to the light. He could see the contents of the room. "Strange animals, statues, and gold," Carter would later write. "Everywhere the glint of gold."

10   Carter was in awe. He couldn't speak. Lord Carnarvon, standing beside him, couldn't stand the suspense. "Can you see anything?" he asked. "Yes," replied Carter, "wonderful things."

11   It took eight years before all those wonderful things had been removed from Tutankhamun's tomb. The tomb was remarkably complete. It was perhaps the greatest find in the history of Egyptian archaeology. The name of the man who found it will be remembered forever beside the name of Tutankhamun.

### Comprehension Check

1. Based on information in the text, what was Howard Carter's success as an archaeologist mainly a result of?

   a. his father's influence

   b. his relationship with Carnarvon

   (c.) his skill and hard work

   d. his consistent good luck

2. What trait described in the text helped Carter most at the beginning of his career?

   a. his ability to organize and plan

   b. his knowledge of archaeological techniques

   c. his love of Egyptian history

   (d.) his artistic ability

### Research to Build Knowledge

Remind students that King Tut's tomb is in Egypt. Explain that Egypt has a rich history and there is much more to know about the country. Put students in small groups, and challenge them use the Internet to find five interesting facts about the pyramids, mummies, the Sphinx, Cleopatra, and the Nile River, as well as any other topic related to Egypt that might be of interest to your students. Extend this activity by asking students to make a digital or print poster for their assigned topic that features visuals and the five facts they researched. Then have students present their posters to the class and explain their topic. Display the posters on a wall (print the digital ones) for students to view.

## Multiple Readings for Critical Comprehension

Have students reread this selection and pose questions that focus on critical comprehension. Remind them to annotate text in a way that will support their comprehension.

- *Which details help you understand that Carter had a passion for archaeology?* (Carter learned as much as he could about archaeology. He spent years searching for and then digging up Tut's tomb.)

- *Which details help you understand that Lord Carnarvon was the boss and that Carter worked for him?* (Lord Carnarvon had the power to say there would be just one more dig. Carter waited to explore the stairs until Lord Carnarvon could be there weeks later.)

## Self-Select Text

As preparation for Connect Across Texts, have students select one of the four selections in this unit and reread it independently. Students can access full pdf versions of the selections at **sadlierconnect.com**.

### Comprehension Check

Begin scoring students' understanding of unit skills and texts from Comprehension Check on this page through Connect Across Texts on page 79. Use students' total score to determine their readiness for the Unit 3 Review on page 81.

## Multiple-Choice Questions: *1 point each*

1. Students should recognize that Carter had success because he developed skills and worked hard.

2. Students should recall that Carter got his first job in archaeology because of "his artistic ability."

## Short-Answer Questions:
## 2 points each

### Item 3 Rubric

| | |
|---|---|
| 2 | Students are able to describe how Carter must have felt, citing evidence from the text to support the idea that seeing the contents of the tomb was the greatest event of his life. |
| 1 | Students are able to either describe how Carter must have felt or cite evidence to support the idea that this was the greatest moment in his life. |
| 0 | Students cannot describe how Carter must have felt or cite evidence. |

### Item 4 Rubric

| | |
|---|---|
| 2 | Students are able to logically describe the complete series of events. |
| 1 | Students are able to describe some of the events, still putting them in a logical order. |
| 0 | Students cannot describe the series of events. |

## Theme Wrap-Up

Lead students in a group discussion on the theme "echoes of the past." *How do past events still affect us today?* Talk about the different discoveries discussed in this unit. (Students should understand that scientists, archaeologists, and explorers can find and study animals, people, and places from long ago, and that studying things from the past helps us understand our history and our place in the world today.)

---

**3.** Paragraph 10 states that "Carter was in awe" when he first saw the contents of the tomb. Describe further how Carter must have felt at this moment. What details in the text support the idea that this was the greatest event of Carter's life.

Sample answer: Carter had worked long and hard to find the tomb, and now he was looking inside for the first time. He was also the first person to see inside the tomb for many centuries. He must have felt very excited and eager to see what was there.

**4.** In paragraph 4, we learn that Carnarvon was injured in a car accident. Using evidence from the text, describe the series of events that links his accident to the discovery of the tomb of Tutankhamun.

Sample answer: Carnarvon was injured in a car accident. Because of his injuries, he suffered in cold weather. He avoided cold winter weather by going to Egypt. In Egypt, he began to take an interest in the country's ancient history. Soon, he met Howard Carter and began the search for Tutankhamun's tomb.

---

## Extend Thinking: Hypothesize

Assign one of the unit texts to each student. Tell students to reread their text, making notes about how the discovery described in it was made. Then tell them to suppose that the person who made the discovery had never made the discovery. Ask them to form a hypothesis about whether someone else would have made the discovery later, or if the discovery would have likely remained unknown. Have students write one paragraph explaining their hypothesis, supporting it with evidence from the text. Then have students present their hypotheses to the class.

## CONNECT ACROSS TEXTS

### Compare and Contrast Texts

In this unit, you read about the discovery of Lyuba, King Tut's tomb, and Machu Picchu and Howard Carter's achievement. Choose two of these events and compare and contrast them using the Venn diagram below. List key details and other evidence from the texts to show similarities and differences. Be prepared to discuss your ideas with the class.

"The 40,000-Year-Old Baby"

Khudi stumbled upon his discovery

discovery in 2007

discovery in Russia

fascinating discovery made

years of scientific work followed discovery

people around world quickly learned of discovery

"Finding Machu Picchu"

Bingham searched for years

discovery in 1911

discovery in South America

### Return to the Essential Question

How do authors convey a main idea and use details to support it?

In small groups or as a class, discuss the Essential Question. Think about what you have learned about asking and answering questions, determining the main idea, and recognizing relationships in a text. Use evidence from the four unit texts to answer the question.

Unit 3 ■ Reading Informational Text: Key Ideas and Details  **79**

### Connect Across Texts: *4 points*
### Review Reading Selections

Assign pairs of students one of the four texts to summarize. Encourage students to build on each other's ideas. Repeat for the remaining three texts.

### Compare and Contrast Texts

Review the directions on page 79 with students. Instruct students to write the two events they have chosen in the outer parts of each circle.

#### Venn Diagram Rubric

| | |
|---|---|
| 4 | Student has identified two events and recorded four or more key details and pieces of evidence in their proper places. |
| 3 | Student has identified two events and recorded at least three key details and pieces of evidence in their proper places. |
| 2 | Student has identified two events and recorded at least three key details and pieces of evidence but may have had trouble categorizing them properly. |
| 1 | Student has identified two events and recorded at least one key detail or piece of evidence. |
| 0 | Student did not complete assignment or demonstrated no understanding of selections. |

### Support Essential Question Discussion

Have students reread the Essential Question. Challenge small groups to finish this sentence: *One way an author conveys details to support a main idea is to . . .* If students have difficulty responding, prompt them to think about how dates help a reader understand the events in a text.

### Assess and Respond (pages 77–79)

| If | Then |
|---|---|
| Students scored 0–4 points, they are **Developing** their understanding of unit skills. | ▶ Provide students with reading support and more intensive modeling of skills. |
| Students scored 5–7 points, they are **Improving** their understanding of unit skills. | ▶ Use students' scores to target areas that are weak and review those specific skills. |
| Students scored 8–10 points, they are **Proficient** in their understanding of unit skills. | ▶ Have these students move on. They are ready for more formal assessment. |

## OBJECTIVE
**Understand how words in texts connect to real life.**

## Guided Instruction

Review the Guided Instruction section on page 80 with students. Be sure they understand that "real-life" means their own world or life, not a world or life that they have read about. Discuss how paying attention to words used in texts can help them develop a more accurate vocabulary for describing their own experiences.

## Guided Practice

If students are having difficulty, have them make a list of six or seven experiences they have recently had. Have them review their lists to see if they can use either of the words in the table to describe any of the experiences. You might also have them do this exercise with a partner.

## Independent Practice

If students are having trouble writing sentences, then discuss events and experiences in their own lives that relate to the two words until students have made a real-life connection to each word.

## Apply to Reading

Have students return to "The 40,000-Year-Old Baby" (pages 56–61) and circle three challenging words to which they can make a real-life connection. Then have them write a sentence for each word, describing a real-life experience. They may make a real-life connection to *discovery* (paragraph 1), *tending* (paragraph 2), and *traveled* (paragraph 4).

---

# LANGUAGE

## Real-Life Word Connections

**Guided Instruction** Identify **real-life word connections** with your own life. Describing your own experiences can help you practice new words, phrases, and meanings.

Lord Carnarvon "couldn't stand the suspense" while Howard Carter peered into Tutankhamun's tomb. In the example below, a student has used the same phrase to describe a personal experience.

*I had to wait until after dinner to open my presents on my last birthday. Sitting at the table, I couldn't stand the suspense.*

| original | (adj.) independent and creative in thought or action |
|---|---|
| assume | (v.) to suppose something true without knowing the facts |

Look at the chart to find definitions of two words from "Howard Carter's Last Chance." Use the definitions to complete the exercise below.

**Guided Practice** Use each word in the table to describe two real-life experiences.

1. Sample answer: My dancing at the party was original.
2. Sample answer: My grandmother dresses differently. She is original.
3. Sample answer: I assumed it was sunny yesterday and got wet.
4. Sample answer: My friends assume they know the real me.

**Independent Practice** Make real-life connections using the words from "Finding Machu Picchu" below. If necessary, use a dictionary to determine word meanings.

culture

Sample answer: My friend Spiro is from another culture.

dominate

Sample answer: I wish I could dominate a soccer game like my brother does.

---

## Support English Language Learners

In order for English language learners to make real-life connections to vocabulary, they must have a clear and deep understanding of the words. Review the definition of *original* and *assume*. Then provide sets of example sentences for each word, with the first sentence in each set reflecting a real-life connection, and the second sentence not reflecting a connection. **Real-life connection:** *I assume I will get better if I take this medication.* **No real-life connection:** *The doctor assumed her patient was taking her medication.* Point to the use of *I* in the first sentence and explain how the sentence describes your own experience. Discuss how the second one does not.

## UNIT 3 REVIEW

Read the following passage. Pay attention to the important details and the relationship between ideas to help you understand the text. Then answer the questions on pages 81 and 82.

# Vikings in America

(Genre: Textbook Article)

1   Columbus was not the first person to discover the Americas. The first inhabitants of North America migrated from Asia over 16,000 years ago. There is also evidence that Vikings reached the mainland about 500 years before Columbus's journey.

2   Stories of Vikings finding North America were centuries old. Without evidence, these claims remained just legends. In 1960, however, a Norwegian explorer discovered the remains of a Viking village in northeastern Canada. The site was excavated. Many items were found. Studies of these items show that Vikings lived at the site. Workshops for metalwork, carpentry, and boat repair had things unknown to Native Americans until the arrival of Europeans. Other items associated with Viking culture were found, including a stone used to sharpen metal objects, an oil lamp, and a bronze pin. The discovery proved there was truth in the old Viking legends.

**Fill in the circle of the correct answer choice.**

1. Vikings came to North America

   ○ before anyone else

   ● 500 years before Columbus

   ○ only in legends

   ○ the same time as Columbus

2. In paragraph 2, *show* means

   ○ a TV program or play

   ○ to put on display

   ● to provide evidence

   ○ to teach or instruct

## Self-Assessment: Progress Check

Have students revisit the Progress Check on page 53 and respond to the questions again. Ask them to compare their Before and After responses.

You may wish to have students rate their answers on a scale of 0–2 rather than simply checking (or not checking) the box. Instruct them to write a 0 if they feel they do not understand the given skill at all, a 1 if they feel they have some understanding, and a 2 if they feel they have a solid grasp of the skill.

## Unit Summary

At this point, students have had instruction and practice in reading informational texts, with a focus on learning about important discoveries related to human history. Students have also learned to ask and answer questions to deepen their understanding of the text, to determine the main idea and key details of a text, and to describe the relationship between ideas. Students have done an independent close reading of text, practiced working with concepts across texts, and practiced making real-life connections to unfamiliar words. They should be well prepared for the review section.

## Introduce the Review

Explain to students that they will read a new passage that is related to the unit's theme and the selections they have already read. Instruct students to read the passage carefully and then answer the questions on pages 81–82.

### Answer Explanations

Scoring: Items 1–4 on pages 81–82 are worth 1 point each. See the rubrics on the next page for guidance scoring the short-answer questions on page 82.

1. The text explicitly states that "the Vikings reached the mainland about 500 years before Columbus's journey," so the second choice, "500 years before Columbus" is correct.

2. The text states that "studies of these items *show* that Vikings lived at the site." So *show* means "to provide evidence," the third choice. The sentence makes sense if you say it with "provided evidence" instead of *show*.

## Answer Explanations

**3.** The legends did not prove the discovery, the reverse occurred, so the second choice is correct.

**4.** Only "metalwork" is mentioned, so the first choice is correct.

### Item 5 Rubric

| | |
|---|---|
| **2** | Student underlines the word and writes a sentence describing a personal trip, using "journey." |
| **1** | Student underlines the word but either does not about a personal trip or does not use "journey." |
| **0** | Student does not underline the word or write a sentence using the word. |

### Items 6 and 8 Rubric

| | |
|---|---|
| **2** | Student identifies the main idea, including Vikings and Columbus, and the correct series of events. |
| **1** | Student either does not identify the main idea, or does not describe the correct series of events. |
| **0** | Student does not identify the main idea or describe a series of events. |

### Item 7 Rubric

| | |
|---|---|
| **2** | Student describes how the items found prove that Vikings were in mainland North America long ago. |
| **1** | Student mentions either the Viking items or North America, but does not make a correct connection. |
| **0** | Student does not provide a response or provides a completely inaccurate response. |

### Items 9 and 10 Rubric

| | |
|---|---|
| **2** | Student lists the three discoveries and indicates no evidence of sailing ships. |
| **1** | Student lists either the three discoveries or indicates no evidence of sailing ships. |
| **0** | Student does not list the three discoveries or indicate no evidence of sailing ships. |

---

# UNIT 3 REVIEW

**3.** The last sentence in the article suggests that legends

- ○ can never be trusted
- ● sometimes contain truths
- ○ do not inform about history
- ○ are for entertainment only

**4.** Which technology did the Vikings use 1,000 years ago?

- ● metalwork
- ○ steam engines
- ○ electricity
- ○ mass production

**5.** Underline the word *journey* in paragraph 1, line 4. Describe a journey you have had.

Answers will vary but should give real-life details about a journey.

**6.** What is the main idea of "Vikings in America"?

Vikings likely reached North America 500 years before Columbus.

**7.** How did items that were found help prove that Vikings were in mainland North America long ago?

The items were unknown to Native Americans at the time.

**8.** Describe the series of events that is proof of the Viking legends.

A village an explorer found in 1960 was excavated and Viking

artifacts were found.

**9.** The article mentions three "discoveries" of the Americas. List them in order.

16,000 years ago; Vikings 500 years before Columbus; Columbus

**10.** Does the article provide evidence indicating whether the Vikings had sailing ships?

Not enough evidence. The article only says that they used boats.

## Analyze Student Scores

| | |
|---|---|
| **12–16 pts Strong** | Student has a good grasp of the skills and concepts taught in this unit. Point out any mistakes the student has made and explain the correct answers if necessary. |
| **6–11 pts Progressing** | Student is struggling with some skills or concepts. Identify the specific skills that are problematic to target a review of instruction. |
| **0–5 pts Emerging** | Student is having serious problems understanding the skills and concepts taught in this unit. Student may need to redo the work with a higher level of support. |

## Introducing UNIT 4

In this unit about amazing things from our past, you will learn how to write an informative or explanatory text. When you do this kind of writing, you give information about a topic that interests you.

When you write an informative or explanatory text, you want to think carefully about the organization. You should introduce the topic in the beginning, and then group related information about the topic together. Your essay should end with a statement or paragraph that tells what the reader just learned. Linking words such as *also, another,* and *but* can help you show how ideas are related.

To be effective, an informative or explanatory text should use facts, definitions, and details to explain the ideas and develop the topic.

**Before Unit 4**

**Progress Check** Can I?

**After Unit 4**

- [ ] Introduce a topic. [ ]
- [ ] Group related information together. [ ]
- [ ] Use facts, definitions, and details to develop a topic. [ ]
- [ ] Use linking words to connect ideas. [ ]
- [ ] Complete my writing with a concluding statement. [ ]
- [ ] Write using pronouns. [ ]
- [ ] Write using pronouns and antecedents that agree. [ ]
- [ ] Spell high-frequency words correctly. [ ]
- [ ] Use commas in addresses. [ ]

Unit 4 ■ Text Types and Purposes: Write Informative/Explanatory Texts

**Student Page 83**

## Progress Check

The Progress Check is a self-assessment feature that students can use to gauge their own progress. Research shows that when students take accountability for their own learning, their motivation increases.

Before students begin work on Unit 4, have them check the boxes next to any item that they feel they can do well. Explain that it is fine if they don't check any of the boxes. Tell them that they will have an opportunity to learn about and practice all of these items while studying the unit. Let them know that near the end of the unit they will have a chance to reconsider how well they can do each item on this list.

Before students begin the Unit 4 Review on page 95, have them revisit this page. You can use this information to work with students on any items they don't understand before they tackle the Review.

## HOME ◆ CONNECT...

In this unit, children will learn about **writing to inform or explain a topic** to the reader. Discuss with your child different types of explanatory and informative texts, such as recipes, instruction guides, encyclopedias, informative websites, and textbooks.

Informative writing topics are developed with **facts, definitions,** and **details.** Ask your child to tell you about his or her writing topic, and to give details by describing something or defining a term. If your child has difficulty describing a topic, find a related image—an illustration or a photo. Encourage your child to describe the image and then incorporate some of these details into his or her writing.

Think of other topics that interest both you and your child. Together, research and write down facts and details about the topic. Have your child write an **introduction** that explains what the topic is. Then work with him or her to **link ideas** to make the writing flow. Distribute your informative text to friends or other family members.

**On the Go:** Encourage your child's curiosity about topics. Guide him or her to resources that can help answer questions. Model for your child how to use the Internet to search for good sources of information. Talk about different resources you use when you want to find out information or learn how to do something new.

### IN THIS UNIT, YOUR CHILD WILL...

- Learn to write an informative or explanatory text that introduces a topic, groups related information, and ends with a conclusion.
- Use facts, definitions, and details to support the topic.
- Learn to use linking words, such as *also, another, more,* and *but,* to connect ideas.
- Learn specific language skills and use them in writing an explanatory or informative text:
  - Use pronouns, such as *he, we,* or *they,* to take the place of a noun.
  - Check sentences for proper pronoun agreement.
  - Spell high-frequency words correctly.
  - Use a comma between the city and state in an address.

### WAYS TO HELP YOUR CHILD

Help your child practice using descriptive words by playing a game called "Stretch It." Choose a word such as *frog.* Take turns adding a description to the word, such as *the tiny, wet, slippery, green frog.* Discuss how writers use descriptions to explain and inform.

ONLINE
For more Home Connect activities, continue online at sadlierconnect.com

84   Unit 4 ■ Text Types and Purposes: Write Informative/Explanatory Texts

**Student Page 84**

## HOME ◆ CONNECT...

The Home Connect feature is a way to keep parents or other adult family members apprised of what their children are learning. The key learning objectives are listed, and some ideas for related activities and discussions are included.

Explain to students that they can share the Home Connect page with their parents or other adult family members in their home. Let students know how much time the class will be spending on this unit so they can plan their time accordingly at home.

Encourage students and their parents to share their experiences using the suggestions on the Home Connect page. You may wish to make a place to post some of this work.

## UNIT PLANNER

| Theme: Echoes of the Past<br>Curriculum Connection:<br>Social Studies | Focus |
|---|---|
| **WRITING MODEL**<br>*pp. 86–88* | *The Mystery of King Tut* |
| **WRITING PRACTICE**<br>*p. 89* | **ORGANIZATIONAL STRUCTURE:** Outline |
| **LANGUAGE MINI-LESSONS**<br>*pp. 90–93* | • Pronouns<br>• Pronoun-Antecedent Agreement<br>• Spelling High-Frequency Words<br>• Commas in Addresses |
| **SPEAKING AND LISTENING**<br>*p. 94* | Discuss the Essential Question |
| **UNIT 4 REVIEW**<br>*pp. 95–96* | • Language Skills Summary<br>• Writing Process Summary |

Essential Question: How do writers develop a topic to inform or explain?

UNIT 4

## Objective(s)

Write an informative/explanatory text with a clear topic, evidence, linking phrases, and a concluding statement.

Plan an informative/explanatory text with an introduction, supporting facts, definitions and details, and a concluding statement.

- Use the correct pronoun in writing.
- Use correct pronoun-antecedent agreement in writing.
- Use correct spelling in writing.
- Use commas correctly in addresses.

- Come to discussion prepared, having read the required text, citing evidence when building on others' ideas.
- Follow conventions of discourse, including agreed-upon rules for discussion.

## Unit Assessment

- Unit 4 Review *pp. 95–96*

## Additional Assessment Options

- Performance Task 1 *pp. 141A–145 and 146*
  ( ALSO ONLINE )
- Performance Task 2 *pp. 259A–263 and 264*
  ( ALSO ONLINE )

**Optional Purchase:**

- iProgress Monitor ( ONLINE )
- Progress Monitor Student Benchmark Assessment Booklet

## ( ONLINE ) Digital Resources

- Home Connect Activities
- Additional Practice
- Teacher Resources
- iProgress Monitor (optional purchase)

**Go to SadlierConnect.com to access your Digital Resources.**

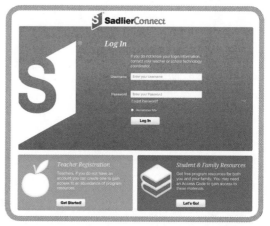

**For more detailed instructions see page T3.**

## LEARNING PROGRESSIONS

In this unit, students will learn how to write an informative/explanatory text on a topic that interests them. In order to learn the skills necessary to craft an informative/explanatory text, students will further develop skills learned in second grade. They should be encouraged to retain these skills, as they will continue to build on them in fourth grade.

**Introducing the Topic**

- Proficient second-grade students should complete the year able to write an informative/explanatory text in which they introduce the topic about which they are writing.

- In grades 3 and 4, students will build on this skill by not only stating the topic of the text in the introduction, but also stating what they will examine about the topic.

**Developing the Topic**

- By the end of grade 2, students should be able to use facts and definitions to develop points in their text.

- Students in grade 3 will be asked to develop their topics with facts and definitions, as well as details, and to group related information together.

- This will prepare them for grade 4, when they will be asked to develop the topic not only with facts, definitions, and concrete details, but also with quotations and other related information and examples, grouping related information together, and adding illustrations and multimedia to aid reader comprehension of the topic.

**Using Linking Words and Phrases**

- In grade 3, students will learn to add linking words and phrases (e.g., *also, another, and, more, but*) to connect ideas in their texts.

- When students move on to grade 4, they will be expected to include more complex linking words (e.g., *for example, because*) in their texts.

**Providing a Concluding Statement**

- In grades 2 and 3, students learn the importance of providing a concluding statement or section.

- In grade 4, students will build on this skill by including a concluding statement or section that relates to the information or explanation presented in the text.

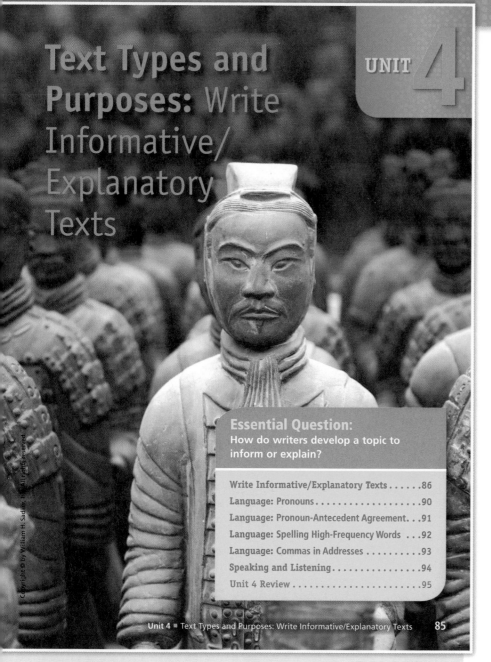

# Text Types and Purposes: Write Informative/ Explanatory Texts

**Essential Question:**
How do writers develop a topic to inform or explain?

**Essential Question:**
How do writers develop a topic to inform or explain?

In this unit, students will explore how a topic is developed with facts, definitions, and details in order to examine that topic and clearly convey ideas and information about it.

## Theme: Echoes of the Past
Students will continue their investigation of long-ago events as they read and analyze an informative/explanatory text writing model.

## Curriculum Connection: Social Studies
Students will use what they have already learned about human history as they work on their own informative/ explanatory text.

## Connect Reading to Writing
Remind students that they read an historical text entitled *The Amazing Tomb of Tut* in Unit 3 (Student Book pages 62–67). Review how the author introduces the topic and develops it with facts, definitions, and details.

## Writing Handbook

If students need extra practice with writing an informative/explanatory text, refer them to the *Writing Handbook* on pages 275–283. The Writing Handbook gives students detailed instruction on planning, drafting, revising, and editing their writing. They will also find tips on producing, publishing, and presenting their writing.

## OBJECTIVE

**Write an informative/explanatory text with a clear topic, evidence, linking phrases, and a concluding statement.**

## Introduce: Organizational Structure

Draw students' attention to the informative/explanatory text outline in the left margin, and point out the key elements. Ask students to look for these key elements as you read and analyze the Student Model together.

## Analyze a Student Model

**TITLE:** Tell students that the title of an informative/explanatory text should clearly identify the topic of the essay. You might read the title aloud and then point out the words *King Tut* in the title. Explain that they signal that the text examines something about him. Then you might point out the word *Mystery* in the title and explain that it signals that Janine's text examines a mystery, or something unknown, about King Tut.

**INTRODUCTION:** Help students find the sentences that state the topic: *I know from the title that the text is about a mystery related to King Tut, so I will look for sentences that suggest something mysterious about him.* Help students identify that the last two sentences state the mystery.

### CREATING AN ORGANIZATIONAL STRUCTURE

Janine used the outline below. It is divided into three sections: introduction, explanation, and conclusion.

### TITLE

Identifies the main topic for the reader

### INTRODUCTION

The introduction states the topic.
*Underline the pair of sentences that tell what this report is about.*

# WRITE INFORMATIVE/EXPLANATORY TEXTS

# Read a Student Model

Janine has been asked to write an informative/explanatory report about King Tutankhamun, a ruler in Egypt over 3,000 years ago. Janine has used an introduction to state her topic and facts to explain what she learned about King Tutankhamun. As you read her report, think about the topic for your report and how you can use facts, definitions, and details to explain it.

### The Mystery of King Tut

Many people think that all of the kings of ancient Egypt were buried in the pyramids. A huge number of these rulers were actually buried in an area called the Valley of the Kings. The famous King Tutankhamun, or King Tut, was buried there. His tomb and his mummy were discovered in 1922. <u>We have learned many things about King Tut since then. Yet, there are many things we don't know.</u> Everyone loves a good mystery. This may be why people continue to be so interested in King Tut.

## Genre: Informative/Explanatory Texts

Draw students' attention to the base words *inform* and *explain* in the text type "informative/explanatory texts." Then ask students to tell what they think is the purpose of this text type. Point out informative/explanatory texts students may have read, such as an encyclopedia entry or a news article. Be sure students understand that writers write this type of text to examine a topic and to inform or explain something about it to the reader.

Explain that in order to effectively communicate ideas about a topic, a writer must group related information together and develop the topic with facts, definitions, and details. Discuss how it might be tempting to add your own opinion when writing this type of text and why it is important to refrain from doing so—as an opinion would be out of place or feel jarring.

## King Tut's MRI Results

King Tut became a ruler in Egypt when he was young. He ruled for only nine years. <u>In 2013, an MRI was used to look at his mummy.</u> An MRI is a special scanner that takes pictures and sends them to a computer. From the pictures, scientists learned that Tut was around 19 years old when he died.

Many people wonder why King Tut died so young. One rumor said that he was hit from behind. The MRI scans of his head, however, did not show he had been hit. Another idea was that he was hurt in battle. One scan did find a broken bone above his knee. Scientists do not know when this happened, but it could have happened when the mummy was first moved.

## Was King Tut Sick?

Scientists thought King Tut's foot looked odd. In 2003, they took DNA from his mummy. The DNA showed that some of the bone had died. It may have made King Tut limp and use a cane. Still the scientists do not think this killed King Tut. Scientists also took DNA from an ancient insect in the pyramid. The insect carried a disease called malaria. This disease can be deadly. However, they do not know if this caused his death.

### DEVELOP THE TOPIC
Facts, definitions, and details help the reader understand the topic.

*In this section, underline a fact and circle a word and its definition.*

### ORGANIZATION
Related information is grouped together.

*Put boxes around two sentences that tell what scientists learned about King Tut's body.*

### LINKING WORDS
Linking words (such as *and, also,* and *but*) and phrases help connect the ideas.

*Circle the linking words in the section "Was King Tut Sick?"*

## Analyze a Student Model

**DEVELOP THE TOPIC:** Remind students that a fact is something that can be proven, like the date something happened, unlike an opinion, which is someone's idea about something. Ask students to identify a fact about an MRI in the text. ("In 2013, an MRI was used to look at his mummy.") Ask students to identify the type of information Janine provides in the next sentence—a fact, definition, or detail. (definition) Ask students what does she define? (an MRI)

**ORGANIZATION:** Model identifying the information that is grouped together: *I know from the first paragraph that scientists used an MRI to study King Tut's mummy. I'll look for information in this paragraph that tells what they learned from the scans of his body.* ("did not show he had been hit" and had "a broken bone above his knee") Read aloud the first paragraph, adding the first circled sentence from the second paragraph to the end of the first paragraph. Then read aloud the second paragraph, leaving out the first circled sentence. Help students see that the paragraphs do not make sense when related information is not grouped together.

**LINKING WORDS:** Ask students to identify the linking word Janine uses to connect the idea that dead bone in King Tut's foot may have made him limp and use a cane to the idea that scientists do not think this killed King Tut. (*Still*) Point out that this information relates to one test scientists conducted with DNA. Have students identify the linking word Janine uses to show that scientists conducted a second test related to DNA. (*also*) After giving students time to find the third linking word (*However*), ask a volunteer to explain the ideas Janine connects with that linking word. ("malaria can be deadly" and "scientists do not know if this caused his death")

---

## Support English Language Learners

Help English language learners build and connect to background knowledge before they read this text so that they can focus their energy on comprehending the ideas the author presents rather than on trying to make sense of unfamiliar references.

Be sure English language learners understand that the King Tut discussed in this text is the same King Tut that they read about in Unit 3. Explain that MRI and DNA are both initialisms. (*magnetic resonance imaging* and *deoxyribonucleic acid*)

Show students pictures and videos related to King Tut, MRIs, and DNA to help them build background knowledge.

## Analyze a Student Model

**CONCLUSION:** Review Janine's conclusion with students. Students should recognize that the questions serve to summarize the ideas in the text; they are not new questions. Students should also recognize that Janine wraps up these ideas with the last sentence, but adds an interesting thought before wrapping up the topic.

## Evaluate a Writer's Work

Have partners discuss the informative/explanatory text. Remind students that the purpose of an informative/explanatory text is to inform or explain something to the reader. Have students recall what Janine stated in her introductory paragraph that she would examine in the text: "We have learned many things about King Tut since then. Yet, there are many things we don't know." Ask students if Janine effectively follows up on this purpose in her text. Have partners share their thinking with the class.

## Model: Organizational Structure

Ask students to think about how the writer might have completed her outline for the informative/explanatory text. On a board or projector, post the outline on page 89. Then have students help you fill in the outline based on the model text. Review the notes in the margins alongside the model text. Fill in the introduction, explanation, and conclusion. Point out that well-written informative/explanatory texts have strong organization, which requires planning and prewriting.

Students will next use the blank outline found in their books to plan their own informative/explanatory text, and then they will draft the text based on their outline.

**CONCLUSION**
The conclusion wraps up the topic by telling what was learned. It also adds an interesting idea related to the topic.
*Underline the concluding statement.*

What caused this young ruler to die? He was not hit in the head. He did not die from a deformed foot. Did he get sick? Was it something else? The scans and tests ruled out some ideas. Yet, we still are not sure what caused King Tut to die so young. As scientists invent new tests and technology, they may find the answers to some of these questions. Until then, King Tut will be remembered as much for what we do know as for what we still wonder.

**88** Unit 4 ■ Text Types and Purposes: Write Informative/Explanatory Texts

## Review: Determining Main Idea and Key Details

Remind students that when they read the historical text "The Amazing Tomb of Tut," they learned that an author usually points out the main idea in the title and then tells the reader the main idea early in the text. They also analyzed how the author supported the main idea with details.

Ask students to recall the main idea that they identified for this text at the start of the lesson. ("We have learned many things about King Tut since then. Yet, there are many things we don't know.") Then ask them to identify a word or phrase in each subheading that points to the main idea of that section. (*MRI Results; Sick*) Finally, have students identify one detail that supports the main topic in the section "Was King Tut Sick?" (They do not know if malaria caused his death.)

Use an outline like the one below to organize your informative/ explanatory essay on a history or science topic that interests you. Then write a first draft of your essay on a separate sheet of paper. Make sure to develop your topic using facts and details and group related information together. Remember to use linking words in your draft to connect pieces of information. Lastly, make sure your draft ends with a conclusion that summarizes your topic. You will use this draft to write your final essay in the Unit 4 Review section on page 96.

**Title:** _____

   **I. Introduction**
      **Topic:** _____
      _____

  **II. Explanation**
      **Subtopic 1:** _____
      **Facts:** _____
      _____

      **Subtopic 2:** _____
      **Facts:** _____
      _____

  **III. Conclusion**
      _____
      _____
      _____

Unit 4 ■ Text Types and Purposes: Write Informative/Explanatory Texts   **89**

## Differentiate Instruction

Work individually with students who are not yet ready to pick a topic and plan and draft their text on their own. Be sure students understand the meaning of *subtopic, fact, definition,* and *detail*. Point to an example of each from the Student Model to reinforce understanding. Consider creating a tree diagram (with the topic box at the top, subtopic boxes in the next row, and evidence boxes in the bottom row with arrows leading down) for students to use in place of the outline for organizing ideas to help them "see" how the subtopics relate to the topic, and how the facts, definitions, and details support the subtopics. Help students select a topic from the list of topics the class brainstormed. Then guide them as they complete their tree diagram to organize their ideas.

## Create: Organizational Structure

### Brainstorming

Tell students that writers write informative/explanatory texts about topics that interest them. Have students name their favorite history and science topics. Make a list of students' topic ideas on the board or projector for them to use as they plan their writing.

### Planning

Students will use the outline on page 89 to plan their text. Students should first decide on a topic and then fill in what they will examine about the topic.

- Students should decide how to best examine their topic through two subtopics and record facts related to each subtopic.
- Remind students that Janine added an interesting idea about the topic to her conclusion. Ask students what idea they can add to their conclusion.

### Drafting an Informative/ Explanatory Text

Instruct students to refer to their outline as they draft their informative/ explanatory text on a separate sheet of paper. Remind them to use linking words to connect their ideas.

## Introduce the Writing Process

Remind students that in order to do a good job on an essay, they must plan, draft, revise, and edit it. These are all steps of the writing process. For more on the writing process, see the *Writing Handbook* on page 275 of this guide.

| Assess and Respond |
| --- |
| **If** students have difficulty breaking their topic into subtopics, |
| **Then** have students list facts they know about the topic and help them group the facts into two subtopics, leaving out any facts that do not fit. |

## OBJECTIVE
**Use the correct pronoun in writing.**

### Guided Instruction

Make sure students understand what a noun is and then review how a pronoun takes its place. Explain that *they* in the first example set takes the place of *statues*. Ask students to identify what *he* and *it* take the place of in the next example sets. Have students read each sentence set aloud, emphasizing the nouns and pronouns in bold, to reinforce learning verbally.

### Guided Practice

Help students identify the pronouns in the first two sentences. Then discuss whether each word in the remaining sentences could take the place of a noun, and thus be a pronoun. Allow students to identify the pronoun in these sentences.

### Independent Practice

Challenge students to explain why the pronoun that they selected is correct. Then have them read aloud the sentence, replacing the underlined noun with the pronoun.

---

**Assess and Respond**

**If** students have difficulty identifying pronouns to replace nouns,

**Then** create several two-sentence sets—with the second sentence containing a pronoun replacing a noun (which is underlined) in the first sentence. Have them circle the pronoun in the second sentence that replaces the underlined noun.

---

## LANGUAGE

### Pronouns

**Guided Instruction**  A **pronoun** takes the place of a noun. Some of the most common pronouns are *I, he, she, it, we, they,* and *you.*

> *Statues* were found in China. [noun]
> *They* were found in China. [pronoun]

> The *Emperor* had the statues made. [noun]
> *He* had the statues made. [pronoun]

> The *book* is from the museum gift shop. [noun]
> *It* is from the museum gift shop. [pronoun]

**Guided Practice**  Write the pronoun in each sentence.

1. We went to the museum to see the Terra Cotta Warriors. ___We___
2. To my surprise, she knew a lot about them. ___she___
3. Have you heard of the statues? ___you___
4. They are very old statues of warriors. ___They___
5. I liked how each statue looked different. ___I___

**Independent Practice**  Replace the underlined words with a pronoun.

1. <u>Mrs. Ling</u> is our teacher. ___She___
2. Mrs. Ling took us to see <u>the exhibit</u>. ___it___
3. <u>Our class</u> saw pictures of the pits where the warriors were found. ___We___
4. <u>The guides</u> told us how they found the warriors. ___They___
5. <u>Mr. Hurd</u> showed us the tools they used. ___He___

90    Unit 4 ■ Text Types and Purposes: Write Informative/Explanatory Texts

---

**Turn and Talk**

During Guided Practice, promote discussion participation by all students by having partners turn to each other and talk over which word in the sentence is the pronoun in sentences 1–5. Have partners take turns sharing the pronoun they selected with the class. Then, after Independent Practice, have different partners turn to each other and discuss the pronouns they chose to replace the underlined words. Have volunteers share the pronouns they chose, explaining their choice.

## Pronoun-Antecedent Agreement

**Guided Instruction**  Some pronouns have antecedents. The **antecedent** is the noun the pronoun refers to. The pronoun and antecedent must match. Both must be singular or plural.

The **scientists** work for **their** museum.
[antecedent]        [pronoun]

The **scientist** works for **her** museum.
[antecedent]        [pronoun]

**Guided Practice**  Correct the sentences.

1. The tourists brought his camera.

Sample answer: The tourists brought their cameras.

_____

2. Kayla left its camera on the bus.

Sample answer: Kayla left her camera on the bus.

_____

3. The students took pictures of her visit to the pyramid.

Sample answer: The students took pictures of their visit to the pyramid.

_____

4. Curt and Diego drew pictures of his favorite sites.

Sample answer: Curt and Diego took pictures of their favorite sites.

_____

**Independent Practice**  Use a pronoun and antecedent in a sentence. Underline the pronoun and its antecedent.

Sample answer: The pyramid had steps leading to its top.

_____

Unit 4 ■ Text Types and Purposes: Write Informative/Explanatory Texts        **91**

### OBJECTIVE
**Use correct pronoun-antecedent agreement in writing.**

## Guided Instruction

Explain that students will build on their knowledge of pronouns in this lesson. Then explain that sometimes a pronoun does not replace a noun; instead it refers back to a noun that comes before it. Have students draw an arrow from the pronoun back to the noun in each example sentence. Discuss how each pronoun matches its noun.

## Guided Practice

Read the first sentence aloud and then model correcting it: *This sentence sounds strange. I know that* his *is a pronoun that refers to a singular, masculine noun, but there is no singular masculine noun before* his *in this sentence. The only noun before the pronoun is* tourists, *so the correct pronoun must be* they—*a plural, gender-neutral pronoun.* Talk students through the second sentence. Then allow them to rewrite the last two sentences on their own.

## Independent Practice

Have students repeat the rules of pronoun-antecedent agreement. Then have them write their sentences.

| Assess and Respond |
| --- |
| **If** students have a difficult time with pronoun-antecedent agreement, |
| **Then** give students more practice correcting sentences by repeating the process under Guided Practice with additional examples. If needed, provide a list of pronouns to draw from for the first few sentences. |

## Support English Language Learners

Reinforce understanding of pronouns for native speakers of Mandarin and other languages that do not rely heavily on pronouns.

First reinforce basic understanding of pronouns. Write the pronouns *I, me, he, him, she, her, they, them, their, we, us, it, its* each on a separate index card. Then write one noun, each on a separate index card, that relates to each pronoun. (Put the students' name on cards for *I, me, we,* and *us.*) Then have students place a pronoun card on top of a noun card to correctly "replace" it. Go on to reinforce understanding of pronoun-antecedent agreement. Have students place a pronoun card after a noun card that it can correctly refer to and use their finger to "draw" an arrow from the pronoun card back to the noun card.

## OBJECTIVE
**Use correct spelling in writing.**

### Guided Instruction

Explain that when you write a text, you want your reader to focus on the ideas you are presenting in your text. You do not want them to be distracted by spelling errors. Then explain that high-frequency words are words that are used often and that students should memorize how to spell these words. Review the spelling of each word. Point out common misspelling errors for each word (e.g., writing *u* instead of *o* in *another*; leaving out the *i* or writing two *e*'s in the second syllable in *believe*). Have students say and spell each word.

### Guided Practice

Have students cover up the word box at the top of their page. Help students circle the correctly spelled word in the first example. Then have partners work together on the remaining sentences and share their answers with the class.

### Independent Practice

Ask students to write another sentence for each misspelled word, using the correctly spelled version of it.

| Assess and Respond |
|---|
| **If** students have difficulty finding the misspelled word and spelling it correctly, |
| **Then** give them additional Independent Practice examples, providing a "correct spelling" word bank to draw from at first. |

---

## LANGUAGE

### Spelling High-Frequency Words

**Guided Instruction** It is important to spell words correctly when you are writing. You should remember how to spell high-frequency words that you use often when you write.

| High-Frequency Words | | |
|---|---|---|
| another | especially | question |
| believe | friendly | ready |
| caught | important | thought |
| does | knew | usually |

**Guided Practice** Circle the correct spelling of the word in parentheses.

1. Chichen Itza is an (importent, **important**) pyramid in Mexico.
2. Scientists (**believe**, beleeve) that the Mayans built the pyramid.
3. (Anuther, **Another**) Mayan pyramid is El Castillo.
4. Pyramids were (espeshelly, **especially**) important in Mayan society.

**Independent Practice** Find the misspelled word and spell it correctly on the line.

1. Chichen Itza has meny steps leading to the top. _____many_____
2. Some peeple like to climb the stairs. _____people_____
3. You should place your feet carfully as you climb, so you don't fall. _____carefully_____
4. Be reddy for a tough climb, but know that it is well worth it in the end. _____ready_____

---

## Differentiate Instruction

Help struggling students master correct spelling with several activities.

First, have students say the word. Then, have them spell the word, tapping each letter with a pencil tip as they spell it. Finally, have them say the word again. Repeat for each word.

Then show an index card to the student with the word written on it. Hide the word and have the student spell it. Show the word to the student again. Ask the student to explain if he or she spelled it correctly or incorrectly, and identify the misspelling. Repeat for each word.

Finally, give students a handout that lists the spelling words with a misspelling of the word next to it. Have them circle the correct version.

## Commas in Addresses

**Guided Instruction**  A comma is used to separate words or ideas.
In an address, a comma separates a city from a state.

*Dinosaur National Monument*
*4545 E. Highway 40*
*Dinosaur, CO 81610*

**Guided Practice**  Add a comma to the sentences below.

1. Dinosaur National Park is near Boulder, Colorado.

2. On your way to the park, you may want to visit the craters near Twin Falls, Idaho.

3. You can also travel to Salt Lake City, Utah, which is nearby.

**Independent Practice**  Using correct punctuation, write your address below.

Answers will vary.

## OBJECTIVE
Use commas correctly in addresses.

### Guided Instruction
Make sure students understand that homes, businesses, and institutions (such as schools and museums) are located in a certain place, and that the place has an address. People use the address to find or send letters to the people in the homes, businesses, or institutions. Then discuss how commas separate words or ideas to clarify information for readers. Point out how if there was no comma in the example address, it would be unclear if *CO* was part of the city name or the abbreviation for the state.

### Guided Practice
Discuss with students why a comma is needed to separate *Boulder* from *Colorado* in the first sentence. Then have partners identify the words that need to be separated in the remaining sentences. Have volunteers share their answers and explain them to the group.

### Independent Practice
Have students explain where they placed the comma and why the information in their address would be confusing if they had omitted the comma.

| Assess and Respond |
| --- |
| **If** students have difficulty correctly using commas in addresses, |
| **Then** give them additional Guided Instruction examples, talking through how to correct the first one, providing corrective feedback for the second one, and allowing them to complete the remaining ones independently. |

## Differentiate Instruction

Some students might not be aware that cities or towns are located in states. Display a map to students. Point first to a city or town on the map. Then draw attention to the state the city or town is in. Present the information orally while pointing to the map. For example, *Boulder is located in Colorado.*

Then review the Guided Instruction and Guided Practice examples. For each example, have students identify the city. Then have them identify the state. Reinforce that these are two different ideas—a city and a state—so they need to be separated by a comma to help readers understand the addresses.

## OBJECTIVES

- Come to discussion prepared, having read the required text, citing evidence when building on others' ideas.
- Follow conventions of discourse, including agreed-upon rules for discussion.

## Discuss the Essential Question

Before beginning a group discussion, copy and distribute the "Did I?" checklist, available on **sadlierconnect.com**.

### Leading the Class Discussion

Give students time to think about the questions before the class discussion.

**1.** Guide students to identify how the section headings give a clue as to how information is grouped in each section.

**2.** Have students skim the text for the linking words used to connect ideas.

---

### Discuss the Essential Question

How do writers develop a topic to inform or explain?

Think about the Essential Question by responding to the questions below. Support your point of view with reasons and experience.

**1.** How does the writer of "The Mystery of King Tut" group related information, or facts, together?

The author tells us that scientists used an MRI to find out the age and cause of

death of King Tut. Then, we learn what scientists know from King Tut's DNA.

**2.** What linking words does the writer of "The Mystery of King Tut" use to connect ideas?

The author uses linking words such as "yet," "however," "another," "but,"

"still," "also," and "as" to connect ideas.

Use your notes above to discuss the Essential Question in small groups or as a class. Follow agreed-upon rules for discussion. Use the organizer below to record what you heard and how you participated.

| Ideas I Agree or Disagree With | | Questions I Asked |
|---|---|---|
| Agree | | |
| Disagree | | |
| New Ideas I Had During Discussion | | Questions I Answered |
| | | |

---

## Discussion Skills

Before discussing each question as a class, have partners build on and clarify each other's ideas by sharing their responses to the questions with each other. Have each partner make one statement, building on the other partner's responses to the questions. Then have each student ask their partner for clarification about their responses. Provide sentence starts if necessary. Encourage students to revise their answers based on their discussions with their partners. Then have volunteers share their responses and explain how they revised their responses through building on and clarifying ideas with their partner. As students participate in the discussion, rephrase what they say, adding to it to model building on and clarifying each other's ideas.

# UNIT 4 REVIEW

This letter has mistakes in spelling, punctuation, and use of pronouns. Write the paragraph correctly on the lines below.

> 238 Elm Street
> Nashville TN 37240
>
> Dear Dr. Frank,
>
> I would like to ask your a few questuns. I am intrested in how you use planes to map your sites. How did your team members get his information about Peru? Do you beleeve that technology will help you find more artifacts? Thank you for the infermation.
>
> Tomas

238 Elm Street

Nashville, TN 37240

Dear Dr. Frank,

I would like to ask you a few questions. I am interested in how you use

planes to map your sites. How did your team members get their information

about Peru? Do you believe that technology will help you find more

artifacts? Thank you for the information.

Tomas

## Introduce the Review

Explain to students that this review will give them an opportunity to apply the language and writing skills that they have studied and practiced in this unit.

**Language Skills Summary**

Let students know that they are going to use what they learned about pronouns, spelling, and commas to make their writing better. Good writers follow grammar rules, can spell correctly, and understand the mechanics of writing.

- Ask students to tell what a pronoun takes the place of (a noun) and name some common pronouns. (*I, he, she, it, we, they, you*)

- Have students explain the rules of pronouns and antecedents. (The pronoun and antecedent must match. Both must be singular or plural.)

- Prompt students to explain what a high-frequency word is and then to correctly spell one or two high-frequency words. (*another, friendly, ready*)

- Have students tell what a comma separates in an address. (a city from a state)

## Test-Taking Tips

Give students the following tips to help with taking assessments focused on editing skills.

- Tell students to read the text slowly and mark suspected errors lightly on the text in pencil as they find them. Tell them to then reread the text, reconsidering the suspected error they marked. If they decide it is not actually an error, they can erase their marking. If they decide that it is an error, they can mark the error more clearly so that they do not omit correcting it when they rewrite the paragraph.

- Have students read the text backward to help them identify misspelled words.

## Writing Process Summary

Remind students that planning helps them organize their ideas before drafting, and revising and editing make a draft better.

### Planning and Drafting

Have students look at the outline and draft they created earlier (page 89). They should check that the draft includes an introduction, subtopics, and ends with a conclusion.

### Informative/Explanatory Text Rubric

| | |
|---|---|
| 4 | The text clearly introduces the topic and states what the writer will examine in the introduction; groups related information and develops the topic with facts, definitions, and details; concludes by wrapping up what was learned and adds an interesting thought; and uses linking words. There are few or no editing errors. |
| 3 | The text has the elements listed under "4" above, though they are executed less successfully. Minor editing errors do not detract greatly from the overall text. |
| 2 | The text is missing one or more of the required elements. There are many editing errors, some of which are serious. |
| 1 | The text is unfinished or shows a minimal understanding of required elements. Serious editing errors make it difficult to read. |
| 0 | The assignment was not attempted. |

### Self-Assessment: Progress Check

Have students revisit the Progress Check on page 83 and compare their answers now with the answers they gave before they started Unit 4.

---

**Assignment:** Write an informative/explanatory text about a history or science topic that interests you.

On the lines below, write your final copy of the informative/explanatory essay you created on page 89. Be sure to introduce the topic and end with a concluding sentence or paragraph. Make sure to use facts, definitions, and details to explain the topic. Do not forget to use linking words to connect ideas. See the Writing Handbook (pages 275–283) for ways to improve your writing as you revise.

Students should write an informative/explanatory essay by using facts, details, and definitions. They should group related information together and use linking words to connect ideas. Each student's essay should include an introduction to make the reader familiar with the topic, a middle to develop ideas further, and a conclusion to wrap up the essay.

**96** Unit 4 ■ Text Types and Purposes: Write Informative/Explanatory Texts

---

## Digital Connection: Digital Slide Presentation

Once students have finished writing their essays, they can turn them into digital slide presentations.

Display a sample digital slide presentation that includes a title slide, sections that group related information, and a concluding slide. Point out that the digital slide presentation does not simply display chunks of text on screen; rather, it displays key headings and bullet points, as well as visuals (images and videos), and audio. The presenter clicks through slides that support what he or she says during the presentation.

Have students create their digital slide presentations and present them to the class.

# Introducing UNIT 5

**W**hat makes friendship special? Do you take time to look for and keep good friends? In this unit, you will read about different pairs of best friends who help each other to be their best.

In the fiction selections that follow, you will look at how authors use language. You will read examples of literal language, where authors say just what they mean, and nonliteral language, where authors use words to create images or associations. You will also find examples of different text structures, including a drama and a narrative poem. As you read, you can look at how fiction can present points of view that may be different from your own.

Learning about the craft and structure of the works that follow will help you better understand the stories of friendship. Then you can talk about them with a friend!

**Before Unit 5**

## Progress Check   *Can I?*

**After Unit 5**

☐  Understand literal and nonliteral language.   ☐

☐  Recognize the different parts of a drama.   ☐

☐  Distinguish my point of view from those of the narrator and characters.   ☐

Unit 5 ■ Reading Literature: Craft and Structure

**Student Page 97**

# HOME ◆ CONNECT...

The Home Connect feature is a way to keep parents or other adult family members apprised of what their children are learning. The key learning objectives are listed, and some ideas for related activities and discussions are included.

Explain to students that they can share the Home Connect page with their parents or other adult family members in their home. Let students know how much time the class will be spending on this unit so they can plan their time accordingly at home.

Encourage students and their parents to share their experiences using the suggestions on the Home Connect page. You may wish to make a place to post some of this work.

# Progress Check

The Progress Check is a self-assessment feature that students can use to gauge their own progress. Research shows that when students take accountability for their own learning, their motivation increases.

Before students begin work on Unit 5, have them check the boxes next to any item that they feel they can do well. Explain that it is fine if they don't check any of the boxes. Tell them that they will have an opportunity to learn about and practice all of these items while studying the unit. Let them know that near the end of the unit they will have a chance to reconsider how well they can do each item on this list.

Before students begin the Unit 5 Review on page 125, have them revisit this page. You can use this information to work with students on any items they don't understand before they tackle the Review.

# HOME ◆ CONNECT...

**C**reative writers use **nonliteral** phrases to create images in a reader's mind. The **literal**, or actual, meaning of the words might be different from what the author is really trying to say. Help your child see the difference. In a children's story or poem, highlight a phrase that is not meant literally. Talk with your child about what it means. Have your child find other examples.

Good readers can talk about the parts of stories, poems, and plays. To help your child understand the **parts of a drama**, find a children's play online or in the library. Read it together, and talk about what happens in each scene. Discuss how scenes in a play are like chapters in a book.

In stories, a narrator or character often feels strongly about something. Readers learn to understand those **points of view** and distinguish them from their own. Read together a children's story or play with a strong point of view. Ask your child about the narrator or character's feelings. Discuss whether you both share these feelings.

**Conversation Starter:** With your child, talk about a favorite story. Ask your child:

- *Can you name examples of figurative language or idioms in the story? What are they?*
- *If you turned the story into a play, how many scenes would there be? What would happen in each scene?*
- *How would you describe the main character's point of view? Do you agree with that point of view?*

## IN THIS UNIT, YOUR CHILD WILL...

- Figure out the meanings of unfamiliar words in texts.
- Distinguish literal language from figurative words and phrases, such as idioms.
- Understand parts of a drama, including scenes, setting, character list, and stage directions.
- Understand the point of view of a narrator or character in a story and distinguish it from his or her own point of view.
- Compare and contrast four texts with the same theme: realistic fiction, drama, a narrative poem, and historical fiction.

### WAYS TO HELP YOUR CHILD

Help your child understand how writers use language to spur readers' imaginations. Read stories and poems together, and point out lines and phrases that you particularly enjoy. Encourage your child to find examples of favorites, too. You might also listen for oral language that creates images on the internet, radio, or television.

**ONLINE**
For more Home Connect activities, continue online at sadlierconnect.com

98   Unit 5 ■ Reading Literature: Craft and Structure

**Student Page 98**

## UNIT PLANNER

| Theme: Best Friends | Focus |
|---|---|
| **DISTINGUISHING LITERAL/ NONLITERAL LANGUAGE** *pp. 100–105* | *The Best Friend Possible* **GENRE:** Realistic Fiction   **LEXILE®:** 640L <br><br> **WORDS TO KNOW:** orientation, mobility, instructor, mature, isolated, nonprofit organization, bond, specialist, evaluate, assigned, suspense |
| **UNDERSTANDING PARTS OF A DRAMA** *pp. 106–111* | *Singing Your Blues Away* **GENRE:** Drama   **LEXILE®:** NP* <br><br> **WORDS TO KNOW:** bragging, invisible, proportion, tradition, spotlight, react, strum, applaud |
| **DISTINGUISHING POINTS OF VIEW** *pp. 112–117* | *Forever Friends* **GENRE:** Narrative Poem   **LEXILE®:** NP* <br><br> **WORDS TO KNOW:** treasure, embarrassed, sulked, separated, interfere, prospect, imperiously, anew |
| **CLOSE READING** *pp. 118–122* | *We Must See the Queen!* **GENRE:** Historical Fiction   **LEXILE®:** 580L |
| **CONNECT ACROSS TEXTS** *p. 123* | Compare and Contrast Texts |
| **LANGUAGE** *p. 124* | Literal and Nonliteral Meanings |
| **UNIT 5 REVIEW** *pp. 125–126* | *Friendship—Yum!* **GENRE:** Poem   **LEXILE®:** NP* |

\* The NP code is given to selections comprising more than 50% non-standard or non-conforming prose. NP selections do not receive a Lexile measure, merely the NP code.

## Objective(s)

Use vocabulary strategies to determine the meaning of words and phrases, distinguishing literal from nonliteral language.

Use terms such as *scene* to describe how parts of a drama build on each other.

Differentiate between a personal point of view and the narrator's or character's point of view.

- Use vocabulary strategies to determine the meaning of words and phrases, distinguishing literal from nonliteral language.
- Use terms such as *scene* to describe how parts of a story build on each other.
- Differentiate between a personal point of view and the narrator's or character's point of view.

Determine the meaning of figurative language, such as idioms.

## Unit Assessment

- Unit 5 Review *pp. 125–126*
- Unit 5 Performance Task  ONLINE

## Additional Assessment Options

- Performance Task 1 *pp. 141A–145 and 146*
  ALSO ONLINE
- Performance Task 2 *pp. 259A–263 and 264*
  ALSO ONLINE

**Optional Purchase:**
- iProgress Monitor  ONLINE
- Progress Monitor Student Benchmark Assessment Booklet

## ONLINE  Digital Resources

- Home Connect Activities
- Unit Performance Task
- Additional Practice
- Full-Length Reading Selections
- Foundational Skills Practice
- Teacher Resources
- iProgress Monitor (optional purchase)

**Go to SadlierConnect.com to access your Digital Resources.**

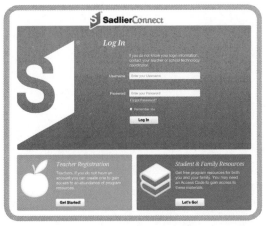

**For more detailed instructions see page T3.**

## LEARNING PROGRESSIONS

In this unit, students will learn how the craft and structure of a literary text contribute to their understanding of it. In order to learn the skills in this unit, students will further develop skills learned in second grade. They should be encouraged to retain these skills, as they will continue to build on them in fourth grade.

**Distinguishing Literal/Nonliteral Language**

- By the end of grade 2, students should have been able to describe how words and phrases add rhythm and meaning in a story, poem, or song.

- In grade 3, students will build on this skill by not only describing how words supply meaning, but also determining the meaning of words and phrases and distinguishing literal from nonliteral language.

- When students move on to grade 4, they will be asked to determine the meaning of more complex words and phrases, including those that refer to specific characters found in mythology.

**Understanding Parts of a Drama**

- Proficient second-grade students should have ended the school year knowing how to discuss the beginning and end of a story.

- As third graders, they should be able to refer to specific parts of stories, dramas, and poems, using appropriate terms such as chapter, scene, and stanza. By the end of third grade, students should master the ability to describe how parts of works build on earlier sections.

- These skills will prepare them for fourth grade, when they will explain the differences between poems, drama, and prose and refer to their structural elements.

**Distinguishing Points of View**

- By the end of second grade, students should have been able to acknowledge differences in the points of view of characters.

- As third graders, students must take this concrete knowledge of characters' points of view and distinguish it from their own point of view.

- This ability to distinguish points of view will become even more complex in fourth grade, when they will learn to compare and contrast the differences between first- and third-person narration.

# Reading Literature: Craft and Structure

## Essential Question:
How do authors craft stories?

**Distinguishing Literal/
Nonliteral Language** . . . .100

**Understanding Parts of
a Drama** . . . . . . . . . . . . .106

**Distinguishing Points
of View** . . . . . . . . . . . . . .112

**Close Reading** . . . . . . . .118

**Connect Across Texts** . . . .123

**Language: Literal and
Nonliteral Meanings** . . . . .124

**Unit 5 Review** . . . . . . . .125

Unit 5   Reading Literature: Craft and Structure   **99**

## Essential Question:
How do authors craft stories?

In this unit, students will learn about the craft and structure of literary texts, specifically how authors use vocabulary, text structure, and point of view to tell stories in different genres.

## Theme: Best Friends
Students will read selections related to the theme of best friends. They will read about friendships between humans and animals, friends supporting each other during difficult times, and loyalty.

## Curriculum Connection: English/Language Arts
Students will learn about the theme of friendship in literature.

## Vocabulary Overview

**General Academic Vocabulary**

anew 116, assigned 104, bond 102, bragging 106, embarrassed 113, evaluate 104, imperiously 116, instructor 100, interfere 114, invisible 107, isolated 102, mature 101, proportion 107, prospect 114, react 110, separated 114, sulked 113, suspense 104, tradition 108, treasure 112

**Domain-Specific Vocabulary**

applaud 110, mobility 100, nonprofit organization 102, orientation 100, specialist 104, spotlight 109, strum 110

## Guided Instruction

### OBJECTIVE
**Use vocabulary strategies to determine the meaning of words and phrases, distinguishing literal from nonliteral language.**

### Genre: Realistic Fiction

Explain to students that realistic fiction tells a story in a real and believable way. Point out to students that *realistic* is related to *real*.

### Set the Purpose

Help students understand the purpose for learning the reading skill by asking *Do you think words can have different meanings? What do you do to figure out the meaning?*

### Model and Teach

Read the selection as students follow along in their books.

### CITE EVIDENCE

**A** *I'm looking for a word in the first sentence of paragraph 1 that means something different from the literal meaning. The literal meaning of* flipped *is "to do a flip in the air." I don't think this is what the character actually did. The character is excited about getting a dog.*

*What is the nonliteral meaning of the word* flipped? (excited)

---

**WORDS TO KNOW**
instructor
mature
mobility
orientation

> **Nonliteral language** gives different meanings to **words and phrases** from those of **literal language**.

**CITE EVIDENCE**

**A** Writers may use **literal words** that say exactly what they mean. Or they may use **nonliteral, figurative words** that mean something other than what the words say. Circle the nonliteral word in paragraph 1, sentence 1. What is the literal meaning of the word? What does the word mean here?

## The Best Friend Possible
(Genre: Realistic Fiction)

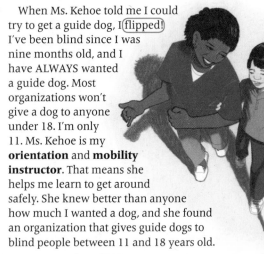

1   When Ms. Kehoe told me I could try to get a guide dog, I flipped! I've been blind since I was nine months old, and I have ALWAYS wanted a guide dog. Most organizations won't give a dog to anyone under 18. I'm only 11. Ms. Kehoe is my **orientation** and **mobility instructor**. That means she helps me learn to get around safely. She knew better than anyone how much I wanted a dog, and she found an organization that gives guide dogs to blind people between 11 and 18 years old.

2   My parents weren't sure it was a good idea. "Honey, you get around with your cane very well," my mother said. "Do you really think you need a dog?"

3   "Mom, a dog can signal what's around me. Yes, a cane is good, but a dog is better!"

4   "But a dog could be trouble," added my dad. "What if it starts to bite?"

5   "Don't worry! These dogs are trained for at least 18 months. They behave better than I do!" I laughed.

---

## Words to Know

**General Academic Vocabulary**
**instructor** (*noun*): a person who teaches something
**mature** (*adjective*): acting in an adult manner

**Domain-Specific Vocabulary**
**mobility** (*noun*): movement
**orientation** (*noun*): position or place in space

**Working with Word Meaning** Encourage students to rephrase the definitions, putting them in their own words.

## CRAFT AND STRUCTURE

6  "But what about the money?" he argued. "A dog like that must cost an arm and a leg."

7  "Dad, you don't have to worry about money. The organization donates the dogs. The main problem will be that we'll probably have to wait a million years for a dog. Come on, let's look at how to join the program."

8  My parents had finally run out of arguments. Together, we filled out an application and started the long wait for a dog.

9  Every day, I asked my mother if the guide dog people had called. Every day, the answer was no. Finally, after many months, the answer was yes! They said that I could come to meet some guide dogs. I was over the moon! By now, my parents were excited about a guide dog, too. They knew that they could count on me. Not many 11-year-old girls could handle the responsibility of caring for a service dog, but I've always been **mature**.

### Comprehension Check

Reread paragraph 9. Find the phrase "count on me" in sentence 7. What does the narrator mean?

### Guided Instruction

**CITE EVIDENCE**

**B**  Idioms are figurative language phrases that are usually used in informal writing and speech. Circle the idiom in paragraph 6. What does this idiom mean?

**C**  Context clues can help you figure out literal meanings of unfamiliar words. Look for hints in surrounding words to help you understand a word. Circle the word *application* in paragraph 8. Then underline the surrounding words that help you figure out its meaning.

**D**  Find and box the idiom in paragraph 9. What does this idiom mean?

101

### Guided Instruction

**CITE EVIDENCE**

**B**  *The text says that a dog "...must cost an arm and a leg." I think this is an idiom. A dog doesn't really cost body parts.*

*What does this idiom mean about the cost of a dog?* (A dog is expensive.)

**C**  *I want to look around the word* application *for clues about what it means.*

*Which words tell what you do with an application?* (filled out) *Based on these clues, what is an application?* (a form)

**D**  *I know that an idiom is a phrase used in informal speech and writing. I'm looking for a phrase that is not literal.*

*Which phrase has a nonliteral meaning?* (over the moon) *What does being over the moon mean?* (being very excited)

### Comprehension Check

**Sample Answer:** The narrator uses the phrase "count on me" to say that her parents can rely on her or trust her.

**Answer Explanation:** Students should realize that the phrase "count on me" is an idiom. It has a nonliteral meaning. The narrator's parents are not actually counting anything. Students can use the sentences following the phrase to understand that "count on me" means "rely on me." The narrator's parents can trust her to care for the dog.

## Listening and Viewing Skills

Read paragraph 8 aloud to students and instruct them to look at the picture on page 101. Ask students what they think the family is doing in the picture.

### Support English Language Learners

Students who are learning English will have a more difficult time with nonliteral language than native speakers. Idioms and other figurative language vary among languages, so generally there is no way to adequately translate these phrases.

As students read the passage, have them make a list of nonliteral phrases. Give students practice with the phrases by asking them to use the most recent phrase they have added to their list. For example, ask them to use the phrase "count on me" in a sentence.

## Guided Practice

### Recap Reading Selection

Let students know that they will read more about the blind girl who hopes to get a guide dog. Review what they read about the girl and the events leading up to her getting to go meet some dogs.

### Read and Practice

Have partners take turns reading the selection as you circulate to provide support. Model practicing interpreting an idiom with Cite Evidence callout A. For callout B, circulate and provide partners with scaffolding as needed. You might use the following suggestions to help students who are having difficulty.

### CITE EVIDENCE

**A** Point out the clues in paragraph 11 that can help students determine the emotion behind "raring to go." The exclamation point alerts readers that the author is excited. This may help them understand that "raring to go" means "excited to go."

**B** Help students see that "on pins and needles" is a nonliteral phrase. She is not actually sitting on pins and needles; rather, she is excited and nervous about getting a dog. The author might use the expression to make the writing more interesting and allow the reader to visualize the emotions.

---

# DISTINGUISHING LITERAL/NONLITERAL LANGUAGE

## Guided Practice

**The Best Friend Possible** *continued*

### WORDS TO KNOW

**bond**
**isolated**
**nonprofit organization**

### CITE EVIDENCE

**A** Reread paragraph 11. Underline the phrase *raring to go* in sentence 6. What does it mean?

**B** Reread paragraph 12. Circle the idiom that means "excited and nervous." Why did the author use this expression?

10   Since I don't remember being able to see, being blind is what I know. I go to a regular public school in the small town where I live, and I do pretty well. Still, I'm the only kid who is blind at the school. A dog might help me feel less **isolated**. Not only would it help me get around—it might even help me make friends!

11   There was just one hitch. I'd have to go to the **nonprofit organization** in Canada for a month to get to know a service dog and learn how to work with it. My father is a teacher, so he had time in the summer. Before long, our plans were set. We would travel near Montreal to meet some guide dogs. I was <u>raring to go</u>!

12   I did have one other worry. The guide dog people said that they couldn't promise that I would get a dog. They had only six dogs ready to work as guide dogs, and other kids were coming, too. It's really important that a guide dog forms a strong **bond** with its human. Sometimes, there just isn't the right dog for a person (or person for a dog). I was (on pins and needles.) What if none of the dogs liked me? I tried not to lose heart.

102

---

## Words to Know

**General Academic Vocabulary**

**bond** (*noun*): a force that ties things or people together
**isolated** (*adjective*): being alone or separate from others

**Domain-Specific Vocabulary**

**nonprofit organization** (*noun*): a company or business that does not have the goal of making money and works for the benefit of people and society

**Working with Word Meaning** Encourage students to make up an original sentence for each word.

## CRAFT AND STRUCTURE
### Guided Practice

13    Finally, the day came when my father and I left for Montreal. My mother broke down at the airport, but I promised to stay in touch.

14    When we got there, I met some teenagers who were also hoping to get a guide dog. At age 11, I was the spring chicken in this group!

### Comprehension Check

**1.** Circle the letter that shows a nonliteral phrase in the story.

   **a.** *the right dog for a person*

   **b.** *my father and I left for Montreal*

   **c.** *was the spring chicken*

   **d.** *ready to work as guide dogs*

**2.** Circle the letter that tells what the phrase *broke down* means in paragraph 13.

   **a.** The narrator's mother stopped walking.

   **b.** The narrator's mother started crying.

   **c.** The narrator's mother fell on the ground.

   **d.** The narrator's mother stopped showing emotion.

**3.** Work with a partner. Reread paragraph 12. Discuss the phrase *lose heart* in sentence 8. What does the phrase mean here? Why is the narrator trying not to lose heart?

The phrase means "give up hope." She is worried that she won't find

a partner dog, but she is trying to stay hopeful.

_____

_____

Unit 5 ■ Reading Literature: Craft and Structure    **103**

### Guided Practice

### Comprehension Check

**Answer Explanations:**

**1.** Choice C, *was the spring chicken*, is a nonliteral phrase. The girl is not really a chicken; rather, she is younger than the others.

**2.** Choice B, *The narrator's mother started crying*, explains the nonliteral phrase *broke down*. The picture on page 102 shows the mother and daughter in tears.

**3.** Have students look closely at paragraph 12 and discuss the meaning of the phrase "lose heart." Students should understand that "lose heart" means "give up hope." The narrator is worried about not getting a dog, but she wants to remain hopeful. Students should understand that if they read everything literally, they may misunderstand the meaning of a text or miss out on the emotions behind the words.

## Peer Collaboration

You might have students work in pairs so that peers can support each other in responding to callouts A and B on page 102 and Comprehension Check 1 and 2 on page 103.

Ask students to finalize their answers and then share them with a partner. Students should then make changes to their answers based on the discussion with their partner. Finally, ask pairs to report their answers to the whole group.

## Digital Connection: Online Reference Resources

Let students know that they can use an online dictionary or thesaurus to determine the difference between literal and nonliteral language. These resources can help students clarify the meaning of words and phrases.

Challenge students to write two short paragraphs. One should use only literal language. The other should use only figurative language. Students can then compare their writing to see the differences.

## Independent Practice

### Recap Reading Selection

Remind students that they have been reading about a blind girl who hopes to get a guide dog. Have them recall the major events in the story so far: The girl has filled out an application, been selected, and is now on her way to meet some guide dogs.

### Read and Apply

Have students read the selection independently as you circulate. If you notice students struggling, you can provide support with the suggestions that follow.

#### CITE EVIDENCE

**A** Help students see that the word *haze* is a figurative word that suggests an image of a blur. It means the days were busy and went by very quickly for the girl.

**B** The sentence "The suspense was killing me" is an idiom that shows how nervous the girl is. Students can check this by verifying that the phrase is nonliteral because suspense can't actually kill someone. The reader should understand just how anxious the girl is to find out if she has received a guide dog. Students should see that nonliteral phrases help the reader understand the emotions of a character.

---

## DISTINGUISHING LITERAL/NONLITERAL LANGUAGE

### Independent Practice

**The Best Friend Possible** *continued*

**WORDS TO KNOW**
assign
evaluate
specialist
suspense

**CITE EVIDENCE**

**A** Reread the first sentence in paragraph 17. Underline the figurative word that suggests an image in the sentence.

**B** Reread paragraph 18. Circle an idiom that has to do with being nervous. What feelings do these words give you about the narrator?

15 The **specialists** said we would each work with several dogs. That way, they could **evaluate** which dog worked best with each of us. By the end of the week, if all went well, we would be **assigned** a dog.

16 "Did you like your first day?" Dad asked me that night. I had to admit it was really nice to be around other people who knew what it was like to be blind.

17 The next few days were a <u>haze</u>. It was really tiring to spend all day learning how to work with the dogs, but I loved meeting the different animals. Most of them were a mix of Bernese Mountain Dogs and Labradors. They're known as Labernese, and they're big and smart and lovable. All of them had been trained how to follow commands since they were puppies. We traveled on paths in a park. I tried to get used to the feeling of walking with a guide dog. When we were done working, we could play with the dogs.

18 On the fifth day, I worked with a really friendly dog named Metro. I liked all the dogs but Metro seemed special. He responded to my commands before I finished saying them. I could only hope the specialists thought we clicked as well as I did. And what if they didn't think I'd make a good partner for any of the dogs? The **suspense** was killing me.

19 Finally, Saturday came—the day I'd find out which dog (if any) would be my partner. I really enjoyed working with all of the dogs, but Metro had my HEART.

104 Unit 5 ■ Reading Literature: Craft and Structure

---

## Words to Know

**General Academic Vocabulary**
**assigned** (*verb*): to be given a job or task; to be matched up
**evaluate** (*verb*): to figure out the value of something
**suspense** (*noun*): a feeling of nervousness or uncertainty

**Domain-Specific Vocabulary**
**specialist** (*noun*): an expert in a particular field

**Working with Word Meaning** Encourage students to reread the text with the definitions in mind to increase comprehension.

20    The specialist called, "Maxine, you'll partner up with Monk. Jorge, you'll work with Muppet. Nashaya, you'll work with Minty. Lucy, Mosh will be your guide dog. Carl, you'll work with Millie." I heard the dogs come to the teenagers. Why wasn't my name being called?

21    Finally, the specialist said, "Oh, I almost forgot! Amanda, you work with Metro." My heart leaped! Before I knew it, Metro was at my feet. We had a lot to learn, but we would learn it together.

### Comprehension Check    ( MORE ONLINE )  sadlierconnect.com

1. Circle the letter that tells what the word *clicked* means in paragraph 18, sentence 4.

   a. made a snapping sound

   b. pressed, like a button

   (c.) got along well

   d. made things fall apart

2. Circle the letter that tells what the phrase *had my heart* means in paragraph 19.

   (a.) had my love

   b. worried me

   c. tugged at me

   d. made me sad

3. Why do you think an author might use idioms and other nonliteral language?

   Sample answer: They make the emotions in a story seem more real.

   They make the tone friendlier. They create pictures in the mind.

Unit 5 ■ Reading Literature: Craft and Structure    **105**

### Extend Thinking: Develop a Logical Argument

Help students extend their thinking by developing a logical argument for why most organizations only give guide dogs to people age 18 and over. Have students consider all of the factors involved in training and caring for a guide dog. Ask students to develop the argument, even if they personally disagree with the idea.

Have students or groups of students present their ideas to the class. Speakers should speak clearly, in complete sentences, and at a reasonable rate. Listeners should pay attention and ask questions to check their understanding.

### Comprehension Check

**Answer Explanations:**

1. Choice C, *got along well*, explains the nonliteral meaning of the word *clicked* as used in the passage to describe the relationship between Amanda and Metro.

2. Choice A, *had my love*, gives the nonliteral meaning of the phrase *had my heart*.

3. Have students look back at all of the idioms used throughout the passage and consider how they add to the reader's experience. Authors use idioms and other nonliteral language to make emotions seem more real and help readers visualize the story better.

## Critical Comprehension

Use the following questions to help students think more deeply about the text. Students should be prepared to support their answers with evidence from the text.

*Why might it be nice for Amanda to be around other blind people?* (They understand the struggles she faces.)

*In what ways can guide dogs help blind people?* (They can help them move freely and safely.)

### Assess and Respond

**If** students have difficulty answering the questions in the Comprehension Check…

**Then** have students make a list of the idioms in the selection and write the meaning of each. Have students reread the selection using the translations to aid comprehension.

## Guided Instruction

### OBJECTIVE
Use terms such as *scene* to describe how parts of a drama build on each other.

### Genre: Drama

Explain to students that a drama is a form of writing that is the basis for a play. It includes notes to the actors called stage directions as well as specific lines, called dialogue, for each character to say. A drama is written for the purpose of the actors acting it out.

### Set the Purpose

To activate students' prior knowledge about the reading skill, ask *How is reading a play different from reading a story?*

### Model and Teach

Read the selection as students follow along in their books.

### CITE EVIDENCE

**A** *I know that a play has a list of characters at the beginning, so I will look at the top of the page.*

*Who are the characters?* (Nathan, Fremont, Kevin, Mr. and Mrs. Jones, Mrs. Ordway)

**B** *The setting is usually mentioned in the stage directions at the beginning of the scene.*

*What is the setting?* (a playground) *Why is it important?* (It shows where the action takes place.)

---

## UNDERSTANDING PARTS OF A DRAMA

### Guided Instruction

### WORDS TO KNOW
**bragging**
**invisible**
**proportion**

> Refer to and explain the importance of the parts of a **drama**, including **setting**, **stage direction**, and **scene**.

#### CITE EVIDENCE

**A** A **drama** has many parts. A list of **characters** tells who is in the play. Circle the characters in this play.

**B** The **setting** tells where and when the play takes place. Underline the setting for Scene 1. Why is the setting important?

## Singing Your Blues Away
(Genre: Drama)

### CHARACTERS
Nathan, a 10-year-old boy who plays the guitar
Fremont, Nathan's friend, also a 10-year-old boy
Kevin, Fremont's brother, 12, a soccer player
Mr. and Mrs. Jones, Kevin and Fremont's parents
Mrs. Ordway, Nathan's mother

### Scene 1

*A playground at an elementary school during recess in late autumn.*

1   **NATHAN:** Hey, Fremont, what's got you down?

**FREMONT:** Same old story. My brother's got a soccer tournament this weekend and that's all anyone in the family can talk about. I hear my parents on the phone talking to *their* parents, **bragging** about Kevin all the time.

106

## Words to Know

**General Academic Vocabulary**

**bragging** (*verb*): making statements that show too much pride in yourself
**invisible** (*adjective*): not able to be seen
**proportion** (*noun*): an amount that is part of a whole

**Working with Word Meaning** Help students remember the vocabulary words by asking them to give an example and non-example of each word's meaning.

## CRAFT AND STRUCTURE

**NATHAN:** Well, he is pretty good, you know.

**FREMONT:** Believe me, I KNOW. Look, I'm proud of him, too, but I'm beginning to feel **invisible**.

5 **NATHAN:** Try not to blow it out of **proportion**. At least they're not worrying about you.

**FREMONT:** What do you mean?

**NATHAN:** My parents get all worried that I spend too much time alone—just because I like to spend my time playing guitar. What's so wrong with that?

**FREMONT:** Nothing, I'm pretty sure. Hey, what kind of music do you play?

**NATHAN:** Well, I'm just learning, really, but I could play you a few songs I know sometime. Hey, you want to come over after school?

10 **FREMONT:** Sure. But don't you have to check with your parents?

**NATHAN:** They won't mind. They'll be happy I'm bringing a friend home.

**FREMONT:** All right. There are two things going for this plan. One: I get to hear you play your songs. Two: I won't have to hear about Kevin the Great every minute. (*laughs*)

(*Bell rings. Kids head to classroom doors.*)

**NATHAN:** Cool. See you after school. ★

### Comprehension Check

How does the setting help you better understand what's happening in the drama?

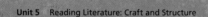

### Support English Language Learners

Students who are learning English may not understand words and phrases with nonliteral meanings, such as "Kevin the Great" and "cool." Point out "Kevin the Great" in the text. Tell students that Fremont is using those words to describe his brother because he feels his parents are treating him as if he were a king. Point out the word *cool*. Explain that Nathan is not saying that he feels cold. Tell students that *cool* is a word people use to say that things are okay. Ask students to use the word *cool* in a sentence.

---

**CITE EVIDENCE**

**C** **Stage directions** tell what the characters in a drama are supposed to do. Underline the two stage directions on this page.

**D** **Scenes** are parts of a play. Just like with chapters in a book, each new scene in a play builds on the one before. Put a star next to the end of the scene. Since this is Scene 1, you know that more scenes will follow. Why might a play have more than one scene?

---

**CITE EVIDENCE**

**C** *I'm looking for stage directions with instructions for the characters. Stage directions are in parentheses and italics.*

*What do the stage directions tell the characters to do?* (laugh, head to the classroom doors)

**D** *Just like a chapter, a scene ends with some sense of closure. This scene ends when the boys go back inside their classroom after recess.*

*Where does the star go to show the end of the scene?* (after Nathan says, "See you after school.") *Do you think the next scene will take place on the playground?* (no) *Why do plays have more than one scene?* (so there can be action in different locations)

### Comprehension Check

**Sample Answer:** The setting helps me understand what is happening in the drama because I can picture where the characters are located.

**Answer Explanation:** Students should realize that knowing the setting helps them visualize the characters and action of the play.

### Review: Distinguishing Literal/Nonliteral Language

Have students use the information they learned about idioms and other nonliteral language to determine the meaning of a nonliteral phrase in the text. You could suggest the first line of the play as an example of an idiom.

## Guided Practice

### Recap Reading Selection

Have students recall what they have learned so far about Nathan and Fremont. They might mention that Fremont's brother plays soccer, that Nathan plays guitar, and that the boys are going to play together after school. Let students know that they will read more about these characters in the next scene of the play.

### Read and Practice

Have partners take turns reading the selection as you circulate to provide support. Model finding scene breaks with Cite Evidence callout A. For callout B, circulate and provide partners with scaffolding as needed. You might use the following suggestions to help students who are having difficulty.

### CITE EVIDENCE

**A** Point out the subheadings for Scenes 2 and 3. Ask students where to place the star to show the last line of dialogue for Scene 2 (next to "NATHAN: I say okay!") Ask where to place the star to show the first line of dialogue for Scene 3. (next to "MRS. JONES: Kevin, we're so proud of you!") Make sure that students star the dialogue and not the stage directions.

**B** By this point, students should know that the setting is written in italics under the scene subheading. *What is the setting for Scene 2?* (Nathan's kitchen) *What is the setting for Scene 3?* (a park)

---

## UNDERSTANDING PARTS OF A DRAMA

**Guided Practice**

**WORDS TO KNOW**
**spotlight**
**tradition**

**CITE EVIDENCE**

**A** Put a star next to the last line of dialogue in Scene 2 and the first line of dialogue in Scene 3.

**B** Circle the setting for Scene 3. How is this setting different from the setting for Scene 2?

*Singing Your Blues Away continued*

### Scene 2

*The kitchen in Nathan's house in the afternoon.*

(*Nathan is strumming on his guitar. Fremont starts to sing some made-up words.*)

**NATHAN:** (*smiling*) Hey, nice voice!

15 **FREMONT:** (*surprised*) Thanks, Nathan. You sound really good on the guitar.

(*Mrs. Ordway pokes her head in.*)

**MRS. ORDWAY:** You guys should take that act on the road! (*laughing*) Really, you sound great. (*She leaves.*)

**FREMONT:** Hey, Nathan, I think I've got an idea. You know how your parents are worried you spend too much time alone?

**NATHAN:** Yeah.

**FREMONT:** And you know how my brother gets all the attention because of his soccer?

20 **NATHAN:** Uh-huh. What's your idea?

**FREMONT:** This Saturday, there's a soccer family picnic. A bunch of kids from school will be there.

**NATHAN:** But why would you want to go to that? You don't even like soccer.

**FREMONT:** True, but there's a **tradition** of people giving speeches and stuff. I'm thinking we could surprise everyone and play a song.

**NATHAN:** Really? I like it. But what song can we play?

25 **FREMONT:** I say we write one ourselves.

**NATHAN:** I say okay! ★

---

## Words to Know

**General Academic Vocabulary**
**tradition** (*noun*): a custom or belief that is handed down from one generation to another

**Domain-Specific Vocabulary**
**spotlight** (*noun*): a light that shines on one particular place on a stage

**Working with Word Meaning** Have students look at how the words are used in the text. Ask students to look in a dictionary for other meanings of the words. Then ask students to use the words in sentences that reflect the meanings in the text.

## CRAFT AND STRUCTURE
### Guided Practice

**Scene 3**

*(A park in late fall. Families with children in soccer uniforms are gathered.)*

**MRS. JONES:** Kevin, we're so proud of you! ★

**MR. JONES:** You really helped your team out there, son.

**KEVIN:** Thanks, Dad.

*(Behind them, Fremont nods to Nathan.)*

30 **NATHAN:** *(picking up his guitar)* Are you ready to grab some **spotlight**?

**FREMONT:** *(smiling)* It's now or never.

### Comprehension Check

1. What do Nathan and Fremont do in Scene 2?

   a. They play a song at a soccer picnic.

   b. They meet at the playground and discuss their problems.

   c. They go to a picnic and hear Mr. and Mrs. Jones praising Kevin.

   (d.) They play and sing and decide to play a song at a picnic.

2. What new characters are introduced in Scene 3?

   (a.) Mr. Jones, Mrs. Jones, Kevin

   b. Mrs. Ordway, Nathan, Fremont

   c. Mr. Jones, Mrs. Jones, Fremont

   d. Kevin, Mrs. Ordway, Mrs. Jones

3. How does Scene 2 build on what happened in Scene 1?

   In Scene 1, the boys discussed their problems and agreed to meet. In

   Scene 2, the boys meet and think of a possible solution to their problems.

Unit 5 ■ Reading Literature: Craft and Structure  **109**

### Guided Practice

### Comprehension Check

**Answer Explanations:**

1. Choice D, *They play and sing and decide to play a song at a picnic*, describes what the boys do in Scene 2. Students can determine the answer by locating the Scene 2 subheading and rereading the scene.

2. Choice A, *Mr. Jones, Mrs. Jones, Kevin*, lists the characters that are introduced in Scene 3. Students can refer back to the text to see which new characters were introduced in the scene.

3. Students should consider the events of both scenes. Students should understand that the events in Scene 2 continue building the story from Scene 1, with the boys meeting and thinking of a solution to the problem introduced in Scene 1.

## Reciprocal Teaching

Form groups of four and assign one of the following roles to each group member: Summarizer, Questioner, Clarifier, and Predictor. In a group discussion, the Summarizers should say what they have learned so far about characters in the play. Questioners should think of something else to ask about the characters. The Clarifiers should answer the question or say where they could look for the answers, and the Predictors should say what they think they will learn next in relation to the characters. Call on different groups to share their ideas with the class.

## Foundational Skills: Fluency

Explain to students that they can read more fluently if they pay attention to words that are treated with special type. These words need extra emphasis. Words that are italicized or written in all capital letters should be emphasized when reading. Model fluent reading of the opening dialogue of Nathan and Fremont in Scene 1 on page 106.

Give students a chance to practice fluent reading with a partner. They may also want to record themselves reading the selection so that they can play it back and listen to their own phrasing for improving prosodic skills. Additional fluency passages and activities can be found at **sadlierconnect.com** and in the *Foundational Skills Handbook*.

## Independent Practice

### Recap Reading Selection

Have a short group discussion about what students have read so far. Ask students if they remember what Fremont and Nathan plan to do at the soccer picnic. Have students discuss the major plot points.

### Read and Apply

Have students read the selection independently as you circulate to provide support. As you circulate, provide students with targeted scaffolding as needed.

### CITE EVIDENCE

**A** Students should look at the stage directions under the Scene 3 subheading for information about the setting. They should notice that "the two boys walk to the center of a stage, where a microphone stands." Students should understand that the boys are performing on a stage.

**B** Students should recognize that the three scenes have different settings. The writer breaks the play into three scenes so the action can take place in three different locations.

---

## UNDERSTANDING PARTS OF A DRAMA

**Independent Practice**

**Singing Your Blues Away** continued

**WORDS TO KNOW**

applaud
react
strum

**CITE EVIDENCE**

**A** Put a star next to the information that helps you understand where the two boys are when they perform in the scene.

**B** Circle the last line of dialogue in the scene. Why did the writer break the play into three scenes?

**Scene 3** continued

(*The two boys walk to the center of a stage, where a microphone stands.*) ★

**FREMONT:** (*speaking into microphone*) Hi, everybody. I'm Kevin's brother Fremont, and this is my buddy, Nathan.

**NATHAN:** Today, we want to sing a song to celebrate the soccer season. Ready?

(*People are unsure how to* **react**. *A few people start to clap, then stop.*)

**NATHAN AND FREMONT:** (*singing*)
Everybody's good at something.
Everybody has a skill.
You all love to play soccer,
And you never have your fill.
(Chorus) So play that soccer, heroes.
Just play it while you can.
Your families love to watch you,
And we are all your fans.

35 **FREMONT:** So while Nathan **strums** his guitar,
And while I sing out the song,
We will celebrate your season,
And you can sing along—(*shouts*) Everybody now!
(Chorus) So play that soccer, heroes.
Just play it while you can.
Your families love to watch you,
And we are all your fans.

(*Crowd* **applauds** *wildly, as Nathan and Fremont bow and walk back to Fremont's family.*)

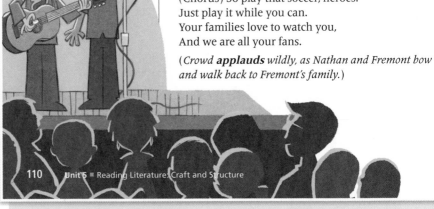

110 Unit 5 ■ Reading Literature: Craft and Structure

---

### Words to Know

**General Academic Vocabulary**
**react** (*verb*): to act in response to someone or something else

**Domain-Specific Vocabulary**
**applaud** (*verb*): to clap hands together in appreciation of someone or something
**strum** (*verb*): to use one's fingers to move an instrument's strings to make music

**Working with Word Meaning** Encourage students to work in partners or small groups to create a brief skit that exemplifies the vocabulary words.

**KEVIN:** (*slapping Fremont on the back*) You're okay, little bro.

**FREMONT:** (*smiling*) Thanks, Kevin. (*looks at Nathan*) Thanks, Nathan.

**NATHAN:** Thank *you* for getting me out of the house!

**FREMONT:** (*laughing as he nudges Nathan*) Thanks to our song for helping us both out!

(*Nathan strums some exit music as curtain closes.*)

**Comprehension Check**  (MORE ONLINE) **sadlierconnect.com**

1. What happens in Scene 3 that the boys prepared for in Scene 2?

   a. Nathan and Fremont talk to Mrs. Ordway.

   **b.** Nathan and Fremont sing at the picnic.

   c. Nathan and Fremont write a song for the picnic.

   d. Nathan and Fremont meet at school.

2. How is Fremont different at the end of Scene 3 from how he was in the first scene?

   a. He is sad.

   b. He is scared.

   **c.** He is happy.

   d. He is jealous.

3. Why did the writer continue Scene 3 on page 110, rather than begin a new scene?

   The action on page 110 (Kevin and Fremont performing) is a

   continuation of the action from pages 108–109, and it all takes place

   in the same setting—the picnic in the park.

Unit 5 ■ Reading Literature: Craft and Structure  **111**

## Independent Practice

**Comprehension Check**

**Answer Explanations:**

1. To arrive at choice B, students must remember that the boys prepare to write a song in Scene 2.

2. Students can arrive at choice C, *He is happy*, by looking at the stage directions at the end of the play. Specifically, Fremont is smiling and laughing.

3. Students should understand that scenes are dependent on continuous action and setting rather than page breaks. A new page does not mean a new scene.

## Critical Comprehension

Use the following questions to help students think more deeply about the text. Students should be prepared to support their answers with evidence from the text.

*In what ways do both boys change over the course of the play?* (Nathan enjoys being out of the house, and Fremont is happy to get some attention at soccer.)

*How would this play be different as a story?* (Answers will vary, but may include that there would not be as much dialogue and the setting might not change as much.)

| **Assess and Respond** |
| --- |
| **If** students have difficulty answering the questions in the Comprehension Check… |
| **Then** assign students roles and have them read the play out loud or act it out. |

## Foundational Skill Review: Consonant Blends

Review consonant blends with students, reminding them that they are two consonants put together. Reinforce to students how they should clearly say the sounds of both letters in the blend. Model how this sounds, exaggerating each specific sound using common words such as *fruit*, *trip*, and *snow*. Explain that students can use this knowledge when they sound out longer or uncommon words, such as these from the passage: *proud*, *grab*, *spotlight*, and *smiling*.

Additional phonics activities can be found in the *Foundational Skills Handbook* at the end of this guide and at **sadlierconnect.com**.

## Guided Instruction

### OBJECTIVE
**Differentiate between a personal point of view and the narrator's or character's point of view.**

### Genre: Narrative Poem

Explain to students that a narrative poem is a story told in poem format. It has characters and a plot like a story. It has common elements of poems such as stanzas and rhyme as well.

### Set the Purpose

Help students understand the purpose for learning the reading skill by asking *Have you ever thought about a situation in a different way from the way someone else thought about it? What did that help you understand?*

### Model and Teach

Read the selection as students follow along in their books.

### CITE EVIDENCE

**A** *I know that a pronoun takes the place of a noun and a stanza is like a paragraph in a poem. Some pronouns are: I, he, she, it, we, etc.*

*Which pronouns are used in stanzas 1 and 2? (they, I, in stanza 1; it, you in stanza 2)*

**B** *The characters in the poem are mentioned by name.*

*What are their names? (Jane, Jack)*

---

# DISTINGUISHING POINTS OF VIEW

## Guided Instruction

**WORDS TO KNOW**
**embarrassed**
**sulked**
**treasure**

> A reader may have a different **point of view** from that of a text's narrator or characters.

### CITE EVIDENCE

**A** Pronouns can help you figure out to whom a **point of view** belongs. Circle all the pronouns in stanza 2.

**B** How many characters are in this poem? Put a star by each character name.

## Forever Friends
### (Genre: Narrative Poem)

1   In any life, people come and they go;
   I know; I've had many a friend.
   But while some friendships have lasted,
   Others have come to an end.
   I've heard about friendships, and
   I've been glad that I had
   Friends so good, so great,
   Why, they've always been rad.

2   For friendship, dear friendship,
   Is more precious than gold.
   It's more valued than money:
   Onto it you must hold.
   Though you can't spend a friend,
   What you earn you should **treasure**.
   You can earn it and save it,
   And that's a great pleasure.

3   Think of what happened
   To young Jack and Jane.
   They were fast friends soon as Jack
   Came into town on a plane.
   When he showed up,
   The new kid in town,
   Three older boys teased him
   And put poor Jack down.

4   Though she'd only just met him,
   Jane thought Jack no fool.
   She told the three bullies,
   "Knock it off, guys, he's cool."

---

## Words to Know

**General Academic Vocabulary**

**embarrassed** (*verb*): felt uncomfortable or foolish in front of others
**sulked** (*verb*): felt unhappy or in a bad mood, and silent about it
**treasure** (*verb*): to hold dear

**Working with Word Meaning** Help students remember the vocabulary words by asking them to give an example and non-example of each word's meaning.

# CRAFT AND STRUCTURE

**Embarrassed** by her scolding,
The boys slunk away,
And Jack and Jane have
Been friends to this day.

5 From that day on,
Jack and Jane were not parted.
They did all together,
And couldn't wait to get started.
When Jack didn't feel well,
Jane for him would care.
When Jane forgot lunch money,
Jack would always share.

6 When Jane's dog got sick,
Jack stayed by her side,
Came along to the vet,
And filled her with pride.
When Jack got braces, he **sulked**;
His teeth were too sore.
But Jane made jokes,
And he laughed once more.

7 Sometimes other kids got jealous
Of what Jack and Jane had.
They tried separating the friends,
Or making them mad.
But Jack and Jane
Could see through it all.
They vowed never to part,
Since they were having a ball.

### Comprehension Check

How do the descriptive words in this passage help you understand what the narrator, Jack, and Jane each think about friendship?

### CITE EVIDENCE

**C** Use of comparisons can show a character's or narrator's point of view. Underline where the writer compares things to friendship in stanza 2. Do you agree or disagree with these ideas?

**D** Third-person pronouns (such as *he* and *her*) can indicate point of view. Box each third-person pronoun in stanza 6. What do they tell you about how these characters view friendship?

## Guided Instruction

### CITE EVIDENCE

**C** *I know that when authors make comparisons, they mention how two different things are alike or different. I'll look in stanza 2 for two things the author thinks are the same or different.*

*The author is saying that two things are the same. What are they?* (friendship and gold/money)

*What is the narrator's point of view about friendship?* (It is very valuable.)

**D** *I'll look in stanza 6 for third-person pronouns. What pronouns are in stanza 6?* (her, he, his)

*Whose point of view is shared in stanza 6?* (Jack's and Jane's) *Do they have the same or different point of view?* (the same)

### Comprehension Check

**Sample Answer:** The descriptive words in the passage give examples of the kind of friendship that Jack and Jane have. I know that Jack and Jane value their friendship, and the narrator thinks it is something special.

**Answer Explanation:** Students should understand that descriptive words help explain a character's point of view.

## Review: Understanding Parts of a Drama

Bring students' attention to the way that the poem is broken up. Ask students if they remember what these parts of poems are called. (stanzas) See if they can recall the way a drama is broken up and what the parts of a drama are called. (scenes) Ask students to compare stanzas and scenes.

### Support English Language Learners

English language learners may need support in understanding idioms. Point out the idiom "having a ball" in stanza 7. Point out to students that the expression does not mean that Jack and Jane are playing with an actual ball. Explain that the expression "having a ball" means that Jack and Jane are having fun together. Ask students to share a time they had a ball with someone.

# Distinguishing Points of View

## Guided Practice

### Recap Reading Selection

Have students recall what they have learned so far about Jane and Jack and friendship in general. They should be able to say that Jane and Jack have a close friendship and that the narrator thinks a friendship like this is something special.

### Read and Practice

Have partners take turns reading the selection as you circulate to provide support. Model distinguishing point of view with Cite Evidence callout A. For callout B, circulate and provide partners with scaffolding as needed. You might use the following suggestions to help students who are having difficulty.

### CITE EVIDENCE

**A** Remind students that they can use pronouns as a clue to determine point of view. The narrator's point of view uses the pronoun *I* in stanza 9.

**B** Students should know that Jane values her friendship with Jack. Tell students to look in stanza 11 for words that show she values their friendship. (loved, feel really blue)

Ask students to brainstorm a list of words they could use to describe how they would feel about moving away from a best friend.

---

## DISTINGUISHING POINTS OF VIEW

### Guided Practice

Forever Friends *continued*

**WORDS TO KNOW**
interfere
prospect
separated

**CITE EVIDENCE**

**A** Find and circle the two stanzas that are from the narrator's point of view.

**B** Underline the words in stanza 11 that show Jane's feelings about her friendship with Jack. How would you feel about moving away from a best friend?

114

8 Jack and Jane never imagined
They'd be **separated**.
They were always together,
As though it were fated.
Each day after school,
They'd race to the park,
And play knights and aliens
Until it got dark.

9 Now let me just say,
If I'd friends like these,
I'd be beside myself;
Life would be full of ease.
It's not easy to find
A good friend like this:
Someone who stays by your side.
Someone you'd miss.

10 But sometimes such friendships
Aren't up to just us.
Life **interferes**,
And creates a fuss.
This was the case
For Jack and for Jane,
As later that year,
Bad news fell like rain.

11 While Jack was relaxing,
It was Jane's turn to worry.
Her mom had a new job;
They had to move in a hurry.
Jane wasn't ready; she <u>loved</u>
School and Jack too.
And the **prospect** of leaving
Made her <u>feel really blue</u>.

---

### Words to Know

**General Academic Vocabulary**

**interfere** (*verb*): to get in the way; slow something down
**prospect** (*noun*): the chance that something will happen
**separated** (*verb*): pulled apart things or people

**Working with Word Meaning** Ask students to use each word in an original sentence. Challenge students to use the new vocabulary terms in a short story about a girl who has to start at a new school.

## CRAFT AND STRUCTURE
### Guided Practice

12  Thoughts of telling Jack
Filled her with dread.
Sure enough, when she told him,
He was so mad he saw red.
"It's not fair," he cried,
"You're my best friend!
"I don't want to lose you.
"Will this be the end?"

### Comprehension Check

**1.** According to stanzas 9 and 10, what does the narrator think about Jack and Jane's friendship?

**a.** The narrator wishes he or she had a friendship like this.

**b.** The narrator explains that he's actually Jack in disguise.

**c.** The narrator says that she had a friend like this once.

**d.** The narrator states that all good friendships must end.

**2.** What problem do Jack and Jane face at this point in their friendship?

**a.** Jack is moving away and wants Jane to come with him.

**b.** Jane is transferring schools, but will stay in the same town.

**c.** Jack has decided that he needs other friends besides Jane.

**d.** Jane is moving away, but they still want to be friends.

**3.** What is the narrator's point of view about friendship? Point out descriptive words used by the narrator to support your answer. Is your point of view the same as the narrator's? Explain.

Sample answer: The narrator thinks friendship is really important and uses

words like "ease" and "miss." I agree that friendship is very important.

My best friends support me and make me laugh.

Unit 5 ■ Reading Literature: Craft and Structure **115**

## Discussion Skills

Remind students that it is acceptable to agree or disagree with something that someone else has said. Students should always strive to come up with their own reasoned conclusions, but they must be able to support them.

Give students some sentence stems to help scaffold an agreement or disagreement:

• *I agree/disagree with that because…*

• *I agree/disagree because of this evidence from the text…*

• *Based on my personal experience…*

• *Based on my understanding…*

• *What makes you agree/disagree with what I said?*

### Guided Practice

### Comprehension Check

**Answer Explanations:**

**1.** The answer, choice A, can be found in stanza 9: "If I'd friends like these, I'd be beside myself."

**2.** Choice D, *Jane is moving away, but they still want to be friends*, best describes the problem that the friends face. All of the other answer choices contain information that is not in the text.

**3.** The narrator's point of view about true friendship is that it is special. Students should note words and phrases, such as *ease* and *stays by your side* in stanza 9. The author also views friendship as sometimes out of one's control. Descriptive words that support this are *not easy to find* and *miss* in stanza 9. Students' own points of view about friendship may differ.

## Numbered Heads Together

Another way to engage students in a comprehension review is to give them a chance to discuss their answers with a small group of their peers. Ask students to number off in their teams from one to four. Announce a question, such as *What is the author's view of Jack and Jane's relationship?* or *How does Jack feel about Jane leaving?* Then set a time limit. Each group of students should try to decide on an answer. Call a number and ask all students with that number to stand and answer the question. Recognize each response and engage in discussion.

## Independent Practice

### Recap Reading Selection

Remind students that they have been reading about Jane and Jack's friendship, which the narrator feels is special. Ask students to tell you the last thing that happened in the poem. (Jane told Jack she is moving away.)

### Read and Apply

Have students read the selection independently. As you circulate, provide students with targeted scaffolding as needed.

### CITE EVIDENCE

**A** Students should know that Jack feels sad about Jane's news, so they should look for words that signal this. (downhearted) He also wants to make sure they stay in touch. (Call me whenever.)

**B** Students should reread stanza 16 to look for forms of communication. (text, talk, phone)

---

**WORDS TO KNOW**
**anew**
**imperiously**

**CITE EVIDENCE**

**A** Underline each word that describes Jack's feelings in stanzas 13 and 14.

**B** Put a star by each of the ideas Jack and Jane have to keep their friendship going in stanza 15. What will they try to do?

Forever Friends *continued*

13 "Me neither," said Jane.
"But what will we do?"
"I'm moving next week;
"How will we stay true?"
"We need a solution,"
Jack said oh so <u>seriously</u>.
"You mustn't forget me," Jane
Ordered **imperiously**.

14 "What, me? Forget you?"
Jack said, <u>downhearted</u>.
"But please promise to help me
Keep up what we've started."
"It's a deal," said Jane.
"Shake on it, will you?"
They shook hands, and with that
Started planning **anew**.

15 Then, "Oh, no," Jane added.
"I'll be all alone,
"With no friends in sight—"
Jack interrupted, "Just phone. ★
"Call me whenever, ★
"And I'll call you too." ★
"Of course, we can e-mail," ★
Jane added. "Well, phew!"

---

## Words to Know

**General Academic Vocabulary**
**anew** (*adverb*): for more time; again
**imperiously** (*adverb*): in the manner of a ruler

**Working with Word Meaning** To help students retain the meaning of the new vocabulary, ask them to restate the definitions in their own words. Then they can try to use each new word in a sentence.

## CRAFT AND STRUCTURE

16  "We'll always be friends,"
    Jack promised, "I swear.
    "And one of these days,
    "You'll come back. That's just fair."
    Jane smiled. "Until then,
    "We'll text, talk, and phone.
    "You'll tell me what's new,
    "And I won't feel alone."

### Comprehension Check          (MORE ONLINE) sadlierconnect.com

**1.** Who is most worried about being alone?

   **(a.)** Jane

   **b.** Jack

   **c.** the narrator

   **d.** Jane and Jack

**2.** Which term below best describes Jane's point of view in stanza 13 about the future of their friendship?

   **(a.)** nervous

   **b.** relaxed

   **c.** happy

   **d.** jealous

**3.** In the end, what viewpoint do Jack and Jane share about their future as friends? Do you have the same viewpoint about their future? Use the poem and your own experiences to explain.

Sample answer: They are hopeful about their future. I do not share their

viewpoint. Although they will try hard, I have had friends who moved

away, and we lost touch.

Unit 5 ■ Reading Literature: Craft and Structure   **117**

### Speaking and Listening Presentation

Have students create a presentation about friendship and its challenges. Have students present to the class. Presenters should:

- state their topic and present appropriate facts and descriptive details.

- use formal language and precise words for effect.

- speak clearly, in complete sentences, and at a reasonable rate.

- answer questions in complete sentences, giving elaboration and detail.

- provide engaging visuals to enhance their presentation.

Listeners should listen attentively and ask questions to better understand the information.

---

### Comprehension Check

**Answer Explanations:**

**1.** Choice A, *Jane*, is supported by the first three lines of stanza 15.

**2.** Choice A, *nervous*, best describes how Jane feels in stanza 13. Students can eliminate *relaxed* and *happy* because they are positive emotions. Jane is not *jealous* of anyone.

**3.** Students should understand that Jane and Jack feel hopeful that they can maintain their friendship despite the distance. Answers will vary about students' viewpoints.

## Critical Comprehension

Use the following questions to help students think more deeply about the text. Students should be prepared to support their answers with evidence from the text.

- *What kind of experiences with friendships do you think the narrator has had?* (The narrator has never had a friendship like Jack and Jane's. He/she may have been disappointed by people in the past.)

- *How would this poem have been different if it were a story or play?* (Sample answers: It would not rhyme. The characters would speak in dialogue.)

### Assess and Respond

**If** students have difficulty answering the questions in the Comprehension Check…

**Then** assign students the characters of Jack and Jane and the narrator. Have students read their parts of the poem aloud.

### OBJECTIVES

- Use vocabulary strategies to determine the meaning of words and phrases, distinguishing literal from nonliteral language.
- Use terms such as *scene* to describe how parts of a story build on each other.
- Differentiate between a personal point of view and the narrator's or character's point of view.

## Genre: Historical Fiction

Explain to students that historical fiction is a fictional story that is set at a time in history. Readers learn about the time period through the story. Authors of historical fiction may alter their word choice or style to fit the time period about which they are writing.

## Path Options

You may want to do a close reading with students; if so, use the supports provided on these pages. Or, you may wish to have the students read the text independently and apply the skills learned in this unit. In either case, students should read the text more than once to facilitate understanding and to be able to answer the Comprehension Check questions correctly.

---

# We Must See the Queen!

(Genre: Historical Fiction)

### Chapter 1
June 28, 1838

1   It was a beautiful day. Mariah was squirming with excitement as soon as she woke up. It was June 28, a day she and her best friend, Laura, who was a few years older, had been looking forward to for months. Today, Victoria would be crowned Queen of Britain.

2   There was going to be a huge parade in the Queen's honor. Mariah and Laura really wanted to go. Things like this didn't happen every day. It was a once-in-a-lifetime experience.

3   Mariah and Laura had spent weeks begging their parents for permission to watch the parade. "Opportunities like this don't grow on trees, Mama!" Mariah said at one point. "Please, can we go?"

4   Her mother had rolled her eyes, having already said she wasn't sure it was a good idea. "Hope springs eternal, eh? Young lady, why do you want to go so badly?"

5   Mariah had clasped her hands together, and her eyes had gleamed with excitement, like two blue stars. "Because it may be my only chance ever to see the Queen! And it's the best day to see her, because it's the day she becomes Queen!"

6   Eventually, Mariah had won, and so had Laura. The two of them were getting to go to the parade.

---

## Support English Language Learners

English language learners may struggle reading this selection independently due to unfamiliar vocabulary. Many of the longer unfamiliar words in the passage, however, are compound words (*lifetime*, *courtyard*, *forehead*, *something*, etc.). Instruct English language learners to pause when they get to a long word and consider if it is a compound word that can be broken into parts for easier decoding.

## CRAFT AND STRUCTURE

**Chapter 2**

7   After breakfast that morning, Mariah hurried over to Laura's house. She didn't have far to go to pick up her best friend. Laura, who was like her big sister, lived just next door. As she rushed past the beautiful old house, Mariah only got more excited. Today, she'd get to see the most famous woman in the world.

8   When she got to Laura's house, Mariah didn't even have to ring the bell. Laura was waiting for her in the courtyard. The two girls hugged, and then Laura tugged on her best friend's sleeve. "We'd better go, Mariah. I don't want to miss anything!"

9   The girls set off on their way to Constitution Hill. Once they got there, they'd be perfectly set up to watch the whole parade, especially the arrival of Queen Victoria.

10   After a few blocks, though, they had a problem. The roads were full of people who were all dressed up for the coronation. It seemed as if people were getting more excited with every passing minute. They were shooting around like hot sparks from a fireplace. They were talking loudly, pushing, and shoving as they tried to get closer to the parade route.

11   Mariah's head started aching with worry. She knew she could count on Laura to figure something out, though. "What should we do, Laura? Do you think we have any chance of getting there in time?"

12   Laura frowned. She wrinkled her forehead like she always did when she concentrated. This made her face as full of creases as an old map. "Hold on, Mariah, let me think." She paused for a few seconds. "What if we cut through the butcher shop? You'll have to be careful not to get your dress dirty," she added, since Mariah was pretty clumsy. "And of course it'll have to be our secret."

Unit 5 ■ Reading Literature: Craft and Structure   **119**

## Support First Reading

Circulate to check students' understanding. As needed, use the following comprehension and strategy check-ins to support basic understanding of the selections as students read.

### Check-in Questions

- *During what time period does the story take place?* (1838) *What is the important historical event that is the basis for the story?* (the coronation of Queen Victoria)

- *What is the problem that Laura and Mariah encounter when they try to watch the parade?* (There are too many people trying to get to the parade and their path is blocked.)

## Review: Distinguishing Literal/Nonliteral Language

Have students determine the meaning of the nonliteral sentence from paragraph 10: "They were shooting around like hot sparks from a fireplace." (Students should be able to explain that the people were moving here and there quickly.)

## Differentiate Instruction

Stopping at multiple points while reading to summarize information is a good strategy that striving readers can employ to aid in comprehension. At the end of each page, have students write down or underline in the text the one or two most important events from that page. As they continue reading, they can review these important events to help aid in comprehension of the general plot development.

## Check-in Question

- *What is Laura's idea for how to get closer to the parade?* (to go through the butcher shop)

## Review: Understanding Parts of a Drama

Remind students that a drama is broken up into scenes. Ask students what parts this story is broken into. (chapters)

## Review: Distinguishing Points of View

Review how to distinguish the points of view of the reader, narrator, and characters. *What are the girls' feelings about the coronation? Find sections of text that support your conclusion.*

*How does the girls' point of view compare with their parents' point of view?*

*If you had lived during this time, how do you think you might have felt about the coronation of the Queen?*

13  "Sure!" said Mariah happily. What were best friends for, after all, if they couldn't share secrets? She and Laura were keeping several secrets already. One was their dislike of the Brickstones' nanny. Another was Laura's wish to someday become an actress. Keeping their shortcut a secret would be a piece of cake. "All right, let's go! Hold on to your hat, Laura," Mariah called over her shoulder as they began to run.

14  The two girls raced across the street to the butcher's. There, they slid through the door and around the greasy counter. The store was much emptier than usual. All the customers were probably on their way to the parade, too.

15  Laura and Mariah ran past the cashier on duty. He looked at them with surprise and maybe a bit of envy. *He's probably jealous he can't go to the parade with us*, Mariah thought. She grinned at her best friend. The two girls hurried to the back of the shop and scampered through the back door.

16  Mariah and Laura stepped into a much less busy street. Now they were one step closer to Constitution Hill. There were only a few blocks to go. They should arrive at the route with plenty of time to see the whole parade.

17  The girls hurried down the street and made a right at the corner by the hat seller's. Just another block and they'd be at the route. Too excited to wait any longer, Mariah broke into a sprint. "Wait for me!" Laura called out.

18  Mariah looked back over her shoulder but didn't stop. "Come on, you slowpoke! What are you waiting for?"

120

## Strategic Reading

You can support all readers by offering them a strategic reading tip: Make predictions as you read. This can help keep readers engaged because they are making inferences and drawing conclusions about the characters and plot. Encourage students to pause as they read to make predictions. As they continue reading, they can check to see if their predictions were accurate or not.

## CRAFT AND STRUCTURE

19   Mariah then bumped straight into a group of people. "Oh, no!" she sighed as Laura caught up and rounded the corner. Laura yelled back, "It's almost as crowded here as it was before!"

20   Mariah looked dejected. "What are we going to do?"

21   Laura spun around slowly, trying to come up with something. "I know! Follow me!" She grabbed Mariah's hand and pulled her along. "We can climb the oak tree two houses down. If we get high enough, we'll have a perfect view!"

22   Mariah's face broke into a wide smile, and she nodded. She and Laura rushed over to the tree. Laura made a basket with her hands and boosted Mariah up to the first branch. Then she jumped and followed Mariah up until they found a wide, comfortable branch to perch on.

23   Mariah giggled. "Look at us! We're like jaguars."

24   Laura grinned and said, "Yeah! Jaguars about to see the Queen."

25   Then they heard the roar of the crowd. The parade had started, and the Queen was on her way.

### Comprehension Check

**1.** Reread paragraph 5. What comparison is being made in this paragraph through figurative language?

**(a.)** A comparison of Mariah's eyes and two stars

**b.** A comparison of two stars with each other

**c.** A comparison of Mariah's eyes and excitement

**d.** A comparison of two stars and excitement

**2.** If this were a play, how many scenes would it have?

**a.** 1

**(b.)** 2

**c.** 3

**d.** 4

Unit 5 ■ Reading Literature: Craft and Structure   **121**

### Research to Build Knowledge

Let students know that there is still a monarchy in Great Britain today. Challenge them to find the members of the royal family online, and see if they can figure out the lineage from Queen Victoria in 1838 until present day. You may wish to assign specific members of the royal family to student pairs or groups and have them report some brief biographical information to the class. Extend this activity by encouraging students to watch videos of the royal wedding of Prince William and Kate Middleton to see the crowds of people who witnessed it.

## Multiple Readings for Critical Comprehension

Have students reread this selection and pose questions that focus on critical comprehension. Remind them to annotate text in a way that will support their comprehension.

● *Do the girls act in a way that they should not? What do they do that might get them in trouble?* (sneak through the butcher's shop, climb a tree)

● *Why might the author have chosen to write this story as historical fiction?* (The event of the coronation is a good way to show how close friends support each other and have an adventure. It makes the story more interesting to have it set in an historical time.)

## Self-Select Text

As preparation for Connect Across Texts, have students select one of the four selections in this unit and reread it independently. Students can access full pdf versions of the selections at **sadlierconnect.com**.

### Comprehension Check

Begin scoring students' understanding of unit skills and texts from Comprehension Check on this page through Connect Across Texts on page 123. Use students' total score to determine their readiness for the Unit 5 Review on page 125.

## Multiple-Choice Questions: *1 point each*

**1.** Students should realize that the word *like* helps make clear the comparison between Mariah's eyes and blue stars, choice A.

**2.** The story is broken up into two chapters. The logical conclusion is that if it were a play, it would be broken up into two scenes, choice B.

## Short-Answer questions:
### 2 points each

### Item 3 Rubric

| | |
|---|---|
| 2 | Students can use pronouns and descriptive words to describe the girls' point of view and give their own point of view. |
| 1 | Students can give their point of view with reasons but have trouble connecting pronouns and descriptive words with the girls' point of view. |
| 0 | Students cannot give supporting reasons for their opinion or describe the girls' point of view. |

### Item 4 Rubric

| | |
|---|---|
| 2 | Students correctly identify the figurative language in the paragraph and use the text to support assertions about the characters' feelings. |
| 1 | Students are able to identify the figurative language but have trouble explaining how it connects to the characters' feelings. |
| 0 | Students cannot identify the figurative language or connect that to the characters' feelings. |

## Theme Wrap-Up

Lead students in a group discussion on the theme of best friends. *What are some challenges that friends face? What are some of the rewards of friendship?* (Students should be able to discuss some of the complexities and varieties of friendships. Answers will vary.)

3. How do the pronouns and descriptive words in the story help you understand Laura and Mariah's point of view about seeing the Queen of England? How would you feel about fighting the crowd for a view of the Queen?

Sample answer: In this story, the third-person pronouns "she" and "her" refer to Laura or Mariah. They tell us about these characters' points of view, such as their feelings about seeing the Queen. Descriptive words like "beautiful," "excited," and "famous" in paragraph 7 show how thrilled Mariah is at the possibility of seeing the Queen. This is a point of view Laura has too. It would be fun to see the Queen, but I think I would be less thrilled, since I don't like crowds.

4. Put a star by the example of figurative language in paragraph 12. How does this language emphasize the characters' feelings? Support your answer with text evidence.

Sample answer: In paragraph 12, figurative language is used in the phrase "made her face as full of creases as an old map." This helps the reader understand that Laura is worried and trying really hard to come up with a plan to see the Queen. She's trying so hard, that she doesn't look like herself. The descriptive words "concentrated," "wrinkled," and "frowned" also show Laura's upset, and serious about not missing the Queen.

## Extend Thinking: Assess

Ask students to consider the friendships discussed in each of the reading selections: *Which friendship do you think is the most rewarding and why?* Instruct students that they should be able to cite evidence from the texts in their arguments. You may wish to have students with different answers argue their points to sway their classmates.

## CONNECT ACROSS TEXTS

### Compare and Contrast Texts

In this unit, you have read four stories about friendship. You learned about relationships between people and service dogs, between two boys, between a boy and a girl, and between two girls in Victorian England. Now, pick out two of the four texts you read for this unit. Using the Venn diagram below, map out what the stories have in common and what is unique about them. Think about the ways friendship is presented in each text. Be prepared to discuss your ideas.

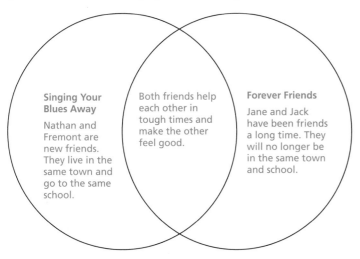

**Singing Your Blues Away**

Nathan and Fremont are new friends. They live in the same town and go to the same school.

Both friends help each other in tough times and make the other feel good.

**Forever Friends**

Jane and Jack have been friends a long time. They will no longer be in the same town and school.

### Return to the Essential Question

How do authors craft stories?

In small groups or as a class, discuss the Essential Question. Think about what you have learned about figurative language, sections of a text (like scenes or chapters), and point of view. Use evidence from the four unit texts to answer the question.

Unit 5 ■ Reading Literature: Craft and Structure  **123**

### Connect Across Texts: *4 points* Review Reading Selections

Put students into groups, giving each the responsibility to summarize one of the four reading selections. Ask volunteers from each group to help the class recall the main ideas from each selection.

### Compare and Contrast Texts

Review the directions on page 123 with students. Instruct students to write the titles of their chosen selections in the outer parts of each circle.

**Venn Diagram Rubric**

| | |
|---|---|
| 4 | Student has identified two selections and recorded four or more characteristics in their proper places. |
| 3 | Student has identified two selections and recorded at least three characteristics in their proper places. |
| 2 | Student has identified two selections and recorded at least three characteristics but may have trouble categorizing them properly. |
| 1 | Student has identified two selections and recorded at least one characteristic. |
| 0 | Student did not complete the assignment or demonstrated no understanding of selections. |

### Support Essential Question Discussion

Have students reread the Essential Question. Challenge them to finish this sentence: *When they write stories, authors use…*

If students have difficulty responding, prompt them by asking how figurative language, structure of a text, and point of view play a part in stories.

### Assess and Respond (pages 121–123)

| If | Then |
|---|---|
| Students scored 0–4 points, they are **Developing** their understanding of unit skills. | Provide students with reading support and more intensive modeling of skills. |
| Students scored 5–7 points, they are **Improving** their understanding of unit skills. | Use students' scores to target areas that are weak and review those specific skills. |
| Students scored 8–10 points, they are **Proficient** In their understanding of unit skills. | Have these students move on. They are ready for the formal assessment. |

## OBJECTIVE
**Determine the meaning of figurative language, such as idioms.**

### Guided Instruction

Review the Guided Instruction section on page 124 with students. Be sure they understand that an idiom is a type of nonliteral, or figurative, phrase. The nonliteral meaning has little to do with the literal meaning. By understanding the meaning of nonliteral phrases, they can understand the meaning of the text.

### Guided Practice

If students are having trouble, help to work through the possibilities by reviewing both the literal and nonliteral meanings in the Guided Instruction. Students can use the definitions to help determine which meaning is used in the sentences.

### Independent Practice

If students are having trouble using the idiom *hold on to your hat*, have them first explain what the nonliteral meaning of the phrase is. Then have them use it in a sentence.

### Apply to Reading

Have students return to "We Must See the Queen!" to hunt for phrases that have nonliteral meanings. They may find "Opportunities like this don't grow on trees" (page 118, paragraph 3) and "Keeping their shortcut a secret would be a piece of cake" (page 120, paragraph 13).

---

**LANGUAGE**

## Literal and Nonliteral Meanings

**Guided Instruction** Nonliteral, or **figurative**, language is language that means something other than what the words say.

An idiom is an example of figurative language. Idioms are popular expressions that have been used for a long time. The meaning of an idiom can be much different from the literal meanings of its words. Read this sentence from "We Must See the Queen!": *Keeping their shortcut a secret would be a piece of cake*. The idiom *that's a piece of cake* means "that is really easy."

| | |
|---|---|
| **bend over backwards** | 1. nonliteral meaning: to do whatever is needed to help |
| | 2. literal meaning: to completely bend one's back |
| **a green thumb** | 1. nonliteral meaning: someone good at gardening |
| | 2. literal meaning: someone's thumb is the color green |

Look at the chart to find other examples of nonliteral idiomatic phrases.

**Guided Practice** Determine whether each sentence uses an idiom or not. In the blank before each sentence, write "n" for *nonliteral* or "l" for *literal* meaning.

___l___ **1.** As he painted, he saw that he had a green thumb.

___n___ **2.** Look at her garden; she has a real green thumb.

___n___ **3.** His mom bent over backwards to make his birthday happy.

___l___ **4.** She had to bend over backwards to get under the fence.

**Independent Practice** Using the phrase *hold on to your hat*, write one sentence that contains an idiom, or nonliteral meaning, and one that contains a literal meaning.

_____

_____

_____

_____

---

## Support English Language Learners

Students whose first language is not English may have difficulty knowing when a phrase is supposed to have a nonliteral meaning. Work with these students to complete the Guided Practice and point out how context can help one determine if the author is using the phrase in a literal or nonliteral way. Students should see if a literal interpretation makes sense in the context of the sentence.

Knowing idioms requires memorization and familiarity with the language, so provide additional example sentences for each idiom.

**UNIT 5 REVIEW**

Read the following passage in which nonliteral language and a narrator's point of view appear in the stanzas of a poem. Then answer the questions on pages 125 and 126.

# Friendship—Yum

(Genre: poem)

1 What does the word *friendship*
Mean to you?
Is it about being faithful
To friends pure and true?
Does it mean trusting others
With all your might?
Does it mean always agreeing
With never a fight?

2 I think friendship's like chocolate
And fruit combined.
It's delicious and nutritious,
And sometimes it's mine.
Look out for nice friends,
And if a fine one you meet,
Hold on; a great friendship
Is good enough to eat.

**Fill in the circle of the correct answer choice.**

**1.** Which word in stanza 2 shows the opinion belongs to the narrator?

● I

○ delicious

○ nice

○ you

**2.** In which stanza of the poem does the narrator compare friendship to food?

○ stanza 1

● stanza 2

## Unit Summary

At this point, students have had instruction and practice in reading literary text, with a focus on learning about different kinds of friendships. Students have also learned different strategies for determining the meaning of nonliteral language, understanding the parts of dramas and stories, and distinguishing points of view. Students have done an independent close reading of text, practiced working with concepts across texts, and practiced working with idioms. They should be well-prepared for the review section.

## Introduce the Review

Explain to students that they will read a new passage that is related to the unit's theme and the selections they have already read. Instruct students to read the passage carefully and then answer the questions on pages 125 and 126.

### Answer Explanations

Scoring: Items 1–6 on pages 125–126 are worth 1 point each. See the rubrics on the next page for guidance scoring the short answer questions on page 126.

**1.** The narrator telling the story in the poem uses the pronoun *I* to express his or her point of view.

**2.** Stanza 2 compares friendship to chocolate and fruit.

## Self-Assessment: Progress Check

Have students revisit the Progress Check on page 97 and respond to the questions again. Ask them to compare their Before and After responses.

You may wish to have students rate their answers on a scale of 0–2 rather than simply checking (or not checking) the box. Instruct them to write a 0 if they feel they do not understand the given skill at all, a 1 if they feel they have some understanding, and a 2 if they feel they have a solid grasp of the skill.

# Unit 5 Review

## Answer Explanations

**3.** The sentences in stanza 1 sound like a person talking. The equivalent in a drama is dialogue.

**4.** The word *like* suggests a figurative expression will follow.

**5.** Students should underline the first and last two lines in stanza 2.

**6.** "Hold on" means that people should keep their good friends.

### Item 7 Rubric

| | |
|---|---|
| 2 | Student rewrites one idea about friendship using figurative language. |
| 1 | Student identifies one idea about friendship but does not use figurative language correctly. |
| 0 | Student does not identify an idea about friendship or use figurative language. |

### Item 8 Rubric

| | |
|---|---|
| 2 | Student correctly identifies points of view of both stanzas. |
| 1 | Student correctly identifies point of view of one stanza. |
| 0 | Student does not correctly identify point of view of either stanza. |

### Item 9 Rubric

| | |
|---|---|
| 2 | Answer characterizes the narrator's point of view correctly. |
| 1 | Answer mentions the narrator's point of view. |
| 0 | Answer does not mention point of view. |

### Item 10 Rubric

| | |
|---|---|
| 2 | Student clearly states point of view and gives logical support. |
| 1 | Student states point of view and gives limited reasons in support. |
| 0 | Student does not state point of view. |

---

## UNIT 5 REVIEW

**3.** If the poem was instead a drama, what part of a drama would stanza 1 be?

- ● dialogue
- ○ setting
- ○ characters
- ○ stage directions

**4.** Which word in stanza 2 hints that figurative language will follow?

- ○ it's
- ○ fine
- ○ good
- ● like

**5.** Underline the nonliteral language in stanza 2.

**6.** Write what the author means by the idiom "Hold on."

The author means you should keep your good friends.

**7.** Select one idea about friendship from the poem. Rewrite the idea using figurative or nonliteral language.

Sample answer: being faithful to friends Rewrite: How does a good friend show her worth? Will she follow you to the ends of the earth?

**8.** How does the point of view change from stanza 1 to 2?

Stanza 1 asks for the reader's point of view, using a series of questions. Stanza 2 states the writer's point of view directly.

**9.** What is the narrator's point of view about friendship?

Sample answer: Friendship is "delicious and nutritious." We should "hold on" to good friends because they're important and wonderful.

**10.** Do you share the narrator's point of view on friendship?

Sample answer: I would not compare friendship to food, but I agree it's important to hold on to good friends when you find them.

## Analyze Student Scores

| | |
|---|---|
| **11–14 pts Strong** | Student has a good grasp of the skills and concepts taught in this unit. Point out any mistakes the student has made and explain the correct answers if necessary. |
| **7–10 pts Progressing** | Student is struggling with some skills or concepts. Identify the specific skills that are problematic to target a review of instruction. |
| **0–6 pts Emerging** | Student is having serious problems understanding the skills and concepts taught in this unit. Student may need to redo the work with a higher level of support. |

## Introducing UNIT 6

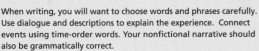

In this unit about friendship, you will learn how to write a nonfictional narrative. A nonfictional narrative is a story about a real experience or event.

When you write a nonfictional narrative, you want to carefully think about the event sequence. The story is told in the order it happened. As a writer, you will include a beginning, middle, and end.

When writing, you will want to choose words and phrases carefully. Use dialogue and descriptions to explain the experience. Connect events using time-order words. Your nonfictional narrative should also be grammatically correct.

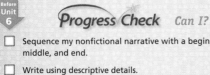

### Progress Check    Can I?

Before Unit 6 | | After Unit 6

- [ ] Sequence my nonfictional narrative with a beginning, middle, and end. [ ]
- [ ] Write using descriptive details. [ ]
- [ ] Write using time-order words to show the order of events. [ ]
- [ ] Use dialogue to develop events. [ ]
- [ ] Write using the correct tense of a verb. [ ]
- [ ] Write using regular and irregular verbs. [ ]
- [ ] Write using correct subject-verb agreement. [ ]
- [ ] Spell correctly when adding suffixes to base words. [ ]

Unit 6 ■ Text Types and Purposes: Write Nonfictional Narratives

**Student Page 127**

## Progress Check

The Progress Check is a self-assessment feature that students can use to gauge their own progress. Research shows that when students take accountability for their own learning, their motivation increases.

Before students begin work on Unit 6, have them check the boxes next to any item that they feel they can do well. Explain that it is fine if they don't check any of the boxes. Tell them that they will have an opportunity to learn about and practice all of these items while studying the unit. Let them know that near the end of the unit they will have a chance to reconsider how well they can do each item on the list.

Before students begin their Unit 4 Review on page 139, have them revisit this page. You can use this information to work with students on any items they don't understand before they tackle the Review.

## HOME ◆ CONNECT...

The Home Connect feature is a way to keep parents or other adult family members apprised of what their children are learning. The key learning objectives are listed, and some ideas for related activities and discussions are included.

Explain to students that they can share the Home Connect page with their parents or other adult family members in their home. Let students know how much time the class will be spending on this unit so they can plan their time accordingly at home.

Encourage students and their parents to share their experiences using suggestions on the Home Connect. You may wish to make a place to post some of this work.

### HOME ◆ CONNECT...

In this unit, children will learn to write about real events and experiences as part of the **nonfictional narrative** form. Explain that many people enjoy recording their experiences in diaries, journals, or blogs. These can be records of special events and exeriences. Encourage your child to retell the events of a special experience, such as a trip to the zoo or losing a tooth.

When writing a nonfictional narrative, your child will be asked to **sequence events** in the order they occurred. As your child retells a special event, ask: *What happened first? What happened next? What happened last?* Help your child think of some **descriptive details** about his or her special event. Ask what was said during the event. This will add **dialogue** and interest to your child's narrative. Encourage him or her to **provide a good ending** by explaining what made the event special and how he or she felt.

**On the Go:** Show your child examples of child-friendly blogs—perhaps a travel blog or movie blog for family movies. Then, ask your child to write about his or her experiences. Encourage him or her to select one important recent event. If you wish, ask your child to share the blog with family or friends who don't live nearby.

128    Unit 6 ■ Writing: Text Type and Purposes—Nonfictional Narratives

### IN THIS UNIT, YOUR CHILD WILL...

- Learn to write a nonfictional narrative using dialogue, descriptive details, and a clear sequence of events.
- Learn to use time-order words such as *next, then,* and *last* to show the order of events.
- Learn specific language skills and use them in writing a nonfictional narrative:
  - Write verbs to show actions in the narrative.
  - Use the correct verb tense to show when the action happened.
  - Correctly use regular and irregular verbs such as *I blow a bubble* and *I blew a bubble.*
  - Use correct singular and plural subject-verb agreement.
  - Recognize suffixes that change the meaning of a base word.

### WAYS TO HELP YOUR CHILD

Discuss special events with your child. For example, instead of telling about the weekend, encourage your child just to tell about dinner at Grandma's. Ask questions: *What did it look like? How did you feel?* Descriptive details add to the event.

**ONLINE**
For more Home Connect activities, continue online at sadlierconnect.com

**Student Page 128**

# UNIT PLANNER

| Theme: Best Friends<br>Curriculum Connection:<br>Language Arts | Focus |
|---|---|
| **WRITING MODEL**<br>pp. 130–132 | *A Hand to Help* |
| **WRITING PRACTICE**<br>p. 133 | **ORGANIZATIONAL STRUCTURE:** Organizer |
| **LANGUAGE MINI-LESSONS**<br>pp. 134–137 | • Verbs and Verb Tenses<br>• Regular and Irregular Verbs<br>• Subject-Verb Agreement<br>• Suffixes |
| **SPEAKING AND LISTENING**<br>p. 138 | Return to the Essential Question |
| **UNIT 6 REVIEW**<br>pp. 139–140 | • Language Skills Summary<br>• Writing Process Summary |

## Objective(s)

Write a nonfictional narrative that develops a real experience or event using effective techniques, descriptive details, and clear event sequences.

Plan and develop a nonfictional narrative with effective techniques, descriptive details, and clear event sequences.

- Use the correct verb tenses in writing.
- Use the correct forms of regular and irregular verbs in writing.
- Use subject-verb agreement in writing.
- Use conventional spelling for adding suffixes to base words.

- Engage effectively in a range of collaborative discussions.
- Follow agreed-upon rules of discussion, including asking and answering questions.

## Unit Assessment

- Unit 6 Review *pp. 139–140*

## Additional Assessment Options

- Performance Task 1 *pp. 141A–145 and 146*
  **ALSO ONLINE**
- Performance Task 2 *pp. 259A–263 and 264*
  **ALSO ONLINE**

**Optional Purchase:**

- iProgress Monitor **ONLINE**
- Progress Monitor Student Benchmark Assessment Booklet

## **ONLINE** Digital Resources

- Home Connect Activities
- Additional Practice
- Teacher Resources
- iProgress Monitor (optional purchase)

**Go to SadlierConnect.com to access your Digital Resources.**

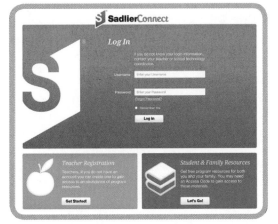

**For more detailed instructions see page T3.**

## LEARNING PROGRESSIONS

In this unit, students will learn how to write a nonfictional narrative about friendship. In order to learn the skills necessary to craft a nonfictional narrative, students will further develop skills learned in second grade. They should be encouraged to retain these skills, as they will continue to build on them in fourth grade.

**Establishing a Situation**

- By the end of grade 2, students should be able to write a narrative in which they recount a well-elaborated event or sequence of events.

- In grade 3, students will learn to use effective narrative techniques, such as by establishing a situation and a narrator.

- When students move to grade 4, they will continue to develop their narrative writing techniques by orienting the reader with a situation and a narrator.

**Dialogue, Details, and Descriptions**

- By the end of grade 2, students will be able to write nonfictional narratives that include details to describe actions, thoughts, and feelings.

- In grade 3, students will build on their abilities by using temporal words and phrases to show the sequence of events.

- During grade 4, students will continue to develop their narrative technique by using transitional words and phrases to clarify sequences of events and concrete words and sensory details to convey experiences.

**Conclusions**

- In grade 2, students learned to provide a concluding statement.

- In grade 3, students will learn to provide a sense of closure to their narrative.

- These skills prepare them for grade 4, when they will learn to provide a conclusion that follows from the narrated experiences and events.

# Text Types and Purposes: Write Nonfictional Narratives

## Essential Question:
How do writers develop nonfictional narratives?

## Essential Question:
How do writers develop nonfictional narratives?

Students will learn how writers craft nonfictional narratives using effective techniques such as dialogue, details, and a clear sequence.

### Theme: Best Friends
Students will write a nonfictional narrative about friendship. The friendship can be with a person or a pet.

### Curriculum Connection: Language Arts
Students will use what they have already learned about reading fictional narratives as they write their own nonfictional narrative.

### Connect Reading to Writing
Remind students that they read several forms of fictional narratives in Unit 5 including realistic fiction, drama, poetry, and historical fiction. In this unit, students will build upon what they have learned to write their own nonfictional narrative.

## Writing Handbook

If students need extra practice with writing a nonfictional narrative, refer them to the *Writing Handbook* on pages 275–283. The Writing Handbook gives students detailed instruction on planning, drafting, revising, and editing their writing. They will also find tips on producing, publishing, and presenting their writing.

# Write Nonfictional Narratives

## OBJECTIVE

Write a nonfictional narrative that develops a real experience or event using effective techniques, descriptive details, and clear event sequences.

## Introduce: Organizational Structure

Draw students' attention to the nonfictional narrative organizer in the left margin and point out the key elements. Ask students to look for these key elements as you read and analyze the Student Model together.

## Analyze a Student Model

**EVENT SEQUENCE:** Tell students that a narrator is the person telling the story, and an event is something that happens. *I know that writers tell about events in a narrative.*

*What event is described in the first paragraph?* (The narrator is crying at a skating party because she doesn't know how to skate.) *How does the writer get the reader's attention?* (by describing the balloons and the loud music)

### CREATING AN ORGANIZATIONAL STRUCTURE

Abbey used an outline to organize her nonfictional narrative. It divides the sequence of events into three sections: beginning, middle, and end.

Title: _____
Characters: _____

Story Events:

Beginning:

Middle:

End:

### EVENT SEQUENCE

- The beginning of the narrative introduces the event and the narrator.
- It uses words for effect and gets the reader's attention.

*Underline a sentence that tells what happened at the beginning.*

## Read a Student Model

Abbey is in the third grade. She has been asked to write a nonfictional narrative about a special day with a friend. She has been asked to use a clear event sequence and to describe her thoughts, feelings, and actions. As you read her nonfictional narrative, think about what event you will share and what words you will use to describe the event.

### A Hand to Help

Lots of colored balloons clung to the ceiling. Loudspeakers blared my favorite music. <u>It was a party, so why was I sitting in the middle of the floor crying?</u> It was a skating party, and I had never been on skates before.

My mom had carefully fastened my bubblegum-pink skates. She turned around to help my little brother with his black ones. I tried to stand up, but instead I wobbled and fell on the shiny hardwood floor. My knees buckled and my hands stung as I tried to break my fall. I felt embarrassed.

**130**   Unit 6 ■ Text Types and Purposes: Write Nonfictional Narratives

### Genre: Nonfictional Narrative

Explain to students that in a nonfictional narrative, the writer recounts an event or experience that actually happened. By using effective storytelling techniques, such as descriptive details and dialogue, the writer can tell a compelling personal story.

Not all nonfictional narratives are personal stories. History books, newspaper and magazine articles about current events, and biographies are also nonfictional narratives that retell real events not experienced by the writer. These forms of nonfiction narratives require the writer to do research and conduct interviews to get the facts behind the true stories.

As I watched my friends skating effortlessly around and around the rink, I wanted to crawl into a hole. Emma waved from across the room. "Oh no! She's coming over here," I thought.

Emma glided to a graceful stop in front of me. I peeked up at her. She had a big smile on her face.

★ "Would you like to go for a spin?" she asked.

I shook my head no. She tried to bend down closer but lost her balance. Her hands were flying around as she tried to break her fall. Then she ended up on the floor just like me.

Emma laughed. "I think I spend more time falling than I do skating!"

"At least you can stand up. I can't skate at all," I replied.

"You will, too. We'll hold onto the rail until you can go on your own."

Having a friend by my side gave me a lot of confidence. I grabbed the rail and Emma's hand in a tight grip as I slowly pulled myself off the floor. I wobbled but eventually managed to stand on my own two feet. In the beginning, I held on to the rail and pulled myself along.

**DIALOGUE AND DESCRIPTIONS**

- Dialogue shows thoughts and feelings of characters.
- Descriptions give details about how things look, smell, sound, or feel.

*Underline descriptive words in the first paragraph on this page that show how the narrator feels.*

*Put a star next to Emma's first line of dialogue.*

**EVENT SEQUENCE**

The middle of the nonfictional narrative continues the sequence of events in the order they happened.

**TIME-ORDER WORDS AND PHRASES**

Words such as *before*, *until*, and *eventually* tell when events happen. Use time-order words and phrases to signal the order of events and make the event sequence clear.

*Circle words that show the sequence of events.*

## Analyze a Student Model

**DIALOGUE AND DESCRIPTIONS:** Tell students that the writer uses dialogue to show the thoughts and feelings of the narrator and other people in the narrative. Ask them to point out an example of dialogue in the text. ("Would you like to go for a spin?") Ask how they know the words are dialogue. (The words are set inside quotation marks.)

Point out that the writer includes details of the party to enhance her story. Ask students how these details help them imagine the scene.

**EVENT SEQUENCE:** Point out to students that the events are told in the order they happened. *What happened when Emma tried to bend closer?* (She fell beside Abbey.)

**TIME-ORDER WORDS AND PHRASES:** Tell students that time-order words indicate the order of events in the sequence. Point out the time-order word *as*. Help students identify other time-order words in Abbey's narrative. (*as*, *eventually*, *in the beginning*)

## Support English Language Learners

Help English language learners by previewing time-order words. Write this list of common time-order words and phrases on the board: *first, second, last, before, after, now, later, next, then, in the beginning, eventually,* and *finally*). Define the words if necessary, and then create a time line showing how they relate to each other. Invite students to tell about something that happened to them recently. Guide them as they retell the event by pointing out the relevant time-order words that will help make the story coherent.

# Write Nonfictional Narratives

## Analyze a Student Model

**PROVIDE A STRONG ENDING:**
Review the end of Abbey's story with the students. Ask if any of them have been in a similar situation, either needing help from or giving help to a friend. *What are Abbey's final feelings about her party that day?* (She learned what a great friend Emma was.) Point out how Abbey's conclusion brings the narrative to a close.

## Evaluate a Writer's Work

Organize a group discussion about Abbey's narrative. Remind students that effective nonfictional narratives include details and dialogue, and use time-order words to show a clear sequence of events. *How well did Abbey include the elements of a good nonfictional narrative?* Students should cite evidence from the Student Model to support their answers. If they don't think Abbey included enough details or dialogue or showed a clear sequence of events, have them explain their thinking.

## Model: Organizational Structure

Ask students to think about how Abbey might have used an organizer to plan for her nonfictional narrative. On a board or projector, post the organizer on page 133. Have students help you fill in the organizer using details from Abbey's narrative. Ask them to include time-order words that tell when events happened.

Students will use the blank organizer in their books to plan their own nonfictional narrative. Once they have completed an organizer, they will draft their own nonfictional narrative based on their notes.

## WRITE NONFICTIONAL NARRATIVES

Then, I released my grip on the rail but my hand stayed close to it.

By the end of the party, I was skating around and around with everyone else. It was so much fun to glide and coast. It felt a little like flying. I felt brave for trying something new and scary. I couldn't have done it without my friend. Emma never left my side. She helped me laugh when I would get upset. She cheered me on when I was doing well. It wasn't learning to skate that made the day special. It was learning what a great friend Emma had been to me.

**PROVIDE A STRONG ENDING**
The ending tells how the events worked out or how the writer felt about the events.
*Underline the words that Abbey used to signal the ending.*

**132** Unit 6 ■ Text Types and Purposes: Write Nonfictional Narratives

### Review: Distinguishing Literal/Nonliteral Language

Remind students that when they read the realistic fictional narratives in Unit 5, they learned how to distinguish literal language from nonliteral language. If necessary, remind students that nonliteral language includes figures of speech, such as "bend over backwards" or "a green thumb." The meaning of the words taken together is different from the dictionary definitions of the individual words. Tell students that they should consider using nonliteral language in their own nonfictional narratives. Nonliteral language is colorful and can make their writing more interesting.

**MORE ONLINE** sadlierconnect.com

Use an organizer like Abbey's to plan your own nonfictional narrative about a special day with a friend. Then write a first draft of your story on a separate piece of paper. Don't forget to use dialogue, descriptions, and time-order words in your narrative. You will use this draft to write your final story draft in the Unit 6 Review section on page 140.

**Title:** _____

**Characters:** _____

_____

**Story Events:**

| Beginning: |
| --- |
| |

| Middle: |
| --- |
| |

| End: |
| --- |
| |

Unit 6 ■ Text Types and Purposes: Write Nonfictional Narratives **133**

## Create: Organizational Structure

### Brainstorming

Remind students that some nonfictional narratives are about the writer's personal experiences. As a class, brainstorm common experiences that students could write about. Make a list of the students' topic ideas on the board or projector for them to use as they plan their writing.

### Planning

Students will use the organizer on page 133 to plan their nonfictional narrative.

- Students should first choose an event or experience to write about.
- Next, they should make a list of the characters that will be in the narrative.
- Have students list the events in chronological order, using time-order words to show the sequence.

### Drafting a Nonfictional Narrative

Instruct students to refer to their organizer as they draft their nonfictional narrative on a separate piece of paper. Be sure students have a beginning, a clear sequence of events, dialogue, descriptive details, and an ending.

## Introduce the Writing Process

Remind students that in order to write their best nonfictional narrative, they must plan, draft, revise, and edit it. These are all steps of the writing process. For more on the writing process, see the *Writing Handbook* on page 275 of this guide.

| Assess and Respond |
| --- |
| **If** students have difficulty turning their organizer into a draft, |
| **Then** draw a flow chart on the board. Ask students to tell you events as you write them in the chart. Then ask students to orally retell the events you wrote by using time-order words. |

| Differentiate Instruction |
| --- |

Struggling students might not yet be ready to write a nonfictional narrative on their own. Form a writing group to support these students.

Lead the group in a shared writing experience in which students brainstorm experiences, decide on a topic, collaborate to complete the organizer, and then draft a nonfictional narrative. Be sure that every member of the group gets a chance to contribute.

## OBJECTIVE
**Use the correct verb tenses in writing.**

### Guided Instruction

Make sure students understand that verb tense helps readers determine when an action happened. Have students study the boldface words in the example, and ask them to identify when the actions happen—in the past, in the present, or in the future. Point out that singular verbs in the present tense end in -s or -es, but plural verbs in the present tense do not have any suffixes. Verbs in the past tense usually end in –ed. Future tense verbs have the helping verb *will* in front of them.

### Guided Practice

Point out how the word at the beginning of each sentence helps identify the tense. Ask students how to change the verb *walk* from the present tense to the past and future tenses.

### Independent Practice

Provide additional examples of sentences with different verb tenses. Have students identify the verb tense in each.

---

**Assess and Respond**

**If** students are having trouble determining which tense the verb should be in,

**Then** have them look for time-order words such as *yesterday*, *today*, *tomorrow*, *next*, and *before* to help them decide when the action takes place.

---

# LANGUAGE

## Verbs and Verb Tenses

**Guided Instruction** A **verb tense** tells when an action happens. When an action happens now or regularly, the verb is in the **present tense**.

> *Kylie **visits** Beth at her house.*
> *Kylie and Sarah **visit** Beth at her house.*

When an action has already happened, the verb is in the ***past tense***.

> *Last week, Kylie **visited** Beth at her house.*

When an action is going to happen, the verb is in the ***future tense***.

> *Tomorrow, Kylie **will visit** Beth at her house.*

**Guided Practice** Write the correct tense of the word in parentheses.

**1.** Today, I _____walk_____ to Tom's house. (walk)

**2.** Yesterday, I _____walked_____ to Tom's house. (walk)

**3.** Tomorrow, I _____will walk_____ to Tom's house. (walk)

**4.** Every month, I _____walk_____ to Tom's house. (walk)

**Independent Practice** Use the correct tense of the verb in parentheses to complete each sentence.

**1.** The friends _____work_____ on a group project right now. (work)

**2.** The group _____talked_____ about the plans a month ago. (talk)

**3.** They _____started_____ it yesterday. (start)

**4.** Tomorrow, the boys and girls _____will look_____ for poster board and paints. (look)

**5.** They _____will finish_____ the project next week. (finish)

---

## Support English Language Learners

Identifying tenses of verbs can be difficult for English language learners, as not all languages conjugate verbs the same way as English. To help students, draw a three-column chart on the board with the headings *Past*, *Present*, and *Future*. Then fill in a couple of rows with the verb tense forms of a common regular verb, such as *walk* or *wish*. You might also include a row showing the verb tense forms of an irregular verb, such as *run* or *sing*. Call out another verb, and ask a volunteer to come up to the board to write the three tenses in the chart, using the words you wrote in it as models. If time allows, call out other verbs for students to write in the chart. Keep the chart up throughout the unit.

---

## Regular and Irregular Verbs

**Guided Instruction** Most verbs form the past tense by adding *-ed* to the end. **Irregular verbs** change their spelling when forming the past tense.

| work (regular verb) | worked | We **worked** on the group project last night. |
|---|---|---|
| come (irregular verb) | came | We **came** home late. |

**Guided Practice** Underline the verb that correctly completes the sentence.

1. Two friends (goed, <u>went</u>) to the park.
2. They (<u>brought</u>, bringed) a picnic lunch.
3. After they (eated, <u>ate</u>), they threw away the trash.
4. Then they (<u>took</u>, taked) the water bottles home.

**Independent Practice** Write the correct past tense of the verbs in parentheses on the line.

1. Arjun _____ran_____ the race last week. (run)
2. Arjun's friend _____broke_____ his leg. (break)
3. Arjun _____pushed_____ his friend in a wheelchair. (push)
4. They_____knew_____ how to finish the race. (know)
5. Their parents _____came_____ to watch. (come)
6. The crowd _____saw_____ a great race. (see)

Unit 6 ■ Text Types and Purposes: Write Nonfictional Narratives  **135**

**OBJECTIVE**
**Use the correct forms of regular and irregular verbs in writing.**

### Guided Instruction

Explain that regular verbs follow a set pattern when changed to the past tense. To change a regular verb from present tense to past, add *–ed* to the word. Give students more examples: *roll, rolled; add, added; allow, allowed; ask, asked.*

Tell students that irregular verbs don't follow a set pattern. Their spelling changes when they shift from present tense to past tense. There is no rule to go by. Students must memorize them. Examples include: *drink, drank; run, ran; forget, forgot; is, was; go, went.*

### Guided Practice

Help students draw on their understanding of how English works. If students can't determine the correct form of a verb, ask them questions like this: *Which is correct? I goed to the park, or I went to the park?*

### Independent Practice

Read aloud each verb in the parentheses and ask students whether it is regular or irregular. Have them form the past tense form of each verb before writing the word in the blank.

| **Assess and Respond** |
|---|
| **If** students are having difficulty recognizing irregular verbs, |
| **Then** provide them with a list of common irregular verbs and their tenses. |

## Numbered Heads Together

Divide students into teams of four. Give each student a number from one to four. Give each group a list of eight verbs—four regular and four irregular. Have students work together in their teams to identify the verbs as regular or irregular and to form the past tense of each. Then call out a number, and ask all students with that number to stand and identify one of the verbs from the list as regular or irregular and give its past tense. Ask the rest of the class if the student's answer is correct. Work together as a class to reach the correct answer. Repeat until all students have given answers to the class.

## OBJECTIVE
Use subject-verb agreement in writing.

## Guided Instruction

Remind students that the subject is who or what the sentence is about, and the verb tells the action, or what the subject does. Explain that the subject and verb must both agree in number. They must both be singular or plural. Point out that when a subject is singular, the verb usually ends in an *–s*. When a subject is plural, the verb does not end in *–s*.

## Guided Practice

Have students read the sentences. Ask whether the sentence is missing its subject or verb. Remind them to fill in the missing word after checking the subject or verb that is present to see if it requires a singular or plural verb or subject.

## Independent Practice

Provide additional examples of sentences that are missing either the subject or verb. Have the students fill in the missing word, making sure it matches the number.

| Assess and Respond |
| --- |
| **If** students are having trouble identifying plural nouns, |
| **Then** work as a class to generate a list of singular and plural nouns. Write the words on the board. Then have students tell you whether to put the letter *P* for plural or the letter *S* for singular next to each. |

---

## LANGUAGE

## Subject-Verb Agreement

**Guided Instruction** The subject and verb in a sentence must both be singular or both be plural.

- If the subject is a singular noun or pronoun, add *-s* to the verb.
  The **lizard runs** across the sand.

- If the subject is a plural noun or pronoun, do not add *-s* to the verb.
  The **lizards run** across the sand.

**Guided Practice** Write the word in parentheses that correctly completes each sentence.

1. Many animals _____live_____ on or around the cactus. (live, lives)
2. The wren _____makes_____ a nest on the branch. (make, makes)
3. The _____owl_____ hunts at night. (owl, owls)
4. Some _____insects_____ eat cactus. (insect, insects)

**Independent Practice** Correct the mistakes in subject-verb agreement. Write the new sentences.

1. The woodpecker make a hole in the cactus.
   The woodpecker makes a hole in the cactus.

2. Inside the nest, the babies sleeps safely.
   Inside the nest, the babies sleep safely.

3. When the babies leave, other birds uses the nest.
   When the babies leave, other birds use the nest.

4. A woodpecker eat insects.
   A woodpecker eats insects.

5. Gila woodpeckers lives as long as 10 years.
   Gila woodpeckers live as long as 10 years.

136   Unit 6 ■ Text Types and Purposes: Write Nonfictional Narratives

---

## Differentiate Instruction

Some struggling students may have trouble understanding the relationship between a subject's number and the form of the verb it takes. Place students in pairs. Create a set of flash cards that students can use. On four index cards, write a singular or plural subject on the front. On the back, identify the subject as singular or plural. On another four index cards, write a singular form of a verb on the front and the plural form on the back. Mix up the cards. Have students work together to sort the cards to create sentences from the words. The subjects and verbs should agree.

## Suffixes

**Guided Instruction** A **suffix** is a word part that is added to the end of a word to change its meaning. Suffixes can be added to the end of verbs to change them into a different part of speech. Sometimes the spelling of the base word is changed when a suffix is added. Here the *e* is dropped before adding *-ing*.

*I like to **bake** cookies.*
*Mom likes **baking** pies in the winter.*

Suffixes can also be added to nouns and adjectives to change their meaning. When a base word ends in *y* preceded by a consonant, the *y* changes to *i* before the suffix is added.

*What makes you feel **happy**?*
*I feel **happiness** when I play at the park with friends.*

**Guided Practice** Add the suffix to the base word and spell the new word on the line.

1. shop + er _____ shopper _____
2. cute + est _____ cutest _____
3. penny + less _____ penniless _____
4. silly + est _____ silliest _____

**Independent Practice** Complete each sentence with the correct base word and suffix.

1. He is the _____ bravest _____ person I know. (brave + est)
2. The child picked up the _____ wrapper _____ on the floor. (wrap + er)
3. Liam's hair was _____ curlier _____ than any I've ever seen! (curly + er)
4. Joni would _____ happily _____ help the young child. (happy + ly)
5. Rene was a _____ skater _____ in the ice show. (skate + er)

### OBJECTIVE
**Use conventional spelling for adding suffixes to base words.**

### Guided Instruction
Explain that suffixes are letters added to the end of base words to change their meaning. When suffixes are added, the spelling of the base word can often change. Remind students that the best way to learn the spellings of these words is to memorize them. Write several words on the board, and demonstrate how to change their spelling.

### Guided Practice
Help students by reviewing the rules for spelling changes to the words in the activity. When adding *-ing* to a word that ends in *e*, the *e* is dropped. When adding *-er* to a word that ends in a consonant, the final consonant is repeated. When adding *-est* or *-less* to a word that ends in *y*, turn the *y* into an *i*.

### Independent Practice
Have students tell you the rules for adding suffixes to words. Write the rules on the board. Have students consult the board as they write the words in the blanks.

#### Assess and Respond

**If** students are having trouble spelling words with suffixes,

**Then** provide them with a list of words with suffixes, and ask students to provide the correctly spelled base words.

## Differentiate Instruction

Struggling students may have trouble forming new words by adding suffixes to base words because the rules for spelling might strike them as arbitrary. Place students in groups of three. Assign each group a suffix—*-y, -er, -est, -less, -ly*. Tell each group to review the rule that applies to the suffix. Then have group members work together to generate a list of five words that use it. Students may consult a dictionary, if necessary. Go around the room and ask students for a word that uses a particular suffix and to spell it. Write their answers on the board.

## OBJECTIVES

- **Engage effectively in a range of collaborative discussions.**
- **Follow agreed-upon rules of discussion, including asking and answering questions.**

## Discuss the Essential Question

Before beginning a group discussion, copy and distribute the "Did I?" checklist available on **sadlierconnect.com**.

### Leading the Class Discussion

Give students time to think about the questions before the class discussion.

**1.** Point students to the body of the Student Model to find time-order words that indicate sequence.

**2.** Have students skim the narrative for descriptive details.

---

## SPEAKING AND LISTENING

### Discuss the Essential Question

How do writers develop nonfictional narratives?

Think about the Essential Question by responding to the questions below. Support your point of view with details from Abbey's story.

**1. What words does the writer use to signal the order of the story?**

then; as; eventually; in the beginning; by the end

**2. What are some words or phrases the writer uses to describe events?**

loudspeakers blaring; glided to a graceful stop; her hands were flying around;

I grabbed the rail and Emma's hands in a tight grip; I released my grip; glide

and coast

Use your notes above to discuss the Essential Question in small groups or as a class. Follow agreed-upon rules for discussion. Use the organizer below to record what you heard and how you participated.

| | Ideas I Agree or Disagree With | Questions I Asked |
|---|---|---|
| **Agree** | | |
| **Disagree** | | |
| | **New Ideas I Had During Discussion** | **Questions I Answered** |
| | | |

---

## Discussion Skills

Remind students of the sentence starters they can use during a discussion that will help them build on each other's reasoning:

- *I am not sure I agree with you. Here's why . . .*
- *I see what you are saying, but I think the evidence shows that . . .*

Then tell students that they are responsible for encouraging everyone in a group to participate. They can use these questions:

- *Would someone like to add to that?*
- *Would you please say more about that?*

## UNIT 6 REVIEW

This paragraph has mistakes in the use of regular and irregular verb tenses, subject-verb agreement, as well as suffixes. Write the paragraph correctly on the lines below. Use a dictionary to help you spell the words.

> Last week, Kate and I had a lemonade stand. We want to raise money for the hospital that is careing for our sick friend. First, we will ask our parents for permission. Then, we puts together our supplies. Kate mixes the lemonade, and I carefully poured it into the glasses. We selled the tastyest lemonade ever for fifty cents. At the end of the day, we raised twenty dollars. It gave us both great happyness to help our friend.

Last week, Kate and I had a lemonade stand. We wanted to raise money for the

hospital that is caring for our sick friend. First, we asked our parents for permission.

Then, we put together our supplies. Kate mixed the lemonade, and I carefully

poured it into the glasses. We sold the tastiest lemonade ever for fifty cents.

At the end of the day, we raised twenty dollars. It gave us both great

happiness to help our friend.

_____

_____

_____

_____

_____

_____

Unit 6 ■ Text Types and Purposes: Write Nonfictional Narratives **139**

## Introduce the Review

Explain to students that this review will give them an opportunity to apply the language and writing skills that they have studied and practiced in this unit.

### Language Skills Summary

Let students know that they are going to have to use what they have learned about using regular and irregular verb tenses, subject-verb agreement, and suffixes to make their writing better. Good writers follow grammar rules, and they know how to use different kinds of sentences to make their writing more interesting for the reader.

- Have students explain how to form the present, past, and future tense of verbs.

- Ask students to give examples of regular and irregular verbs.

- Ask students how to determine whether verbs and subjects are singular or plural.

- Prompt students to explain how the spelling of a base word changes when they add certain suffixes to it.

## Test-Taking Tips

Provide the following tips to students to help with taking assessments based on editing skills.

- Students should make a list of at least five common editing errors. Then they should read through their answer five separate times, checking for one item on the list each time. Students' lists should include the errors they typically make in their writing, such as capitalization of proper nouns, correctly using easily confused words (*there*, *their*, *they're*), and end punctuation.

- Tell students to place a ruler or piece of paper beneath each line as they check it for errors.

## Writing Process Summary

Remind students that planning helps them organize their ideas before drafting, and that revising and editing make a draft better.

### Planning and Drafting

Have students look at the graphic organizer and draft they created earlier (page 133). They should be sure that the draft includes the sequence of events listed in the graphic organizer, dialogue, descriptions, and a strong ending.

### Nonfictional Narrative Rubric

| | |
|---|---|
| 4 | The narrative includes: characters, a clear sequence of events with time-order words, dialogue and descriptions, and a conclusion. There are few or no editing errors. |
| 3 | The narrative includes the elements listed in "4" above, though they are executed less successfully. Minor editing errors do not detract from the overall piece. |
| 2 | The narrative is missing one or more of the required elements. There are many editing errors, some of them serious. |
| 1 | The narrative is unfinished or shows a minimal understanding of the required elements. Serious editing errors make it difficult to read and understand. |
| 0 | The assignment was not attempted. |

### Self-Assessment: Progress Check

Have students revisit the Progress Check on Page 127 and compare their answers now with those they gave before they started Unit 6.

---

## UNIT 6 REVIEW

**Assignment:** Write a nonfictional narrative about a special day with a friend.

On the lines below, write your final copy of the nonfictional narrative draft you created on page 133. Be sure to describe your thoughts, feelings, and actions. Make sure to choose your words carefully and use words to signal the order of events. You may also use dialogue to explain events and tell about the characters. Wrap up your narrative with a conclusion. See the Writing Handbook (pp. 275–283) for ways to improve your writing as you revise.

Students should write a nonfictional narrative that establishes a situation with characters. They should use detailed descriptions and possibly dialogue to describe events, and the narrative should have a clear beginning, middle, and end. Time-order words should signal event order. The strong ending should provide closure to the events.

---

## Digital Connection: Online Publishing

Once students have completed their nonfictional narratives, they can publish them online for other classmates, family, and friends to read. Guide students to an appropriate website for publishing their work. Before students post, they should enhance the final versions of their narratives by adding relevant illustrations or photos. Some students might even want to draw their own illustrations, which they can scan into a computer and then paste into their final drafts.

## Performance Task Overview

The Performance Tasks in *Progress English Language Arts* are designed to determine a student's ability to closely read and understand a complex text, locate textual evidence to support analysis of the text, and create an extended response that shows deep comprehension of the text. Writing prompts in each part of the Performance Task address requirements for creating opinion pieces, informative texts, and narratives. Each Performance Task has three main parts: a Literary Analysis Task, a Narrative Writing Task, and a Research Simulation Task.

Each Performance Task requires students to read multiple thematically related texts—literature, a nonfiction narrative, and a research-based informational text—and to respond to two types of assessment items:

- **Selected response items** require students to choose the correct answer from a number of options. Selected response items are divided into two parts: Part A requires students to answer a question related to the content or language of the text; Part B requires students to identify textual evidence that supports the answer to Part A.

- **Constructed response items** require students to create a brief written response—a literary analysis, a narrative, or an informational text—in response to a prompt.

You can help your students by introducing the overall topic of the Performance Task, orienting students to the requirements of each part of the task, and communicating helpful reminders that will enable students to approach each part successfully. Once students have completed each part, go over the items and correct responses with them, especially focusing on the connection between textual evidence and acceptable responses.

In **Performance Task 1,** students will read and respond to three texts relating to Antarctica.

- *The Missing Glove* (realistic fiction)
- *A Famous Voyage to Antarctica* (historical narrative)
- *Continent of Ice* (informational/explanatory text)

Specific information about how these texts are used with each section of **Performance Task 1** is shown in the chart at the right.

---

**ONLINE Digital Resources**

Go to **sadlierconnect.com** to download the following resources for **Performance Task 1:**

**Texts:**
- *The Missing Glove*
- *A Famous Voyage to Antarctica*
- *Continent of Ice*

**Answer Keys and Rubrics:**
- Literary Analysis Task
- Narrative Writing Task
- Research Simulation Task

---

## RECOMMENDED PACING

Administer the entire Performance Task over a three-day period. Students should complete one part per day, accompanied by instructional support and review.

| Performance Task 1 |
| --- |
| **PART 1: LITERARY ANALYSIS** *(30 minutes)* |
| **TASK** <br> Students will respond to questions that require careful analysis of a literary text. Then they will write a brief literary analysis text in response to a prompt. |
| **SELECTION** <br> *The Missing Glove* |
| **PART 2: NARRATIVE WRITING** *(30 minutes)* |
| **TASK** <br> Students will respond to questions that require careful analysis of a narrative text. Then they will respond to a prompt by writing a short narrative. |
| **SELECTION** <br> *A Famous Voyage to Antarctica* |
| **PART 3: RESEARCH SIMULATION** *(30 minutes)* |
| **TASK** <br> Students will respond to questions that require careful analysis of an informational text and a narrative text. Then students will respond to a writing prompt that requires them to synthesize information from the two texts. |
| **SELECTIONS** <br> *Continent of Ice* and *A Famous Voyage to Antarctica* |

## PERFORMANCE TASK 1

There are three parts to this performance task. Your teacher will provide you with copies of three reading selections.

- *The Missing Glove*  Genre: Realistic Fiction
- *A Famous Voyage to Antarctica*  Genre: Historical Narrative
- *Continent of Ice*  Genre: Informational Text

### Part 1: Literary Analysis

☐ Read *The Missing Glove* carefully. Take notes that will help you understand the passage.

☐ Answer Items 1–3 on pages 142–143.

☐ Then read the prompt for Item 4 and write a paragraph on your own paper. You may want to make some notes on scratch paper first.

### Part 2: Narrative Writing

☐ Read *A Famous Voyage to Antarctica* carefully. Take notes that will help you understand the passage.

☐ Answer Items 1–2 on page 144.

☐ Then read the prompt for Item 3 and write two or three paragraphs on your own paper. You may want to make some notes on scratch paper first.

### Part 3: Research Simulation

☐ Read *Continent of Ice* carefully. Take notes that will help you understand the passage.

☐ Answer Items 1–3 about *Continent of Ice* on pages 145–146.

☐ Review *A Famous Voyage to Antarctica*. You will use it in addition to *Continent of Ice* in this task.

☐ Then read the prompt for Item 4 and write an essay on your own paper. You may want to make some notes on scratch paper first.

Performance Task 1  **141**

## Test-Taking Tips

**Selected response items:** Remind students to . . .

- read each question closely and follow the directions carefully.
- read every answer choice carefully before deciding on an answer.
- use a pencil so that a wrong answer can be corrected.

**Constructed response items:** Remind students to . . .

- focus on a clear main idea.
- be well-organized and stay on topic.
- provide details from the passage to support their responses.
- use clear language and include linking words to connect ideas.
- follow rules of formal writing (spelling, punctuation, capitalization, and grammar).

## Administration Procedure

### STEP 1  Introduce the Task

Tell students that this Performance Task may cover any of the skills they have learned and practiced in Units 1–6 of *Progress English Language Arts*.

Explain that students will read three texts. After each reading, they will answer questions and then write about what they read. Familiarize students with the types of items they will see:

- Selected response items have two parts. Part A asks students to answer a question about the reading selection; Part B asks them to identify textual evidence—details from the selection—that point to the correct answer.

- Constructed response items are writing prompts based on one or more of the reading selections. Students should use textual evidence from the selections to support their responses to these items. They can make notes before writing.

**\* Repeat Steps 2–4 for each part of the Performance Task.**

### STEP 2  Reading

Tell students that they will read a text about Antarctica. Remind them that they should read the text closely and that they can take notes about key ideas and details as they read. Have students read the text(s) for that part.

### STEP 3  Selected Response

Have students complete the selected response items.

### STEP 4  Constructed Response

Read the writing prompt, and make sure students understand the directions. Explain: *Your task is to write a paragraph. You may use your notes. Also, you may go back to the text to find ideas and details you want to use in your paragraph.* Answer any questions. Then have students respond to the writing prompt.

### STEP 5  Check the Task

Go over the selected response items so students understand why each answer is correct; help them identify the textual evidence that supports each item. Review the writing prompt and discuss what an effective response should include.

## Part 1: Literary Analysis Task

**Selection:** *The Missing Glove* ONLINE

**Genre:** Realistic fiction

**Core Task:** Students will read a literary text and respond to three selected response items. Then students will write a literary analysis of the text.

**Text Summary:** In this story, Dr. Lin works in Antarctica. One morning, she cannot find one of her gloves required to withstand the extreme cold; the camp store has no extras in her size. After an anxious search, she finally finds it in an unusual place: the refrigerator! Her friends had filled it with flowers to surprise her on her birthday.

**Score Points:** Up to **9 points** total

- Selected response items: Up to 6 points (1 point for each part of three 2-part items)

- Constructed response item: Up to 3 points for one item

**Depth of Knowledge Levels:**

| Item 1: | Item 2: | Item 3: | Item 4: |
| Level 1 | Level 1 | Level 2 | Level 3 |

ONLINE Download the reading selection and the Answer Key and Rubric.

---

**Selected Response Items:** When students have completed the items, go over the correct answers with them. Help them locate the evidence in the text that supports each answer.

**Constructed Response Items:** While reading the prompt, have students circle the most important words that explain what they must do to respond to the prompt.

**Analyzing the Constructed Response:** When students have finished writing, present the rubric's key elements to students and discuss their importance. Ask volunteers to share how they could improve the answer by paying attention to the elements the rubric outlines for an excellent answer.

---

**How this task contributes to reading and writing grounded in evidence from literary text:** In order to complete the task, students 1. analyze and select information from a realistic fiction selection; 2. answer questions about the selection and identify the evidence the author presents as support; 3. write an explanatory paragraph about how a character changes in the selection; 4. organize ideas by stating and maintaining a focus; 5. develop a topic, including citing supportive evidence and details; 6. effectively present ideas, transitions, and a relevant conclusion; 7. follow conventions and rules of grammar, usage, and mechanics.

---

### Part 1 Literary Analysis

**Read all parts of the question before responding. Circle the correct answer to Items 1–3. Use your own paper to respond to Item 4.**

**Item 1**

**Part A** In the story *The Missing Glove*, what makes Dr. Lin so upset?
a. She receives special clothes for very cold weather.
b. She loses a piece of gear that is very important.
c. She thinks that no one remembers it is her birthday.
d. She hasn't seen flowers in her six months in Antarctica.

**Part B** Which sentence from the story best supports the answer to Part A?
a. "The government has issued her all the items . . . "
b. "Every Antarctica worker got the same items."
c. "Dr. Lin started feeling more and more anxious."
d. "She could not perform her work without that glove . . ."

**Item 2**

**Part A** In the story *The Missing Glove*, what happens that makes Dr. Lin feel warm and happy?
a. Her friends surprise her by turning away when they see her.
b. Her friends surprise her with flowers for her birthday.
c. Her friends surprise her by putting her glove in the refrigerator.
d. Her friends surprise her with a new glove made just for her.

---

**Part B** Which detail from the story best supports the answer to Part A?
a. It is the first time she has seen a flower in the six months she has been in Antarctica.
b. It is a shock to find her glove because it is in the kitchen refrigerator.
c. It is unusual that her friends turn away and then yell, "Surprise!"
d. It is a comfort to find the lost glove so that she can do her work.

**Item 3**

**Part A** What does the word *extremely* mean in this line from *The Missing Glove*?
"She was *extremely* careful to keep track of it all."
a. briefly
b. easily
c. gently
d. very

**Part B** Which sentence from the story best helps the reader understand the meaning of *extremely*?
a. "She was nearing the end of her six-month job . . . "
b. "She worked outside . . . "
c. "She even kept a detailed checklist."
d. "She also got hats, hoods, and goggles."

**Item 4**

Think about how Dr. Lin's feelings change throughout the story. How does she feel at the end of the story? How are her feelings at the end of the story different from those at the beginning? Write a paragraph to explain your answer. Use details from the story to support your answer. See online rubric for scoring.

## NARRATIVE WRITING

### Part 2 Narrative Writing

Read all parts of the question before responding. Circle the correct answer to Items 1–2. Use your own paper to respond to Item 3.

**Item 1**

**Part A** What is the main idea of *A Famous Voyage to Antarctica*?
a. Sir Ernest Shackleton never reached the South Pole.
b. Exploring Antarctica is too dangerous and shouldn't be tried.
c. Iron ships are better for Antarctic expeditions than wooden ones.
d. The crew of the *Endurance* survived two years trapped in ice.

**Part B** Which text detail does NOT support the answer to Part A?
a. "Shackleton made four trips to the frozen continent."
b. "They would not return to civilization for two long years."
c. "If they survived the trip, they would return with help."
d. "Not a single life had been lost."

**Item 2**

**Part A** What is the meaning of *hazardous* in this sentence from the text?
"Men wanted for *hazardous* journey."
a. calm   b. unsafe   c. exciting   d. enjoyable

**Part B** Which detail helps readers understand the meaning of *hazardous*?
a. Many men applied to be on the *Endurance* crew.
b. Shackleton was buried on South Georgia Island.
c. The crew had to camp on an ice floe for many months.
d. Shackleton's advertisement warned of "constant danger."

**Item 3**

Think about the events described in *A Famous Voyage to Antarctica*. Then write two paragraphs to tell what might have happened to the last crew members to be rescued from Elephant Island. Use ideas and facts from *A Famous Voyage to Antarctica* to help your writing. See online rubric for scoring.

## Part 2: Narrative Writing Task

**Selection:** *A Famous Voyage to Antarctica*  ONLINE

**Genre:** Historical narrative

**Core Task:** Students will read a narrative text and respond to two selected response items. Then they will write a response to tell what happens after the end of the narrative.

**Text Summary:** Sir Ernest Shackleton's hazardous third voyage to Antarctica in 1914 turned out to be his most famous, although Shackleton and his crew did not achieve their goal of crossing Antarctica. Disaster struck when their ship became trapped in ice, stranding them on an ice floe. The story is an incredible tale of survival.

**Score Points:** Up to **7 points** total

- Selected response items: Up to 4 points (1 point for each part of two 2-part items)
- Constructed response item: Up to 3 points for one item

**Depth of Knowledge Levels:**

| **Item 1:** | **Item 2:** | **Item 3:** |
|---|---|---|
| Level 1 | Level 2 | Level 3 |

ONLINE Download the reading selection and the Answer Key and Rubric.

### Test-Taking Tips

Remind students to . . .

- read the directions carefully.
- determine clearly what is being asked.
- read the entire question and all of the choices.
- pay close attention to words that will help you identify how to answer, e.g., *in paragraph 2*.
- narrow down possible answers by getting rid of incorrect choices.
- answer all parts of the question and use text evidence.
- review your responses after you are done to check for errors.
- plan what you want to say before you begin writing.
- write as neatly and legibly as possible.

**Selected Response Items:** Remind students to carefully read each of the answer options in Part B of each item. Only one will make sense as support for the Part A answer.

**Constructed Response Items:** To make sure students understand the writing prompt, have them answer specific questions that you ask about it, such as *What are you going to write about? Where will you find details to support what you write?*

**Analyzing the Constructed Response:** Have student volunteers share their responses. Discuss key elements of the scoring rubric and ask students to make one significant change to improve their response.

**How this task contributes to reading and writing grounded in evidence from informational text:** In order to complete the task, students 1. analyze and select information from a historical narrative selection; 2. answer questions about the selection and identify the evidence the author presents as support; 3. write one or two paragraphs to tell a story, using ideas and facts from the selection; 4. organize ideas with clear event sequences; 5. develop a narrative, including descriptive details and elaboration consistent with the source selection; 6. effectively present ideas, transitions, and a conclusion; 7. follow conventions and rules of grammar, usage, and mechanics.

## Part 3: Research Simulation Task

**Selections:** *Continent of Ice* and *A Famous Voyage to Antarctica* **ONLINE**

**Genres:** Informational text and historical narrative

**Core Task:** Students will read nonfiction texts and respond to three selected response items. Then students will write an essay that requires them to synthesize information from the two texts to respond to the research question.

**Text Summary:** The article *Continent of Ice* describes the extreme continent of Antarctica as an ice-covered desert where there are no trees or bushes. Because it is so frigid, people stay for only a short time for tourism or for scientific investigation.

**Score Points:** Up to **9 points** total

- Selected response items: Up to 6 points (1 point for each part of three 2-part items)
- Constructed response item: Up to 3 points for one item

**Depth of Knowledge Levels:**

| **Item 1:** | **Item 2:** | **Item 3:** | **Item 4:** |
| Level 1 | Level 1 | Level 2 | Level 4 |

**ONLINE** Download the reading selections and the Answer Key and Rubric.

---

**Selected Response Items:** Tell students that one way to tell which Part B answer is correct is to locate each choice in the text and check the words and sentences around it. This will help them understand what each choice does and does not mean.

**Constructed Response Items:** Remind students that they should combine information from both texts in their response to the writing prompt.

**Analyzing the Constructed Response:** Discuss key elements of the scoring rubric with students. Have students underline their claim and specific details that support it.

---

**How this task contributes to reading and writing grounded in evidence from informational texts:**
Students 1. analyze and select information from informational selections; 2. answer questions about a selection and identify the evidence the author presents as support; 3. write an explanatory paragraph describing challenges the Antarctic environment presents; 4. organize ideas by stating and maintaining a focus; 5. develop a topic, including citing supportive evidence and details, and elaboration consistent with the source selections; 6. effectively present ideas, transitions, and a conclusion; 7. follow conventions and rules of grammar, usage, and mechanics.

---

### Part 3 Research Simulation

Read all parts of the question before responding. Circle the correct answer to Items 1–3. Use your own paper to respond to Item 4.

**Item 1**

**Part A** In *Continent of Ice*, where would the reader find facts about things scientists can learn in Antarctica?
- a. in the first paragraph
- b. in "What Is Antarctica Like?"
- c. in "Who Lives in Antarctica?"
- **d.** in "Why Do Scientists Study in Antarctica?"

**Part B** Which sentence from the text best supports the answer to Part A?
- a. "Antarctica covers Earth's South Pole."
- b. "Antarctica is the coldest place on Earth."
- **c.** "Antarctica is a good place to find meteorites . . . "
- d. "Antarctica has no trees or bushes."

**Item 2**

**Part A** What does the text say that scientists might find out about from studying Antarctica?
- a. deserts
- **b.** Mars
- c. many types of whales
- d. seals and penguins

**Part B** Which details from the text best support the answer to Part A?
- a. Antarctica has a warmer temperature on its coasts than at its center.
- b. Antarctica has only moss and algae for plants.
- c. Antarctica has meteorites, or rocks from space.
- **d.** Antarctica has cold weather and is dry like Mars.

---

**Item 3**

**Part A** What does the word *analyze* mean in this part of *Continent of Ice*?
"Also, meteorites that fall in Antarctica are protected by the ice for a long time. This gives scientists more time to *analyze* them in order to learn more about these rocks."
- a. to clean something well
- b. to do something quickly
- **c.** to study something carefully
- d. to keep something cold

**Part B** Which set of words from the passage best help the reader understand the meaning of *analyze* in Part A?
- a. protected; ice; long time
- **b.** scientists; more time; learn
- c. in order; more; these rocks
- d. that fall; protected; gives

**Item 4**

You have read two texts describing Antarctica. Think about the facts in *A Famous Voyage to Antarctica* and the facts in *Continent of Ice*. What challenges do people face when they are working and exploring in Antarctica? Write a paragraph to explain how these challenges affect people. Use details from the passages to support your answer. See online rubric for scoring.

## Introducing UNIT 7

In this unit about extreme weather, you will learn about what makes up craft and structure in informational text. Craft and structure refers to the tools that authors use to create a text.

When you read a magazine article or a history book, you are reading informational text. This unit deals with a science topic. Authors may use words that you do not know in their explanations of scientific ideas. Knowing how to figure out or find the meanings of words you do not know is especially important to understanding what you read. Authors of informational text may also use text features, such as sidebars and hyperlinks, to present ideas. It's important to know how to use these sources of information.

Thinking about an author's point of view and the way that the author uses words and language can also help you understand what you read. You will learn more about this and the other tools as you complete this unit.

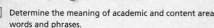

### Progress Check  *Can I?*

<table>
<tr><td>Before Unit 7</td><td></td><td></td><td>After Unit 7</td></tr>
</table>

☐ Determine the meaning of academic and content area words and phrases. ☐

☐ Use text features and search tools to locate information. ☐

☐ Distinguish my point of view from the author's point of view. ☐

☐ Find the meaning of a new word when a familiar prefix or suffix is added. ☐

Unit 7 ■ Reading Informational Text: Craft and Structure

**Student Page 147**

## Progress Check

The Progress Check is a self-assessment feature that students can use to gauge their own progress. Research shows that when students take accountability for their own learning, their motivation increases.

Before students begin work on Unit 7, have them check the boxes next to any item that they feel they can do well. Explain that it is fine if they do not check any of the boxes. Tell them that they will have an opportunity to learn about and practice all of these items while studying the unit. Let them know that near the end of the unit they will have a chance to reconsider how well they can do each item on this list.

Before students begin the Unit 7 Review on page 175, have them revisit this page. You can use this information to work with students on any items they don't understand before they tackle the Review.

## HOME ◆ CONNECT...

The Home Connect feature is a way to keep parents or other adult family members apprised of what their children are learning. The key learning objectives are listed, and some ideas for related activities and discussions are included.

Explain to students that they can share the Home Connect page with their parents or other adult family members in their home. Let students know how much time the class will be spending on this unit so they can plan their time accordingly at home.

Encourage students and their parents to share their experiences using the suggestions on the Home Connect. You may wish to make a place to post some of this work.

## HOME ◆ CONNECT...

**N**ewspaper writers and editors are good about providing context clues for tough words in their articles. **Context clues** are words that give readers the help they need to understand the meanings of unfamiliar words. Choose a print or online news article your child might enjoy. Highlight any difficult words defined in context. Then ask your child to help you use context clues to find the meanings of the highlighted words.

**Text features** such as subheads, charts, and sidebars can help children see what is important in an article. Choose an online article with an appealing topic. Before reading, have your child point out subheads and predict what the article will be about. Talk about sidebars, maps, and charts, and discuss why information is shown this way.

Understanding an **author's point of view** about a subject is an important reading skill. Find an editorial in a newspaper or children's magazine. Read it with your child. Have your child state the author's opinion and say whether they agree with the author.

**Activity:** With your child, explore interesting Web links related to extreme weather. Use correct terms for the text features you see on screen, such as *sidebar, heading, caption, hyperlink, boldface type*. Talk about why some of the texts you explore are easier to follow or more appealing than others. List the interesting new facts you learn, and create your own fact sheet on the computer.

**148**  Unit 7 ■ Reading Informational Text: Craft and Structure

### IN THIS UNIT, YOUR CHILD WILL...

■ Use clues in a text to figure out the meaning of unfamiliar words and words with multiple meanings.

■ Learn how text features such as headings or visuals (charts, photos, hyperlinks, etc.) help readers locate information within the text.

■ Identify an author's point of view, or opinion, about a topic, and decide whether or not he or she agrees with it.

■ Combine the meaning of a base word, such as agree, with those of prefixes and suffixes, such as *dis-* and *-able*, to understand word meanings.

■ Compare and contrast four texts on the same theme: an explanatory text, a magazine article, an editorial, and a personal narrative.

### WAYS TO HELP YOUR CHILD

Show respect for your child's point of view on topics while also helping your child develop the thinking and speaking skills needed to express and support opinions. Whether you are discussing sports, current events, or daily life, ask for your child's point of view. Encourage him or her to offer supporting reasons for it.

ONLINE
For more Home Connect activities, continue online at sadlierconnect.com

**Student Page 148**

## UNIT PLANNER

| Theme: Extreme Weather | Focus |
|---|---|
| **DETERMINING WORD MEANINGS**<br>*pp. 150–155* | *Water Everywhere*<br>**GENRE:** Explanatory Text   **LEXILE™:** 720L<br><br>**WORDS TO KNOW:** levee, barrier, system, debris, disaster, snowmelt, absorb, contaminated |
| **USING TEXT FEATURES**<br>*pp. 156–161* | *Watch Out for Weather!*<br>**GENRE:** Journal Article   **LEXILE™:** 760L<br><br>**WORDS TO KNOW:** atmosphere, destroy, crew, predict, severe, dangerous, prairie |
| **DISTINGUISHING POINTS OF VIEW**<br>*pp. 162–167* | *Stop the Droughts!*<br>**GENRE:** Editorial   **LEXILE™:** 730L<br><br>**WORDS TO KNOW:** conserving, vapor, condense, devastating, adapted, continent, wildfire, precious |
| **CLOSE READING**<br>*pp. 168–172* | *Dust Bowl Disaster*<br>**GENRE:** Personal Narrative   **LEXILE™:** 700L |
| **CONNECT ACROSS TEXTS**<br>*p. 173* | Compare and Contrast Texts |
| **LANGUAGE**<br>*p. 174* | Prefixes and Suffixes |
| **UNIT 7 REVIEW**<br>*pp. 175–176* | *Lightning Strikes!* |

Essential Question: How can an author present informational text effectively?

UNIT 7

## Objective(s)

Use vocabulary strategies to determine the meaning of general academic and domain-specific words in text.

Use text features and search tools to locate information in a text.

Distinguish personal and author's point of view.

- Use vocabulary strategies to determine the meaning of general academic and domain-specific words in text.
- Use text features and search tools to locate information in a text.
- Distinguish personal and author's point of view.

Determine the meanings of words with prefixes and suffixes.

## Unit Assessment

- Unit 7 Review *pp. 175–176*
- Unit 7 Performance Task ( ONLINE )

## Additional Assessment Options

- Performance Task 1 *pp. 141A–145 and 146*
  ( ALSO ONLINE )
- Performance Task 2 *pp. 259A–263 and 264*
  ( ALSO ONLINE )

**Optional Purchase:**

- iProgress Monitor ( ONLINE )
- Progress Monitor Student Benchmark Assessment Booklet

## ( ONLINE ) Digital Resources

- Home Connect Activities
- Unit Performance Task
- Additional Practice
- Full-Length Reading Selections
- Foundational Skills Practice
- Teacher Resources
- iProgress Monitor (optional purchase)

**Go to SadlierConnect.com to access your Digital Resources.**

**For more detailed instructions see page T3.**

## LEARNING PROGRESSIONS

In this unit, students will learn how the craft and structure of an informational text contribute to their understanding of it. In order to learn the skills in this unit, students will further develop skills learned in second grade. They should be encouraged to retain these skills, as they will continue to build on them in fourth grade.

**Determining Word Meanings**

- By the end of grade 2, students should have been able to determine the meaning of words and phrases in a text relevant to a grade 2 topic or subject area.

- In grade 3, students will learn to determine the meaning of both academic and domain-specific words and phrases relevant to a grade 3 topic or subject area.

- In grade 4, students will be determining the meaning of academic and domain-specific words and phrases relevant to more complex texts.

**Using Text Features**

- Proficient second-grade students should have ended the school year knowing how to use various text features to locate key facts or information in a text.

- As third graders, they should be able to use these same text features as well as search tools in order to locate information relevant to a given topic. The ability to distinguish between information that is relevant and information that is irrelevant is one that students should master by the end of third grade.

- This skill will prepare them for fourth grade, when they will learn to use these text features as well as the text itself to describe the overall structure of events, ideas, concepts, or information in a text.

**Distinguishing Points of View**

- By the end of second grade, students should have been able to identify the author's purpose in an informational text, including what he or she wants to answer, explain, or describe.

- As third graders, students must take this concrete knowledge of the author's purpose and point of view and distinguish it from their own point of view.

- This ability to distinguish between points of view will become even more complex in fourth grade, when they will learn to compare and contrast firsthand and secondhand accounts of the same event or topic.

# Reading Informational Text: Craft and Structure

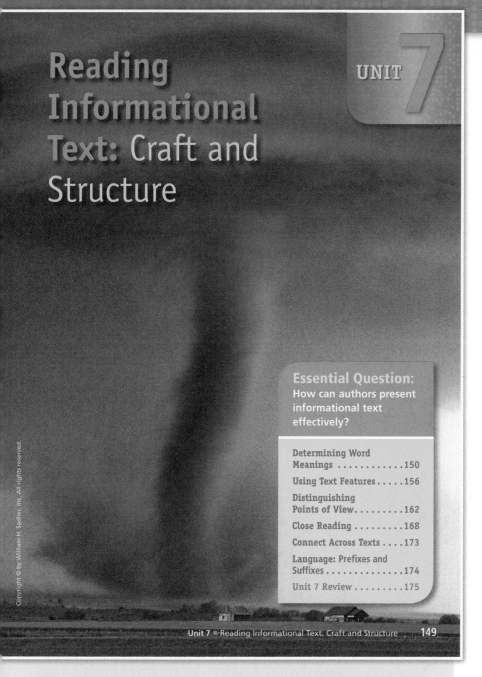

**UNIT 7**

**Essential Question:**
How can authors present informational text effectively?

**Essential Question:**
How can an author present informational text effectively?

In this unit, students will learn about the craft and structure of informational text, specifically how authors use vocabulary, text features, and point of view to communicate information and ideas.

## Theme: Extreme Weather

Students will read selections related to the theme of extreme weather. They will read about floods, droughts, and storms—including tornadoes, hurricanes, and blizzards—and a personal account of the Dust Bowl.

## Curriculum Connection: Science

Students will learn about weather patterns and storm systems, the water cycle, and how essential water is for living things.

---

## Vocabulary Overview

**General Academic Vocabulary**

absorb 154, barrier 150, conserving 162, contaminated 154, crew 158, dangerous 160, destroy 157, devastating 164, disaster 152, precious 166, predict 158, severe 160, system 150

**Domain-Specific Vocabulary**

adapted 164, atmosphere 156, condense 163, continent 166, debris 152, levee 150, prairie 160, snowmelt 154, vapor 163, wildfire 166

## Guided Instruction

### OBJECTIVE
**Use vocabulary strategies to determine the meaning of general academic and domain-specific words in text.**

### Genre: Explanatory Text

Explain to students that explanatory text gives the reader information about a topic. Point out that the word *explanatory* is related to the word *explanation*.

### Set the Purpose

Help students understand the purpose for learning the reading skill by asking *Do you ever find a new word while reading? What do you do to figure out the meaning?*

### Model and Teach

Read the selection as students follow along in their books.

### CITE EVIDENCE

**A** *The text says that "water went over the first barrier," and that houses were lifted up by the water. The photograph also shows many houses under water.*

*What does submerged mean, based on the clues?* (under water)

**B** *I will look for a word that means the same thing as* halt. *I will put that word in place of* halt *and see if the sentence still makes sense.*

*What synonym for* halt *is in the last sentence of paragraph 3?* (stop) *So what does* halt *mean?* (stop)

---

## DETERMINING WORD MEANINGS

### Guided Instruction

**WORDS TO KNOW**
**barrier**
**levee**
**system**

To determine the **meaning of a word**, readers can use context clues located in the same sentence as the word or in nearby sentences.

**CITE EVIDENCE**

**A** **Inference** clues help you figure out the **meaning of an unknown word**. By using the text, readers can infer—or figure out—what a word means. Circle the word *submerged* in paragraph 2. Underline the nearby words that help you figure out its meaning.

**B** **Synonyms** are words that have the same or similar meanings, such as *big/large*. Sometimes synonyms can be context clues. Circle the word *halt* and its synonym in the last sentence of paragraph 3. Why are synonyms often good context clues?

## Water Everywhere
(Genre: Explanatory Text)

1 The worst flood in the United States took place in 1993. It is known as "The Great Flood of 1993." It rained for five months, causing the Mississippi and Missouri rivers to overflow. This extra water resulted in flooding across nine states.

**Too Much Rain**

2 **Levees** stand along the sides of the rivers and keep the river water from going into nearby towns. This time, there was too much rain. Water went over the first **barrier** on June 7. Seventy-five towns were soon submerged. Garbage, bridge parts, and lumber floated on the river. The river water even lifted entire houses.

**Floods in the Future**

3 We can protect ourselves from floods. Better levees can be built to hold back floodwaters. Rainfall can be measured by taking pictures from space. A flood warning **system** is also important. It can send an alert to people to leave their homes. Human beings can't stop the rain, but we may be able to halt its flow.

---

## Words to Know

**General Academic Vocabulary**
**barrier** (*noun*): something that gets in the way of or stops something else
**system** (*noun*): a group of things that work together for the same purpose

**Domain-Specific Vocabulary**
**levee** (*noun*): land along a river that is built up higher than the water to prevent flooding

**Working with Word Meaning** Encourage students to rephrase the definitions, putting them in their own words.

## CRAFT AND STRUCTURE

4    Flooding is a big problem in places that are below sea level. The Netherlands is a country in Europe. That country has been dealing with floods for a long time. And people there have some new ideas.

### Fighting Floods

5    In the Netherlands, the Dutch fight floods by letting some water in. As sea levels rise, levees and other barriers do not work as well. So the Dutch government created a flood zone. <u>Floodwaters can spill there. No one is hurt.  No property is damaged.</u>

6    In the United States, during Hurricane Katrina in 2005, the levees around New Orleans failed. The city was badly flooded. New levees kept the city mostly (dry) during Hurricane Isaac in 2012, but other areas were (swamped.) It may not be possible to protect everyone with levees. The East Coast also experienced massive flooding in 2012 during Hurricane Sandy. Now some people there are wondering if they should create flood zones as people have done in the Netherlands.

### Comprehension Check

How does determining the meaning of *flood zone* help you understand solutions to flooding? Give specific examples.

Unit 7 ■ Reading Informational Text: Craft and Structure    151

### Guided Instruction

**CITE EVIDENCE**

**C** **Restatement** occurs when a text restates what a word means—similar to a definition. Sentence 3 in paragraph 5 includes the term *flood zone*. Underline the restatement that helps you figure out the meaning of *flood zone*. How does the restatement help you?

**D** **Antonyms** are words that are opposite in meaning, like *glad/sad*. Sometimes antonyms can be used as context clues. Circle the word *swamped* and its antonym in paragraph 6.

## Guided Instruction

**CITE EVIDENCE**

**C** *I want to look after the term* flood zone *for some clues that tell what a flood zone is.*

*What sentences restate the meaning of* flood zone? ("Floodwaters can spill there. . . . No property is damaged") *Based on the restatement, what is a* flood zone? (an area where flood waters can flow without damage to people or property)

**D** *I'm looking for a word that is opposite in meaning from* swamped. *The text says that "New levees kept the city mostly dry . . . but other areas were swamped." I think this is a clue, because* dry *and* swamped *are set up as opposites.*

*What word in paragraph 6 is an antonym of* swamped? (dry) *What does* swamped *mean?* (flooded)

### Comprehension Check

**Sample Answer:** Understanding the meaning of *flood zone* helps me understand the solution the people in the Netherlands have created to deal with their flooding problem.

**Answer Explanation:** Students should realize that the text says that a flood zone is a place where floodwater can go without hurting anyone or damaging any property. It follows that this is a good solution for places that have many floods, because flood zones can keep floodwaters away from places where people live.

## Support English Language Learners

Students who are learning English are going to encounter many more unknown words in this passage than are native speakers. If English language learners speak a Romance first language, i.e., one with roots in Latin such as Spanish or French, they can look for cognates. A cognate is a word in one language that is similar in form and meaning to a word in another language.

For native Spanish speakers, some cognates that students might find include: *important/importante, completely/completamente, disaster/desastre.* Native French speakers might also recognize *debris/débris.*

# Determining Word Meanings

## Guided Practice

### Recap Reading Selection

Let students know that they will read more about floods. Review what they read about the Great Flood of 1993, Hurricane Katrina, and the idea of using flood zones as a way to keep flooding away from people and property.

### Read and Practice

Have partners take turns reading the selection as you circulate to provide support. Model practicing determining word meanings with Cite Evidence callout A. For callout B, circulate and provide partners with scaffolding as needed. You might use the following suggestions to help students who are having difficulty.

### CITE EVIDENCE

**A** Point out the clues in the text that can help students determine what *dampness* means. It is something "left behind by water," and it "causes mold to grow." Suggest that this sounds like a bathroom after a shower. This may help them understand that *dampness* means "a slight wetness."

**B** Help students see that *strike* and *hit* are used in the same way in the first two sentences of paragraph 9. *Hit* is a synonym for *strike*, and both words describe the action of a flood on a place.

---

## DETERMINING WORD MEANINGS

### Guided Practice

Water Everywhere *continued*

**WORDS TO KNOW**
debris
disaster

**CITE EVIDENCE**

**A** Underline the words in paragraph 7 that help you determine what the word *dampness* means.

**B** Read paragraph 8. Circle the text that helps explain the word *assistance*. In paragraph 9, underline the context clue that helps you figure out what the word *strike* means.

#### Flood and Funds

7    Floods are expensive. Floodwater is powerful, lifting buildings off the ground and sending cars sailing. Floodwater is also dirty. When the water drains away from buildings, mud and other **debris** are left behind. The dirty water can ruin furniture, electrical appliances, and other household items. Dampness <u>left behind by water</u> causes mold to grow, and wood and other building materials <u>can be ruined by water.</u> Even a few inches of water can mean thousands of dollars in cleaning and repairs. Many buildings cannot be repaired.

8    A major flood can cost billions of dollars. After Hurricane Sandy, some neighborhoods were completely destroyed. New York City subway tunnels were underwater. That flood was a **disaster**, and many people needed assistance. Government workers rescued those who were stranded. They provided food and water. The government also gave people money to fix their homes and businesses.

#### Finding Solutions

9    Floods can strike almost anywhere. But they tend <u>to hit</u> the same places over and over. Low-lying places near water are at the greatest risk. People build homes where there may be floods. When a flood hits, they may get money from the government to rebuild. Sometimes they rebuild in the same spot.

**152**    Unit 7 ■ Reading Informational Text: Craft and Structure

---

## Words to Know

**General Academic Vocabulary**
**disaster** (*noun*): a terrible event that destroys things or harms people

**Domain-Specific Vocabulary**
**debris** (*noun*): small scattered pieces left over when something has been destroyed

**Working with Word Meaning** Encourage students to draw images that help them remember these words. In this case, because the words are related, students could draw a single image titled "Disaster" with a label for the debris.

10 Some say these owners should be allowed to rebuild where they want. It's their home. Others say that when government pays, everyone pays. They think the owners should not be allowed to rebuild in the same place. What do you think?

### Comprehension Check

**1.** Circle the letter next to the word that helps you figure out the meaning of *appliances* in paragraph 7.

  **a.** dirty

  **b.** ruin

  **c.** furniture

  **(d.)** electrical

**2.** Circle the letter next to the word that is a synonym of *provided* in paragraph 8.

  **a.** rescued

  **b.** stranded

  **(c.)** gave

  **d.** fix

**3.** Work with a partner to determine the meanings of unknown words on pages 152–153. Why is it important to know what the words mean in order to understand information in the passage?

Sample answer: It's important to know what words in the text mean so that the reader won't miss any details and will completely understand the topic.

## Foundational Skills: Fluency

Explain to students that they can read more fluently if they pay attention to punctuation marks—for example, pausing at periods and raising intonation at question marks. Model fluent reading for the section "Finding Solutions" on page 152 in the Student Book.

Give students a chance to practice fluent reading with a partner. They may also want to record themselves reading the selection so that they can play it back and listen to their own phrasing for improving prosodic skills. Additional fluency passages and activities can be found at **sadlierconnect.com** and in the *Foundational Skills Handbook*.

## Guided Practice

### Comprehension Check

**Answer Explanations:**

**1.** Choice D, *electrical*, is a clue to the meaning of *appliances* because it is the adjective that describes the noun.

**2.** Choice C, *gave*, is a synonym for *provided*. The text would also make sense if you used *gave* in place of *provided* in sentence 5.

**3.** Have students use context clues to determine the meanings of the boldface words on page 152. They can use inferencing, synonyms, antonyms, or restatements. Students should understand that if they do not know what a word in the passage means, they might miss an important piece of information.

## Peer Collaboration

You might have students work in pairs so that peers can support each other in responding to callouts A and B on page 152 and Comprehension Check questions 1 and 2 on page 153.

Ask students to finalize their answers and then share them with a partner. Students should then make changes to their answers based on the discussion with their partner. Finally, ask pairs to report their answers to the whole group.

# Determining Word Meanings

## Independent Practice

### Recap Reading Selection

Remind students that they have been reading about floods and flooding. Have them recall the kind of damage that floods do (ruining things and leaving them dirty and moldy) and a possible solution (creating a flood zone, so the water can go someplace that will not cause damage).

### Read and Apply

Have students read the selection independently as you circulate. If you notice students struggling, you can provide support with the suggestions that follow.

### CITE EVIDENCE

**A** Help students see that the word *safe* is the opposite of the word *treacherous*, so *treacherous* clearly means something like "dangerous."

**B** The word *leave* is a synonym for *evacuate*. Students can check this by using the word *leave* twice: "If you are asked to *leave*, *leave* as quickly as you can." Since this substitution does make sense, the two words are synonyms.

Students should see that the synonyms and antonyms on the page help the reader understand the text better by giving clues to the meanings of unknown words.

---

## DETERMINING WORD MEANINGS

**Independent Practice**

Water Everywhere *continued*

**WORDS TO KNOW**
absorb
contaminated
snowmelt

**CITE EVIDENCE**

**A** Circle an antonym that helps you determine the meaning of the word *treacherous* in the first sentence of paragraph 13.

**B** In paragraph 13, bullet point 3, underline a synonym for *evacuate*. How did these synonyms and antonyms help you understand this section on flood safety?

### What Causes Floods?

11    Floods are caused by storms and heavy rain. But other conditions cause flooding as well. Melting snow can turn into gallons of water. **Snowmelt** can flow downhill and fill rivers and streams. When they get too full, they overflow. Wildfires can also lead to flooding. Fire burns away the trees and other plants that **absorb** water. Without plants to soak up the water, floodwaters take longer to go down.

12    Finally, dam failures also cause floods. Dams control the flow of rivers. They can create lakes that we use for fun or to supply us with drinking water. Dams can also turn the flow of water into a source of electrical power. But if a dam fails, all that water rushes out, crushing everything in its path. The floodwater from a dam break is like a tidal wave because the water moves with great force. A dam failure was the cause of the tragic Johnstown flood in Pennsylvania. It happened in 1889 after heavy rains. More than 2,200 people died.

### Flood Safety

13    Floods can be treacherous. Take steps to stay safe.

- Listen to the weather forecast if you are at risk. A flood watch means a flood is possible. A flood warning means flooding has begun.
- Unplug electrical appliances.
- If you are asked to evacuate, leave as quickly as you can. Keep a bag packed with essential items that you can grab fast.
- Do not try to walk through moving water. It can knock you down. And floodwater can be **contaminated** with waste.

---

## Words to Know

**General Academic Vocabulary**
**absorb** (*verb*): to soak in or soak up
**contaminated** (*adjective*): unclean or harmful

**Domain-Specific Vocabulary**
**snowmelt** (*noun*): the water created when snow melts

**Working with Word Meaning** Help students remember the vocabulary words by asking them to give an example and nonexample of each word's meaning.

14    After a flood you may need to boil water to make it safe to drink. Be sure electrical appliances are completely dry before you use them. Watch out for snakes or other creatures that might have floated into your home. Floods are the most common natural disaster. So stay safe!

**Comprehension Check**    (MORE ONLINE) sadlierconnect.com

1. Circle the letter next to the word in paragraph 13 that helps you figure out the meaning of the word *contaminated*.

   a. float
   (b.) waste
   c. water
   d. flood

2. Circle the letter next to the words in paragraph 11 that help you determine the meaning of the word *overflow*.

   (a.) get too full
   b. gallons of water
   c. flow downhill
   d. fill rivers and streams

3. The section "What Causes Floods?" discusses the conditions that bring about flooding. What context clues tell you the meaning of *conditions* in paragraph 11? How does knowing the meaning of the word help you understand this section?

   Sample answer: "Floods are caused by storms and heavy rain" followed

   by "other" and "cause flooding as well" help me understand that

   *conditions* means "things that cause something else." The meaning helps

   me understand the things that cause flooding.

## Extend Thinking: Create

Help students extend their thinking by doing a short creative project. Have groups of students make a public service advertisement for a public solution to flooding. They could advocate for flood zones, more levees, or other, more fanciful solutions that they imagine.

Students should create a visual to represent the flood-control solution and then present their solution to the rest of the class.

Speakers should speak clearly, in complete sentences, and at a reasonable rate. Listeners should pay attention and ask questions to check their understanding.

**Comprehension Check**

**Answer Explanations:**

1. Choice B, *waste*, should help students figure out that *contaminated* means "unclean."

2. Choice A, the phrase *get too full*, shows the cause of overflow and gives a clue to that word's meaning.

3. The first sentence in paragraph 11 says that "floods are caused by storms and heavy rain," and the second sentence says that "other conditions cause flooding as well." This means that storms and heavy rain are also conditions, which leads to the conclusion that *conditions* are things or situations that can cause flooding.

## Critical Comprehension

Use the following questions to help students think more deeply about the text. Students should be prepared to support their answers with evidence from the text.

- *Why are some parts of the U.S. at greater risk of flooding than others?* (Areas close to or below sea level or near the coastlines are at greater risk.)

- *How can people lower their chances of losing their home to a flood?* (ask the local government to put more flood-control measures in place; build their homes away from low-lying areas; build their homes on posts)

**Assess and Respond**

**If** students have difficulty answering the questions in the Comprehension Check…

**Then** create a reading group to review the selections, summarizing each section as you go and modeling the skills that had been practiced independently.

## Guided Instruction

### OBJECTIVE
**Use text features and search tools to locate information in a text.**

### Genre: Journal Article

A journal article is a form of writing that explains a topic. It often includes photographs and other features that offer additional information to the reader. A journal article might appear in print or online.

### Set the Purpose

To activate students' prior knowledge about the reading skill, ask *What does it mean if you see words in an article that look different from other words? Why might some text be in a box?*

### Model and Teach

Read the selection as students follow along in their books.

### CITE EVIDENCE

**A** *I know that a hyperlink might be set in a different color or with underlining to show that it can be clicked on.*

*What is the hyperlink in paragraph 1?* (www.weather.gov) *What word in the link tells you what kind of information is on this site?* (weather)

**B** *I will look for a subhead on a line by itself. What is the subhead on this page?* (Twirling Tornadoes) *Based on the subhead, what do you predict you will learn about in this section of the passage?* (tornadoes)

---

## USING TEXT FEATURES

**Guided Instruction**

**WORDS TO KNOW**
atmosphere
destroy

> Text features and search tools help readers locate information.

#### CITE EVIDENCE

**A** A **hyperlink** is a search tool that is used to find **information** on the Internet. The words in the link tell what information can be found there when you click on it. Circle the hyperlink in paragraph 1. Underline the word that tells what information you might find when you click on it.

**B** A **subhead** is a title within a selection. This text feature introduces a specific part of a reading passage. Subheads are included on a separate line above the part of the passage they introduce. Put a star next to the subhead on this page. What might you learn in this section?

# Watch Out for Weather!
### (Genre: Journal Article)

1 Tornadoes, hurricanes, and blizzards are all extreme weather events. They are often called natural disasters. Scientists at the National Weather Service (**www.weather.gov**) watch and study weather. They warn people when a dangerous storm is on its way. Each year, the National Weather Service sends out 50,000 warnings for extreme weather events. The warnings give people time to prepare for storms and protect themselves.

#### Twirling Tornadoes ★

2 *Twister, funnel,* and *whirlwind* are all nicknames for one dangerous weather event: a tornado. Tornadoes develop from thunderstorms. Before a tornado appears, warm air near the ground meets cold air higher in the **atmosphere**. The two masses of air push against each other in a circular motion. Then they form a funnel of water droplets. If the funnel touches the ground, the storm is a tornado. Winds inside a tornado may reach 200 miles per hour. The funnel picks up dust and dirt in its path. It can even uproot trees and pick up cars. One big tornado picked up a train. It carried the train in the air for 80 feet. All the passengers were still inside!

**156**   Unit 7 ■ Reading Informational Text: Craft and Structure

---

## Words to Know

**General Academic Vocabulary**
**destroy** (*verb*): to completely break or ruin something, leaving nothing but scattered pieces

**Domain-Specific Vocabulary**
**atmosphere** (*noun*): the layer of air that surrounds a planet

**Working with Word Meaning** Have students make flash cards of the two words. The word and a picture that represents the word should be on one side of the card. On the other side should be a word they associate with the vocabulary word and a sentence using the word. Have students use the cards to help them remember the meanings of the words.

## CRAFT AND STRUCTURE

3   Tornado funnels can be a mile wide. Most of them do not stay on the ground for long. Still, they do a lot of damage. Tornadoes can **destroy** everything in their paths. Hospitals, schools, and homes may be completely ruined. Because they twist and turn as they race across the ground, tornadoes may destroy one house and leave the next one untouched.

4   Sometimes a tornado travels over water. It forms a waterspout. It picks up water and fish along the way. Some fish have been carried hundreds of miles in water spouts.

**TORNADO ALERT!**

People may be injured or killed by objects tossed by the funnel. That is why it is important to know what to do when a tornado approaches.

- Stay inside.
- Go to the basement or ground floor.
- ★ Stay away from windows.
- Get under a table or stairs that can protect you from falling objects.

### Comprehension Check

How does each text feature in this passage improve your understanding of tornadoes?

**CITE EVIDENCE**

**C** A **sidebar** is a text feature that provides extra information about the topic of an article. Circle the "Tornado Alert!" sidebar.

**D** A **bulleted list** is a text feature that organizes information. A bullet is a small circle. Each bullet introduces a fact or piece of information. Put a star next to a bulleted piece of information about staying safe during a tornado. What else do you learn from this list?

**CITE EVIDENCE**

**C** *I know that a sidebar is not part of the main text. I will look for something that seems to be set apart from the text.*

*What is the title of the sidebar on this page?* (Tornado Alert!) *What do you predict this sidebar will be about?* (knowing what to do in case of a tornado)

**D** *Bullets are small circles or dots, so I will look for a list with dots in front of them. Where is the bulleted list on the page?* (in the sidebar) *How many safety tips are in the list?* (four)

### Comprehension Check

**Sample Answer:** The hyperlink gives me more information about weather. The subhead helps me find the part of the article that is just about tornadoes. The sidebar gives me extra information about what to do in case of a tornado.

**Answer Explanation:** Students should understand that the various text features help the reader locate more information about the topic of the article.

## Listening and Viewing Skills

Reread paragraph 4 as students listen and look at the photograph. *What is the funnel of a tornado over water made of?* (water) *What else can get picked up when a tornado goes over water?* (fish, and possibly other things that are in the water)

## Review: Determine Word Meanings

Have students use the vocabulary strategies they learned earlier in the unit to determine the meaning of an unfamiliar word. You might suggest the word *develop* (used with its synonym *appear*) in paragraph 2 on page 156.

## Digital Connection: Hyperlinks

Let students know that when they are reading an article online it may sometimes be difficult to identify a hyperlink. However, if they put their cursor over a hyperlink, the cursor will change from an arrow into a pointing finger.

Challenge students to go to the National Weather Service Website, by typing in the address in the hyperlink on page 156 (www.weather.gov). Have them look for another hyperlink at that site and click through. Ask students to a make a list or a branch diagram of the web pages they visited and what they learned on each one.

## Guided Practice

### Recap Reading Selection

Have students recall what they have learned so far about tornadoes. They should understand that these are destructive storm clouds that rotate and reach down to the ground. Let students know that in this section they will read about hurricanes, another kind of storm.

### Read and Practice

Have partners take turns reading the selection as you circulate to provide support. Model finding text features with Cite Evidence callout A. For callout B, circulate and provide partners with scaffolding as needed. You might use the following to help students who are having difficulty.

### CITE EVIDENCE

**A** By this point, students should be able to tell the difference between sidebar text and the article's main text. Guide students to look at the green sidebar labeled "Hurricane Facts." Ask them what kind of text feature appears in the sidebar. (a bulleted list)

**B** Remind students that a subhead is a text feature authors can use to organize information. Have students scan pages 158–159 for the subhead that mentions famous hurricanes.

**C** Help students think about what information might be located at the web page. Guide students to understand that the link will provide readers with additional information the author does not have room to provide.

---

## USING TEXT FEATURES

### Guided Practice

**Watch Out for Weather!** *continued*

**WORDS TO KNOW**

crew

predict

#### CITE EVIDENCE

**A** Circle the text feature that gives you facts about hurricanes.

**B** Put a star next to the text feature that tells you that you will be reading about famous hurricanes.

**C** Underline the hyperlink. Why does the author include it?

### Horrible Hurricanes

5  A hurricane can be as dangerous as a tornado. A hurricane is a storm that brings strong winds and heavy rain. Hurricanes begin as tropical storms near Earth's equator. They form over warm ocean waters. As the water becomes warmer, the winds become faster. Once wind speeds reach 75 miles per hour, the storm is a hurricane. The winds spin in a closed circle.

**HURRICANE FACTS**

- Hurricanes in the Pacific Ocean are usually called typhoons.
- Hurricanes in the Indian Ocean are usually called cyclones.
- When the eye of a hurricane passes overhead, the weather is sunny, calm, and quiet.
- Most hurricanes travel about 10–20 miles per hour.

### Too Much Wind

6  Scientists on the ground need to get information about a storm. Hurricane hunters fly right into storms to get the facts. They bravely go into the storm's eye through fierce winds. The eye is the hurricane's calmest part. There the plane's **crew** drops instruments into the air. The instruments check wind speed and temperature. Scientists on the ground study the information and use it to **predict** how serious the storm will be. It's also important to try to figure out in what direction the storm will travel. Scientists can't stop a hurricane. But they can warn people who might be in the path of a natural disaster.

To see a video about hurricane hunters, visit http://oceantoday.noaa.gov/hurricanehunters/welcome.html.

---

## Words to Know

**General Academic Vocabulary**

**crew** (*noun*): a team of people who work together, especially on board a ship or an airplane

**predict** (*verb*): to make an informed guess about something that has not happened yet

**Working with Word Meaning** Encourage students to use new vocabulary words in speaking and in writing. Ask students to use the words in discussions when appropriate. You might use a signal, such as finger snapping, to recognize when someone uses a vocabulary word.

## CRAFT AND STRUCTURE
### Guided Practice

**Famous Hurricanes** ★

7     The Galveston hurricane hit Texas in 1900. Its highest winds reached 140 miles per hour. Hugo hit the Atlantic Coast in 1989. Its highest winds reached 160 miles per hour. Andrew hit Florida in 1992. Its highest winds reached 165 miles per hour. Katrina hit and destroyed much of New Orleans in 2005. Its highest winds reached 170 miles per hour.

### Comprehension Check

1. Circle the letter next to the sentence that is NOT included in a sidebar text feature.

    a. Hurricanes in the Indian Ocean are usually called cyclones.

    b. Most hurricanes travel about 10–20 miles per hour.

    c. When the eye of a hurricane passes overhead, the weather is sunny, calm, and quiet.

    (d.) The Galveston hurricane hit Texas in 1900.

2. Circle the letter next to the text feature that a reader would use to see a video about hurricane hunters.

    a. Too Much Wind

    b. Hurricane Facts

    (c.) http://oceantoday.noaa.gov/hurricanehunters/welcome.html

    d. Famous Hurricanes

3. With a partner, read and discuss the "Hurricane Facts" sidebar on page 158. Why does the author include this text feature? How does it help you understand "Horrible Hurricanes"?

Sample answer: The sidebar adds extra important facts. It helps me

understand the essay because it gives me more information.

Unit 7 ■ Reading Informational Text: Craft and Structure    **159**

### Comprehension Check

**Answer Explanations:**

1. Choice D, the only fact about the Galveston hurricane, was not mentioned in the sidebar.

2. Students can see that the words *hurricane hunters* are in the hyperlink. Therefore, choice C is correct. They can also revisit the text at the bottom of page 158.

3. Students should understand that the sidebar gives additional information that is helpful for learning more about hurricanes.

## Reciprocal Teaching

Form groups of four, and assign one of the following roles to each group member: Summarizer, Questioner, Clarifier, and Predictor. In a group discussion, the Summarizers should say what they have learned so far about the topic of hurricanes. The Questioners should think of at least two questions to ask about the topic. The Clarifiers should answer those questions or identify where the answers could be found. The Predictors should say what they think they will learn about the topic in the next section. Call on different groups to share their ideas with the class.

## Supporting English Language Learners

Build background information for English language learners by telling them that larger hurricanes and tropical storms are given human names. *Hugo*, *Andrew*, and *Katrina* are all names given to storms. Over the course of a hurricane season, the storms are named in alphabetical order. If storms have names, people who work in weather-related fields can more easily talk about and distinguish them.

As students read the last paragraph on page 159, they should be able to read more fluently and with less confusion because they know that the proper names are the names of hurricanes, not people.

## Independent Practice

### Recap Reading Selection

Have a short group discussion about what students have learned so far about tornadoes and hurricanes. Ask students if they remember how tornadoes and hurricanes form. (Tornadoes form when cold and warm air meet; hurricanes form when warm ocean water causes wind speed to increase.) Let them know they are next going to read about another kind of storm called a blizzard. Depending on where they live or have lived, students may not be familiar with this type of storm.

### Read and Apply

Have students read the selection independently as you circulate to provide support. As you circulate, provide students with targeted scaffolding as needed.

### CITE EVIDENCE

**A** Remind students to scan the text for the words *Great Lakes*. Once they find the words, have them identify the subhead under which the information appears.

**B** Have students scan pages 160–161 for text features. If necessary, remind students what a bulleted list is. Guide them to identify the bulleted text in the sidebar on page 161.

---

## USING TEXT FEATURES

### Independent Practice

**Watch Out for Weather!** *continued*

**WORDS TO KNOW**
**dangerous**
**prairie**
**severe**

**CITE EVIDENCE**

**A** Under which subhead would you find information about blizzards in the Great Lakes area? Find that information and underline it.

**B** Underline the sentence in the text feature that states a fact about ground blizzards. What kind of text feature is inside the sidebar?

#### What Is a Blizzard?

8    A blizzard is usually any serious snowstorm with strong winds of at least 35 miles per hour. To count as a blizzard, there has to be a lot of wind. While blizzards often mean lots of snow, there are no rules about how low the temperature has to be or how much snow must fall—if any—for a storm to be called a blizzard. **Severe** blizzards make it impossible to see buildings or trees just a few yards away.

9    Blizzards can be very **dangerous**. Since it is so hard to see outside, it is dangerous to travel. People can even get lost walking around their own backyard. Also, being out in cold temperatures and strong winds can cause frostbite, or frozen fingers and toes. Before weather could be predicted, blizzards could happen with almost no warning, such as when temperatures were warm. For an example, go to the link about the "Children's Blizzard" that happened in the late 1800s. **(http://www.farmersalmanac.com/weather/2012/01/09/the-childrens-blizzard/)**

#### Where and Why Do Blizzards Happen?

10    In North America, blizzards appear most in the **prairie** states, the Great Lakes, the northeastern United States, and Canada. Blizzards over the prairie happen when cold, dry northern air hits warm, wet southern air. In the Northeast, blizzards usually come from hurricanes moving down from the northern Atlantic Ocean. The poor Great Lakes area! It gets hit by both types of storms. This land is also affected by heavy lake snow and wind, which create even more chance of blizzards.

**160**    Unit 7 ■ Reading Informational Text: Craft and Structure

---

## Words to Know

**General Academic Vocabulary**
**dangerous** (*adjective*): able to cause harm
**severe** (*adjective*): harsh and strong

**Domain-Specific Vocabulary**
**prairie** (*noun*): a large, flat grassland area

**Working with Word Meaning** Have students write a weather forecast using the vocabulary words. Invite student volunteers to read their forecasts aloud.

## CRAFT AND STRUCTURE

### How to Prepare for a Blizzard

11    First, pay attention to the weather forecasts. Next, make sure you have flashlights, batteries, food, water, first aid supplies, and a backup heater in your home. Most importantly, stay inside!

**BLIZZARD FACTS**

- Some unusual blizzards bring no precipitation, or snow.
- Strong winds can pick up ground snow to create a "ground blizzard."
- The strength of a blizzard's wind is more important than the snowfall.

**Comprehension Check**    MORE ONLINE  sadlierconnect.com

1. If you click the link mentioned in paragraph 9, you would expect to find information about

   (a.) a blizzard that happened without warning.

   b. children who played in the snow.

   c. the importance of having flashlights, batteries, and food.

   d. how farmers prepare for blizzards.

2. Circle the letter next to the sentence that is included in the sidebar.

   a. What is a blizzard?

   (b.) Some unusual blizzards bring no precipitation, or snow.

   c. Where and why do blizzards happen?

   d. Blizzards can be very dangerous.

3. Review the text features on pages 160–161. What did each text feature help you understand about blizzards? Cite text evidence to support your answer.

   Sample answer: The text features help me because they organize the passage and

   let me know what information is coming next, like "what" comes before "where"

   and "why." The facts give me information, like some blizzards have no snowfall.

---

**Comprehension Check**

### Answer Explanations:

**1.** Based on the details in paragraph 9, students should understand that the link will give more information about the Children's Blizzard, which happened suddenly and without warning. Therefore, choice A is correct.

**2.** The sentence identified in choice B appears in the sidebar.

**3.** Students should identify subheads, sidebars, and hyperlinks. Students should understand text features help readers find information in a text.

## Critical Comprehension

Use the following questions to help students think more deeply about the text. Students should be prepared to support their answers with evidence from the text.

- *What safety precautions are common to the types of weather discussed in the article?* (Stay inside and keep emergency supplies handy.)

- *What do you think the author's purpose might have been in writing this article?* (to provide safety information to readers)

**Assess and Respond**

**If** students have trouble answering the questions in the Comprehension Check…

**Then** ask them some comprehension questions about the article to determine whether they understood what they read. If not, you may wish to form a reading group to support them.

---

## Foundational Skill Review: *R*-controlled Vowels

Review *r*-controlled vowels with students by reminding them how the letter *r* after a vowel changes the sound of that vowel. Model how this sounds, using small words such as *car, her, stir, or,* and *fur.* Explain that students can use this knowledge when they sound out longer words, such as *blizzard, southern, temperature, dangerous, forecasts, batteries,* and *importantly.*

Additional phonics activities can be found in the *Foundational Skills Handbook* on pages 265–274.

## Guided Instruction

### OBJECTIVE
**Distinguish personal and author's point of view.**

### Genre: Editorial

Explain that an author uses an editorial to take a position on an issue. In this editorial, the author expresses a point of view, or opinion, about the problem of droughts and what people can do about them.

### Set the Purpose

To activate students' thinking about the reading skill, ask *How has someone successfully persuaded you to think or do something?*

### Model and Teach

Read the selection as students follow along in their books.

### CITE EVIDENCE

**A** *I am going to look in the first paragraph for words, such as* should *or* must. *These words are often used to express a point of view, or opinion.*

*What sentence in paragraph 1 states a point of view?* (the last sentence) *How do you know this is a point of view and not a fact?* (The ideas cannot be proven true or false, as facts can.)

**B** *I am going to look for facts that support the author's point of view that people must change their behavior. What text in paragraph 1 can be checked to see if it is true or false?* (the first three sentences)

---

## DISTINGUISHING POINTS OF VIEW

### Guided Instruction

**WORDS TO KNOW**
condense
conserving
vapor

> The author's **point of view** is the author's opinion on a topic. The reader can agree or disagree with this point of view.

**CITE EVIDENCE**

**A** In an editorial, the author's **point of view** is directly and clearly stated. Underline the sentence in paragraph 1 that states the author's point of view.

**B** The purpose of an editorial is to persuade the reader to share the author's point of view. To do this, the author gives evidence to support the opinion. Circle each fact in paragraph 1 that supports the author's point of view.

## Stop the Droughts!
### (Genre: Editorial)

1   Our state is currently in the middle of the third worst drought in history. Our land is drying up. Plants and animals are dying. People must change their behavior so that we can end this crisis soon.

2   Droughts happen when the earth is very dry. Because we depend on the water cycle to keep the earth wet, it's a problem when there is not enough rain. Things get worse when high temperatures dry out the land fast. Plants can't grow, and animals don't have enough to eat or drink. Without them, people have no food.

3   People can help lessen the effects of droughts by **conserving** water. We must always try to save water. Doing this before a problem arrives can help an area when it is hit by a drought. Here are a few things we can do to conserve water:

- Take shorter showers.
- Water lawns less often.
- Don't let faucets drip or run.

---

### Words to Know

**General Academic Vocabulary**
**conserving** (*verb*): saving, or using carefully

**Domain-Specific Vocabulary**
**condense** (*verb*): to turn a gas into a liquid by cooling it
**vapor** (*noun*): the gaseous, invisible form of a liquid

**Working with Word Meaning** Help students retain the meaning of words they learn by asking them to think of examples and nonexamples for each word. Invite student volunteers to share them with the class.

## CRAFT AND STRUCTURE
### Guided Instruction

4   It's essential to prepare for a drought. It's even more important to help keep droughts from coming in the first place. Earth is getting warmer. Cars and smokestacks burn fossil fuels, such as coal and oil. These fuels cause air pollution. The pollution traps heat in the atmosphere, affecting global climate.

5   We should care about global warming because higher temperatures help cause drought. In the water cycle, the sun causes water to evaporate into an invisible gas called water **vapor**. Cooler temperatures cause the vapor to **condense** and form rain. In an unusually hot area, the clouds take the water away. The water condenses and falls where the air is cooler. That is why droughts are worse in hotter areas.

### Rules for Saving Water

6   Water conservation is more important than ever in places with low rainfall. The American Southwest has been suffering from major droughts for years. Many places have water restrictions that affect how often people can water gardens or fill their swimming pools.

7   Restrictions help save water for more important things, such as for drinking! Water conservation saves water for growing crops.

### Comprehension Check

What two weather-related reasons does the author give for drought? What is the author's point of view about the responsibility that people have to limit the effects of droughts? Cite text evidence in your answer.

#### CITE EVIDENCE

**C**  Often, an editorial asks the reader to take action. Underline the two sentences in paragraph 4 that tell the reader what he or she should do.

**D**  Sometimes an author states opinions related to the main opinion. Circle the sentence that tells how the author feels about global warming. What information supports this point of view?

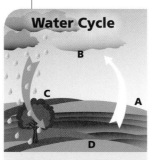

**Water Cycle**

A  Evaporation—Sun turns water into steam.

B  Condensation—Steam turns into liquid.

C  Precipitation—Rain or snow falls.

D  Collection—Water gathers in the ground or ocean.

### Guided Instruction

## CITE EVIDENCE

**C**  *I know that when authors are trying to persuade readers to take action, they often use phrases such as "it is necessary to," "it is important to," and "people must." I will look in paragraph 4 for phrases like these.*

*What action is the author asking readers to take?* (to prepare for a drought; to keep droughts from occurring in the first place)

**D**  *I will look for some of the words that I know authors use when giving an opinion or point of view.*

*What word in paragraph 5 gives a clue that the author is giving his point of view, or opinion?* (should)

### Comprehension Check

**Sample Answer:** The author says that drought is caused by lack of rain and high temperatures. People need to conserve water and to help lessen the effects of drought.

**Answer Explanation:** Students should understand that the author's point of view is that people need to take responsibility for global warming and conserving water so we can have enough water to drink, use, and grow food.

## Review: Using Text Features

Bring students' attention to the Water Cycle diagram on page 163. Ask students to identify the type of text feature (a sidebar) and its purpose (to illustrate the water cycle). Challenge students to tell you the best time to stop and read this text feature (before or after "Rules for Saving Water").

## Support English Language Learners

Help English language learners with the spelling pattern *gh*. Review the sounds this letter combination can make—an *f* sound and no sound. Point out the selection words *enough* and *drought* as examples.  Work with students to fill in a two-column chart with words in which the *gh* sounds like *f* (*cough, tough, rough, laugh, paragraph*) and those in which the *gh* is silent (*thought, bought, caught, fought, daughter, taught, night, fight, sight, right, light, high*).

## Guided Practice

### Recap Reading Selection

Have students recall what they have learned so far about droughts. They should be able to say that droughts happen when not enough rain falls in a place. They should be able to say that higher temperatures can worsen the effects of droughts. Students should also remember that people can help during a drought by using less water.

### Read and Practice

Have partners take turns reading the selection as you circulate to provide support. Model practicing distinguishing points of view with Cite Evidence callout A. For callout B, circulate and provide partners with scaffolding as needed. You might use the following to help students who are having difficulty.

### CITE EVIDENCE

**A** Point out the last three sentences of paragraph 8. Ask students, *According to the author, why should someone care about drought if that person is not living in an area affected by drought?* (The price of food goes up for everyone.)

**B** Students should realize that causing thousands of deaths is devastating, as are famine and the loss of crops around the world.

---

## DISTINGUISHING POINTS OF VIEW

### Guided Practice

**Stop the Droughts!** *continued*

**WORDS TO KNOW**
adapted
devastating

**CITE EVIDENCE**

**A** What does the author think you should care about in paragraph 8? Circle that piece of information.

**B** Put a star next to the evidence that the author gives in paragraph 9 to show that droughts are devastating. Explain to a partner why you do or do not share the author's point of view.

### Drought and Famine Hurt Us All

8　(Severe droughts are happening around the world.) During a severe drought, the rainfall for the year remains less than average. If this goes on for years, reservoirs begin to dry up. Reservoirs are natural or human-made lakes that hold our drinking water. The plants and farm animals can die from thirst when this happens. There may not be a drought where you are, but you can be still affected. Drought can kill crops. Then the price of food goes up for everyone.

9　In places like East Africa, droughts can be **devastating**. The drought there has caused thousands of people to ★ die. In places with a lot of poverty, people cannot afford to pay higher food prices. So they eat less or go hungry. When this happens to many people at once, it is called a famine. Droughts are affecting crops around the world. So other countries have less to share to help people affected by famine.

10　Another place that is experiencing drought is the Amazon rainforest. The rainforests in Brazil are going through a "megadrought." That means that before they could recover from the last drought, another drought struck. The living things in the rainforest have **adapted** to a wet environment. They suffer when it is too dry. Many of the plants and animals are not found anyplace else. And this is bad news for us. Some of the plants in the Amazon are used to make important medicines.

---

## Words to Know

**General Academic Vocabulary**
**devastating** (*adjective*): terrible in a way that causes a great deal of damage

**Domain-Specific Vocabulary**
**adapted** (*verb*): changed in a way that makes it easier to survive in a certain place

**Working with Word Meaning** Challenge students to use the new vocabulary terms in a short story about an animal that survives by changing in a new environment.

## CRAFT AND STRUCTURE
**Guided Practice**

11    So even if there is plenty of rain where you live, there are still a lot of reasons to be concerned. Your source of food may depend on rain in other parts of the country or the world. Many thousands of lives depend on rain. Plants and animals that don't live anyplace else depend on it. Conserving water is an important issue we should all care about!

### Comprehension Check

1. Circle the letter next to the word that best describes how the author feels about droughts.

  **a.** hopeful

  **b.** angry

  **(c.)** worried

  **d.** sad

2. Circle the letter next to the reason that the author gives for thinking you might not care about droughts.

  **a.** You think food is too expensive.

  **(b.)** You do not live in an area with drought.

  **c.** You have never been to Africa.

  **d.** You think the rainforests have enough rain.

3. The author gives many reasons to care about droughts. With a partner, discuss which reasons you think are best at making you share his point of view. Why are these reasons so effective?

Sample answer: Droughts are killing many people through famine. The Amazon rainforest is in trouble. These are effective reasons because they show that droughts are a serious problem that we need to do something about.

Unit 7 ■ Reading Informational Text: Craft and Structure    **165**

## Guided Practice

### Comprehension Check

**Answer Explanations:**

1. Choice C, *worried*, is the best answer because the author is writing about a serious problem and calling the reader to action.

2. Choice B is supported by text in paragraph 8: "There may not be a drought where you are, but you can still be affected."

3. Students should articulate at least two reasons and explain why they were effective. Students should suggest that the author's discussion of famine, crop failure, water shortages, and the deaths of plants and animals are all reasons for everyone to care about drought.

## Turn and Talk

Another way to engage students in a comprehension review is to give them a chance to discuss their answers with a peer. Have students take turns sharing their answers with a partner. Then give them a chance to change or add to their answers based on anything they learned in the discussion. You might wish to have students record the ideas they heard from their partner in order to effectively practice listening skills.

## Discussion Skills

Remind students that when they are having discussions, they should listen carefully to each other's ideas and try to add on to them. This makes discussions more interesting and productive rather than each participant only introducing new ideas.

Give students some sentence stems to help scaffold a discussion that builds on ideas.

• *What you said makes me wonder if . . .*

• *That comment makes me think that . . .*

• *That thought reminds me of . . .*

## Independent Practice

### Recap Reading Selection

Remind students that they have been reading about droughts. Ask students to summarize what they have learned so far. They should recall that droughts can cause famines in places where crops fail and people cannot afford to buy more expensive food.

### Read and Apply

Have students read the selection independently as you circulate to provide support. As you circulate, provide students with targeted scaffolding as needed.

### CITE EVIDENCE

**A** Guide students to see that the last sentence of paragraph 12 states what the author thinks is the worst part about droughts: "droughts will happen often."

**B** Students should understand after reading paragraph 13 that water is not always present in adequate amounts where it is needed most. Help them understand that the author recommends conserving water and using less energy as a way of lessening the effects of droughts.

---

## DISTINGUISHING POINTS OF VIEW

### Independent Practice

Stop the Droughts! *continued*

**WORDS TO KNOW**
continent
precious
wildfire

### CITE EVIDENCE

**A** What does the author think is the worst thing about droughts? Put a star next to that sentence in paragraph 12.

**B** If there is the same amount of water in the world, why is the author worried? Underline the reason in paragraph 13. How does the author feel we should deal with droughts?

12  Drought is a problem that is happening around the world. Every **continent** is affected by it. In some places, people have to live with water restrictions. They can't water their lawns or wash their cars. In other places, food crops are dying because droughts are drying out the land. Droughts are causing famines and **wildfires**. The worst part is that ★ scientists say droughts will happen more often.

13  The world has always had the same amount of water in it. The water we have evaporates into the sky and comes back down as rain. The water in your glass might be the same water that the dinosaurs drank. The problem is that the water isn't always where we need it. We need it in the places that people live and in places where food is grown. If some are wasting water, others may not have enough. So we have to be careful with our water supplies, conserve them, and keep them clean for ourselves and for all other living things on this planet. And because droughts are happening more often, we all need to pitch in and save our most **precious** resource.

14  By now, maybe you are serious about helping. Do you turn off the faucet while you brush your teeth? That could save gallons. Do you run tap water until it gets cold when you want a drink? That's a lot of clean water down the drain. Instead, fill a pitcher and put it in the refrigerator. Time yourself when you take a shower. The quicker you are, the more water you will save. But that's not all. We also need to use less energy to keep the planet from getting even hotter. Turn off the lights when you leave the room. Ride a bike. It's everyone's job to help the environment.

---

### Words to Know

**General Academic Vocabulary**
**precious** (*adjective*): having great value

**Domain-Specific Vocabulary**
**continent** (*noun*): one of the seven large landmasses of the globe (North America, South America, Europe, Africa, Asia, Australia, Antarctica)
**wildfire** (*noun*): a fire that burns out of control, usually in forests and grasslands

**Working with Word Meaning** To help students retain the meanings of the new vocabulary, ask them to restate the definitions in their own words.

CRAFT AND STRUCTURE
**Independent Practice**

15 Remember, you can still be affected by a drought even if you live in an area with lots of rain. Remember also that by saving water at your home, you could be helping people who are experiencing drought somewhere else. Think of how amazing if would be if, through your actions, you could help people all over the world.

**Comprehension Check**   MORE ONLINE   sadlierconnect.com

**1.** Circle the letter next to a problem caused by droughts.

a. famine

b. wildfires

c. restrictions

d. all of the above

**2.** Circle the letter next to the BEST summary of the author's point of view.

a. We should help the victims of famine and send them food.

b. We should turn off the water when we brush our teeth.

c. We should care about droughts and help deal with them.

d. We should learn more about the history of water.

**3.** What should people be doing about droughts, in this author's point of view? List as many of the author's specific recommendations as you can.

Sample answer: Conserve water by taking shorter showers; turn off the tap while brushing teeth; water lawns less often; don't run water waiting for it to get cold; care about droughts all over the world; conserve energy by turning off lights or riding a bike.

Unit 7 ■ Reading Informational Text: Craft and Structure   **167**

## Speaking and Listening Presentation

Have students create a presentation on an extreme weather topic in this unit. Have students interview each other about the event they or their families experienced. Students should take turns presenting to the class. Presenters should:

• state their topic clearly, and present appropriate facts.

• use formal language, and choose words for effect.

• speak clearly, in complete sentences, and at a reasonable rate.

Elicit responses from students of different cultural backgrounds. Listeners should listen attentively and ask questions.

## Independent Practice

**Comprehension Check**

**Answer Explanations:**

**1.** Students should know that droughts cause famine, wildfires, and restrictions. Choice D is correct.

**2.** Choice C, *We should care about droughts and help deal with them*, is the best answer because it explains the main idea of the text.

**3.** The author's recommendations for dealing with droughts include turning water off while brushing teeth, using the refrigerator for cold water instead of running the tap, taking shorter showers, turning off chargers and lights, and riding a bike.

## Critical Comprehension

Use the following questions to help students think more deeply about the text. Students should be prepared to support their answers with evidence from the text.

• *Would the author have written this editorial if he or she had not experienced a drought? Why or why not?* (The author says that people who have not lived with drought tend not to care about it. He or she likely lives in a place with drought.)

• *What is the connection between drought and conserving water?* (People should conserve water so that they have enough during a drought.)

**Assess and Respond**

**If** students have difficulty answering the Comprehension Check…

**Then** ask them to tell you where they had the most difficulty: reading the text, finding information, or understanding questions. Provide assistance according to students' responses.

## OBJECTIVES

- **Use vocabulary strategies to determine the meaning of general academic and domain-specific words in text.**
- **Use text features and search tools to locate information in a text.**
- **Distinguish personal and author's point of view.**

### Genre: Personal Narrative

Explain to students that in a personal narrative, the author tells a story about an event or events from his or her own life. Generally, these events are told in time order with descriptive information.

### Path Options

You may want to do a close reading with students; if so, use the supports provided on these pages. Or, you may wish to have the students read the text independently and apply the skills learned in this unit. In either case, students should read the text more than once to facilitate understanding and to be able to answer the Comprehension Check questions correctly.

## CLOSE READING

# Dust Bowl Disaster
### (Genre: Personal Narrative)

1    My name is Jack Blanchard. I'm an elderly man now, but I'll never forget my childhood during the Dust Bowl. In 1925, my family moved to the Texas Panhandle. I was just 5 years old then. My parents dreamed of farming on their own land, so they bought a farmhouse with acres and acres of land. In a few years, they had transformed the land into great wheat fields. With the profits from the wheat, they were able to buy cows and chickens, too. We were real pioneers!

2    But the good times did not last long. By 1930, a severe drought turned the rich fields to sand and dust. The earth cracked and split open. Nothing would grow, not even weeds. Thick, choking dust covered everything.

3    Back then, I was just a young boy. I lived with my parents, grandpa, and five sisters. We were simple people who worked long hours, seven days a week. My sisters and I would wake up early before school to milk the cows or plow the fields. We took time off only to go to church on Sunday.

**168**    Unit 7 ▪ Reading Informational Text: Craft and Structure

## Support English Language Learners

English language learners may struggle to read this selection independently. You may wish to assign them reading buddies who have strong reading skills. Instruct reading buddies to take turns reading and summarizing each paragraph. Encourage them to use the pictures as well as words in their summaries.

## CRAFT AND STRUCTURE

4    We took pride in our crops and animals. We weren't rich, but we had what we needed. Or we did until the drought came. The bone-dry conditions were constant and never let up. <u>Those were the worst years of my life.</u>

5    With the drought came fearful storms, nicknamed "dusters." The dust storms stung our eyes and itched our hair. It was hard to breathe. It got so bad that we had to cover our noses and mouths with wet cloths to block the dirt. To protect our eyes, we wore goggles to school.

6    The worst dusters were called "black blizzards." Those were scary because in the middle of the day, the world was dark. Night seemed to last all day.

7    It's hard to explain the impact of this disaster. During it, everyone and everything suffered. Farmers and ranchers couldn't work the land. The bodies of horses, cows, and pigs lay by the roads, filled with dirt. Jackrabbits invaded, eating everything in sight, and the birds flew far, far away. People got sick. Some died of lung disease from breathing in too much dust. Others died from not having food or water.

8    Filthy dust settled on buildings, automobiles, people, and animals. Sand piled up high outside homes. Sometimes we had to climb out of windows because it blocked doors. There was no escaping it. We used rags and tape to seal all the cracks in the windows and doors, but the dust still got in.

9    We had dust in our food and water. We ate dinner and ended up with grit in our teeth. My sisters and I could draw pictures in the dirt that lay on our dining table. Ma said there was no use hanging laundry out to dry. When we did, it looked dirtier than before it was cleaned!

## Support First Reading

Circulate to check students' understanding. As needed, use the following comprehension and strategy check-ins to support basic understanding of the selection as students read.

### Check-in Questions

- *Who is Jack Blanchard, and what historical event is he looking back on?* (Jack Blanchard is the author, and he is looking back on the Dust Bowl that he lived through as a child.)

- *What was it like when the dust storms hit? Describe what happened inside and outside the author's home.* (Inside the house dust got into food, clothing, and water and covered the furniture. Outside the house farm animals died, birds flew away, jackrabbits ate all the plants, and dust storms made seeing and breathing difficult.)

## Review: Determining Word Meanings

Have students use their vocabulary strategies to determine the meaning of the word *constant* in paragraph 4. (Students should be able to figure out that "never let up" is another way of saying *constant*.)

## Differentiate Instruction

Assigning reading buddies to assist striving readers is a good strategy to use. Create heterogeneous pairings, so that proficient students can help those who are unable to read on grade level. Have both partners restate the meaning of the paragraphs they read. This will aid striving readers' comprehension of text as they listen to restatements and read carefully to formulate their own.

**Check-in Question**

• *When did the author and his family leave, and where did they go?* (The author and his family decided to leave after three years of the dust storms. They headed to California, as did many other people escaping the Dust Bowl.)

## Review: Using Text Features

Ask students if they can find the text feature on page 170 and if they remember what it is called (a sidebar). See if they can tell you what information it supplies (the causes of the dust bowl) and when the best time to stop and read it is (in between paragraphs).

## Review: Distinguishing Points of View

Review the author's point of view with students. *What do you think Jack Blanchard's feelings are about the Dust Bowl? Find sections of text that support your conclusion.*

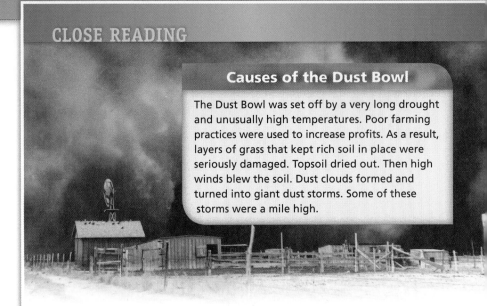

### CLOSE READING

#### Causes of the Dust Bowl

The Dust Bowl was set off by a very long drought and unusually high temperatures. Poor farming practices were used to increase profits. As a result, layers of grass that kept rich soil in place were seriously damaged. Topsoil dried out. Then high winds blew the soil. Dust clouds formed and turned into giant dust storms. Some of these storms were a mile high.

10    My teacher, Miss Evans, read us big-city newspaper accounts of what was going on. Our region in the middle of the country became known as the Dust Bowl. Many states, including Texas, Oklahoma, and Kansas, were affected. But the dusters were so powerful, people as far away as New York and Boston breathed in the dust, too. My grandpa said he felt like he was living in a desert. I said it looked like the moon.

11    We tried to stick it out, but it was clear we had to leave. We had survived three years of drought and dust storms. We said goodbye to our farm and friends, then we packed what we could fit in two old cars and left. The dust storms would continue for seven more years.

12    We headed west, just like millions of others, including folksinger Woody Guthrie. He also lived in Texas during that period and became famous as the "Dust Bowl Troubadour." He wrote and sang great songs about his experience in the Dust Bowl and about traveling west to California. His songs really captured what it was like to live through the great dust storms and then to pack up all you have and move west.

**170**    Unit 7 ■ Reading Informational Text: Craft and Structure

### Strategic Reading

You can support all readers by offering them a strategic reading tip: Create a mental picture as you read. This can aid comprehension and help keep readers engaged, so encourage students to pause as they read and try to picture the events as the author describes them. Challenge students to think about how things might have looked, sounded, felt, smelled, and tasted.

## CRAFT AND STRUCTURE

13  During our travels, no one knew what to expect from life out west. Unfortunately, life in California was hard, too. Jobs weren't always easy to find. The days were long and the pay was low. We lived in one-room shacks with no running water. But we escaped the dust, and at least we could breathe clean air.

14  My family was in California's Central Valley for 10 years. We picked lettuce, grapes, and oranges—whatever was in season. But we could never call California home. I was 23 and married, and I had two children when we returned to Texas. We rebuilt my parents' house and bought a new herd of cows. Now my children and grandchildren work the land.

15  This is Texas. It gets hot, and droughts still come and go. But in 2011, we had the driest year ever recorded. Some were calling it the New Dust Bowl. I just hope we learned a lesson from the Dust Bowl of my childhood. We must all do what we can to care for the earth.

To see more photos of the Dust Bowl, visit:
**http://www.pbs.org/kenburns/dustbowl/photos/**

### Comprehension Check

1. Reread paragraph 11. Use context clues to choose the meaning of the word *stick* below. Circle the correct answer.

   **a.** to remain

   **b.** to poke

   **c.** to fasten

   **d.** a part of a tree

2. What information do you expect to find at the hyperlink on page 171?

   **a.** causes of the Dust Bowl

   **b.** Jack Blanchard's Dust Bowl memories

   **c.** images of the Dust Bowl

   **d.** the history of droughts

Unit 7 ■ Reading Informational Text: Craft and Structure  **171**

### Research to Build Knowledge

Let students know that they may already know a Woodie Guthrie song, "This Land Is Your Land." Challenge them to find the lyrics to his Dust Bowl ballads online, and see what new information they can find about the Dust Bowl from these songs. You may wish to assign specific songs to student pairs or groups and have them report what they learned back to the class. Extend this activity by asking students to suggest songs that people might listen to in order to learn about the time that we live in.

## Multiple Readings for Critical Comprehension

Have students reread this selection and pose questions that focus on critical comprehension. Remind them to annotate text.

- *Does the author view the Dust Bowl as caused by people or by nature?* (both) *How do you know?* (He says human farming practices and natural causes worked together.)

- *Reread the last paragraph of the narrative. What does it tell you about the author's purpose?* (The author is concerned because there is another drought in Texas. He wants people to understand that they must prevent another Dust Bowl.)

## Self-Select Text

As preparation for Connect Across Texts, have students select one of the four selections in this unit and reread it independently. Students can access full pdf versions of the selections at **sadlierconnect.com**.

### Comprehension Check

Begin scoring students' understanding of unit skills and texts from Comprehension Check on this page through Connect Across Texts on page 173. Use students' total score to determine their readiness for the Unit 7 Review on page 175.

## Multiple-Choice Questions: *1 point each*

1. *Stick* is a multiple-meaning word. The context determines the answer. Here, *stick* means the opposite of "to leave," so choice A, to *remain*, is correct.

2. The hyperlink's introduction and the word *photos* inside it indicate the link will take students to a site where they can see images of the Dust Bowl.

## Short-Answer Questions: 2 points each

### Item 3 Rubric

| | |
|---|---|
| 2 | Students are able to discuss the contents of the sidebar and describe how that information informs specific parts of the text. |
| 1 | Students are able to discuss the contents of the sidebar and connect it generally to the text. |
| 0 | Students cannot discuss what is in the sidebar or connect that information to the text. |

### Item 4 Rubric

| | |
|---|---|
| 2 | Students can find text evidence from the author's life to support the point of view he has now and can give their own opinion with supporting reasons. |
| 1 | Students can give their opinion with reasons but have trouble connecting the author's point of view with his life experience. |
| 0 | Students cannot give supporting reasons for their opinion or connect the author's point of view with his life experience. |

## Theme Wrap-Up

Lead students in a group discussion on the theme of extreme weather. *What are some things that people can do about dangerous floods, storms, and droughts?* Talk about what things people can control and what they cannot. (Students should understand that people cannot control the weather, but they can take safety precautions for floods and storms, and they can practice water and energy conservation to combat droughts.)

---

3. How does the text feature on page 170 help you understand "Dust Bowl Disaster"? Support your answer with text evidence.

Sample answer: The text feature gives me the reasons behind the Dust Bowl.

For example, I learned that it all started with a drought. Then it got too hot.

Farmers kept farming, and the grass and topsoil were damaged and dried.

Then the winds came. Then the terrible storms formed.

_____

_____

_____

_____

4. Underline the last sentence of paragraph 4. Why does the author have this opinion? If you were the author, would you agree? Include details from the text to support your answer.

Sample answer: The author was fine before the dust storms. He was a

kid on a farm. Then the storms ruined everything: his farm, the animals,

and his way of life. He was scared of not being able to breathe. I

would feel the same way because the dust storms make you think

you might die.

_____

_____

_____

_____

_____

---

## Extend Thinking: Apply Concepts

Invite students to design a questionnaire for their friends and family about their readiness for extreme weather conditions. Challenge students to think of questions about storm and flood preparedness as well as water and energy usage.

You may wish to ask students to determine a scoring scale that will rate those who take the questionnaire on their readiness for extreme weather conditions. See if students can add recommendations for those who are unprepared.

## CONNECT ACROSS TEXTS

### Compare and Contrast Texts

In this unit, you read about hurricanes and tornadoes, floods, droughts, and an important event known as the Dust Bowl. Think about what you learned from these four texts. Then choose two of the texts and compare and contrast them using the Venn diagram below. List key details and important points from the texts to show the similarities and differences between them. Be prepared to discuss your ideas with your class.

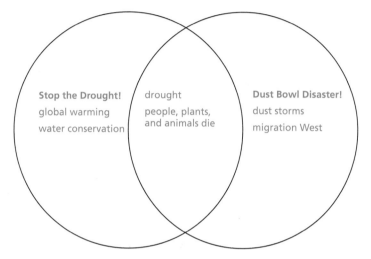

Stop the Drought!
global warming
water conservation

drought
people, plants,
and animals die

Dust Bowl Disaster!
dust storms
migration West

### Return to the Essential Question

How can authors present informational text effectively?

In small groups or as a class, discuss the Essential Question. Think about what you have learned about word meanings, text features, and point of view. Use evidence from the four unit texts to answer the question.

### Connect Across Texts: *4 points* Review Reading Selections

Put students into groups, giving each the responsibility to summarize one of the four reading selections.

### Compare and Contrast Texts

Review the directions on page 173 with students. Instruct students to write the titles of their chosen selections in the outer parts of each circle.

**Venn Diagram Rubric**

| | |
|---|---|
| 4 | Student has identified two selections and recorded four or more characteristics in their proper places. |
| 3 | Student has identified two selections and recorded at least three characteristics in their proper places. |
| 2 | Student has identified two selections and recorded at least three characteristics but may have had trouble categorizing them properly. |
| 1 | Student has identified two selections and recorded at least one characteristic. |
| 0 | Student did not complete assignment or demonstrated no understanding of selections. |

### Support Essential Question Discussion

Have students reread the Essential Question. Challenge them to finish this sentence. *Authors present informational text effectively when they . . .* If students have difficulty responding, prompt them by asking how context clues, text features, and support for the author's point of view help them understand informational text.

### Assess and Respond (pages 171–173)

| If | Then |
|---|---|
| Students scored 0–4 points, they are **Developing** their understanding of unit skills… | Provide students with reading support and more intensive modeling of skills. |
| Students scored 5–7 points, they are **Improving** their understanding of unit skills… | Use students' scores to target areas that are weak, and review those specific skills. |
| Students scored 8–10 points, they are **Proficient** in their understanding of unit skills… | Have these students move on. They are ready for the formal assessment. |

## OBJECTIVE
**Determine the meanings of words with prefixes and suffixes.**

### Guided Instruction

Review the Guided Instruction section on page 174 with students. Be sure they understand that suffixes and prefixes are word parts that might be added to the beginning or to the end of a base word. Suffixes are added to the end, and prefixes are added to the beginning. By understanding the meaning of the base word and the suffix or prefix, they can understand the meaning of the new word.

### Guided Practice

If students are having trouble, help them work through the possibilities by trying the different suffix and prefix options in each blank and focusing on the meaning needed in the sentence. You might also have them do this exercise in small groups.

### Independent Practice

If students are having trouble writing new sentences using the words, have them turn back to the selection to read the words in context. The words appear on page 170, paragraph 10 (*powerful*) and page 171, paragraph 14 (*rebuilt*).

### Apply to Reading

Have students return to "Dust Bowl Disaster" to go on a word hunt for words that contain these suffixes and prefixes: *pre-, re-, dis-, un-, -ful, -less*. They may find *fearful* (page 169, paragraph 5) and *unfortunately* (page 171, paragraph 13).

---

## LANGUAGE
### Prefixes and Suffixes

**Guided Instruction** **Prefixes** and **suffixes** are word parts that are added to a base word to change its meaning. A prefix is added to the beginning of a base word. A suffix is added to the end of a base word. The new word's meaning is connected to the base word's meaning.

Read this sentence from "Dust Bowl Disaster": *The Dust Bowl was set off by a very long drought and unusually high temperatures.* In this sentence, the word *unusually* has a prefix in it. The prefix *un-* has been added to the beginning of the base word *usually*. The word's meaning has changed from *usually* (or "normally") to *unusually* ("not usually").

The chart shows common prefixes and suffixes and their meaning.

| Prefix | pre- | dis- | un- |
|---|---|---|---|
| **Meaning** | before | opposite of | not |
| **Suffix** | -er | -ful | -less |
| **Meaning** | one who | full of | without |

**Guided Practice** Add a prefix or suffix from the chart to change the base word's meaning so that each sentence below makes sense.

1. When the lights go out, having candles is very use _____ful_____.

2. Mia did not want to ___dis___ obey her parents.

3. The factory smoke made an _____un_____ pleasant smell.

**Independent Practice** Each word below from "Dust Bowl Disaster" contains a prefix or a suffix. Write a separate sentence using each word.

**powerful**          **rebuilt**

Sample answer: Powerful spring storms in the plains often include tornadoes.

Sample answer: After a tornado, a neighborhood may need to be rebuilt.

---

## Support English Language Learners

Students whose first language is not English may have difficulty knowing what affixes make sense with various English words. Work with these students to complete the Guided Practice. Students should substitute each affix into the blank in the sentence and see if the resulting word

- sounds like a word they have heard in English.

- makes sense in the context of the sentence.

For each item, only one affix will complete the word to make sense in the sentence. Understanding suffix and prefix words often relies on memorization, so provide additional example sentences to go with each affix.

Read the following passage in which vocabulary words, text features, and the author's point of view appear. Then answer the questions on pages 175 and 176.

# Lightning Strikes!

(Genre: Magazine Article)

## Stay Safe

1   Lightning kills more people than hurricanes or tornadoes. Only floods kill more people during storms. If a storm is near, stay inside. If you are outside during a storm, try to find shelter. If you can't get inside a building, stay away from tall trees and open fields. If you want to learn more about lightning, try **http://www.lightningsafety. noaa.gov/kids.htm.**

## Zapped

2   No one knows how many people are hit by lightning each year. Even experts are unsure. Some say it's about 200, and others say it's more than 1,000. Although people can be killed by lightning strikes, most survive. People who were hit by lightning often have strange problems that doctors cannot explain. Their symptoms include headaches, forgetfulness, and trouble sleeping. A group of survivors meets every year in Tennessee to share stories. It's good to be around others who understand.

**Fill in the circle of the correct answer choice.**

**1.** What phrase in paragraph 1 is a clue to the meaning of *shelter*?

- ○ it is unsafe
- ○ during a storm
- ○ tall trees and open fields
- ● inside a building

**2.** Another word for *symptoms* in paragraph 2, line 6 is

- ○ explain
- ○ strange
- ● problems
- ○ strikes

## Unit Summary

At this point, students have had instruction and practice in reading informational text, with a focus on learning about floods, storms, droughts, and the Dust Bowl. Students have also learned different strategies for determining word meanings from textual clues, learned about text features, and learned to recognize the author's point of view. Students have done an independent close reading of text, practiced working with concepts across texts, and practiced working with suffixes and prefixes. They should be well prepared for the review section.

## Introduce the Review

Explain to students that they will read a new passage that is related to the unit's theme and the selections they have already read. Instruct students to read the passage carefully and then answer the questions on pages 175 and 176.

### Answer Explanations

Scoring: Items 1–6 on pages 175–176 are worth 1 point each. See the rubrics on the next page for guidance scoring the short-answer questions on page 176.

**1.** The text urges the reader to find shelter in a storm and then says, "But if you can't get inside a building . . ." So the answer is the fourth choice, *inside a building.*

**2.** The text says that the symptoms include "headaches, forgetfulness, and trouble sleeping." These are problems that the survivors have, so the answer is the third choice, *problems.*

## Self-Assessment: Progress Check

Have students revisit the Progress Check on page 147 and respond to the questions again. Ask them to compare their Before and After responses.

You may wish to have students rate their answers on a scale of 0–2 rather than simply checking (or not checking) the box. Instruct them to write a zero if they feel they do not understand the given skill at all, a 1 if they feel they have some understanding, and a 2 if they feel they have a solid grasp of the skill.

## Answer Explanations

**3.** The word *strange* refers to something doctors can't explain, so the best answer is "not well understood."

**4.** *Survivors* refers to people who lived after being struck by lightning, so the answer is "people who lived."

**5.** "Stay Safe" or "Zapped"

**6.** The hyperlink is located at the end of the first paragraph.

### Item 7 Rubric

| | |
|---|---|
| 2 | Answer includes lightning safety. |
| 1 | Answer includes lightning. |
| 0 | Answer does not include lightning. |

### Item 8 Rubric

| | |
|---|---|
| 2 | Students identify the prefix *un-*, the base word *sure*, and the definition "not sure." |
| 1 | Students identify the prefix or base word and define the word. |
| 0 | Students do not identify the word parts or the definition. |

### Item 9 Rubric

| | |
|---|---|
| 2 | Answer characterizes the author's point of view correctly and cites text evidence. |
| 1 | Answer characterizes the author's point of view correctly and cites limited text evidence. |
| 0 | Answer mischaracterizes the author's point of view and/or gives no text evidence as support. |

### Item 10 Rubric

| | |
|---|---|
| 2 | Student states an opinion and gives logical reasons in support. |
| 1 | Student states an opinion and gives limited reasons in support. |
| 0 | Student does not state an opinion and/or does not give any reasons in support. |

---

## UNIT 7 REVIEW

**3.** The word *strange* in paragraph 2 means

- ● not well understood
- ○ not very serious
- ○ cannot be cured
- ○ made-up or fake

**4.** In the last paragraph, *survivors* means

- ● people who lived
- ○ doctors who examine
- ○ lightning that strikes
- ○ groups that meet

**5.** Circle a subhead in the passage.

**6.** Underline the hyperlink in the passage.

**7.** What information do you expect to learn by using the hyperlink?

I expect to learn how to keep safe when there is a lightning storm.

**8.** Put a box around the word with a prefix in paragraph 2, line 2. Give the prefix, the base word, and the word's meaning.

prefix is "un-"; root is "sure"; "unsure" means "not sure"

**9.** What is the author's point of view about the meeting of lightning strike survivors? Use text evidence in your answer.

Sample answer: The author thinks the meeting is a good idea. He or she thinks it helps "to be around people who understand."

**10.** Do you agree with the author's point of view? Give reasons for your answer.

Sample answer: I agree because it helps to talk to people who know what you've gone through because they have, too.

---

## Analyze Student Scores

| | |
|---|---|
| **11–14 pts Strong** | Student has a good grasp of the skills and concepts taught in this unit. Point out any mistakes the student has made, and explain the correct answers if necessary. |
| **7–10 pts Progressing** | Student is struggling with some skills or concepts. Identify the specific skills that are problematic to target a review of instruction. |
| **0–6 pts Emerging** | Student is having serious problems understanding the skills and concepts taught in this unit. Student may need to redo the work with a higher level of support. |

# **I**ntroducing UNIT **8**

**I**n this unit about extreme weather and pet safety, you will learn how to write an opinion piece. An opinion piece is sometimes called an argument.

When you write an opinion piece, you try to change the point of view of your readers or persuade them to do something. You might try to convince them to agree with your opinion on a school topic, a social problem, or a book.

To be effective, an opinion piece must be well organized and clearly written. Opinions should be supported by convincing reasons. Words should be chosen carefully, and the writing should follow grammatical rules.

## Progress Check    *Can I?*

| Before Unit 8 | | After Unit 8 |
|---|---|---|
| ☐ | State my opinion clearly. | ☐ |
| ☐ | Support my opinions with reasons. | ☐ |
| ☐ | Use linking words and phrases to connect my opinion and my reasons. | ☐ |
| ☐ | Include both an introduction and a conclusion. | ☐ |
| ☐ | Write using adjectives and adverbs correctly. | ☐ |
| ☐ | Write using correct spelling. | ☐ |
| ☐ | Write simple sentences. | ☐ |

Unit 8 ■ Text Types and Purposes: Write Opinion Pieces

**Student Page 177**

# **H**OME◆CONNECT...

The Home Connect feature is a way to keep parents or other adult family members apprised of what their children are learning. The key learning objectives are listed, and some ideas for related activities and discussions are included.

Explain to students that they can share the Home Connect page with their parents or other adult family members in their home. Let students know how much time the class will be spending on this unit so they can plan their time accordingly at home.

Encourage students and their parents to share their experiences using the suggestions on the Home Connect. You may wish to make a place to post some of this work.

# Progress Check

The Progress Check is a self-assessment feature that students can use to gauge their own progress. Research shows that when students take accountability for their own learning, their motivation increases.

Before students begin work on Unit 8, have them check the boxes next to any item that they feel they can do well. Explain that it is fine if they don't check any of the boxes. Tell them that they will have an opportunity to learn about and practice all of these items while studying the unit. Let them know that near the end of the unit they will have a chance to reconsider how well they can do each item on this list.

Before students begin the Unit 8 Review on page 189, have them revisit this page. You can use this information to work with students on any items they don't understand before they tackle the Review.

## **H**OME◆CONNECT...

**I**n this unit, children will learn about **writing to express an opinion.** Help your child see all the different types of opinion writing in the world around you, ranging from billboards and signs to movie reviews on websites and editorials in newspapers. Model responding to opinions by giving reasons that you agree or disagree with them.

When writing an opinion piece, it is important to pay attention to the **organization.** A good way for your child to organize his or her piece is to **list a reason to support an opinion,** and then **give details** to explain why that reason is important. Identify reasons and supporting information with your child in a published review or editorial. Decide together if the reasons and supporting details are convincing or not.

👪 **Activity:** Focus on an important community issue. With your child, reach an opinion about it. Then together, write a letter to the editor of a local newspaper or contribute to a blog. In the first paragraph, introduce the topic and state your opinion. In the next paragraphs, give at least three reasons in support of your opinion. In the conclusion, restate your opinion and call for some sort of action. Then sign and submit!

### IN THIS UNIT, YOUR CHILD WILL...

- Learn to write an opinion piece with an introduction, a statement of opinion, reasons supporting it, and a conclusion.
- Learn to use linking words to connect the reasons to the opinion.
- Follow a process when writing an opinion piece, beginning with using an outline to organize ideas.
- Learn specific language skills to use when writing an opinion piece:
  - Use adjectives to describe nouns and adverbs to describe verbs.
  - Spell words using word families.
  - Write a variety of simple sentences.

### WAYS TO HELP YOUR CHILD

Show respect for your child's opinions. Regularly engage in discussion with your child about topics he or she is passionate about, such as sports, hobbies, or movies. Ask for your child's point of view and follow up with questions requesting reasons: *Why do you say that? Do you know any facts that support your feelings?*

ONLINE
For more Home Connect activities, continue online at sadlierconnect.com

178    Unit 8 ■ Text Types and Purposes: Write Opinion Pieces

**Student Page 178**

## UNIT PLANNER

| Theme: Natural Disasters<br>Curriculum Connection: Science | Focus |
|---|---|
| **WRITING MODEL**<br>pp. 180–182 | *Any Pet in a Storm!* |
| **WRITING PRACTICE**<br>p. 183 | **ORGANIZATIONAL STRUCTURE:** Outline |
| **LANGUAGE MINI-LESSONS**<br>pp. 184–187 | • Adjectives<br>• Adverbs<br>• Correct Spelling<br>• Simple Sentences |
| **SPEAKING AND LISTENING**<br>p. 188 | Discuss the Essential Question |
| **UNIT 8 REVIEW**<br>pp. 189–190 | • Language Skills Summary<br>• Writing Process Summary |

## Objective(s)

Write an opinion piece with a clear opinion, supporting reasons, linking phrases, and a concluding statement.

Plan an opinion piece with supporting reasons, linking phrases, and a concluding statement.

- Use comparative and superlative adjectives in writing.

- Use adverbs that compare and tell when and where in writing.

- Use correct spelling in writing.

- Use a variety of sentence types, including simple sentences.

- Engage in collaborative discussion with peers, expressing ideas clearly and in complete sentences.

- Follow conventions of discourse, including asking and answering questions.

## Unit Assessment

- Unit 8 Review *pp. 189–190*

## Additional Assessment Options

- Performance Task 1 *pp. 141A–145 and 146*
  ( ALSO ONLINE )

- Performance Task 2 *pp. 259A–263 and 264*
  ( ALSO ONLINE )

**Optional Purchase:**

- iProgress Monitor ( ONLINE )

- Progress Monitor Student Benchmark Assessment Booklet

## ( ONLINE )  Digital Resources

- Home Connect Activities

- Additional Practice

- Teacher Resources

- iProgress Monitor (optional purchase)

**Go to SadlierConnect.com to access your Digital Resources.**

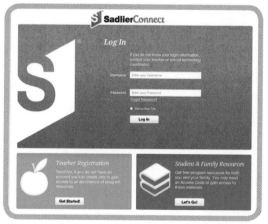

**For more detailed instructions see page T3.**

## LEARNING PROGRESSIONS

In this unit, students will learn how to write an opinion piece on a topic that interests them. In order to learn the skills necessary to craft an opinion piece, students will further develop skills learned in second grade. They should be encouraged to retain these skills, as they will continue to build on them in fourth grade.

**Introducing the Topic**

- By the end of grade 2, students should have been able to write opinion pieces in which they introduce the topic or book they are writing about.

- In grade 3, students will build on this skill by not only introducing the topic or text they are writing about, but also creating an organizational structure, such as an outline, to list the reasons behind their opinion.

- When students move on to grade 4, their organizational structures will become more complex as they group related ideas to support their purpose.

**Providing Reasons that Support the Opinion**

- Throughout grades 2 and 3, students are asked to master supplying reasons that support their opinion about a certain topic or text.

- This skill provides the foundation for what they learn in grade 4. By grade 4, students will need to provide reasons that are supported by facts and details.

**Using Linking Words and Phrases**

- By the end of grade 2, students should have been able to use linking words such as *because*, *and*, and *also* to connect their opinion to their reasons.

- In grade 3, students use not only linking words but also linking phrases to connect opinions and reasons, such as *therefore*, *since*, and *for example*.

- This prepares students for the more complex linking words and phrases in grade 4, including *for instance*, *in order to*, and *in addition*.

**Providing a Concluding Statement**

- In grades 2 and 3, students learn the importance of providing a concluding statement or section.

- This skill prepares them for grade 4, when their concluding statement or section must be related to the opinion presented.

# Text Types and Purposes: Write Opinion Pieces

## UNIT 8

**Essential Question:**
How do writers support their opinions?

---

**Essential Question:**
How do writers support their opinions?

Students will learn how opinions are supported with reasons and evidence in order to make arguments more persuasive.

### Theme: Natural Disasters

Students will continue their investigation of natural disasters as they read and analyze an opinion piece writing model.

### Curriculum Connection: Science

Students will use what they have already learned about natural disasters as they work on their own opinion piece.

### Connect Reading to Writing

Remind students that they read an editorial entitled "Stop the Droughts!" in Unit 7 (Student Book pages 162–167). Review the author's opinion expressed in that editorial article. Tell students they will be reading and writing an opinion piece in this lesson.

---

## Writing Handbook

If students need extra practice with writing an opinion piece, refer them to the *Writing Handbook* on pages 275–283. The Writing Handbook gives students detailed instruction on planning, drafting, revising, and editing their writing. They will also find tips on producing, publishing, and presenting their writing.

## OBJECTIVE
Write an opinion piece with a clear opinion, supporting reasons, linking phrases, and a concluding statement.

## Introduce: Organizational Structure

Draw students' attention to the opinion piece outline in the left margin, and point out the key elements. Ask students to look for these key elements as you read and analyze the Student Model together.

## Analyze a Student Model

**TITLE:** Tell students that an essay title should tell the topic of the essay and also be interesting enough to grab the reader's attention. You might point out that Ruthie's title is a pun on the saying, "any port in a storm," which roughly means "When things are difficult, do whatever works."

**INTRODUCTION:** Help students find the opinion statement: *I know that the opinion is usually at the end of the introduction and that it might contain words like* I think, I believe that, should, *or* must. Point out that Ruthie, the author, first says something about the topic (natural disasters), then gives some background (her own experience with a hurricane), and finally states her opinion on the topic.

---

WRITE OPINION PIECES

### CREATING AN ORGANIZATIONAL STRUCTURE

Ruthie used an outline to organize her essay. It has an opinion, three reasons to support this opinion, and a conclusion.

Title:
I. Introduction
   a. Background: _____
   b. Opinion: _____
II. Supporting Reasons
   a. Reason 1: _____
   b. Reason 2: _____
   c. Reason 3: _____
III. Conclusion
   _____

### TITLE
- Draws the reader into the basic topic.

### INTRODUCTION
- Introduces the topic.
- Gives background.
- States an opinion.
*Underline the writer's opinion.*

# Read a Student Model

Ruthie is a student in Ms. Jenkin's third-grade class. Ruthie has been asked to write an opinion piece on what she would do with a pet during a natural disaster. In her piece, she must support her point of view with three reasons. As you read her essay, think about your opinion, reasons, and organization to prepare to write your own opinion piece.

### Any Pet in a Storm!

I know that there are a lot of natural disasters, such as hurricanes, tornadoes, and droughts, all over the world. The only one I can write about with real experience is a hurricane that hit my town last summer. When the hurricane hit, I was very worried about my beagle, Rudy, and what to do with him. My parents said we might have to leave our home without him. <u>I think pet owners should always take their pets with them in a disaster.</u>

---

## Genre: Opinion Piece

Tell students that a writer writes an opinion piece for a purpose: to give an opinion on a specific topic and to convince readers to agree with this opinion. Sometimes the writer also wants to convince the reader to do something after reading.

To convince readers, the writer constructs a strong argument in support of his or her opinion. The writer gives solid reasons to support the opinion and uses information such as facts, examples, and personal experiences to support each reason. Whether the reader will agree with the writer depends on how good the reasons and support are.

First of all, our pets depend on us for everything—their food, their shelter, their health, and their happiness. These things don't change just because there is an emergency. We must take care of our pets no matter what! How would you feel if you were left alone in a scary emergency?

Also, I know my dog, Rudy, is a part of the family. He comes on trips with us, eats dinner at the same time, and sits on the couch with me as I read. When I am sad, he always cheers me up, and I love him so much. Even thinking of leaving him behind in a hurricane gives me nightmares—imagining him hungry, scared, and alone.

Finally, it can be dangerous for other people when abandoned animals are trapped or roaming around. Imagine a rescue worker trying to search a house for survivors while a scared dog or cat tries to protect the house. The worker or the pet might get hurt. Also, if hungry animals roam the streets, they could get into trouble, like fighting each other and chasing or attacking people.

**LINKING PHRASE**
- Use linking words and phrases to link reasons to the opinion.

**REASON 1**
- Provide reasons that support the opinion.
- Ruthie uses *First of all* to link her reason and opinion.

**REASON 2**
*Underline Ruthie's second reason.*

**REASON 3**
*Underline Ruthie's third reason for never leaving pets behind.*

*Circle the linking word that connects this reason with Ruthie's opinion.*

Unit 8 ■ Text Types and Purposes: Write Opinion Pieces  **181**

## Analyze a Student Model

**LINKING PHRASE:** Explain to students that Ruthie uses a linking phrase (*First of all*) to connect Reason 1 to the opinion that she gives in her introduction. Alert students to watch for other linking words and phrases as they read the rest of Ruthie's essay. (*Also, Finally*)

**REASON 1:** Model identifying Ruthie's first reason: *I'm looking for something that explains why pet owners should take their pets with them in a disaster. I know reasons are usually found near the beginning of the paragraph in an opinion piece.* (First of all, our pets depend on us for everything . . . ) Help students see the close connection between Reason 1 and the opinion statement.

**REASON 2:** If necessary, model identifying the second reason with the same wording as for Reason 1. Ask students to put Reason 2 in their own words. (Pets are part of the family.) Point out that the author uses personal experience as support for this reason. (Her dog goes on family trips, eats dinner with the family, etc.)

**REASON 3:** If students are struggling, model identifying the third reason with the same wording as for Reason 1. Have students state Reason 3 in their own words. (Animals left behind can be a danger.) Point out that Ruthie uses possible situations as support for this reason. Ask volunteers to describe these situations. (pets defending their homes and endangering rescuers; pets fighting each other or attacking people)

## Support English Language Learners

Help English language learners by previewing some basic information that will help students understand this essay. First, be sure they understand that the author, Ruthie, is a young girl who has a pet dog named Rudy. Point out the picture of the beagle on page 180.

Explain that Ruthie is giving her opinion on what pet owners should do with their pets if they have to leave their homes due to a natural disaster. Ruthie is basing her opinion on her own experience with her dog Rudy during a hurricane last summer.

## Analyze a Student Model

**CONCLUSION:** Review Ruthie's conclusion with students. Ruthie gives pet owners some advice for planning ahead. Students should understand how this advice connects to the restated opinion in the last sentence. (Ruthie wants readers to take their pets with them during an emergency.)

## Evaluate a Writer's Work

Begin a group discussion about Ruthie's opinion piece. Remind students that the purpose of an opinion piece is to convince the reader to share the author's point of view. First, have students recall Ruthie's point of view: If there is a big storm or other emergency, people should not leave their pets behind. Then ask students if Ruthie was able to convince them. Have them explain their thinking.

## Model: Organizational Structure

Ask students to think about how Ruthie might have made an outline for her essay. On a board or projector, post the outline on page 183. Then have students help you fill in the outline based on Ruthie's essay. Review the notes in the margins alongside the essay. Fill in Ruthie's introduction, supporting reasons, and conclusion. Point out that well-written pieces have strong organization, which requires planning and prewriting.

Students will next use the blank outline found in their books to plan their own opinion piece, and then they will draft the piece based on their outline.

### WRITE OPINION PIECES

You should plan ahead for your pets in an emergency. Have a supply kit packed. Make sure your pet has its identification and shots, and plan to go to a safe place that allows pets if you have to leave your home. After you do all of this, you will never have to leave your pet behind in an emergency.

**CONCLUSION:**
- Ruthie's concluding statement wraps up her opinion essay and restates her opening opinion in slightly different words.
*Underline Ruthie's concluding statement.*

**182** Unit 8 ■ Text Types and Purposes: Write Opinion Pieces

### Review: Author's Point of View

Remind students that when they read the editorial on droughts ("Stop the Droughts!" on Student Book pages 162–167), they identified the author's point of view. They looked for evidence that the author used to support that point of view, and they thought about whether they agreed with the author.

Ask students to rephrase Ruthie's point of view. (Animals should not be left behind in an emergency.) Ask them to tell what kind of evidence Ruthie used. (examples from life and her own experience)

Use an outline like the one below to organize your opinion essay about something you care about. Then write a first draft of your essay on a separate sheet of paper. Remember to state an opinion and give three supporting reasons. Be sure to use linking words to connect ideas. You will use this draft to write your final essay in the Unit 8 Review section on page 190.

**Title:** _____

I. **Introduction**

   **a.** Background: _____

   _____

   **b.** Opinion: _____

   _____

II. **Supporting Reasons**

   **a.** Reason 1:_____

   _____

   _____

   **b.** Reason 2:_____

   _____

   _____

   **c.** Reason 3:_____

   _____

   _____

III. **Conclusion**

   _____

   _____

   _____

Unit 8 ■ Text Types and Purposes: Write Opinion Pieces   **183**

## Differentiate Instruction

Some students might not yet be ready to write an essay on their own. Form a writing group to support these students.

Lead the group in a shared writing experience in which the group brainstorms ideas, decides on a topic, collaborates to fill in the outline, and then drafts an essay. Be sure that every member of the group gets a chance to contribute. You might subdivide the essay and assign pieces to individuals or small groups to draft.

## Create: Organizational Structure

### Brainstorming

Tell students that writers write opinion pieces on topics they care about. As a class, brainstorm school and community issues that students have opinions about. Make a list of students' topic ideas on the board or projector for them to use as they plan their writing.

### Planning

Students will use the outline on page 183 to plan their opinion piece. Students should first decide on a topic and then begin by filling in their opinion.

- Students should write three clear reasons that they believe would be convincing to a reader.

- Remind students that Ruthie gave advice in her conclusion that would make it easier for people to agree with her. Ask students what kind of advice or extra information they can give in their conclusion.

### Drafting an Opinion Piece

Instruct students to refer to their outline as they draft their opinion piece on a separate piece of paper. Be sure students have an introduction, three reasons, and a conclusion. Remind them to use linking phrases.

## Introduce the Writing Process

Remind students that in order to do a good job on an essay, they must plan, draft, revise, and edit it. These are all steps of the writing process. For more information on the writing process, see the *Writing Handbook* on page 275 of this guide.

| **Assess and Respond** |
|---|
| **If** students have difficulty turning their outline into a draft, |
| **Then** give students some sentence starters that will help them put their ideas into words. |

## OBJECTIVE
Use comparative and superlative adjectives in writing.

### Guided Instruction
Make sure students understand that adjectives give information about the persons, places, or things in a sentence. Explain that adjectives are often used to compare two or more nouns. Have students identify the nouns in the example sentences. (*puppy, dog; puppy, litter*).

### Guided Practice
Have students begin by identifying the nouns in the first sentence. (*rain, barn*) Have them look for any words that tell about those nouns. (*old*) Have students continue identifying the adjectives in the rest of the sentences.

### Independent Practice
Remind students that adjectives usually end in -*er* when one thing is being compared to another, and they end in -*est* when one thing is being compared to two or more. If students struggle, ask them to figure out how many things are being compared in each sentence before choosing their answers.

---

**Assess and Respond**

**If** students have difficulty with comparative and superlative adjectives,

**Then** give students more practice by acting out simple examples with students; for example, "Joe is taller than Zoe" and "Joe is the tallest student in the class."

---

## LANGUAGE

### Adjectives

**Guided Instruction** An **adjective** describes or tells about a noun. Adjectives often answer the questions "What kind?" or "How many?"

> The **strong** wind blew down many houses.

Sometimes adjectives are used to compare. To compare two nouns, add -*er* to the end of most adjectives.

To compare three or more nouns, add -*est* to the end of most adjectives.

> The puppy was **smaller** than the dog.
> The puppy was the **smallest** in the litter.

**Guided Practice** Underline the adjectives in each sentence.

1. The rain leaked through the <u>old</u> barn.
2. There were <u>wet</u> puddles everywhere.
3. The <u>cold</u> wind blew through the sides of the barn.
4. <u>Several</u> animals cuddled in the hay.
5. The <u>nasty</u> storm finally ended in the morning.

**Independent Practice** Circle the correct adjective in parentheses to complete each sentence.

1. The calf was the (younger, (youngest)) animal in the herd.
2. It was the ((smaller,) smallest) brother of the twins.
3. However, the calf was ((smarter,) smartest) than the bull.
4. It found the (drier, (driest)) hay of all in the barn.
5. After the storm, the calf was the (sleepier, (sleepiest)) animal in the barn.

---

## Support English Language Learners

Using comparative and superlative adjectives correctly may be difficult for English language learners who may be inclined to use the words *more* and *most* before adjectives instead of adding endings.

On the board, make a chart showing the forms of several adjectives, such as *high, higher, highest; low, lower, lowest;* and *funny, funnier, funniest.* Model how to compare items in the classroom by using these adjectives. Then have volunteers use these adjectives to discuss other items, such as books and pictures.

## Adverbs

**Guided Instruction** An **adverb** describes or tells about a verb. Adverbs often tell when, where, and how.

> *The wind blew **fiercely**.*
> ***Then,** the rain fell **everywhere**.*

Sometimes adverbs are used to compare. To compare two actions, add *-er* to the end of most one-syllable adverbs.

To compare three or more actions, add *–est* to the end of most one-syllable adverbs.

**Guided Practice** Underline the adverbs in each sentence.

1. <u>Yesterday</u> my cat was lost.

2. We looked <u>outside</u> for it.

3. After we won the baseball game, I ran <u>happily</u> all the way home.

4. My cat was on the front porch, meowing <u>loudly</u>.

**Independent Practice** Write the correct adverb in parentheses on the line.

1. The second lightning bolt flashed (quicker, quickest) than the first one.
   _quicker_____

2. That thunderclap was the (louder, loudest) I had ever heard.
   _louder_____

3. The storm traveled (faster, fastest) than the one last week.
   _faster_____

4. My little brother fell asleep (easier, easiest) than I did.
   _easier_____

5. I was the one who was awake the (longer, longest) in my family.
   _longest_____

## OBJECTIVE
**Use adverbs that compare and tell when and where in writing.**

### Guided Instruction
Tell students that adverbs give information about actions. Adverbs can compare two or more actions; for example, John ran faster than Kam, and Shel ran the fastest of all.

### Guided Practice
Adverbs answer questions about when, where, and how. Have students identify the action in the first sentence (*was lost*) and the word that tells when. (*Yesterday*) Have students continue underlining adverbs.

### Independent Practice
Adverbs that compare one action to another usually end in *-er*; adverbs that compare one action to two or more other actions usually end in *–est*.

| Assess and Respond |
|---|
| **If** students have difficulty with the concept of comparative adverbs, |
| **Then** give students more practice using correct adverbs to compare simple actions. |

## Differentiate Instruction

Some students may have difficulty identifying and understanding how to use adverbs in a sentence.

Have students practice using adverbs by writing the Guided Practice sentences on the board. Erase the adverb in each sentence, and have students generate other possible adverbs that could be used to tell where, when, or how. (For example, <u>Tuesday</u> my cat was lost. We looked <u>everywhere</u> for it. I walked <u>quickly</u> back home. My cat was on the front porch, meowing <u>sweetly</u>.)

## OBJECTIVE
**Use correct spelling in writing.**

### Guided Instruction
Make sure that students understand that all of the example words are related. Point out that the letters *famil* are in each word. Review that *un-* is a common prefix, and *-ity* and *-ize* are common suffixes.

### Guided Practice
Help students identify the base word in the first two items. Point out that the spelling of a base word may change, as when you change a *y* to an *i* before adding *-ed*. Then have students complete items 3 and 4. Answer students' questions as needed.

### Independent Practice
Remind students that the form of the base word needs to make sense in the sentence. Point out that the missing word might take the form of a verb, an adjective, or an adverb.

| Assess and Respond |
| --- |
| **If** students have difficulty spelling related words correctly, |
| **Then** provide them with more examples of word families, and have them identify common spelling patterns. |

# LANGUAGE

## Correct Spelling

**Guided Instruction** When you are writing, it is important to spell the words you use correctly. Use what you know about other words to help you spell new words. You can use word families, syllable patterns, ending rules, and word parts such as suffixes and prefixes to help you spell words.

family    unfamiliar    familiarity    familiarize

You can use a dictionary to look up the correct spelling of words. You can also use a dictionary to look up the meaning of the word you are spelling, to make sure you are using the correct form of the word.

**Guided Practice** Write the base word that can help you spell the two words.

1. taken          mistake          _take_
2. retried        trying           _try_
3. caring         uncaring         _care_
4. interview      viewing          _view_

**Independent Practice** Write a word to complete each sentence, using a form of the base word in parentheses.

1. I was very ___excited___ to get a hamster. (excite)
2. I held it very ___carefully___ so I wouldn't harm it. (care)
3. Mom gave me little food ___dishes___ to put in its cage. (dish)
4. My hamster loves ___using___ its wheel to run around and around. (use)
5. I think my hamster's fur is ___beautiful___. (beauty)

## Grouping Options

Give students an opportunity to learn from peers by creating pairs of students with different levels of spelling ability.

Provide pairs with a list of base words, such as *circle*, *light*, and *fear*. Have the more proficient partner choose a word and then name a related word (for example, *circle—circular*). Have the less proficient partner then write down the related word. Then the more proficient partner should check the spelling, using a dictionary if necessary. Tell partners to switch roles and try again with another pair of related words.

## Simple Sentences

**Guided Instruction** A **simple sentence** has one subject and one verb. It expresses one complete thought or idea.

- Simple: *The ground shakes during an earthquake.*

- Not Simple: *The ground shakes, and buildings move.*

**Guided Practice** Write *simple* or *not simple* to describe each sentence.

1. Yesterday there was an earthquake in our town. _____simple_____

2. I grabbed my dog, and we dashed under our table. _not simple_

3. My dog was shaking so I petted his fur and whispered soft words. _not simple_

4. None of our family was hurt in the earthquake. _____simple_____

5. We helped our neighbors and cleaned up the park. _not simple_

**Independent Practice** Write simple sentences.

1. Sample answer: There were several pets missing after the storm.

2. Sample answer: We helped look for lost pets in the neighborhood.

3. Sample answer: We put posters on trees.

4. Sample answer: Many pets were returned to their families.

5. Sample answer: We were happy to help our neighborhood.

Unit 8 ■ Text Types and Purposes: Write Opinion Pieces  **187**

## OBJECTIVE
**Use a variety of sentence types, including simple sentences.**

### Guided Instruction

Make sure that students understand that a simple sentence has one noun, or subject, and one verb. Point out that in the example sentence, the word *ground* is the subject, and the word *shakes* is the verb. Explain that the word *earthquake* is also a noun, but it does not have a verb (the word *shakes* does not tell about it), so it is not the subject. Show students that in the second example, both nouns are subjects since they are each paired with verbs. Two subjects and two verbs mean the sentence is not simple.

### Guided Practice

Point out that words like *and*, *so*, and *because* may join two simple sentences to create a compound—not simple—sentence.

### Independent Practice

Have students repeat the rules of a simple sentence. Then have them write five simple sentences about natural disasters or another topic that interests them.

| Assess and Respond |
| --- |
| **If** students have difficulty with the concept of simple sentences, |
| **Then** provide students with more practice by writing several simple sentences on the board. Ask volunteers to come up to the board to underline the subjects and circle the verbs. |

## Differentiate Instruction

Help struggling students understand simple sentences by working with them to create a checklist. Guide students to suggest the following:

- *Is there only one subject?*

- *Is there only one verb?*

- *Does the sentence express a complete thought?*

If students answer yes to all three questions, they have a simple sentence. Tell students to write the checklist on a self-stick note and keep it handy while they are writing their opinion pieces.

### OBJECTIVES

- **Engage in collaborative discussion with peers, expressing ideas clearly and in complete sentences.**
- **Follow conventions of discourse, including asking and answering questions.**

## Discuss the Essential Question

Before beginning a group discussion, copy and distribute the "Did I?" checklist, available on **sadlierconnect.com**.

### Leading the Class Discussion

Give students time to think about the questions before the class discussion.

**1.** Point students to the Student Model introduction and conclusion, where Ruthie has stated and restated her opinion.

**2.** Have students skim paragraphs 2–4 for Ruthie's reasons and linking words and phrases.

## SPEAKING AND LISTENING

### Discuss the Essential Question

How do writers support their opinions?

Think about the Essential Question by responding to the questions below. Support your point of view with reasons and experience.

**1.** What words did the writer use to state her opinion?

"I think pet owners should always take their pets with them in a disaster."

_____

**2.** What reasons did the writer state to support her opinion? How did the writer connect her reason to her opinion?

Pets depend on us; pets are part of our family; abandoned pets can be

dangerous. She used linking words such as *first of all, also,* and *finally.*

Use your notes above to discuss the Essential Question in small groups or as a class. Follow agreed-upon rules for discussion. Use the organizer below to record what you heard and how you participated.

| Ideas I Agree or Disagree With | | Questions I Asked |
|---|---|---|
| **Agree** | | |
| **Disagree** | | |
| **New Ideas I Had During Discussion** | | **Questions I Answered** |
| | | |

## Discussion Skills

Remind students of the sentence starters for building on ideas of others:

- *What you said makes me wonder . . .*
- *What you said reminds me of . . .*

Then give students some sentence starters they can use when asking for clarification:

- *Could you repeat what you said about . . . ?*
- *I'm not sure what you meant by . . .*
- *What evidence do you have for . . . ?*

# UNIT 8 REVIEW

This paragraph has mistakes in the use of adjectives and adverbs and in spelling. Write the paragraph correctly on the lines below. If you need help, look in a dictionary to check your spelling.

> Last night a large storm came through. Dad and I spent the night in the barn careing for the animals. Each animal took cover. The chickens climbed to the higher point in the barn. The cows are our larger animals. Surprisingly, the pigs yelled the louder. The horses were very excitied and jittery. We put blankests on their backs. We tryed to keep them calm. Dad turned on the lights and played some soft music. It was a long night, but I am glad that I could help our animals.

Last night a large storm came through. Dad and I spent the night in the barn caring for the animals. Each animal took cover. The chickens climbed to the highest point in the barn. The cows are our largest animals. Surprisingly, the pigs yelled the loudest. The horses were very excited and jittery. We put blankets on their backs. We tried to keep them calm. Dad turned on the lights and played some soft music. It was a long night, but I am glad that I could help our animals.

Unit 8 ■ Text Types and Purposes: Write Opinion Pieces  **189**

## Introduce the Review

Explain to students that this review will give them an opportunity to apply the language and writing skills that they have studied and practiced in this unit.

**Language Skills Summary**

Let students know that they are going to use what they learned about adjectives, adverbs, correct spelling, and simple sentences to make their writing better. Good writers follow grammar rules, and they know how to use adjectives and adverbs to make their writing more interesting to the reader.

- Have students explain why some adjectives end in –er. (One thing is compared to one other thing.) Then have them explain why some adjectives end in -est. (One thing is compared to two or more other things.)
- Ask them to tell what kinds of things an adverb tells about an action. (when, where, and how it took place)
- Prompt students to name the base word in *caring* (*care*), and have them name and spell related words. (*careful*, *carefully*)
- Ask students how to tell if a sentence is simple. (It has one subject and one verb.)

## Test-Taking Tips

Give students the following tips to help with taking assessments focused on editing skills.

- Students should read each sentence or paragraph carefully and slowly, and then read it softly aloud. Students will be able to identify grammar and punctuation errors from text that doesn't sound correct to their trained ears.
- Tell students to read through each sentence or paragraph several times, each time looking for a specific kind of problem. For example, on the first read they might look for capitalization and punctuation errors, on the second read they might look for agreement errors, and on the third read they might look for incomplete sentences.

## Writing Process Summary

Remind students that planning helps them organize their ideas before drafting, and revising and editing make a draft better.

### Planning and Drafting

Have students look at the outline and the draft they created earlier (page 183). They should check that the draft covers all the important points in the outline, especially the reasons that support their opinion.

### Opinion Piece Rubric

| | |
|---|---|
| 4 | The piece includes: a clear opinion statement; three reasons supported by facts, etc.; a conclusion with a restated opinion; linking words/phrases; sentence variety. There are few or no editing errors. |
| 3 | The piece has the elements listed under "4" above, though they are executed less successfully. Minor editing errors do not detract greatly from the overall essay. |
| 2 | The piece is missing one or more of the elements required. There are many editing errors, some of which are serious. |
| 1 | The piece is unfinished or shows a minimal understanding of required elements. Serious editing errors make it difficult to read. |
| 0 | The assignment was not attempted. |

### Self-Assessment: Progress Check

Have students revisit the Progress Check on page 177 and compare their answers now with the answers they gave before they started Unit 8.

---

## UNIT 8 REVIEW

**Assignment:** Write an opinion essay about something you care about.

On the lines below, write the final copy of the opinion essay draft you created on page 183. It should start with an introduction and end with a conclusion. Be sure to include reasons that support your opinion. Make sure to use linking words to connect your reasons with your opinion. See the Writing Handbook (pages 275–283) for ways to improve your writing as you revise.

Students should write an opinion essay that clearly states an opinion and includes

at least three supporting reasons. Students should use linking words to connect

their ideas, and they should provide a concluding statement.

190    Unit 8 ■ Text Types and Purposes: Write Opinion Pieces

---

### Digital Connection: Multimedia Presentations

Once students have finished writing their opinion pieces, they can use them as the basis for a multimedia slideshow.

Have students condense their opinions, reasons, supporting evidence, and conclusion into a brief statement that can be featured on individual slides. If necessary, review how to use bulleted lists to succinctly convey information. Encourage students to find appropriate images that will illustrate or complement their ideas. Ask students to present their slideshows to their classmates or have them post them online.

# Introducing UNIT 9

**H**ave you ever read two stories that were about the same characters? What kind of connections did you make about those characters when you read the second story? Maybe you remembered how they looked or what their personalities were like.

In the upcoming unit, the author has written four stories that involve the same two characters. In each story, the characters find themselves searching for answers in new situations. As you are reading, think about how the settings, events, and themes change with each story.

Pay close attention to the illustrations in each story, as well. What do the illustrations tell you about the stories? By the time you are done, you should be able to use these illustrations to find your own answers and make connections to the characters in the story!

**Before Unit 9**

## Progress Check *Can I?*

**After Unit 9**

- [ ] Explain how illustrations help you understand a story. [ ]
- [ ] Compare and contrast the themes of stories with the same characters. [ ]
- [ ] Compare and contrast the plots of stories with the same characters. [ ]
- [ ] Compare and contrast the settings of stories with the same characters. [ ]
- [ ] Use word roots as a clue to help find the meanings of words. [ ]

Unit 9 ■ Reading Literature: Integration of Knowledge and Ideas

**Student Page 191**

# HOME ✦ CONNECT...

The Home Connect feature is a way to keep parents or other adult family members apprised of what their children are learning. The key learning objectives are listed, and some ideas for related activities and discussions are included.

Explain to students that they can share the Home Connect page with their parents or other adult family members in their home. Let students know how much time the class will be spending on this unit so they can plan their time accordingly at home.

Encourage students and their parents to share their experiences using the suggestions on the Home Connect. You may wish to make a place to post some of this work.

# Progress Check

The Progress Check is a self-assessment feature that students can use to gauge their own progress. Research shows that when students take accountability for their own learning, their motivation increases.

Before students begin work in Unit 9, have them check the boxes next to any item that they feel they can do well. Explain that it is fine if they don't check any of the boxes. Tell them that they will have an opportunity to learn about and practice all of these items while studying the unit. Let them know that near the end of the unit they will have a chance to reconsider how well they can do each item on this list.

Before students begin the Unit 9 Review on page 213, have them revisit this page. You can use this information to work with students on any items they don't understand before they tackle the Review.

# HOME ✦ CONNECT...

**W**hen students are able to combine what they read with what they see in **illustrations**, they are better able to understand the **characters, setting,** and **mood** of a text. As you are reading a story with illustrations, begin by having your child look at the illustrations and tell you what he or she is seeing. Then, read the text. Finally, ask your child about what he or she has seen and read and how the two go together.

Students enjoy reading a series of stories that feature the same characters. When characters are familiar, readers become interested in what will happen next in each story. In this unit, your child will read three stories featuring the same brother and sister duo. Being able to **compare and contrast** each one of these stories to the others is an important skill. As your child reads, ask him or her to pay attention to the details and themes in each story that are the same across texts and to look for ways in which each story is different.

**Activity:** With your child, use descriptions in a text to create illustrations. First, do a web search on well-known illustrators, and look at some of the illustrations they have created. Then, read a favorite text-only story to your child, and work together to create illustrations to go along with the words.

## IN THIS UNIT, YOUR CHILD WILL...

- Use illustrations to help better understand the meaning of the words in a story.
- Learn how to compare and contrast the settings, plots, and themes of texts featuring the same characters.
- Use a known word (for example, *medium*) to help define a lesser-known word with the same root (such as *medieval*).
- Compare and contrast three different texts featuring the same main characters: a mystery story and two adventure stories.

## WAYS TO HELP YOUR CHILD

The ability to compare and contrast situations, characters, and events is an extremely important skill. Help your child develop this skill by asking him or her leading questions, when appropriate. Read two different stories together, back-to-back, and ask your child to tell you how the stories are the same and how they are different. Have your child compare his or her two favorite movies or contrast one favorite sports team with another. Build the concept of comparing and contrasting into everyday conversations.

**ONLINE**
For more Home Connect activities, continue online at sadlierconnect.com

192  Unit 9 ■ Reading Literature: Integration of Knowledge and Ideas

**Student Page 192**

## UNIT PLANNER

| Theme: Searching for Answers | Focus |
|---|---|
| **CONNECTING ILLUSTRATIONS AND TEXT**<br>pp. 194–199 | *The Case of the Missing Fruit*<br>**GENRE:** Mystery  **LEXILE®:** 600L<br><br>**WORDS TO KNOW:** expression, cactus, investigate, abnormal, review, evidence, healthy |
| **COMPARING AND CONTRASTING STORIES**<br>pp. 200–205 | *A Camping Adventure*<br>**GENRE:** Adventure Story  **LEXILE®:** 690L<br><br>**WORDS TO KNOW:** exploration, outskirts, hammock, endangered, environment, observation, wildlife, vein, admiring |
| **CLOSE READING**<br>pp. 206–210 | *Treasure in the Desert*<br>**GENRE:** Adventure Story  **LEXILE®:** 620L |
| **CONNECT ACROSS TEXTS**<br>p. 211 | Compare and Contrast Texts |
| **LANGUAGE**<br>p. 212 | Roots |
| **UNIT 9 REVIEW**<br>pp. 213–214 | *The Missing Pencil Sharpener*<br>**GENRE:** Mystery  **LEXILE®:** 560L |

## Objective(s)

Use illustrations to help understand a story.

Compare and contrast two stories featuring the same characters.

- Use illustrations to help understand a story.
- Compare and contrast two stories featuring the same characters.

Use root words to determine word meanings.

## Unit Assessment

- Unit 9 Review *pp. 213–214*
- Unit 9 Performance Task ( ONLINE )

## Additional Assessment Options

- Performance Task 1 *pp. 141A–145 and 146*
  ( ALSO ONLINE )
- Performance Task 2 *pp. 259A–263 and 264*
  ( ALSO ONLINE )

**Optional Purchase:**

- iProgress Monitor ( ONLINE )
- Progress Monitor Student Benchmark Assessment Booklet

## ( ONLINE ) Digital Resources

- Home Connect Activities
- Unit Performance Task
- Additional Practice
- Full-Length Reading Selections
- Foundational Skills Practice
- Teacher Resources
- iProgress Monitor (optional purchase)

**Go to SadlierConnect.com to access your Digital Resources.**

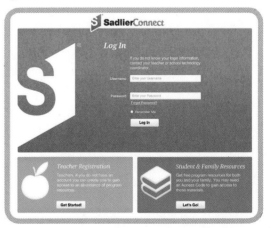

**For more detailed instructions see page T3.**

## LEARNING PROGRESSIONS

In this unit, students will learn how readers can make connections using the elements of literature. In order to learn the skills in this unit, students will further develop skills learned in second grade. They should be encouraged to retain these skills, as they will continue to build on them in fourth grade.

**Connecting Illustrations and Text**

- Second-grade students should have finished the year with the ability to use information from illustrations to build comprehension in literature.

- In third grade, students will continue to develop their skills in connecting specific elements of a text with the accompanying illustration.

- In grade 4, students will be using this knowledge to make connections between a specific text and a visual or oral presentation of that text.

**Comparing and Contrasting Stories**

- Proficient second graders should have learned how to compare and contrast two or more versions of the same story.

- In third grade, students will learn how to compare and contrast two stories written by the same author that feature the same or similar characters.

- This will prepare students for the task of comparing similar themes and events across texts they will encounter in fourth grade.

# Reading Literature: Integration of Knowledge and Ideas

**Essential Question:
What connections can readers make?**

Unit 9 ▪ Reading Literature: Integration of Knowledge and Ideas    **193**

**Essential Question:
What connections can readers make?**

In this unit, students will learn how illustrations in a story can help convey subtle ideas related to character, setting, and plot. Students will also make connections by comparing these elements of fiction across three different texts featuring the same characters.

## Theme: Searching for Answers

Students will read selections based on two recurring main characters. They will read mystery and adventure stories in which the recurring characters work together to solve puzzles and unravel new ideas.

## Curriculum Connection: Language Arts

Students will read stories in which a brother and sister use their curiosity and powers of observation to solve mysteries and discover new things.

## Vocabulary Overview

**General Academic Vocabulary**

abnormal 196, admiring 204, evidence 198, exploration 200, expression 194, healthy 198, investigate 196, observation 202, review 198

**Domain-Specific Vocabulary**

cactus 195, endangered 202, environment 202, hammock 201, outskirts 201, vein 204, wildlife 204

# Connecting Illustrations and Text

## Guided Instruction

### OBJECTIVE
**Use illustrations to help understand a story.**

### Genre: Mystery

Explain to students that a mystery story involves some kind of hidden question that the main characters have to answer.

### Set the Purpose

Help students understand the purpose for learning the reading skill by asking *Did you know that illustrations can be as important to a story as the words you read? What do you think you can learn about a story by looking closely at its illustrations?*

### Model and Teach

Read the selection as students follow along in their books.

### CITE EVIDENCE

**A** *I see that there are three characters in the illustration that look like they are playing basketball.*
*Can you find the names of those three characters in paragraph 1?* (Sofia, Tino, and Ella)

**B** *When you identify setting, you are looking for images and words that tell you where and when a story takes place. I see palm trees, cacti, and a basketball court in the illustration.*
*Where might you see palm trees and cacti?* (warm climate, desert)

## CONNECTING ILLUSTRATIONS AND TEXT

### Guided Instruction

### WORDS TO KNOW
**cactus**

**expression**

> **Illustrations** are pictures of the characters, setting, and events in a story.

#### CITE EVIDENCE

**A** **Illustrations** can help you picture a story's action. Look at the illustration below. In the story, underline the names of the **characters** in the illustration.

**B** The **setting** is where a story takes place. In the illustration, circle any pictures that tell you about the setting. Where does the story take place?

## The Case of the Missing Fruit
### (Genre: Mystery)

1   It was after lunch on Saturday, and <u>Sofia</u> and <u>Tino</u> were playing basketball. Their big sister, <u>Ella</u>, was home from college, and she was watching the children play while their parents were at work. Sofia was beating Tino by six points, and Tino was getting frustrated.

2   Sofia, on the other hand, was enjoying the game a little *too* much. "Hey, Tino, why did the chicken cross the road? To beat you at basketball!"

3   Tino started to get upset, and then he looked at Sofia's face. He had to laugh at her silly **expression**.

4   "Good one. But should you be clowning around when you are only winning by six points?"

5   "I don't know, hermano. Should I be?"

6   Before they could finish their game, a shout rang out from down the block.

7   "What was that?" Tino asked.

8   "I don't know," said Sofia, "but it sounded like it came from Mrs. Moreno's house."

194

## Words to Know

**General Academic Vocabulary**
**expression** (*noun*): the look on a person's face

**Domain-Specific Vocabulary**
**cactus** (*noun*): a flowering plant able to live in dry regions with fleshy stems and branches that bear scales or prickles instead of leaves

**Working with Word Meaning** Encourage students to pay attention to context clues when they encounter new words.

## INTEGRATION OF KNOWLEDGE AND IDEAS

### Guided Instruction

9    Suddenly, another shout pierced the air. The two children and Ella ran toward the sound.

10    When the children arrived at Mrs. Moreno's, she was standing in her backyard, wearing thick gloves, and carrying a metal bucket.

11    "Mrs. Moreno," Ella asked, "are you all right?"

12    "Oh, *niños*, children, I didn't mean to frighten you."

13    "What happened?" asked Sofia.

14    "I came out to pick the fruit from my prickly pear cactus plants. It's time for me to make my prickly pear jam for the Labor Day picnic. When I got here, all of the cacti were bare!"

15    Tino and Sofia gave each other a look. They knew they had to help Mrs. Moreno.

16    "When was the last time you noticed the fruit?" Tino asked.

17    "I came outside this morning, and saw that the prickly pear fruit was ready to harvest. After that, I had to run some errands. Then, I came home, made an early lunch, and took a short nap."

18    "Has anyone asked about your prickly pears lately?" Sofia asked.

#### Comprehension Check

Illustrations can show you the mood of the characters in a story. Look at the picture of Mrs. Moreno. What is her mood? How can you tell?

Unit 9 ■ Reading Literature: Integration of Knowledge and Ideas    **195**

#### CITE EVIDENCE

**C** Illustrations let you see new characters in a story. Look at the picture of Mrs. Moreno. Then, box the words in the story that match the picture.

**D** Illustrations can help the reader visualize unfamiliar things in a story. Circle in the text what Mrs. Moreno is looking at. Have you seen a prickly pear cactus before?

### Guided Instruction

#### CITE EVIDENCE

**C** *In paragraph 10, I see details about how Mrs. Moreno looks. The story talks about what Mrs. Moreno is wearing, what she is doing, and where she is standing.*

*Can you find the words that match the picture?* ("standing in her backyard, wearing thick gloves, and carrying a metal bucket")

**D** *I'm looking for the words on this page that describe Mrs. Moreno's prickly pear cactus. Look carefully in paragraph 14.*

*What does the text tell you about the cactus?* (It bears fruit that can be made into jam; the fruit is missing.)

#### Comprehension Check

**Sample Answer:** In the picture, Mrs. Moreno looks like she is upset or worried. Her eyes look sad, and her hand is pointing at the cactus as if she doesn't understand what has happened.

**Answer Explanation:** Students should look for details in the illustration that help them understand Mrs. Moreno's mood. Direct students to look carefully at her facial expression as well as the way she is standing. Also, guide them to look carefully at where she is standing and what she is doing.

### Support English Language Learners

Illustrations can be a key element in helping English language learners understand more subtle elements of a story, such as mood and expression. With students who are learning English, introduce stories by using a modified version of the Picture Word Inductive Model. Before reading a text, have them brainstorm words to describe the illustrations that accompany the story. Have the students put those words into categories; for instance, "Setting" or "Characters." Then have students look for words that match their brainstorming session within the text itself.

# Connecting Illustrations and Text

## Guided Practice

### Recap Reading Selection

Remind students that they have been reading a mystery story. Have students recall details about what has happened in the story so far. (Tino, Sofia, and their sister Ella are trying to solve a mystery about Mrs. Moreno's missing cactus fruit.) Have students make a prediction about what will happen next in the story.

### Read and Practice

Have partners take turns reading the selection as you circulate to provide support. Model analyzing illustrations with Cite Evidence callout A. For callout B, circulate and provide partners with scaffolding as needed. You might use the following suggestions to help students who are having difficulty.

### CITE EVIDENCE

**A** Remind students to pay close attention to the characters in the illustration to help follow the mystery. Remind them that even a character's clothing can help illustrate details in the story.

**B** Tell students that they should look carefully at the illustration and compare it to the last sentence in paragraph 19. Have students identify what is included in the illustration that is not mentioned in the text. (an empty bird feeder and birdseed)

## CONNECTING ILLUSTRATIONS AND TEXT

### Guided Practice

**The Case of the Missing Fruit** *continued*

**WORDS TO KNOW**
abnormal
investigate

**CITE EVIDENCE**

**A** Look carefully at the illustration. It shows one of the visitors Mrs. Moreno is describing in paragraph 19. Underline the sentences that match the illustration.

**B** Compare the illustration to the words in paragraph 19. What do you notice about the setting in the illustration that is not described in the story?

19   Mrs. Moreno answered Sofia, "Yesterday, Mr. Layton was walking his dog, and he stopped to tell me how good my plants were looking. This morning, Lisa Wu came over with some homemade bread from her mother. She made sure to tell me that she couldn't wait to try some jam soon. <u>Then, Mr. Abbott from the pet store arrived. He told me he had never seen such vibrant red fruit!</u>"

20   Tino could tell that Sofia's brain was working.

21   "I think we can find out what happened to the prickly pear fruit, but we need to **investigate**. Ella, would you mind driving us a few places?" she asked.

22   Ella answered, "Let's go solve a mystery!"

23   The first place they stopped was Lisa Wu's house. Lisa was in the front yard, watching her little brothers.

24   "Hey guys!" Lisa smiled at her visitors.

25   Tino spoke first. "We were wondering if you noticed anything **abnormal** at Mrs. Moreno's house this morning?"

26   Lisa thought for a minute. "Not that I can think of. Is something wrong?"

27   "All of the fruits from her prickly pear plants have been picked." Tino said.

28   "Oh no!" Lisa cried. "I have been looking forward to that jam all week!"

29   The next stop was Mr. Layton's house. No one was outside when Ella stopped, so the children rang the front doorbell. Mr. Layton came to the door.

30   "Hello, kids. How's it going?"

**196**   Unit 9 ■ Reading Literature: Integration of Knowledge and Ideas

### Words to Know

**General Academic Vocabulary**

**abnormal** (*adjective*): different than the expected

**investigate** (*verb*): examine the facts to answer a question or solve a mystery

**Working with Word Meaning** Help students work with words in context by having them write sentences with their partner, focusing on the Words to Know.

## INTEGRATION OF KNOWLEDGE AND IDEAS

**Guided Practice**

31   "Hi, Mr. Layton," Sofia said, "we have a question for you. When you were at Mrs. Moreno's house yesterday, did you notice anything strange?"

32   "Not at all," said Mr. Layton, "unless you count the fact that her prickly pear cactus plants always grow better than anything else in the neighborhood!"

### Comprehension Check

1. Use the illustration to help you determine the meaning of the word *vibrant* in paragraph 19.

   a. sweet

   b. bright

   c. dark

   d. pale

2. Based on both the description of the setting in the story and the illustrations, where do you think this story takes place?

   a. in the mountains

   b. at the ocean

   c. in a forest

   d. in the desert

3. Work with a partner. Think about how you would draw an illustration of the characters and setting in paragraphs 29–32. What would your illustration look like?

   Sample answer: My illustration would show the four kids with Mr.

   Layton at the door of his house. Mr. Layton would be a man

   with gray hair, and his mouth would be open as if he was talking.

Unit 9 ■ Reading Literature: Integration of Knowledge and Ideas    **197**

## Guided Practice

### Comprehension Check

**Answer Explanations:**

1. Choice B, *bright*, is the correct answer, based on the illustration. In the picture, the prickly pear flowers are bright red.

2. Choice D, *in the desert*, is correct. The illustrations show palm trees and cacti. Also, the text of the story describes Mrs. Moreno's prickly pear cactus, which grows naturally in the desert.

3. Have students think about how they would draw Mr. Layton. Remind them to think about how he would look, what he would be doing, and which characters would be with him.

## Peer Collaboration

Have students think about each Comprehension Check question independently, coming up with their own ideas on how to respond. Then have students discuss their responses with a partner. Students should consider each other's ideas and formulate one response for the pair. Have the partners share their response with the whole group.

## Foundational Skills: Fluency

Explain to students that they can read more fluently if they use expression when reading dialogue. Model fluent reading for paragraphs 24–28 on page 196 in the Student Book. Explain that reading dialogue with expression means understanding how different characters may be feeling, such as curious and surprised, in this example.

Give students a chance to practice reading dialogue with expression with a partner. They may also want to record themselves reading the selection so that they can play it back and listen to their own use of expression in dialogue. Additional fluency passages and activities can be found at **sadlierconnect.com** and in the *Foundational Skills Handbook*.

## Independent Practice

### Recap Reading Selection

Remind students that they have been reading about how Tino and Sofia are trying to solve Mrs. Moreno's mystery. Have students recall details from the last section of the story. (They learned who visited Mrs. Moreno.) Have students make predictions about the end of the story, based on the illustrations.

### Read and Apply

Have students read the selection independently as you circulate. If you notice students struggling, you can provide support with the suggestions that follow.

#### CITE EVIDENCE

**A** Help students connect the setting of the illustration with Sofia's explanation of the mystery to Mrs. Moreno. Tell students that in the illustration, Sofia (and later Tino) is explaining what happened to her cactus fruit. Sofia mentions that the fruits were on the cactus when Mr. Abbott filled the empty bird feeder.

**B** Help students find clues to solve the mystery by using both the text and the illustrations. Have them read carefully in paragraph 45 and then identify those details in the illustration. If necessary, direct students to the location of the bird feeder next to the cacti.

---

**WORDS TO KNOW**
evidence
healthy
review

**CITE EVIDENCE**

**A** Put a box around Sofia's dialogue that is connected to what she is saying in the illustration.

**B** Circle the item in the **illustration** that is related to Mr. Abbot's delivery.

33   Sofia smiled, politely. "Thanks, Mr. Layton, that's all we needed to know."

34   The last stop was Mr. Abbott's pet store.

35   "Hey kids! What brings you this way?"

36   "We're helping out Mrs. Moreno," said Sofia. "You made a delivery to her house this morning. Can you tell us what it was?"

37   "Sure, I just dropped by to bring her some seed for her bird feeder."

38   Sofia smiled. "Did you just *deliver* the seed, Mr. Abbott, or did you also put it in the feeder?"

39   "Well, actually, I always fill her bird feeder for her as well."

40   "Thanks for your help, Mr. Abbott!"

41   Once the children were back in Ella's car, Sofia made an announcement. "I know who stole the prickly pear fruits! I'll tell you when we get to Mrs. Moreno's."

42   When they arrived, Mrs. Moreno was sitting on her front porch.

43   "Mrs. Moreno," Sofia said, "I think I know who stole your prickly pear fruit!"

44   "*Niña*, child, have you really solved the mystery? Who did this terrible thing?"

45   "First let's **review** the **evidence**: Mr. Layton noticed how **healthy** your cactus plants were looking. Lisa Wu's mom sent homemade bread, because she knew the fruits were ready to pick. And Mr. Abbott said how red the fruits were, as he filled your bird feeder."

---

### Words to Know

**General Academic Vocabulary**
**evidence** (*noun*): the facts that help answer a question
**healthy** (*adjective*): growing well; not sick
**review** (*verb*): to go over something again

**Working with Word Meaning**  Help students remember the meanings of the words by having them give definitions for the vocabulary, rephrasing the meanings using their own words.

# INTEGRATION OF KNOWLEDGE AND IDEAS

**Independent Practice**

46   Before Sofia could finish, Tino gave a triumphant shout. "Of course! It wasn't a person who stole your cactus fruits, Mrs. Moreno. It was birds. The food Mr. Abbott put in your feeder attracted them to your yard, but they liked your beautiful red fruits even more. A perfect treat!"

47   Mrs. Moreno looked shocked, and then she began laughing. "I guess the case of the missing fruit has been solved!"

**Comprehension Check**   ( MORE ONLINE )  sadlierconnect.com

1. How would you describe the mood of the characters in the illustration on page 198?

   a. sad

   b. bored, uninterested

   c. excited, happy

   d. scared

2. Why is the filled bird feeder important to understanding how the fruit disappeared?

   a. It attracted birds to the cactus fruit nearby.

   b. It was not present when the cactus fruit disappeared.

   c. Mrs. Moreno did not want bird seed in her feeder.

   d. Mr. Abbott saw the cactus fruit when he filled the bird feeder.

3. If you paid close attention to the story and the illustrations, there were clues given to help you solve the mystery. What were those clues, both in the text and in the illustrations?

   Sample answer: Mrs. Moreno talked about Mr. Abbott making a

   delivery, and he said he delivered birdseed. In the illustrations, Mrs.

   Moreno has a bird feeder right next to her prickly pear cactus.

Unit 9 ■ Reading Literature: Integration of Knowledge and Ideas   **199**

## Discussion Skills

During discussion, prompt students to support or disagree with what another student has said. This helps extend a discussion and generate new ideas.

Have students respond to one another by asking:

• *Do you agree or disagree and why?*

• *Is this always true?*

• *Can you think of any examples that would not work?*

## Independent Practice

**Comprehension Check**

**Answer Explanations:**

1. Choice C, *excited, happy,* is correct based on the characters' facial expressions in the illustration on page 198 and the excitement of solving the mystery described in the text.

2. Choice A is correct. The location of the bird feeder next to the cactus helps solve the mystery.

3. In the story, Mrs. Moreno mentions that Mr. Abbott was making a delivery. Once the kids determine that Mr. Abbott was delivering birdseed, and they see where Mrs. Moreno's bird feeder is located, they are able to solve the mystery.

## Critical Comprehension

Use the following questions to help students think more deeply about the text. Students should be prepared to support their answers with evidence from the text.

• *What actions do Tino and Sofia take to help them solve the mystery?* (gather evidence, interview people, look at the scene of the mystery)

• *How would this story have been different if the setting were in the mountains?* (The trees would not be palm trees; there would not be any cactus, but birds might have stolen a different fruit or nuts from a tree.)

| Assess and Respond |
| --- |
| **If** students have difficulty answering the questions in the Comprehension Check… |
| **Then** have students work in pairs to answer the questions, having them brainstorm ideas, referencing the text for answers where necessary. |

## Guided Instruction

### OBJECTIVE
**Compare and contrast two stories featuring the same characters.**

### Genre: Adventure Story

Explain to students that an adventure story introduces characters to exciting new experiences. It includes action and sometimes risk as characters are challenged by nature.

### Set the Purpose

Help students understand the purpose for learning the reading skill by asking *Have you ever read two books that are similar? Maybe they have the same characters, or the same setting. Maybe they even tell the same story, but in two different ways. How were those stories the same? How were they different?*

### Model and Teach

Read the selection as students follow along in their books.

### CITE EVIDENCE

**A** *Remember that the setting describes when and where a story takes place.*

*What are details in paragraph 3 that describe the setting of the story?* (Sonoran Desert, outside the city of Tucson, Arizona)

**B** *The main characters in this story are the same as the main characters in the last story.*

*What are the names of the two new characters in paragraph 4?* (Mamá and Papá)

---

## COMPARING AND CONTRASTING STORIES

### Guided Instruction

**WORDS TO KNOW**
exploration
hammock
outskirts

**Comparing** two stories is looking at how they are the same. **Contrasting** two stories is looking at how they are different.

**CITE EVIDENCE**

**A** The first story took place in a neighborhood. Underline descriptions of the **setting** in this story.

**B** The first story featured many different **characters**. In this story, there are only four characters. Circle their names. What kind of adventure do you predict for the characters?

## A Camping Adventure
### (Genre: Adventure Story)

1   Tino finished rolling his sleeping bag and attached it to his backpack. "Hey, Sofia, I'm ready to go, " he called.

2   "Just give me one minute," his twin sister answered back.

3   Tino, Sofia, and their parents were leaving on an overnight camping trip in the Sonoran Desert, just outside of the city of Tucson, Arizona. They had come to Tucson for spring break. They had already visited many interesting places, including an old western movie set and a World War II airplane museum. Yesterday, the family decided that a camping trip would be the perfect way to end their week of fun and **exploration**.

4   Sofia grabbed her first-aid kit and shoved it into her backpack. "Last item! Let's go down to the hotel lobby and find Mamá and Papá!"

---

## Words to Know

**General Academic Vocabulary**
**exploration** (*noun*): learning about a new place by travelling through it

**Domain-Specific Vocabulary**
**hammock** (*noun*): an outdoor hanging bed made of rope
**outskirts** (*noun*): the outer parts of a city

**Working with Word Meaning** Help students remember word meanings by having them draw a picture of one of the words above, and then use that word in a sentence.

# INTEGRATION OF KNOWLEDGE AND IDEAS

5  They arrived at the Gilbert Ray campground right before lunch. They were given a campsite on the **outskirts** of the campground. They spent 30 minutes setting up camp: a large tent with three rooms, a fire pit, camp chairs, and a **hammock** stretched between two ironwood trees.

6  Sofia wanted to unroll their sleeping bags and get the cabin ready for the evening. Tino stopped her.

7  "What are you doing, sis?"

8  "I thought I would surprise everyone and make their beds for them for tonight."

9  "Well, they would get a surprise, all right."

10  "What do you mean?"

11  "Did you forget about scorpions?" answered Tino. "An unrolled sleeping bag is the perfect place for a scorpion to crawl in during the day. Imagine sliding into your sleeping bag tonight with one!"

12  "Ahh!" Sofia cried. "I can't believe I forgot that. Thanks for reminding me!"

13  "Any time, hermana!"

14  After lunch, Sofia, Tino, and their parents decided it was the perfect time for a nap. In the Sonoran Desert, it's best to sleep or relax during the heat of the day. Many of the animals do the same, in order to conserve their energy.

### Comprehension Check

Based on what you have read so far, how is this story the same as "The Mystery of the Missing Fruit"? How is it different?

## Guided Instruction

### CITE EVIDENCE

**C**  The first story was a **mystery** story, while this story is an **adventure** story. Box the paragraph that makes you think of an adventure story.

**D**  In the first story, Sofia is in charge of solving the problem. Underline the name of the person who solves the problem in paragraph 11. Which problem is more serious?

## Guided Instruction

### CITE EVIDENCE

**C**  *We learned that characters in an adventure story have exciting new experiences in nature.*

*What is Sofia and Tino's new experience in nature in paragraph 11?* (learning how to deal with scorpions)

**D**  *In paragraph 11, we learn that an unrolled sleeping bag is the perfect place for a scorpion to crawl into.*

*Who reminds Sofia about what scorpions like to do?* (Tino) *Do you think sleeping with a scorpion is a more serious problem than finding missing fruit?* (Yes)

### Comprehension Check

**Sample Answer:** In a mystery story, the characters have to solve a problem by using evidence. In an adventure story, the characters have exciting new experiences. Both stories can have mystery and adventure, and a problem to solve.

**Answer Explanation:** Mysteries often involve some element of adventure, but adventure stories don't always have a mystery or problem to solve.

## Listening and Viewing Skills

Reread paragraph 3 as students listen and look at the accompanying illustration on page 200. *Where are Tino and Sofia going camping?* (in the desert) *Who is going with them?* (their parents)

## Review: Connecting Illustrations and Text

Have students look at the illustration on page 201 as you read paragraph 11 aloud. *How does the illustration reflect what's happening in the text?* (Tino is worried about scorpions in the sleeping bag.)

## Digital Connection: Using Online Resources

Tell students that, even though this story is a work of fiction, the Sonoran Desert is a real desert in the Southwest. Have students visit the Sonoran Desert pages on the National Park Service website. Help students locate information about the climate and wildlife in the Sonoran Desert.

Have students compare and contrast the illustrations in the text with the photographs on the National Park Service website. Ask students how illustrations differ from photographs. Have students identify ways the two are the same. Ask students which kinds of images they prefer: illustrations or photographs.

# Comparing and Contrasting Stories

## Guided Practice

### Recap Reading Selection

Have a short group discussion about the first section of the story. Ask students to recall what has happened in the story so far. (Sofia and Tino are camping in the Sonoran Desert with their parents.) Ask what new information students have learned about camping in the desert. (Watch out for scorpions; save energy during the hottest part of the day.)

### Read and Practice

Have partners take turns reading the selection as you circulate to provide support. Model identifying contrasting details with Cite Evidence callout A. For callout B, circulate and provide partners with scaffolding as needed. You might use the following suggestions to help students who are having difficulty.

#### CITE EVIDENCE

**A** Have students recall that the important animals in the first story were the birds that ate Mrs. Moreno's cacti. Help student identify *coyotes* as the animal featured in this story by asking what animal tracks Tino discovers.

**B** Remind students that, in the first story, Tino and Sofia were investigating a mystery about cacti. Students should identify the endangered plant Sofia finds, and her father identifies, in this story. (Kearney's Blue Star)

---

## COMPARING AND CONTRASTING STORIES

### Guided Practice

**WORDS TO KNOW**
endangered
environment
observation

**CITE EVIDENCE**

**A** Circle the animal that is featured among the setting in paragraphs 19 and 20. The first story also has an important animal. **Compare** the important animal from the setting of each story.

**B** Underline the plant that is featured in the setting in paragraph 18. How is it different from the plant in the first story?

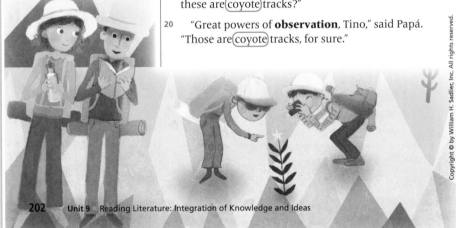

### A Camping Adventure *continued*

15 Once the temperature had dropped, Sofia asked her parents if they could all take a hike. "There are some desert plants I want to see, and I'm hoping to get a picture of some coyote tracks."

16 They decided to take one of the many small trails that intersected with their campground. The plan was to stop along the way to take pictures and explore the natural wonders of the desert.

17 Right away, Sofia noticed some interesting plants. "Take a look at these flowers, Papá. Can you look them up in your guidebook?"

18 Her father looked through his guidebook. "Wow, Sofia, that's a really rare plant. It's called the Kearney's Blue Star, and it's on the **endangered** species list. Make sure you get some good pictures, but don't touch it. We want to leave the **environment** just like we found it." Their father then reminded them of the old hikers' motto: *Take nothing but pictures, leave nothing but footprints.*

19 Tino was the next one to make a discovery. He stopped on the trail when he saw some animal tracks on the ground. "Look over here! Do you think these are coyote tracks?"

20 "Great powers of **observation**, Tino," said Papá. "Those are coyote tracks, for sure."

---

### Words to Know

**General Academic Vocabulary**
**observation** (*noun*): the act of paying close attention to details

**Domain-Specific Vocabulary**
**endangered** (*adjective*): a species that may die out, or become extinct
**environment** (*noun*): the landscape and surroundings

**Working with Word Meaning** Encourage students to find synonyms for each of the Words to Know. For instance, instead of *environment*, they might say *landscape*.

# INTEGRATION OF KNOWLEDGE AND IDEAS

21 They hiked for a little while longer, and were just about to turn back for camp, when Tino spotted a small cave about ten feet off the trail.

22 "Mamá, Papá, can we go explore that cave?"

### Comprehension Check

1. Choose the statement that best describes the settings of the first two stories.

   **a.** The first story mainly takes place in a pet store. This story mainly takes place in Tucson, Arizona.

   **b.** The first story mainly takes place in the desert. This story mainly takes place in a campground.

   **c.** The first story mainly takes place in a neighborhood. This story mainly takes place in the desert.

   **d.** The first story mainly takes place in Mrs. Moreno's yard. This story mainly takes place in Tino and Sofia's tent.

2. There are two new characters introduced in this story. Who are they?

   **a.** Abuela and Mr. Abbott

   **b.** Mamá and Papá

   **c.** Kearney's Blue Star and coyote

   **d.** Leo and Mr. Layton

3. Work with a partner. Name three ways that this story is different from the first story. Base your answer on details from both stories.

   Sample answer: In this story, the setting is different, there are
   different characters, and Tino and Sofia are not solving a mystery.

Unit 9 ■ Reading Literature: Integration of Knowledge and Ideas    **203**

### Comprehension Check

**Answer Explanations:**

**1.** Choice C, *The first story mainly takes place in a neighborhood. This story mainly takes place in the desert,* is correct. The first story takes place in the children's own neighborhood; this one is set in the Sonoran Desert during their family vacation.

**2.** Choice B, *Mamá and Papá*, is correct because they are the only new characters in the story.

**3.** The three main elements that differ between the stories are characters, setting, and genre. Tino and Sofia are on an adventure and not solving a mystery.

## Reciprocal Teaching

Form groups of four and assign one of the following roles to each group member: Summarizer, Questioner, Clarifier, and Predictor. In a group discussion, the Summarizers should say what they have learned so far about the story, the Questioners should think of something else to ask about the story, the Clarifiers should answer the question or say where they could look for the answers, and the Predictors should say what they think they will learn next in the story. Call on different groups to share their ideas with the class.

## Support English Language Learners

Support English language learners by assigning them a reading buddy with stronger reading skills. Have them take turns reading the selection with their reading buddies, and then summarizing each paragraph after it has been read. Have the students pay close attention to the illustrations that accompany the story. Instruct each partner to describe the illustrations to each other before they read, and then read to see if the text matches what they are seeing.

## Comparing and Contrasting Stories

### Independent Practice

### Recap Reading Selection

Remind students that they have been reading about the adventure Tino and Sofia are having in the Sonoran Desert. Have students recall details from the story specific to the setting. (desert, cacti, coyotes, endangered species, cave) Ask students what they think Tino and Sofia will find in the cave.

### Read and Apply

Have students read the selection independently as you circulate. If you notice students struggling, you can provide support with the suggestions that follow.

### CITE EVIDENCE

**A** Have students match the text in paragraph 27 to the illustration. Students should recognize that both the appearance of the cave wall and the missing cacti fruit in the previous story are plot elements based on natural events.

**B** Remind students that the theme of a story is the main message the author is communicating. Have them think about how the message would be different in an adventure story than it would be in a mystery.

---

## COMPARING AND CONTRASTING STORIES

### Independent Practice

**WORDS TO KNOW**
admiring
vein
wildlife

**CITE EVIDENCE**

**A** The plots of this story and the last story both focus on nature. Circle the narrator's description of a natural event.

**B** In paragraph 33, underline the sentences that describe a **theme**, or main idea, of this story. What was the main idea of the first story?

**A Camping Adventure** *continued*

23    Papá considered for a moment. "The cave doesn't look big enough for any **wildlife**, so it's probably safe. But, I would like to check it out first."

24    They hiked over to the cave, and Papá looked inside with his flashlight. It wasn't what he expected. The cave was a large room, big enough for people to stand up. Papá went in first, and the family followed.

25    Papá moved his flashlight around the walls. Suddenly, Sofia gasped. "Papá, shine the flashlight back in that corner."

26    As he moved his light to the back of the room, Tino said, "Wow!" while Mama caught her breath. Papa just looked on in wonder.

27    At the back of the cave was one of the most beautiful rock walls any of them had ever seen. It was covered in sparkling shades of green, blue, and red. A small stream of water curled down the wall, highlighting a colored path as it flowed.

28    "What is it, Papá?" Sofia asked.

29    "I'm not completely certain," her father said, "but I think we may have discovered a rare copper **vein.** When the chemicals in the water mix with the chemicals in the rock, it creates colors on the wall."

30    The family members stood quietly, **admiring** the beauty of the cave. After a few minutes, Mamá reminded them that it was time to leave.

31    "This is spectacular," she said quietly, "but we do need to get back to camp before dark."

**204** Unit 9 ▪ Reading Literature: Integration of Knowledge and Ideas

---

### Words to Know

**General Academic Vocabulary**
**admiring** (*verb*): looking at something with enjoyment

**Domain-Specific Vocabulary**
**vein** (*noun*): a line of metal running through a rock bed
**wildlife** (*noun*): animals and plants

**Working with Word Meaning** Help students reinforce word meanings by having them write each word in an original sentence.

# INTEGRATION OF KNOWLEDGE AND IDEAS

32    As they left the cave to head back into the desert, Tino turned to his sister. "I don't know about you, Sofia, but I feel like we saved the best part of our spring break trip for last."

33    Sofia smiled. "I'm with you, *hermano*. That was the most amazing thing I have ever seen. What a cool adventure!"

## Comprehension Check    MORE ONLINE sadlierconnect.com

1. Based on your understanding of the setting, what is the meaning of the phrase "copper vein" in paragraph 29?

   a. a streak of copper in the rock wall

   b. the way chemicals react

   c. how blood flows through the body

   d. a copper picture in the cave

2. Based on both stories, which character would you describe as intelligent, with a love for the outdoors?

   a. Papá

   b. Sofia

   c. Mrs. Moreno

   d. Mr. Layton

3. Compare and contrast the themes of the first two stories. How are the themes the same? How are they different? Cite text evidence.

   Sample answer: In each story, Tino and Sofia search for answers. In
   the first story, they find an answer to solve a mystery. In this story,
   they explore nature and make discoveries. They find answers to
   nature's secrets.

Unit 9 ■ Reading Literature: Integration of Knowledge and Ideas    **205**

## Foundational Skill Review: Vowel Diphthongs

Review vowel diphthongs with students, reminding them that they are two letters combined to make one sound. Model how these letter combinations look and sound, using words from the text, such as *caught* and *out*. Have students find other words with vowel diphthongs in the text. (for example, *enough*, *around*, *beauty*)

Additional phonics activities can be found in the *Foundational Skills Handbook* at the end of this guide.

## Independent Practice

### Comprehension Check

**Answer Explanations:**

1. The correct choice is A, *a streak of copper in the rock wall.* Students can use the text descriptions in paragraphs 27 and 29 and the illustration to determine the answer.

2. Choice B, *Sofia*, is the best answer because she is the only character that appears in both stories and seems to know a great deal about nature.

3. The stories are similar in that they each contain an element of mystery. The characters make discoveries and find answers. They differ in central theme: helping neighbors and looking at facts versus respect for nature and appreciating new experiences.

## Critical Comprehension

Use the following questions to help students think more deeply about the text. Students should be prepared to support their answers with evidence from the text.

- *How can we keep endangered species and other natural wonders from disappearing?* (Answers will vary, but may include respecting natural environments and leaving nature as it is found.)

- *What are some of the safety precautions you should take on a hike?* (plenty of water, snacks, sun protection, a compass or map)

### Assess and Respond

**If** students have difficulty answering the Comprehension Check questions...

**Then** have them think about what it would be like to hike in the desert. Ask them what they should do if they come upon plants and wildlife on a hike. Have them reread the "Hiker's Motto" in the text.

## OBJECTIVES

- **Use illustrations to help understand a story.**
- **Compare and contrast two stories featuring the same characters.**

## Genre: Adventure Story

Tell students that they will be reading another adventure story featuring Sofia and Tino. Remind students that an adventure story places the main characters in a new or exciting situation. Remind students to play close attention to the ways in which this story is similar to and different from the first two stories.

## Path Options

You may want to do a close reading with students; if so, use the supports provided on these pages. Or, you may wish to have the students read the text independently and apply the skills learned in this unit. In either case, students should read the text more than once to facilitate understanding and to be able to answer the Comprehension Check questions correctly.

---

## CLOSE READING

# Treasure in the Desert

(Genre: Adventure Story)

1   It was 3:05 on Friday, and Sofia Rivera was searching for her twin brother, Tino. School was already over, and it wasn't like Tino to hang around. They were staying with their *abuela*, or grandmother, for the weekend, and she would be waiting. Sofia decided to check the school library. She found Tino putting an old, dusty book in his backpack.

2   "Tino, hurry! Abuela will be waiting outside."

3   "Okay, Sofia, but wait until you see the book I just found!"

4   That evening, after they said goodnight to their grandmother, Tino came into Sofia's room. "We need to talk," he said.

5   "Does this have anything to do with that book you checked out from the library?"

6   "It does. It's a book about finding gold and jewels in Arizona's deserts. I thought it would make an interesting book report. But, as I was reading, I noticed something curious."

7   Tino opened the book and slowly turned the pages in the last chapter. "Look at the bottom of the pages," he said.

8   "It looks like someone has drawn a map in the book," Sofia said. "Do you know what it leads to?"

9   "Well," Tino said slowly, "this is the chapter about gold in the Superstition Wilderness. You know, the place where the Lost Dutchman Mine is located?"

10   "Do you think this map could help us find the most famous lost treasure in Arizona?"

11   "Maybe!" Tino winked at his twin sister.

**206**   Unit 9 ■ Reading Literature: Integration of Knowledge and Ideas

---

## Support English Language Learners

English language learners often benefit from differing methods of vocabulary instruction. Because the unknown words are not explicitly highlighted in the Close Reading section of this unit, allow English language learners to highlight their own new vocabulary. Have each student go through the story once, highlighting unfamiliar words as they read. Then help the students discover the definitions of the words. Finally, have the students reread the Close Reading selection, replacing the unknown words with a definition or synonym.

## INTEGRATION OF KNOWLEDGE AND IDEAS

12  Saturday dawned clear and sunny. Tino and Sofia got up early and cooked breakfast for their abuela.

13  Tino explained to his grandmother about the dusty old book from the library, and how he believed it held a map to the Lost Dutchman Mine.

14  "And you want us to follow the map, to see if we can locate the lost treasure?" Abuela asked.

15  "It would be a fun adventure," Sofia said.

16  Abuela considered for a moment. "Okay!" she said at last. "Let's go find a treasure!"

17  Hiking in the desert requires special precautions. They packed water, trail mix, and sunblock. They wore long pants, protective hats, and hiking boots. At the Superstition Wilderness area, Tino pulled out his map and compass.

18  "We need to take the trail into the Superstition Wilderness for about 300 yards, then veer off to the north."

19  They grabbed their packs and checked in at the ranger station. Then they followed the trail into the desert.

20  Suddenly, Tino stopped. "Look at that saguaro cactus!"

21  In front of the group was a giant saguaro cactus with a peculiar shape. It had four arms that pointed straight down.

22  "Now," Tino said, "look at the map."

23  Sure enough, there was a drawing of a cactus with four arms pointing down.

Unit 9 ■ Reading Literature: Integration of Knowledge and Ideas   **207**

## Support First Reading

Circulate to check students' understanding. As needed, use the following comprehension and strategy check-ins to support basic understanding of the selection as students read.

### Check-in Questions

- *Who is the new character in this story—a character who was not in the earlier stories you read about Sofia and Tino?* (Sofia and Tino's *abuela*, or grandmother) *What is her role in the story?* (Sofia and Tino are staying with her for the weekend, so she is their adult guardian.)

- *What does Tino discover in his library book?* (a map to the Lost Dutchman Mine) *Why is this significant?* (The Lost Dutchman Mine is supposed to be the place where "the most famous lost treasure in Arizona is located.")

## Review: Connecting Text and Illustrations

After reading the first three paragraphs of the story, have students look carefully at the illustration. Ask students how Tino is feeling about his library book, based on his expression in the illustration and his conversation with Sofia. (Tino's face looks excited about his library book. He tells his sister, "Wait until you see the book I just found!" which also indicates excitement.)

## Differentiate Instruction

Offer vocabulary support to students by highlighting the following words: *abuela, curious, wilderness, located, precautions, protective, saguaro.* Have lower-level readers work with a partner to develop their own definitions for these words. Monitor their work. Allow students to use available research materials to formulate accurate definitions. Then ask individual students to use a word in a sentence that fits the context of the story.

# Close Reading

## Check-in Question

- *What do Tino, Sofia, and Abuela take on their hike?* (water, trail mix, sunblock, protective clothing, hiking boots) *Why are these things called* precautions *in the text?*

## Review: Comparing and Contrasting Stories

After reading page 207, have students compare and contrast the adventures that Tino and Sofia have in "A Camping Adventure" and "Treasure in the Desert." Remind students to look for ways in which the stories are the same and ways in which the stories differ.

## Review: Connecting Text and Illustrations

Have students make connections between the illustrations and the text of the stories. Ask students to underline, in the stories, text that describes the images in the illustrations. Then have students describe things they see in the illustrations that are not mentioned in the text.

## CLOSE READING

24    "We're on the right trail!" Tino exclaimed. "Next, we need to turn west until we see a rock shaped like a castle."

25    Abuela was the one who spotted it first. "Children, *niños*, look. Does that giant rock look like a castle to you?"

26    Tino studied his map. "Behind the rock, there should be a small opening. That's where we need to dig!"

27    They started digging, taking turns to avoid overheating. Eventually, Sofia spoke up, "I think I've found something!"

28    She uncovered a small leather pouch.

29    "Whoa," Tino breathed, "I bet this is it. It's probably some old money that's worth millions of dollars today."

30    "Why don't you open it and see?" Abuela chimed in.

31    Tino opened the leather pouch. He carefully pulled out a thin yellow sheet of paper. There was old-fashioned writing.

32    "My name is Josef Walzer," he read. "People around here call me 'The Dutchman,' but I am actually a German immigrant. I came to America to make my fortune. I was driven by a desire for gold.

33    "I spent years searching for gold, but never found anything. I returned to civilization, but I had no money and no place to live. A kind old woman who owned a small restaurant agreed to take me in, if I would work for her. She let me cook for the restaurant, and that's when I found my real treasure—I was a talented chef.

**208    Unit 9** ■ Reading Literature: Integration of Knowledge and Ideas

## Strategic Reading

Provide support for all readers by providing them with reading strategies for improving comprehension as they read. Have students make predictions as they read, based on both the text and the illustrations in the story. As students are reading, have them stop periodically and discuss, either as a group or in pairs, what they think will happen next. For instance, at the end of page 207, you might ask the students: *What do you think Tino, Sofia, and Abuela will find as a result of following the treasure map?*

# INTEGRATION OF KNOWLEDGE AND IDEAS

34   "I created a recipe for Dutch Apple Pie that everyone loved. Customers came from miles around to try my Lost Dutchman Pie. Now I have no one to leave the secret of my famous pie to. I am burying the recipe in the desert. I've left a map in my old guidebook. Hopefully, someone worthy will find my valuable treasure."

35   Tino turned the letter over. Sure enough, on the back, was a recipe for Lost Dutchman Pie.

36   Tino, Sofia, and Abuela looked at each other, not sure what to say. Suddenly, Sofia burst out laughing. "It's not the Lost Dutchman Mine; it's the Lost Dutchman Pie!"

37   Tino and Abuela joined in with her laughter. "Tino," Abuela said, "thank you for this adventure."

38   "But we didn't find any gold," Tino said.

39   "Maybe not, " Abuela answered back, "but we did find a treasure. I don't know about you, but I can't wait to uncover the mysteries of the Lost Dutchman Pie. Dessert, anyone?"

## Comprehension Check

**1.** Compare and contrast this story to "A Camping Adventure." Which new character is introduced in this story?

  **a.** Mamá

  **b.** Leo

  **c.** Abuela

  **d.** Mrs. Johnson

**2.** Based on the text and illustrations, which statement best describes the setting of this story?

  **a.** a neighborhood

  **b.** a classroom

  **c.** the high desert

  **d.** an old movie set

Unit 9 ■ Reading Literature: Integration of Knowledge and Ideas   **209**

## Research to Build Knowledge

Many areas of the country have fables and myths specific to a geographic location, such as Pecos Bill in Texas and Paul Bunyan in the Northwest. Have students research some of the stories told in geographic locations throughout America and write a short research paper on one locale that especially interests them. Extend the activity by having students present their paper to the class.

## Multiple Readings for Critical Comprehension

Have students reread this selection and pose questions that focus on critical comprehension. Remind them to annotate text to support their comprehension.

- *What do the twins and their grandmother discover at the end of this story?* (The Lost Dutchman's treasure is a recipe for pie.) *Why is this a "twist" ending?* (Like Tino, readers are expecting that a real treasure will be found. They are not expecting the "treasure" to be a pie recipe.)

- *What do you think is the main theme, or message, of "Treasure in the Desert"?* (Not all treasure is silver and gold; sometimes your treasures are your talents and ideas.)

## Self-Select Text

As preparation for Connect Across Texts, have students select one of the three selections in this unit and reread it independently. Students can access full pdf versions of the selections at **sadlierconnect.com**.

## Comprehension Check

Begin scoring students' understanding of unit skills and texts from Comprehension Check on this page through Connect Across Texts on page 211. Use students' total score to determine their readiness for the Unit 9 Review on page 213.

## Multiple-Choice Questions: *1 point each*

**1.** The only new character that appears in this story is Tino and Sofia's grandmother; therefore, choice C, *Abuela*, is correct.

**2.** Choice C, *the high desert*, is correct based on both the text descriptions and the illustrations in this story.

# Close Reading

## Short-Answer Questions: 2 points each

### Item 3 Rubric

| | |
|---|---|
| 2 | Students are able to accurately make connections between text and illustrations to describe both the characters and setting in the story. |
| 1 | Students are able to use text and illustrations to describe either the characters or the setting in the story but not both. |
| 0 | Students cannot describe either the characters in the story or the setting of the story. |

### Item 4 Rubric

| | |
|---|---|
| 2 | Students are able to both compare and contrast the main themes in two stories with recurring characters. |
| 1 | Students are able to either compare or contrast the themes of the two stories but cannot do both. |
| 0 | Students cannot compare or contrast themes in the stories. |

## Theme Wrap-Up

Lead students in a group discussion on the theme of Searching for Answers. How are Sofia and Tino searching for answers in each of these stories? Have students get into small groups and brainstorm ideas for a mystery/adventure story. Have students work together to write and illustrate their own mystery/adventure story.

## CLOSE READING

3. Think about the illustrations in this story. How do the illustrations help you learn more about the characters and the setting in this story? Use examples from the story in your answer.

Sample answer: This story has one new character, Abuela, and it takes place in a new setting, the Superstition Wilderness. The illustration helps you create a picture of both the new character and the setting. For example, if you don't know what a saguaro cactus is, you can see a picture of one in the illustration.

4. This story and the second story, "A Camping Adventure," are both adventure stories. But, they have very different themes. Compare and contrast the themes of these two stories.

Sample answer: The theme of "A Camping Adventure" involves exploring nature and making an amazing discovery on a family adventure trip. The theme of this story involves taking a chance and finding a lost treasure. In "A Camping Adventure," Sofia and Tino discover a beautiful cave, and make sure not to harm it. In this story, Sofia and Tino learn a lesson about how different people value different things in life.

## Extend Thinking: Create

Help students extend their thinking by creating a short graphic novel based on a short story. Provide students with a variety of well-known short stories, folk tales, myths, and fairy tales from which to choose. Then have students use illustrations to tell the story. They can use a collage or a computer program if they do not wish to draw. Remind them to focus on the illustration rather than using text.

Students should create their graphic novel and then present their work to the rest of the class. Students should describe their graphic novels to the class, speaking clearly and highlighting appropriate events in the story.

## CONNECT ACROSS TEXTS

### Compare and Contrast Texts

In this unit, you read stories that featured the same characters in different situations. Think about how these stories are the same, and how they are different. Then choose two of the texts and compare and contrast them using the T-chart below. List important details about setting, characters, and theme to show how the texts are similar or different. Be prepared to discuss your ideas with the class.

| Similarities | Differences |
|---|---|
| "A Camping Adventure" and "Treasure in the Desert": | "A Camping Adventure": |
| adventure stories | parents are characters |
| include Sofia and Tino characters | discover a secret cave |
| desert setting | "Treasure in the Desert": |
| amazing discoveries made | grandparent is character |
| | discover a hidden note |

### Return to the Essential Question

**What connections can readers make?**

In small groups or as a class, discuss the Essential Question. Think about what you have learned about making connections between illustrations and texts, and about how you can compare and contrast setting, theme, and characters in different stories. Use evidence from the three unit texts to answer the question.

### Connect Across Texts: *4 points* Review Reading Selections

Have students work in groups of four to identify similarities and differences in two of the unit's stories. Each student should have one topic to answer: characters, setting, events, or theme. Have each student share with the rest of the group.

### Compare and Contrast Texts

Review the directions on page 211, and instruct students to write the titles of their chosen selections on top of the chart.

#### T-Chart Rubric

| | |
|---|---|
| **4** | Student has correctly identified the similarities and differences between two texts in the unit. |
| **3** | Student has correctly identified some of the similarities and differences in two texts in the unit. |
| **2** | Student has correctly identified either the similarities, or the differences, between two texts, but not elements of both. |
| **1** | Student has identified two texts from the unit, but has not compared or contrasted them. |
| **0** | Student has not identified the selections, or included what they learned. |

### Support Essential Question Discussion

Have students reread the Essential Question and finish this sentence. *When I read two stories, I can make connections between…*

If students have difficulty responding, prompt them by asking which elements of literature they compared and contrasted throughout this unit.

### Assess and Respond (pages 209–211)

| If | Then |
|---|---|
| Students scored 0–4 points, they are **Developing** their understanding of unit skills… | Provide students with reading support and more intensive modeling of skills. |
| Students scored 5–7 points, they are **Improving** their understanding of unit skills… | Use students' scores to target areas that are weak and review those specific skills. |
| Students scored 8–10 points, they are **Proficient** in their understanding of unit skills… | Have these students move on. They are ready for the formal assessment. |

## OBJECTIVE
**Use root words to determine word meanings.**

### Guided Instruction

Review the Guided Instruction section on page 212 with students. Be sure they understand that root words provide the basic meaning behind a word. Looking at root words can help a reader decipher the meaning of a word by breaking it down into smaller pieces.

### Guided Practice

If students are having trouble, have them break the words into small pieces, and then try to match those pieces to the roots listed on the word chart in the text. You might also have them do this exercise in small groups.

### Independent Practice

If students are having trouble defining the indicated words, have them turn back to the selection to read the words as they are used there. They appear on page 209, paragraph 37 (*adventure*) and page 208, paragraph 33 (*civilization*).

## Apply to Reading

Have students return to page 208 of "Treasure in the Desert" to find a word that contains one of the word roots listed in the chart. They should identify *eventually* in paragraph 27. Have the students use the word root chart to define the word and use it correctly in a sentence.

## LANGUAGE

### Roots

**Guided Instruction** Looking at the **root** of a word and comparing it to a familiar word with the same root can help you understand a word's meaning.

| Root | port | cause or cus | vent | vac |
|---|---|---|---|---|
| Meaning | carry | reason | come | empty |

| Root | civ | fac | migra | vert |
|---|---|---|---|---|
| Meaning | citizen | do, make | wander | turn |

**Guided Practice** Identify the root of each word below.

**1.** fact: _____ fac _____

**2.** immigrant: _____ migra _____

**3.** report: _____ port _____

**Independent Practice** Identify the root, and its meaning, in each of the words in **bold** below. Then in the sentence that follows, use what you have learned to write the meaning of the bold word with the same root. Use a dictionary if necessary.

**1.** "Tino," Abuela said, "thank you for this **adventure**."
Root/meaning: _____ vent/come _____
The people at the comic book **convention** came from all over the world.
Word meaning: _____ a meeting where people come together _____

**2.** "I gave up and moved back to **civilization**."
Root/meaning: _____ civ/citizen _____
The volunteers who cleaned up the park were very **civic** minded.
Word meaning: _____ relating to the duties of a citizen _____

## Support English Language Learners

Allowing English language learners the opportunity to physically manipulate the word roots will aid them in comprehension of difficult vocabulary. Write each of the words identified in the text (*immigrant*, *report*, *adventure*, *civilization*) on a separate sheet of paper. Model cutting the words up into their individual pieces for the students, leaving the word roots intact. Then have the students physically put the words back together, defining the roots as they do. Finally, have the students go back and identify each word within the text.

## UNIT 9 REVIEW

Read the following mystery story. Think about how this story is the same as the previous stories in this unit and how it is different. Then answer the questions on pages 213 and 214.

# The Missing Pencil Sharpener

### (Genre: Mystery)

1   Sofia and Tino were in their home classroom. Ms. Johnson, their teacher, stood in front of the class with two students.

2   "Class, I have a mystery. When I got to school, my classroom was vacant, and my pencil sharpener had disappeared. Can you discover which one of these two students took it?"

3   Sofia raised her hand and asked one of the students, "Where were you when the sharpener was taken?" The boy smiled and said, "I was outside."

4   Tino quizzed the other student. "Where were you when the sharpener was taken?" "I was in the cafeteria," she said.

5   Sofia closely inspected the students and then said, "The boy did it. His excuse is not true. It's raining, and his shoes are clean. If he'd been outside, they would be muddy and wet!"

6   Ms. Johnson laughed, "I should have known you two would win my mystery challenge!"

**Fill in the circle of the correct answer choice.**

**1.** What is the setting of this story?

- ○ the desert
- ○ a neighborhood
- ● a classroom
- ○ the pet store

**2.** What new character appears in paragraph 1?

- ● Ms. Johnson
- ○ Mr. Abbott
- ○ Abuela
- ○ April

## Unit Summary

At this point, students have had instruction and practice in reading literature, with a focus on connecting texts to illustrations and comparing and contrasting different elements in stories that feature recurring characters. Students have done an independent close reading of a text, practiced working with concepts across texts, and practiced using different strategies for determining word meanings from word roots. They should be well-prepared for the review section.

## Introduce the Review

Explain to students that they will read a new passage that is related to the unit's theme and the selections they have already read. Instruct students to read the passage carefully and then answer the questions that start on page 213.

### Answer Explanations

Scoring: Items 1–7 on pages 213–214 are worth 1 point each. See the rubrics on the next page for guidance on scoring the short-answer questions on page 214.

**1.** The text describes the classroom, so the third choice, *a classroom*, is correct.

**2.** Sofia and Tino are recurring characters, so the first choice, *Ms. Johnson*, is correct.

## Self-Assessment: Progress Check

Have students revisit the Progress Check on page 191 and respond to the questions again. Ask them to compare their Before and After responses.

You may wish to have students rate their answers on a scale of 0–2 rather than simply checking (or not checking) the box. Instruct them to write a *0* if feel they don't understand the given skill at all, a *1* if they feel they have some understanding, and a *2* if they feel they have a solid grasp of the skill.

## Answers Explanations

**3.** This story is a mystery, so the third choice, *"The Case of the Missing Fruit,"* is correct.

**4.** There are only two recurring characters in this unit, so *Tino and Sofia* is correct.

**5.** The root of the word *excuse* is *cus*.

**6.** The story genre is mystery, and the other story in this genre is "The Case of the Missing Fruit."

**7.** Sofia figures out the solution to the mystery in both "The Case of the Missing Fruit" and "The Missing Pencil Sharpener."

## Item 8 Rubric

| | |
|---|---|
| 2 | Answer makes comparisons between Mrs. Moreno and Ms. Johnson. |
| 1 | Answer describes either Mrs. Moreno or Ms. Johnson, but does not make comparisons. |
| 0 | Answer does not reference either Mrs. Moreno or Ms. Johnson. |

## Item 9 Rubric

| | |
|---|---|
| 2 | Student accurately describes setting details based on the story. |
| 1 | Student describes some setting details based on the story. |
| 0 | Student does not describe any setting details based on the story. |

## Item 10 Rubric

| | |
|---|---|
| 2 | Student accurately describes setting details and characters as they appear in the story. |
| 1 | Student describes either setting details or characters as they appear in the story. |
| 0 | Student does not describe setting details or characters as they appear in the story. |

## UNIT 9 REVIEW

**3.** Which story in this unit has a theme most like "The Missing Pencil Sharpener"?

○ "A Camping Adventure"

○ "Treasure in the Desert"

● "The Case of the Missing Fruit"

**4.** Which characters appear in all of the stories in this unit?

○ Sofia and Abuela

● Tino and Sofia

○ Mamá and Papá

○ Ella and April

**5.** Identify the root of the word *excuse* in paragraph 5.

cause or cus

**6.** Name this story's genre. Name another unit story in this genre.

a mystery; "The Case of the Missing Fruit"

**7.** Who announces the solution to the mystery in both stories?

Sofia

**8.** Compare the character of Ms. Johnson in "The Missing Pencil Sharpener" to Mrs. Moreno in "The Case of the Missing Fruit."

Ms. Johnson is Tino and Sofia's teacher. Mrs. Moreno is Tino and Sofia's neighbor. Both want Tino and Sofia to solve a problem.

**9.** What would a picture of this story's setting look like?

Sample answer: There are kids at desks in a classroom, and a teacher and chalkboard at the front. Outside the window, it is raining.

**10.** How would you illustrate "The Missing Pencil Sharpener"?

Sample answer: The teacher stands at the front of the room; Tino and Sofia have their hands raised; a boy and a girl stand next to the teacher.

214   Unit 9 ■ Reading Literature: Integration of Knowledge and Ideas

## Analyze Student Scores

| | |
|---|---|
| **10–13 pts Strong** | Student has a good grasp of the skills and concepts taught in this unit. Point out any mistakes the student has made and explain the correct answers if necessary. |
| **6–9 pts Progressing** | Student is struggling with some skills or concepts. Identify the specific skills that are problematic to target a review of instruction. |
| **0–5 pts Emerging** | Student is having serious problems understanding the skills and concepts taught in this unit. Student may need to redo the work with a higher level of support. |

## Introducing UNIT **10**

**I**n this unit about the desert, you will learn how to research and write a report. The purpose of a research report is to provide information.

When you write an informative text, such as a research report, you will begin by gathering information on your topic. You will want to find several different sources for information, and then organize this information into related ideas. You will introduce the topic in the beginning, and end with a statement or paragraph that tells what the reader just learned. Linking words such as *also*, *another*, and *but* can help you show how ideas are related.

To be effective, a research report should use facts, definitions, and details to explain the ideas and develop the topic.

### Progress Check *Can I?*

| Before Unit 10 | | After Unit 10 |
|---|---|---|
| ☐ | Conduct a research project. | ☐ |
| ☐ | Gather and take notes on information from print and digital sources. | ☐ |
| ☐ | Group related information together. | ☐ |
| ☐ | Provide information that builds knowledge about a topic. | ☐ |
| ☐ | Write using compound sentences correctly. | ☐ |
| ☐ | Write using complex sentences correctly. | ☐ |
| ☐ | Capitalize the important words in a title. | ☐ |

Unit 10 ■ Research to Build and Present Knowledge: Write Research Reports

**Student Page 215**

## Progress Check

The Progress Check is a self-assessment feature that students can use to gauge their own progress. Research shows that when students take accountability for their own learning, it increases their motivation.

Before students begin work on Unit 10, have them check the boxes next to any item that they feel they can do well. Explain that it is fine if they don't check any of the boxes. Tell them that they will have an opportunity to learn about and practice all of these items while studying the unit. Let them know that near the end of the unit they will have a chance to reconsider how well they can do each item on this list.

Before students begin the Unit 10 Review on page 227, have them revisit this page. You can use this information to work with students on any items they don't understand before they tackle the Review.

## HOME ◆ CONNECT...

The Home Connect feature is a way to keep parents or other adult family members apprised of what their children are learning. The key learning objectives are listed, and some ideas for related activities and discussions are included.

Explain to students that they can share the Home Connect page with their parents or the adult family members in their home. Let students know how much time the class will be spending on this unit so they can plan their time accordingly at home.

Encourage students and their parents to share their experiences using the suggestions on the Home Connect page. You may wish to make a place to post any of this work.

## HOME ◆ CONNECT...

**I**n this unit, children will learn about writing a **research report** to share knowledge about a topic. Discuss with your child a topic that you know about, such as repairing a car or baking bread. Share how you continue to learn more. For example, you may read books, talk to other people, or do research on the Internet. Point out that there are a great many resources that can give you the information you need.

Your child will begin the process by **researching a topic**. He or she will use **research materials**, such as books and websites. To practice researching on the Internet, discuss a topic and help your child find good sources of Internet information on it. (Sites ending in .edu and .gov are the most reliable.) As you read information on the topic together, **write down facts and details** that are related. Help your child understand that **related information is grouped together** in a research report.

**Conversation Starter:** A research report is an opportunity to build knowledge on a topic by searching for answers. Discuss these questions with your child: *What is an expert? How does someone become an expert? What are you an expert at? On what topic would you like to become an expert? How might you learn more about that topic?* Emphasize that writing is a great way to learn from and share knowledge with others.

### IN THIS UNIT, YOUR CHILD WILL...

- Learn to write a research report that builds knowledge about a subject.
- Gather information by taking notes from print and digital sources.
- Group related information in a report.
- Learn specific language skills and use them in writing a research report:
  - Write compound and complex sentences, using conjunctions correctly.
  - Capitalize the important words in a title.

### WAYS TO HELP YOUR CHILD

Encourage your child to write often and for a variety of purposes. For example, your child can write thank-you notes and letters to family and friends, a journal entry on a scrapbook page, or a list of instructions for taking care of a pet. As your child writes, discuss the purpose for that kind of writing and how it is unique.

**ONLINE**
For more Home Connect activities, continue online at sadlierconnect.com

216   Unit 10 ■ Research to Build and Present Knowledge: Write Research Reports

**Student Page 216**

## UNIT PLANNER

| Theme: Searching for Answers<br>Curriculum Connection: Science | Focus |
|---|---|
| **WRITING MODEL**<br>*pp. 218–220* | *Life in the Desert* |
| **WRITING PRACTICE**<br>*pp. 221–222* | **ORGANIZATIONAL STRUCTURE:** Note-Taking Organizer and Outline |
| **LANGUAGE MINI-LESSONS**<br>*pp. 223–225* | • Compound Sentences<br>• Complex Sentences<br>• Capitalization |
| **SPEAKING AND LISTENING**<br>*p. 226* | Discuss the Essential Question |
| **UNIT 10 REVIEW**<br>*pp. 227–228* | • Language Skills Summary<br>• Writing Process Summary |

Essential Question: How do writers conduct and present research on a topic?

UNIT 10

## Objective(s)

Research a topic using multiple sources and present the topic in writing with appropriate organization.

Plan a research report with an introduction, subtopics, and a concluding statement.

- Use compound sentences in writing, employing coordinating conjunctions as necessary.
- Use complex sentences in writing, employing subordinating conjunctions as necessary.
- Capitalize titles correctly in writing.

- Ask questions to check understanding.
- Express ideas clearly.

## Unit Assessment

- Unit 10 Review *pp. 227–228*

## Additional Assessment Options

- Performance Task 1 *pp. 141A–145 and 146*
  ( ALSO ONLINE )
- Performance Task 2 *pp. 259A–263 and 264*
  ( ALSO ONLINE )

## Optional Purchase:

- iProgress Monitor ( ONLINE )
- Progress Monitor Student Benchmark Assessment Booklet

## ( ONLINE ) Digital Resources

- Home Connect Activities
- Additional Practice
- Teacher Resources
- iProgress Monitor (optional purchase)

**Go to SadlierConnect.com to access your Digital Resources.**

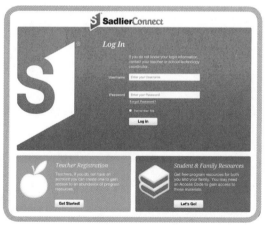

**For more detailed instructions see page T3.**

**217B**

## LEARNING PROGRESSIONS

In this unit, students will learn how to research and write a report on the desert. In order to learn the skills necessary to craft a research report, a type of informational text, students will further develop skills learned in second grade. They should be encouraged to retain these skills, as they will continue to build on them in fourth grade.

**Conducting Research**

- Proficient second-grade students should have ended the year capable of participating in shared research and writing projects (e.g., read a number of books on a single topic to produce a report; record scientific observations).

- As third graders, students will expand on this skill by conducting short research projects that build knowledge about a topic.

- This skill will prepare students for grade 4, when they will conduct short research projects that build knowledge through investigation of different aspects of a topic.

**Gathering Information**

- In grade 2, students should have learned to recall information from experiences or gather information from provided sources to answer a question.

- In grade 3, students will be expected to recall information from experiences, gather information from print or digital sources, take brief notes on sources, and sort evidence into provided categories.

- As fourth graders, students will further develop this skill by categorizing information and providing a list of sources.

# Research to Build and Present Knowledge: Write Research Reports

**Essential Question:**
How do writers conduct and present research on a topic?

Copyright © by William H. Sadlier, Inc. All rights reserved.

## Essential Question:
How do writers conduct and present research on a topic?

In this unit, students will learn how to research and gather information about a topic from multiple sources for the purpose of writing a research report.

### Theme: Searching for Answers
Students will continue their exploration of what it means to search for answers as they read and analyze a research report writing model.

### Curriculum Connection: Science
Students will apply the concept of searching for answers as they research and present information about the desert in their own research report.

### Connect Reading to Writing
Remind students that they read a mystery entitled "The Case of the Missing Fruit" in Unit 9 (Student Book pages 194–199). Discuss how the characters in the story search for answers about missing fruit. Draw a connection to how students, like the characters, will conduct their own search. Explain, however, that they will search for answers about—or research—a nonfiction topic, the desert, and then write about it.

## Writing Handbook

If students need extra practice with writing a research report, refer them to the *Writing Handbook* on pages 275–283. The Writing Handbook gives students detailed instruction on planning, drafting, revising, and editing their writing. They will also find tips on producing, publishing, and presenting their writing.

## OBJECTIVE
Research a topic using multiple sources and present the topic in writing with appropriate organization.

## Introduce: Organizational Structure

Draw students' attention to the research report outline in the left margin. Point out the three subtopics in the outline. Ask students to think about these subtopics as you read and analyze the Student Model together.

## Analyze a Student Model

**TITLE:** Have students read the title. *What can we predict the report is about?* (animals that live in the desert)

**INTRODUCTION:** Help students find the sentence that states the topic: *I know from the title that the report is about life in the desert. That's a pretty big topic that could mean many different things. So, I will look for a sentence that tells me what aspect of life in the desert Bharat focuses on.*

Help students identify that the last sentence in the introduction states what the report is about. Then discuss how Bharat leads up to the topic statement. *Did you notice that Bharat starts his report with a question? That helps engage and get the readers thinking. Then he addresses what readers may be thinking and how it may differ from what is actually true.*

### CREATING AN ORGANIZATIONAL STRUCTURE
Bharat used an outline to organize his report. It is divided into three sections: introduction, explanation, and conclusion.

```
I.  Introduction
    Topic:
    _____
    _____

II. Explanation
    a. Subtopic 1:
    _____
    _____
    _____

    b. Subtopic 2:
    _____
    _____

III. Conclusion
    _____
    _____
    _____
```

**INTRODUCTION**

• Bharat introduces the topic at the beginning, leading up to a statement about what the report will be about.

*Underline the sentence that tells what Bharat's report will be about.*

# Read a Student Model

Bharat has been asked to write a research report about the desert. He has researched sources, taken notes, and then grouped related information together. As you read Bharat's research report, think about how you might research your own report about the desert and how you might use the facts, definitions, and details you find to build readers' knowledge.

### Life in the Desert

What do you think of when you imagine a desert? Many people think of sand, rocks, or cacti. They might be surprised to know that the desert is home to many different animals, from snakes to birds to rabbits. The desert presents many challenges to animals. They must be able to survive the strong heat and the limited rainfall. However, many animals are uniquely suited to living in these harsh conditions. <u>Let's take a look at some animals that make their home in and around the saguaro cactus.</u>

## Genre: Research Report

Remind students that the theme of the unit is "searching for answers." Point out the word *research* within the text type *research report.* Then draw a connection between "searching for answers" and "conducting research." *What is a writer doing when he or she researches something?* Be sure students understand that a writer is looking for answers, in the sense that he or she is trying to find out more about a topic.

Explain that to effectively report on the information a writer has researched about the topic, he or she must present it clearly. This means grouping related information together and developing the topic with facts, definitions, and details. *What other kind of writing has these same requirements?* (A research report is a type of informative/ explanatory text.)

## Inside the Cactus

The saguaro cactus has long arms that reach toward the sky. They are covered with a tough coating and spikes. The spikes help to keep water in and animals out. Yet, some animals make their way through these barriers and nest inside the soft flesh of the cactus. (For example, the woodpecker uses its beak to peck holes in the trunk and branches.) It hollows out the soft inside to make a nest. (Later, when the woodpecker leaves, elf owls, purple martins, and sparrows may use the abandoned nest for their home.)

## Under the Cactus

Under the saguaro cactus stretches the sandy desert floor. Many animals may be found scurrying across the dry landscape in search of food and water. Several animals eat the cactus's flesh. They include such animals as pack rats, jackrabbits, mule deer, and bighorn sheep. In the late summer, the cactus bears fruit. This fruit is a source of energy for several animals. The saguaro cactus has thick channels inside that hold water for the plant. This channel is a source of water for animals when needed.

**ORGANIZATION**

- Bharat has gathered information about desert life from different sources. Some sources are printed materials. Other sources are digital or online.
- He has grouped related information together, using headings to show each grouping.

*Circle two details about different animals that use the inside of the saguaro cactus.*

**DEVELOP THE TOPIC**

- Facts and other details that Bharat has researched help build readers' knowledge about the topic.

*Underline two facts in the section "Under the Cactus."*

## Analyze a Student Model

**ORGANIZATION:** Point out the section headings to students. *Think about the introductory statement that tells what the report is about. Based on the introductory statement and this heading, what do you think this section will tell you about?* (It will tell about animals that make their home in the cactus.) Point out the second section heading. *How has Bharat organized his report?* (He has organized his report by grouping related information.) *So where can we expect to find all the details he includes about animals that live in the cactus?* (We can expect to find those details in the first section.) Ask students to find the first animal that Bharat mentions in this section (the woodpecker). *What information does he provide about the woodpecker?* (It uses its beak to peck holes in the trunk and branches.) Guide students as they look for the detail that relates to how other animals live in the cactus. (Elf owls, purple martins, and sparrows may use the abandoned nest for their home.)

**DEVELOP THE TOPIC:** Model identifying how Bharat builds his topic: *I know from the heading that this section is about animals that live under the cactus. As I read this section, I see that Bharat means the animals that live on the desert floor, not ones that literally live underneath the cactus. He builds this topic by talking about how these animals rely on the cactus for food and water. What is the first fact that Bharat includes to build this idea?* (Several animals eat the cactus flesh.) Point to the sentence "In the late summer, the cactus bears fruit." *Is this a fact or an opinion?* (a fact) *How does this help build this section?* (It helps the reader understand another way some desert animals rely on the cactus for food.) Point out how the first section discussed how the cactus provides shelter, and the second section discusses how the cactus provides food.

## Support English Language Learners

Help English language learners make sense of the many details about desert life presented in the student model by having them highlight key terms as they conduct a first read and then use the highlighted words to create a drawing of the desert. For example, in the first paragraph, students may highlight the words *sand, rocks, cacti, snakes, birds, rabbits, strong heat,* and *limited rainfall.* After they have created their drawings, show them photographs of desert life. Be sure the photographs you show reflect ideas presented in the student model, such as a woodpecker pecking a hole in a cactus. Point out in the photographs any ideas that students did not include in their own drawings. Then have them read the text again, making additional highlights, and revising their drawings.

## Analyze a Student Model

**CONCLUDING STATEMENT:** Review Bharat's conclusion with students. Students should recognize that Bharat summarizes what readers learn from his report, and then he returns to his opening question by urging readers to broaden what they think about when they think about the desert. Finally, he makes his concluding statement.

## Evaluate a Writer's Work

Remind students that the purpose of a research report is to share information collected about a topic from multiple sources. Have students recall how a research report should group information. (A research report should group related information together.) Have students independently write one sentence telling whether they think Bharat organized his report well. Then have students turn to a partner and share and discuss their opinions about Bharat's organization.

## Model: Organizational Structure

Ask students to think about how Bharat might have taken notes for his research and then written summaries and paraphrases to help complete the outline for his research report. On a board or projector, post the graphic organizer on page 221. Briefly discuss how it works. Then post the outline on page 222. Have students help you fill in the outline based on the model text. Fill in the introduction, explanation, and conclusion. Point out that well-written research reports have strong organization, which requires planning and prewriting.

Students will next use the graphic organizer and outline found in their books to research and plan their own research reports, and then they will draft the report based on their outline.

### WRITE RESEARCH REPORTS

**CONCLUDING STATEMENT**
- Bharat's ending wraps up the report by summing up what the reader has learned.
*Underline the sentence that is the concluding statement.*

The desert can be a harsh place to live. The animals living there face many challenges. Despite this, many animals make their homes in the desert. They depend on the natural resources such as the saguaro cactus to survive. So, the next time you think of the desert, you may think of rocks, sand, and cacti. However, you also should think about woodpeckers, hawks, jackrabbits, mule deer, and bighorn sheep. <u>The desert is home to a surprising number of animals.</u>

Sources:
http://www.saguaro.national-park.com/info.htm#Life
http://www.nps.gov/sagu/planyourvisit/upload/The%20Saguaro%20Cactus.pdf
"Saguaro," Encyclopædia Britannica

220

### Review: Comparing and Contrasting Texts

Remind students that when they read the three fictional stories in Unit 9, they compared and contrasted them in order to better understand that the two main characters appeared in all three stories but that the setting changed for each story.

Draw students' attention to the sources Bharat noted at the end of his research report. Explain to students that when they conduct research to write their report on the desert, they will need to look at more than one source, just as Bharat did, and then compare and contrast those sources because different sources sometimes contain different information about a topic. Explain that if several sources note the same information about a topic, then students can feel confident that the information is correct.

Use a graphic organizer like the one below to take notes for your research report on the desert. You may use print or digital sources to find information. You will use these notes to create your outline on page 222.

| Source 1 | Source 2 |
|---|---|
| Summarize or paraphrase information: | Summarize or paraphrase information: |

Unit 10 ■ Research to Build and Present Knowledge: Write Research Reports **221**

## Conduct Research

### Finding Sources

Explain to students that they can find sources by looking for books in the library and searching for websites online. Model using key words to search for sources online, and discuss how to determine if an online source is credible. Point out that spelling errors, poor site design, and obvious bias can indicate that the source is not credible.

### Taking Notes

Students will use the graphic organizer on page 221 to record notes as they conduct their research. Explain that there are two ways they can take notes:

- Students can quote directly from the source—writing down the exact words used in the text and putting quotation marks around them.

- Students can summarize or paraphrase the ideas in the source. Discuss how someone else's idea needs to be credited. Point out that if students do not properly credit these ideas in their report, then they will be guilty of plagiarism.

### Citing Sources

Tell students that they need to cite their sources both when they take notes and at the end of their research report. *If you don't cite your sources as you take notes, you might forget which source a fact or detail is from.*

Provide the structure and examples for citing both print and online sources:

- PRINT: Last name, First name. Name of Book. City published in; Publisher, Date published.

- ONLINE: Last name, First name. "Article title." Date published. Website title. Date accessed. URL.

Students should include this information before each summary or paraphrase in their note-taking graphic organizer.

## Differentiate Instruction

Work individually with students who are not yet ready to conduct research. First, review what a source is—a print or digital publication from which you get facts, details, and other information to use in your own text. Then, discuss why one would need to look at several sources, or conduct research, before writing about a topic. *Do you know everything there is to know about the desert? Do you know what kinds of insects live in the desert? Can you name a plant, other than the cactus, that lives in the desert?* Finally, review finding sources, taking notes, and citing sources with students, asking questions to check that they fully understand the role and significance of each step of conducting research.

# Write Research Reports

## Create: Organizational Structure

### Brainstorming

Tell students that writers write research reports about topics that they want to know more about. As a class, have students name aspects of the desert they want to know more about. Make a list of students' topic ideas on the board for them to use as they plan.

### Planning

Students will use the outline on page 222 to plan their text. After conducting their research, students should write down their topic and what they will examine about the topic.

- Students should divide their topic into two subtopics and record information from their organizer related to each subtopic.
- Have students recall that Bharat summed up the information presented in his report in his conclusion. Ask students how they might sum up their report.

### Drafting a Research Report

Instruct students to refer to their outline as they draft their research report on a separate piece of paper. Be sure students have an introduction, explanation, and conclusion.

## Introduce the Writing Process

Remind students that in order to do a good job on an essay, they must plan, draft, revise, and edit it. These are all steps of the writing process. For more on the writing process, see the *Writing Handbook* on page 275 of this guide.

### Assess and Respond

**If** students have difficulty writing a conclusion in their outline,

**Then** have them sum up the ideas in their outline to a partner to help them think through how to conclude their report.

## WRITE RESEARCH REPORTS

Use an outline like the one below to organize your research report about the desert. Then write a first draft of your report on a separate sheet of paper. Be sure to take good notes and group related information together. You will use this draft to write your final research report in the Unit 10 Review section on page 228.

I. **Introduction**
   Topic:

   _____

   _____

II. **Explanation**
   a. Subtopic 1:

   _____

   _____

   _____

   _____

   b. Subtopic 2:

   _____

   _____

   _____

   _____

III. **Conclusion**

   _____

   _____

   _____

   _____

222    Unit 10 ■ Research to Build and Present Knowledge: Write Research Reports

## Differentiate Instruction

Work individually with students who do not understand how the note-taking graphic organizer relates to the outline. Have them review their notes, color-coding related information. Then help them decide, based on the subtopics that emerge from their color-coding, how best they can convey the information they have researched about their topic through two subtopics. Help them enter those two subtopics on the outline. Then help them pick the best facts and other details from their notes related to their subtopics and enter them on the outline. Guide them as they note a conclusion.

## Compound Sentences

**Guided Instruction** A **compound sentence** combines two simple sentences that have related ideas. A connecting word called a **conjunction** (*and, but, or*) joins the two sentences. Always use a comma before the conjunction in a compound sentence.

Read these related sentences.

*Some desert plants have needles. Not all plants have them.*

To write these two sentences as a compound sentence, use a conjunction.

*Some desert plants have needles, but not all plants have them.*

**Guided Practice** Complete each sentence using a conjunction (*and, but, or*).

1. We will camp in the desert, _____ or _____ we will go to the beach.

2. I like camping in the desert, _____ but _____ it can get cold at night.

Make each pair of sentences into a compound sentence.

3. Be sure to bring sunscreen. You might get a sunburn.

   Be sure to bring sunscreen, or you might get a sunburn.

4. You should wear hiking boots. You might want a hat.

   You should wear hiking boots, and you might want a hat.

**Independent Practice** Write two of your own compound sentences. Use a different conjunction in each sentence. Be sure to use a comma before the conjunction.

1. Sample answer: We can have a snack, and then we can go hiking.

2. Sample answer: We can sleep on cots, or we can use air mattresses.

## OBJECTIVE
Use compound sentences in writing, employing coordinating conjunctions as necessary.

### Guided Instruction

Review that a simple sentence has one subject and one verb to express one complete idea. Explain that a **compound sentence** is made up of two simple sentences connected by a conjunction to express two related ideas. Have students underline the simple sentences in the second example, circle the conjunction, and put a box around the comma. *How are the two ideas related?* (They are both about plants.)

### Guided Practice

Model completing the first sentence with a conjunction. Explain why you choose *or.* Have students test the different conjunctions for the second sentence. Then discuss why *but* is the best fit. Have partners write sentences for items 3 and 4 and explain their answers.

### Independent Practice

After writing their own sentences, have partners see if they can rewrite each other's sentences using a different conjunction and explain why they could or could not replace the conjunction.

| Assess and Respond |
| --- |
| **If** students have difficulty writing compound sentences, |
| **Then** give students more practice completing and writing sentences by repeating the process under Guided Practice with additional examples. |

## Turn and Talk

After completing the activities, have partners engage in a compound sentence game. Hand out a set of index cards to each pair. Each set of index cards should include one index card for each conjunction (*and, but, or*), as well as one index card for each of six sentences of your choosing. (Vary the sentences so every pair has a different set. Check each set to make sure three logical sentences can be created from the index cards.) Ask students to create three compound sentences with the cards by connecting two sentence index cards with a conjunction index card. Challenge them to make necessary capitalization and punctuation corrections. Then have pairs share their sentences with the class.

## OBJECTIVE
Use complex sentences in writing, employing subordinating conjunctions as necessary.

## Guided Instruction

Explain what a **complex sentence** is. Use the second example to point out how the complete idea from the first example, *We went on a hike*, no longer expresses a complete idea when the subordinating conjunction *before* is added to it. *What are you left wondering?* (What happened before the hike?) Explain that adding the subordinating conjunction turns the simple sentence into a subordinating clause. Point out that the first part of the sentence (*We filled our water bottles*) is still a complete idea, and it is the independent clause portion of the complex sentence.

## Guided Practice

Help students test the subordinating conjunctions for items 1 and 2. Have pairs write sentences for items 3 and 4. Ask students to explain their responses and identify the independent clause, dependent clauses, and subordinating conjunction in each sentence.

## Independent Practice

Have students explain what a complex sentence is before writing their sentences. Ask them to identify the parts of their sentences.

### Assess and Respond

**If** students have difficulty with the concept of complex sentences,

**Then** review additional examples with parts that are labeled "independent clause," "dependent clause," and "subordinating conjunction."

---

## LANGUAGE

### Complex Sentences

**Guided Instruction**  A **complex sentence** is made up of two related ideas joined together by a subordinating conjunction. Some common **subordinating conjunctions** are *after*, *as if*, *because*, *before*, *since*, *though*, *when*, and *which*.

Read these related sentences.

> *We filled our water bottles. We went on a hike.*

To write these two sentences as one complex sentence, use a subordinating conjunction.

> *We filled our water bottles **before** we went on a hike.*

**Guided Practice**  Complete each of these complex sentences. Use the subordinating conjunction *until* or *because*.

1. We will walk on the path _____until_____ we get to the ranger station.

2. _____Because_____ we had hiked for so long, I was really tired.

Make each pair of sentences into a complex sentence using a subordinating conjunction.

3. Beth led our hike. She had the map.

   Sample answer: Beth led our hike because she had the map.

4. We were lost. We used our compass.

   Sample answer: Since we were lost, we used our compass.

**Independent Practice**  Write two of your own complex sentences using a subordinating conjunction.

1. Sample answer: After we hiked, we all rested.

2. Sample answer: Dad pointed out animals when he saw them.

### Support English Language Learners

Complex sentences might seem overwhelming to English language learners. Point out the subject/verb/object pattern in complex sentences to help students see these sentences as more approachable. (This will be especially useful to native speakers of Vietnamese and Hmong—languages which also follow the subject/verb/object pattern.)

Build sentences with these students, starting with a simple subject/verb/object sentence. Label the sentence parts, and discuss why it is a simple sentence. Use it as a base for writing a compound and a complex sentence. Discuss the definition of each sentence type, and label the sentence parts. Repeat until understanding of complex sentences (particularly in how they differ from compound sentences) is clear.

## Capitalization

**Guided Instruction** A title tells the name of a book. The first word and all the important words are capitalized. Words such as *a, an, and, but, for, in, of, or, the,* and *to* are not capitalized unless they are the first word.

*A Guide to Deserts*
*Camping in the Desert*

**Guided Practice** Circle the letters that should be capitalized in each title.

1. ⓐnts ⓐnd ⓞther ⓓesert ⓘnsects
2. ⓐ ⓑird ⓛover's ⓛook ⓐt ⓓeserts
3. ⓛooking for ⓢnakes
4. ⓣhe ⓗidden ⓛife of ⓓesert ⓐnimals

**Independent Practice** Write each book title correctly.

1. *look at the sand and rocks*

   *Look at the Sand and Rocks*

2. *lizard's big adventure*

   *Lizard's Big Adventure*

3. *ollie owl flies at night*

   *Ollie Owl Flies at Night*

4. *what's under the rock?*

   *What's Under the Rock?*

5. *a really hot day and a cold night*

   *A Really Hot Day and a Cold Night*

**OBJECTIVE**
**Capitalize titles correctly in writing.**

### Guided Instruction

Hold up a book. Read the title. Ask students to name which words in the title are capitalized. *Do you think the author made up his/her own mind about which words to capitalize? Or do you think there are rules for which words to capitalize in a title?* (There are rules.) Explain that the rules are the same whether the title appears on the actual book, such as the one you are holding, or is noted in print, such as in a review of the book. Discuss the rules for capitalization of titles. Then have students explain why *to, in,* and *the* are not capitalized in the examples.

### Guided Practice

Model circling the letters that should be capitalized in the first sentence. Have partners circle the letters in the third and fourth sentences and share their choices. Then guide students as they circle the letters in the last sentence independently.

### Independent Practice

After students have written each book title correctly, challenge them to come up with a title for the sequel to each book and to write it down using correct capitalization.

| Assess and Respond |
|---|
| **If** students have difficulty identifying which words in a title to capitalize, |
| **Then** discuss additional Guided Instruction examples before giving them additional Guided Practice examples. |

## Differentiate Instruction

Some students might find it difficult to remember when an article or preposition should be capitalized in a book title.

Give students a list of ten made-up or real book titles with the important words capitalized but all the articles and prepositions in lowercase, regardless of placement. Use this title, or one like it, as the first title:

• the Sun Shines Brightly in the Morning

Correct the capitalization error and discuss why the first *the* needs to be capitalized, but the *in* and the second *the* do not need to be capitalized. Then have students correct the remaining titles, explaining their choices.

## OBJECTIVES

- Ask questions to check understanding.
- Express ideas clearly.

## Discuss the Essential Question

Before beginning a group discussion, copy and distribute the "Did I?" checklist, available on **sadlierconnect.com**.

### Leading the Class Discussion

Give students time to think about the questions before the class discussion.

1. Direct students to the research report title and introductory paragraph to identify the topic the writer developed.

2. Guide students to identify how the section headings give a clue as to how information is grouped in each section.

## SPEAKING AND LISTENING

### Discuss the Essential Question

How do writers conduct and present research on a topic?

Think about the Essential Question by responding to the questions below. Support your point of view with reasons and experience.

**1.** What topic did the writer develop into a research report?

Sample answer: The writer talked about animal life in the desert, especially how animals use the saguaro cactus to survive.

**2.** How did the writer group related information together?

Sample answer: The writer used two categories: the animals found in the saguaro cactus, and the animals found under the cactus. He used headings to show how the ideas were related.

Use your notes above to discuss the Essential Question in small groups or as a class. Follow agreed-upon rules of discussion. Use the organizer below to record what you heard and how you participated.

| Ideas I Agree or Disagree With | | Questions I Asked |
|---|---|---|
| **Agree** | | |
| **Disagree** | | |
| **New Ideas I Had During Discussion** | | **Questions I Answered** |
| | | |

## Discussion Skills

Remind students that asking questions is a vital part of any discussion. Be sure students understand that asking questions is important not only for the person who does not understand something, but also for the person who is attempting to express his or her ideas. Give students these questions to ask when they want a speaker to clarify or explain a point:

- *Can you please repeat what you said about … ?*
- *I'm not sure I understand. Can you restate your idea?*
- *Can you explain why you made that connection?*

# UNIT 10 REVIEW

This paragraph has mistakes in compound and complex sentences and in capitalization. Write the paragraph correctly on the lines below.

> We read the book <u>the deserts of texas</u> in class. The book had many interesting facts it showed lots of beautiful pictures. This book was helpful, because we are writing desert reports. Today, our teacher showed us pictures of desert flowers. I was surprised at how many there are. Tomorrow, we will read a book called <u>I live in the desert</u>. The book tells about different desert animals. After that, we will share what we learned. We may create a poster about desert animals or we may write a report about them.

We read the book <u>The Deserts of Texas</u> in class. The book had many interesting facts, and it showed lots of beautiful pictures. This book was helpful because we are writing desert reports. Today, our teacher showed us pictures of desert flowers. I was surprised at how many there are. Tomorrow, we will read a book called <u>I Live in the Desert</u>. This book tells about different desert animals. After that, we will share what we learned. We may create a poster about desert animals, or we may write a report about them.

Unit 10 ■ Research to Build and Present Knowledge: Write Research Reports **227**

## Introduce the Review

Explain to students that this review will give them an opportunity to apply the language and writing skills that they have studied and practiced in this unit.

**Language Skills Summary**

Let students know that they are going to use what they learned about compound sentences, complex sentences, and capitalization of titles to make their writing better. Good writers follow grammar rules, can spell correctly, and understand the mechanics of writing.

- Ask students to tell what a compound sentence is. (A compound sentence combines two simple sentences with a conjunction.) Have students give examples of conjunctions. (*and, but, or*) Ask students to tell how many thoughts a compound sentence expresses. (two or more)

- Have students name the part of speech that connects the two ideas in a complex sentence. (a subordinating conjunction) Ask students to give examples of subordinating conjunctions. (*after, as if, because, before, since, though, when, which*) Prompt students to explain how a complex sentence differs from a compound sentence. (A complex sentence contains a complete thought and a dependent thought. The dependent part of the sentence cannot stand alone as its own sentence.)

- Prompt students to explain the rules for capitalizing the title of a book. (The first word and all the important words are capitalized. Words such as *a, an, and, but, for, in, of, or, the*, and *to* are not capitalized unless they are the first word.)

## Test-Taking Tips

Give students the following tips to help with taking assessments focused on editing skills.

- Tell students to make a list of what they are checking for, and then read the passage multiple times, focusing on one type of correction on the list each time.

- Explain to students that if they read slowly they are less likely to skip over subtle errors that need correcting.

- Have students mark suspected errors lightly in pencil and then reread to confirm whether they are errors, and, if so, mark them darkly.

## Writing Process Summary

Remind students that planning helps them organize their ideas before drafting, and revising and editing make a draft better.

### Planning and Drafting

Have students look at the outline and the draft they created earlier (page 222). They should check that the draft includes an introduction, groups related information in the explanation section, and ends with a conclusion.

### Research Report Rubric

| | |
|---|---|
| 4 | The text clearly identifies the topic of the report in the introduction; groups related information and builds knowledge about the topic with facts, definitions, and details; provides a conclusion that wraps up what is learned from the report; and lists sources at the end of the report. There are few or no editing errors. |
| 3 | The text has the elements listed under "4" above, though they are executed less successfully. Minor editing errors do not detract greatly from the overall essay. |
| 2 | The text is missing one or more of the required elements. There are many editing errors, some of which are serious. |
| 1 | The text is unfinished or shows a minimal understanding of required elements. Serious editing errors make it difficult to read. |
| 0 | The assignment was not attempted. |

### Self-Assessment: Progress Check

Have students revisit the Progress Check on page 215 and compare their answers now with the answers they gave before they started Unit 10.

---

# UNIT 10 REVIEW

**Assignment:** Research and write a report about a desert topic.

On the lines below, write your final copy of the research report draft you created on page 222. Be sure to group related evidence together. As you write, use the evidence you have found to build knowledge about the topic. Remember to list your sources at the end of the report. See the Writing Handbook (pages 275–283) for ways to improve your writing as you revise.

Students should write a research report that clearly states the topic, groups

related evidence together, and builds knowledge about the topic through

a clear presentation of the evidence. Students should use at least two sources

and cite the sources used.

---

## Digital Connection: Social Media

Once students have finished writing their research reports, they can use information from their reports to contribute to a social media account.

Establish a class Twitter account (or some other type of social media account). Call the account: *The Desert! Did You Know . . .*  Or have students vote on another title for the account. (Discuss which words to capitalize in the title.)

Then have students contribute their favorite facts about the desert from their reports to the site. Make sure every student contributes at least one fact. Encourage students to add photographs. Have a discussion about what students learn from other students' posts.

## Introducing UNIT **11**

**W**hat do you see when you look into the sky at night? How much do you know about our solar system? In this unit, you will learn more about the solar system and the ways we study it.

This unit focuses on science topics. It includes a how-to manual, a magazine article, an editorial, and an explanatory text. These are all informational texts. Each one provides the reader with facts about a topic. Authors who write informational texts organize their writing clearly. They also present interesting details. Informational texts usually include photos, graphs, and charts. These images may include additional information that is not stated in the text.

You can learn a lot from an informational text. You also can learn a lot from comparing texts on the same topic. Let's see what you discover as you read this unit!

### Progress Check  *Can I?*

Before Unit 11 / After Unit 11

☐ Connect photos and other visual information to an informational text. ☐

☐ Understand the structure, such as causes and effects and sequence of events, of an informational text. ☐

☐ Compare and contrast important information in two informational texts. ☐

☐ Understand differences of meaning among related words. ☐

**Unit 11** ▪ Reading Informational Text: Integration of Knowledge and Ideas

**Student Page 229**

## Progress Check

The Progress Check is a self-assessment feature that students can use to gauge their own progress. Research shows that when students take accountability for their own learning, it increases their motivation.

Before students begin work in Unit 11, have them check the boxes next to any item that they feel they can do well. Explain that it is fine if they don't check any of the boxes. Tell them that they will have an opportunity to learn about and practice all of these items while studying the unit. Let them know that near the end of the unit they will have a chance to reconsider how well they can do each item on this list.

Before students begin the Unit 11 Review on page 257, have them revisit this page. You can use this information to work with students on any items they don't understand before they tackle the Review.

## HOME ◆ CONNECT...

The Home Connect feature is a way to keep parents or other adult family members apprised of what their children are learning. The key learning objectives are listed, and some ideas for related activities and discussions are included.

Explain to students that they can share the Home Connect page with their parents or the adult family members in their home. Let students know how much time the class will be spending on this unit so they can plan their time accordingly at home.

Encourage students and their parents to share their experiences using the suggestions on the Home Connect page. You may wish to make a place to post any of this work.

## HOME ◆ CONNECT...

**I**t is important for readers to learn how to connect **visual information** (such as photographs, illustrations, graphs, and charts) **and text** to understand what they read. Find a magazine article that includes a number of images. Share it with your child, and discuss how the images add to the text.

Cause and effect is a type of **text structure** that nonfiction authors use to organize their writing. Talk with your child about a recent news event. Discuss the reasons why it happened and what occurred (the cause and effect). Work together with your child to create a two-column chart that lists causes and effects related to the event.

This unit includes a magazine article and an editorial about the same topic: the dwarf planet Pluto. It can be helpful to **compare and contrast texts** about the same subject to better understand a topic. Find a newspaper story and a newspaper editorial on the same subject. Share the two articles with your child. Discuss how they are alike and how they are different.

**Activity:** Work together with your child to search for articles about the universe and space exploration on the Internet. Narrow the topic as you choose links to explore. Use correct terms for the images you see on screen, such as *photograph, illustration, graph,* etc. Discuss why some of the articles are easier to follow or more appealing than others. List interesting facts, and create your own fact sheet about space.

### IN THIS UNIT, YOUR CHILD WILL...

▪ Connect photographs, illustrations, and other examples of visual information to text.

▪ Describe text structure—how information and ideas are related—in an informational text.

▪ Identify causes and effects and sequences of events in a text.

▪ Compare and contrast the most important points in two texts on the same topic.

▪ Understand different meanings among related words.

▪ Compare and contrast four texts on the same theme: a technical text, a magazine article, an editorial, and a scientific text.

### WAYS TO HELP YOUR CHILD

Demonstrate a positive attitude toward reading and learning. Find articles to read with your child. Before you read, pose questions about the topic. You should ask questions you hope the article will address. Encourage your child to ask questions, too. Create a list that includes your questions and those of your child. Then as you read through the article together, search for the answers.

ONLINE
**For more Home Connect activities, continue online at** sadlierconnect.com

**230** Unit 11 ▪ Reading Informational Text: Integration of Knowledge and Ideas

**Student Page 230**

# UNIT PLANNER

| Theme: The Solar System | Focus |
|---|---|
| **CONNECTING VISUAL INFORMATION AND TEXT** pp. 232–237 | *How to Make a Telescope* **GENRE:** Technical Text **LEXILE®:** 770L |
| | **WORDS TO KNOW:** astronomer, solar system, refracting telescope, reflecting telescope, centimeter, excess, crater, constellation, comet |
| **DESCRIBING TEXT STRUCTURES** pp. 238–243 | *Pluto: Planet or Not?* **GENRE:** Magazine Article **LEXILE®:** 780L |
| | **WORDS TO KNOW:** classification, calculation, gravitational pull, orbit, gravity, universe, asteroid, dwarf planet, mnemonic |
| **COMPARING AND CONTRASTING TEXTS** pp. 244–249 | *Pluto Is Our Planet!* **GENRE:** Editorial **LEXILE®:** 800L |
| | **WORDS TO KNOW:** category, ellipsis, interior, diameter, judging, core, tilted |
| **CLOSE READING** pp. 250–256 | *Why the Solar System Moves* **GENRE:** Explanatory Text **LEXILE®:** 810L |
| **CONNECT ACROSS TEXTS** p. 255 | Compare and Contrast Texts |
| **LANGUAGE** p. 256 | Shades of Meaning |
| **UNIT 11 REVIEW** pp. 257–258 | *Comets* |

| Objective(s) |
| --- |
| Use illustrations and words to understand the concepts and events in a text. |
| Understand the use of cause/effect and sequence in a text. |
| Compare and contrast two texts on the same topic. |
| • Use illustrations and words to understand the concepts and events in a text.<br>• Understand the use of cause/effect and sequence in a text.<br>• Compare and contrast two texts on the same topic. |
| Understand shades of meaning in words that describe states of mind or degrees of certainty. |

## Unit Assessment

- Unit 11 Review *pp. 257–258*
- Unit 11 Performance Task  ( ONLINE )

## Additional Assessment Options

- Performance Task 1 *pp. 141A–145 and 146*
  ( ALSO ONLINE )
- Performance Task 2 *pp. 259A–263 and 264*
  ( ALSO ONLINE )

### Optional Purchase:

- iProgress Monitor  ( ONLINE )
- Progress Monitor Student Benchmark Assessment Booklet

## ( ONLINE ) Digital Resources

- Home Connect Activities
- Unit Performance Task
- Additional Practice
- Full-Length Reading Selections
- Foundational Skills Practice
- Teacher Resources
- iProgress Monitor (optional purchase)

**Go to SadlierConnect.com to access your Digital Resources.**

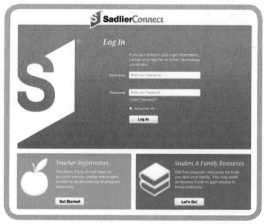

**For more detailed instructions see page T3.**

## LEARNING PROGRESSIONS

In this unit, students will learn how the integration of knowledge and ideas in an informational text contributes to their understanding of it. In order to learn the skills in this unit, students will further develop skills learned in second grade. They should be encouraged to retain these skills, as they will continue to build on them in fourth grade.

**Connecting Visual Information and Text**

- In second grade, students should have learned how images contribute to and clarify their understanding of a text.

- In grade 3, students will extend their knowledge of how to integrate information learned from words and images to gain understanding of a text.

- In fourth grade, students will be examining more advanced images, such as charts, graphs, and time lines, and exploring how these images increase their understanding of a text.

**Describing Text Structures**

- By the end of grade 2, students should have been able to determine how reasons support points an author makes in a text.

- In third grade, students will explore how sequence and cause/effect make logical connections between sentences and paragraphs in a text.

- This will prepare them for fourth grade, in which they will more deeply explore how authors use evidence to support their points in a text.

**Comparing and Contrasting Texts**

- Proficient second graders should have ended the school year understanding how to compare and contrast two texts on the same topic.

- In third grade, students will look at the most important points and key details as they compare and contrast two texts on the same topic.

- This will prepare them for grade 4, in which they will integrate information from two texts on the same topic and write about that topic knowledgeably.

# Reading Informational Text: Integration of Knowledge and Ideas

UNIT 11

**Essential Question:**
How can authors use text structure to connect ideas and information?

Unit 11 ■ Reading Informational Text: Integration of Knowledge and Ideas **231**

**Essential Question:**
How can authors use text structure to connect ideas and information?

In this unit, students will learn about the integration of knowledge and ideas in informational text, specifically how to connect visual information to ideas, analyze text structures, and compare and contrast ideas in two texts on the same topic.

## Theme: The Solar System
Students will read selections related to the theme of the solar system. They will read about how to make a telescope, the history of Pluto and whether or not it is a planet, and the movement of the solar system.

## Curriculum Connection: Science
Students will learn about the solar system and how scientists have made discoveries and decisions about our planets and other objects in the solar system.

## Vocabulary Overview

**General Academic Vocabulary**
astronomer 232, calculation 239, category 244, classification 238, comet 236, excess 234, interior 245, judging 246, mnemonic 243, solar system 232, tilted 248, universe 240

**Domain-Specific Vocabulary**
asteroid 242, centimeter 234, constellation 236, core 248, crater 236, diameter 246, dwarf planet 242, ellipsis 244, gravitational pull 239, gravity 240, orbit 239, reflecting telescope 232, refracting telescope 232

## Guided Instruction

### OBJECTIVE
**Use illustrations and words to understand the concepts and events in a text.**

### Genre: Technical Text

Tell students that technical texts explain a concept or how to do something. How-to articles often include a series of steps.

### Set the Purpose

Help students understand the purpose for learning the reading skill by asking *Why do you look at illustrations, such as maps or pictures, when you read an informational text?*

### Model and Teach

Read the selection as students follow along in their books.

### CITE EVIDENCE

**A** *I read that refracting telescopes use lenses and reflecting telescopes use mirrors. I'll look at the labels on the telescope in the image to figure out what it uses.*

*Based on this clue, what type of telescope is in the picture?* (a refracting telescope)

**B** *We figured out that the image shows a refracting telescope. That's described in paragraph 3.*

*Which paragraph describes the reflecting telescope?* (paragraph 4)

---

## CONNECTING VISUAL INFORMATION AND TEXT

### Guided Instruction

**WORDS TO KNOW**
astronomer
reflecting telescope
refracting telescope
solar system

> Informational text often includes photos, charts, diagrams, or other kinds of **visual information**. These images help support the text.

**CITE EVIDENCE**

**A** Technical text provides information through **images** and written information. Circle the paragraph that describes the image on this page.

**B** Place a box around the paragraph that describes a telescope that is not shown as an image.

# How to Make a Telescope
(Genre: Technical Text)

1 Hello, budding **astronomers**! Do you want to study objects in the **solar system**? This manual provides all the information you need to build your own telescope. When you are done, you will be able to see the stars and the planets. You might even spot a comet or two!

2 Before you begin, it is important to know how telescopes work. A telescope is a tool that makes distant objects look close.

3 This manual explains how to build a **refracting telescope**, which is made with lenses. You will use two magnifying glasses as your lenses. A refracting telescope shows objects upside down.

4 A refracting telescope is different from a **reflecting telescope**, which is made with mirrors. The world's first telescopes were the refracting kind. Today, most telescopes are the reflecting kind. These are more complicated and harder to build on your own.

5 Follow these instructions to put your refracting telescope together. First, make sure you have everything you will need.

**Refracting Telescope**

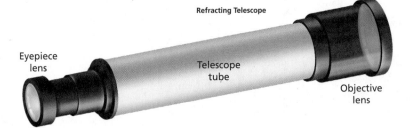

Eyepiece lens

Telescope tube

Objective lens

---

## Words to Know

**General Academic Vocabulary**

**astronomer** (*noun*): a scientist who studies the stars, planets, and other objects in space

**solar system** (*noun*): the planets and other space objects that orbit around the sun

**Domain-Specific Vocabulary**

**reflecting telescope** (*noun*): a telescope that uses mirrors to let users see distant objects

**refracting telescope** (*noun*): a telescope that uses lenses to let users see distant objects

**Working with Word Meaning** Help students understand the meanings of these words by leading an Internet image search for each word.

# INTEGRATION OF KNOWLEDGE AND IDEAS

6    Gather the following items:

- Two magnifying glasses, one big and one small
- A long cardboard tube
- A roll of masking tape
- A black marker
- A piece of newspaper
- A pair of scissors
- Measuring tape
- A friend to lend a hand

7    Now, assemble your telescope.

8    **Step 1:** First, take the newspaper and place it on a table or other flat surface. Hold the big magnifying glass over the paper so the printing appears blurry, or hard to read.

9    **Step 2:** Take the small magnifying glass into your other hand. Hold it between your eyes and the big magnifying glass. Move the small magnifying glass forward and back. Stop when you see the newspaper come into focus in the large magnifying glass. The printing will appear both larger and upside down.

## Comprehension Check

How does the list on this page relate to the image on the page? Include evidence from the text in your answer.

## Guided Instruction

### CITE EVIDENCE

**C** The **illustrations** in a text connect to the words, helping the reader to see key details. Draw a box around the lenses in the text and in the Figure A image.

**D** Illustrations can also help by showing the reader the steps in a process. Circle the text that tells you in what order the telescope assembly occurs. How does seeing the items help you understand the circled text?

**Figure A**

## Guided Instruction

### CITE EVIDENCE

**C** *I'll read through the text first and then look at the image. I don't see the label* lenses, *so I'll have to figure out which are the lenses in the image. I know from the image on page 232 that there are two lenses that are different sizes.*

*Based on this clue, what do you think the lenses are?* (the magnifying glasses)

**D** *Illustrations should work together with the text to give you information. I'll look for words that tell me how to put the telescope together. I'll look for order words, such as* first, *and direction words, such as* take *and* hold.

*Which step or steps use order words and direction words to tell you how to put the telescope together?* (Steps 1 and 2)

## Comprehension Check

**Sample Answer:** The image shows all the items on the list, except the friend. It illustrates the supplies that I must gather to make the telescope.

**Answer Explanation:** Students should be able to integrate the information from the text with that in the image by recognizing that the image illustrates the items in the list, except for the friend. This is the group of supplies that readers would need to build a refracting telescope.

## Support English Language Learners

Help struggling students develop their vocabulary by matching each item on the list at the top of page 233 with the image in the lower right. Students can circle each item and draw a line to the corresponding point in the list. Then have students work with a partner to rephrase Steps 1 and 2 in their own words.

## Guided Practice

### Recap Reading Selection

Remind students that they have discussed two types of telescopes: reflecting and refracting. Ask them to summarize the differences and say which one this text is explaining how to build. Finally, ask them to list some of the supplies that are needed to build the telescope.

### Read and Practice

Have partners take turns reading the selection as you circulate to provide support. For callout A, circulate and provide partners with scaffolding as needed. Model connecting images and text with Cite Evidence callout B. You might use the following suggestions to help students who are having difficulty.

### CITE EVIDENCE

**A** Guide students to read through the text first. Then tell them to look back at each step and scan for the words *cut* and *slot*.

**B** Explain that Step 4 describes how to cut a slot in the tube. Guide students to identify the image (Figure B) that shows a student cutting a tube with scissors.

---

CONNECTING VISUAL INFORMATION AND TEXT

**Guided Practice**

How to Make a Telescope *continued*

**WORDS TO KNOW**
centimeter
excess

**CITE EVIDENCE**

**A** Circle the step that explains how to cut a slot into the tube and what the slot is for.

**B** Draw a box around the letter of the figure that illustrates Step 4. In your own words, what does that illustration show?

**Figure C**

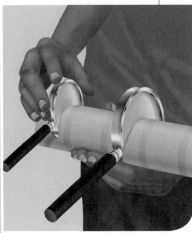

10 **Step 3:** Hold the two magnifying glasses steady, making sure to keep the newspaper in focus in the larger lens. Ask your friend to use the measuring tape to find the distance between the two magnifying glasses, and have him or her write down that number.

11 **Step 4:** Next, measure a distance of 1 inch (2.5 **centimeters**) from one end of the cardboard tube. Draw a line with the black marker, and use the scissors to cut a slot into the tube on the line you marked. Do not cut all the way through the tube. The slot should only be large enough to hold the big magnifying glass.

**Figure B**

12 **Step 5:** Now, measure the distance your friend wrote down from the slot on the tube. Draw a line with the marker, and cut another slot in the tube. This one should only be large enough to hold the small magnifying glass.

13 **Step 6:** Put the two magnifying glasses into their slots. Remember, the big one goes in the front and the small one goes in the back. Use the masking tape to hold the two lenses in place.

14 **Step 7:** Next, measure about 1 inch beyond the small magnifying glass. Draw a line with the marker. The rest is **excess** tube. Cut it off.

---

### Words to Know

**General Academic Vocabulary**
**excess** (*adjective*): extra, not needed

**Domain-Specific Vocabulary**
**centimeter** (*noun*): a small unit of measurement

**Working with Word Meaning** Help students learn these word meanings by asking them to write a sentence using each word.

# INTEGRATION OF KNOWLEDGE AND IDEAS

**Guided Practice**

15 **Step 8:** Finally, test the telescope by looking at the piece of newspaper with it. You may need to adjust the distance between the two magnifying glasses to get the best quality.

**Comprehension Check**

1. What kind of image is Figure C?

   a. a chart

   b. a graph

   c. an illustration

   d. a photograph

2. What does Figure C show?

   a. It shows how to cut off the excess part of the tube.

   b. It shows how to put the magnifying lenses into place.

   c. It shows how to test the telescope to get the best quality.

   d. It shows how to measure 1 inch along the cardboard tube.

3. Work with a partner to discuss how Figure C connects to the text. What does the image show that the text does not say? How does Figure C help the reader?

   Sample answer: Figure C helps explain Step 6 in the text. It shows how to

   put the magnifying lenses into place. The image also shows about how far

   apart the slots should be, which is not directly stated in the text. It helps

   the reader follow the instructions to add the lenses to the telescope.

Unit 11 ■ Reading Informational Text: Integration of Knowledge and Ideas **235**

**Comprehension Check**

**Answer Explanations:**

1. Choice C, *an illustration*, is correct. Students should be able to identify Figure C as an illustration, not a chart, graph, or photograph.

2. Choice B, *It shows how to put the magnifying lenses into place*, is correct. Students can check the answer by looking carefully at Figure C.

3. Help students understand that they will need to integrate information from both the text and the illustration in order to get the full picture of what to do. Prompt them to reread the steps and then compare them to the illustration before they answer the question.

## Peer Collaboration

Follow this procedure for each item: Ask students to think about how they would respond to the question or item. Then have them turn to a partner and discuss their response. Students should be prepared to make changes to their own answer based on the discussion with their partner. Finally, ask pairs to report their answers to the whole group.

## Foundational Skills: Fluency Practice

Explain to students that when they are following a series of steps like these, often one partner will read the step aloud while the other follows the procedure described. The one reading should pause after each sentence to make sure that their partner has understood and has been able to complete the action. At the end of each step, both partners should pause and read back over the step to make sure that the entire step has been completed. Additional fluency passages and activities can be found at **sadlierconnect.com** and in the *Foundational Skills Handbook*.

## Independent Practice

### Recap Reading Selection

Work with the class to summarize each step they read in the previous section. Encourage students to refer back to the text as necessary to recall each step.

### Read and Apply

Have students read the selection independently as you circulate to provide support. If you notice students struggling, you can provide support with the suggestions that follow.

### CITE EVIDENCE

**A** Students should identify the label "Constellations" at the beginning of paragraph 19 and find the information in this paragraph.

**B** Students should review paragraph 19. They should then look at the images on the page in order to select the caption of the one (the Big Dipper) that illustrates the information conveyed in the paragraph.

---

## CONNECTING VISUAL INFORMATION AND TEXT

### Independent Practice

**How to Make a Telescope** *continued*

**WORDS TO KNOW**
comet
constellation
crater

**CITE EVIDENCE**

**A** Underline the paragraph that explains what a constellation is and names the two best-known constellations.

**B** Which image on this page helps you understand the information in paragraph 19? Draw a box around the caption that explains what the image is.

16   Wait for a clear night to try out your telescope. Stare at the sky through the end with the two lenses. Any objects you see will appear upside down. That is how they looked to the astronomers who built the first telescopes.

17   Here are some things to observe with your new telescope.

18   **The Moon:** The moon is the largest object in the night sky. You can use your telescope to get a better look at **craters** on the moon's surface.

19   **Constellations:** <u>A **constellation** is a collection of stars that forms a pattern. Two of the most well-known constellations are the Big Dipper and Orion.</u>

20   **Planets:** There are seven other planets in the solar system. It is possible to see up to five of them in the sky at night: Mercury, Venus, Mars, Jupiter, and Saturn.

21   **Comets:** A **comet** is a huge ball of ice and dust, streaking across the sky. Comets are often named after the first person who reports seeing them, which is a good reason to look for them!

A comet

The Big Dipper

---

## Words to Know

**General Academic Vocabulary**
**comet** (*noun*): an icy space object that sometimes develops a tail

**Domain-Specific Vocabulary**
**constellation** (*noun*): a group of stars that forms a picture
**crater** (*noun*): a hole made by an impact of something

**Working with Word Meaning** Help students understand these word meanings by asking them to draw an illustration of each word.

# INTEGRATION OF KNOWLEDGE AND IDEAS

22 **Objects on Earth:** You can also use your telescope to view faraway objects right here on Earth. It is also great for bird watching or for studying landscapes in the distance. You might learn just as much about life on our planet as you do about outer space.

23 Keep a journal of the objects you see in your telescope. Record your observations, or draw illustrations of everything you see. It is another way to enjoy your homemade telescope!

**Comprehension Check**    MORE ONLINE  sadlierconnect.com

1. Circle the answer that completes the following sentence. The image of the Big Dipper shows you what _____ looks like.

   (a.) a constellation

   b. a comet

   c. Orion

   d. the moon's craters

2. Which text connects to what you see in the image of the comet?

   a. Comets are named after the first person who finds them.

   b. Keep a journal of the objects you see in your telescope.

   c. There are seven other planets in the solar system.

   (d.) A comet is a huge ball of ice and dust, streaking across the sky.

3. What does the image of the comet show that the text does not say? Why was the image included?

   Sample answer: The text in paragraph 21 explains what a comet is.

   The photograph shows what a comet looks like. The image helps the

   reader understand what you can see with a telescope.

   _____

## Independent Practice

**Comprehension Check**

**Answer Explanations:**

1. Choice A, *a constellation*, is correct. According to paragraph 19, the Big Dipper is a constellation.

2. Choice D is the correct answer. It is the best and most accurate description of the image of the comet.

3. Students should compare the information in the text with the image. Both describe a comet, but the image shows the comet's tail and helps the reader see what a comet looks like.

## Critical Comprehension

Use the following questions to help students think more deeply about the text. Students should be prepared to support their answers with evidence from the text.

- *How does this text change your ideas about telescopes?* (Students may be surprised that a telescope could be made with such simple materials.)

- *Could you have understood this text in the same way without the images?* (Most students will say no, that they needed the illustrations to understand how things look.)

**Assess and Respond**

**If** students have difficulty answering the questions in the Comprehension Check,

**Then** lead a reading group to review the selection, summarizing each section and modeling the skills that had been practiced independently.

## Extend Thinking: Analyze and Compare

This article tells readers how to make a refracting telescope. Ask students to research how the more complicated reflecting telescopes are made. They should examine how these telescopes are made and why they have become the more common type of telescope used today. Then they should discuss whether or not they could make one on their own as simply as they could make a refracting telescope.

# Describing Text Structures

## Guided Instruction

### OBJECTIVE
**Understand the use of cause/effect and sequence in a text.**

### Genre: Magazine Article

Remind students that magazine articles can be about a variety of subjects. They often are written in an objective tone and give an overview of an issue.

### Set the Purpose

Help students understand the purpose for learning the reading skill by asking *Have you ever thought about how an essay is structured? How do you think a problem/solution essay might present its information?*

### Model and Teach

Read the selection as students follow along in their books.

### CITE EVIDENCE

**A** *I see that the first sentence reads "The year was 1930." That sounds like the opening of a movie trailer! I'll expect to find out what happened in 1930 next. What happened in 1930?* (Astronomers discovered a new object in space.)

**B** *Authors can use clue words, such as* first, second, *or* third *to indicate a sequence of events. They also use dates. I see dates that tell when Uranus and Neptune were discovered. Which was discovered first?* (Uranus)

---

## DESCRIBING TEXT STRUCTURES

### Guided Instruction

**WORDS TO KNOW**
calculation
classification
gravitational pull
orbit

> **Text structure** is the way a text is organized. Different texts can have different structures.

**CITE EVIDENCE**

**A** **Sequence** is one type of text structure. Sequence tells when things happened. In paragraph 1, underline an event that happened in 1930. Box an event that happened after.

**B** Sequence explains the **order of events in a series**. It tells which one happened first, which happened second, and so on. Circle the sentence that describes the discoveries of Uranus and Neptune. Which of these two planets was discovered first?

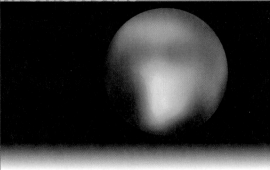

## Pluto:
### Planet or Not?
(Genre: Magazine Article)

1    The year was 1930. <u>Astronomers in Arizona had discovered an unknown object in space</u>. What was it? They were not sure. However, it seemed to behave like a planet, so it must be a planet. They declared it was the ninth planet in our solar system. It became known as Pluto.

2    For decades, that **classification** remained in place. But in 2006, everything changed. Scientists were no longer sure what to call Pluto. Was it a planet or not? Here is the strange story of the former planet Pluto.

**The Search for "Planet X"**

3    For years, students were taught the solar system contained nine planets: Mercury, Venus, Earth, Mars, Jupiter, Saturn, Uranus, Neptune, and Pluto. The last three planets were discovered across centuries as astronomers used increasingly sophisticated tools to study space. Uranus was discovered in 1781, and Neptune was found in 1846.

**238**    Unit 11 ■ Reading Informational Text: Integration of Knowledge and Ideas

---

### Words to Know

**General Academic Vocabulary**
**calculation** (*noun*): figuring something out, often by using math
**classification** (*noun*): the action of placing something in a group

**Domain-Specific Vocabulary**
**gravitational pull** (*noun*): the effect one object's gravity has on another
**orbit** (*noun*): the path an object in space takes around a planet, moon, or the sun

**Working with Word Meaning** Help students learn these word meanings by having them play a simple game of charades.

# INTEGRATION OF KNOWLEDGE AND IDEAS

4   About 50 years after Neptune's discovery, an astronomer named Percival Lowell suspected there might be a ninth planet in the solar system. So, in 1905, he decided to search for it. He called it "Planet X." Lowell spent more than a decade searching for this planet, but he could not find it.

### The Discovery of Pluto

5   In 1929, an astronomer named Clyde Tombaugh was working at an observatory that Percival Lowell had founded in Arizona. He wondered if Percival Lowell might be right about a ninth planet in the solar system. So, he took up the search. He started with Lowell's **calculations** and then expanded his search.

6   The following year, Tombaugh's search uncovered a tiny, distant planet on the far edges of the solar system. It appeared no bigger than a bit of dust in a photograph. Could this be it? One clue was the **gravitational pull** of the unknown object, which affected the **orbits** of Neptune and Uranus.

### Comprehension Check

Clyde Tombaugh decided to continue Percival Lowell's search. What was the effect? Include evidence from the text in your answer.

Percival Lowell

Unit 11 ■ Reading Informational Text: Integration of Knowledge and Ideas   **239**

## Guided Instruction

**CITE EVIDENCE**

**C** **Cause and effect** is another type of text structure. A cause is the reason something happens, and the effect is what happened. Paragraph 4 uses this structure. Circle the effect of Lowell's suspicions in paragraph 4.

**D** Underline the sentence that tells what Tombaugh did when he first took up the search for Lowell's "Planet X." Why did Tombaugh expand his search?

## Guided Instruction

### CITE EVIDENCE

**C** *I'll read paragraph 4 to look for any causes it describes. I see that Lowell thought there might be a ninth planet and decided to look for it. These are both causes. The effect will come next. What is it?* (He spent more than a decade searching for the planet.)

**D** *I see the sentence "So, he took up the search." I think the sentence after that will tell me how he started. It actually begins with "He started"!*

*What did Tombaugh do first?* (He started with Lowell's calculations.) *What did he do next, and why?* (Tombaugh expanded his search because Lowell never found anything.)

### Comprehension Check

**Sample Answer:** The effect of Tombaugh continuing the search was the discovery of Pluto. The heading "The Discovery of Pluto" and the text "Tombaugh's search uncovered a tiny, distant planet" make this clear.

**Answer Explanation:** Some students may be confused because the text does not directly state that Tombaugh discovered Pluto. Students will have to put together the text that reads "Tombaugh's search uncovered a tiny, distant planet" with the heading "The Discovery of Pluto" and the information in the first paragraph about when Pluto was discovered to figure out the effect of Tombaugh's search.

### Review: Connecting Visual Information and Text

In a magazine article, images don't always explain information the way they do in a technical text, but they can still help readers understand the topic. Have students consider what they can learn about Pluto from the image on page 238.

## Extend Thinking: Investigate

Ask students to find and research another astronomer and his or her contribution to our current understanding of the solar system or universe. Tell them to prepare a brief presentation for the class about what they learned. Encourage students to include at least one visual that supports their presentation. Students should make sure they speak clearly and use academic language in their presentation.

# Describing Text Structures

## Recap Reading Selection

Work with students to make a time line of the events described in the first section of the text.

## Read and Practice

Have partners take turns reading the selection as you circulate to provide support. Model identifying the sequence of events with Cite Evidence callout A. For callout B, circulate and provide partners with scaffolding as needed. You might use the following suggestions to help students who are having difficulty.

## CITE EVIDENCE

**A** Guide students to locate the date in paragraph 8, and then find out what happened next. (A ninth planet was found.)

**B** Students may be confused because there are no further dates included in paragraph 8. Remind students that the schoolgirl's idea for the name of the ninth planet and her grandfather's passing on the suggestion occurred after the planet was discovered. In paragraph 9, however, there is a date that serves as a clue to when the events occur.

---

## DESCRIBING TEXT STRUCTURES

**Guided Practice**

**Pluto:** Planet or Not? *continued*

**WORDS TO KNOW**

gravity

universe

**CITE EVIDENCE**

**A** Clyde Tombaugh did not have to search as long as Percival Lowell did to find "Planet X." Underline the event that happened on March 13, 1930.

**B** Circle two things from paragraph 8 that occurred after March 13, 1930. In paragraph 9, circle the detail that tells you if the paragraph describes events from 1930 or refers to an earlier time.

7    **Gravity** is a force that acts to draw objects together. The bigger an object is, the greater the object's gravitational pull. Gravity on Earth pulls objects to the ground, which is a good thing. Without Earth's gravitational pull, everything on Earth would float into space! The impact of Pluto's gravitational pull on Neptune and Uranus was great enough to make scientists look for its source.

8    On March 13, 1930, the Lowell Observatory announced the discovery. This object was celebrated as the ninth planet in our part of the **universe**. An 11-year-old schoolgirl from England suggested the name *Pluto*, after the name of a Roman god. Her grandfather was friends with an astronomer and passed on her suggestion.

9    Unfortunately, Percival Lowell, who died in 1916, did not live to see the discovery of his mystery planet. But one reason the name *Pluto* was selected was because the first two letters are Percival Lowell's initials.

### A Dwarf Planet

10    Pluto was called a planet for decades. Astronomers continued to study it. Around 1950, a scientist named Gerard Kuiper used a high-powered telescope to study Pluto. In 1978, other scientists discovered one of Pluto's moons. They named it Charon.

Mercury   Venus   Earth   Mars     Jupiter     Saturn    Uranus   Neptune   Pluto

**240**    Unit 11 ■ Reading Informational Text: Integration of Knowledge and Ideas

---

## Words to Know

**General Academic Vocabulary**

**universe** (*noun*): all the stars and planets; everything that is known to exist

**Domain-Specific Vocabulary**

**gravity** (*noun*): the force that pulls every object toward the center of the Earth or toward other objects

**Working with Word Meaning** Help students learn these word meanings by drawing an illustration of each word.

# INTEGRATION OF KNOWLEDGE AND IDEAS

11    Everything changed in 2006 when scientists decided to define the planets. Gravitational strength was a big part of this new definition, and Pluto no longer fit the definition of a planet.

### Comprehension Check

**1.** What is the effect of Earth's gravity?

   a. It pushes against Pluto.

   **b.** It pulls objects to the ground.

   c. It makes objects float into space.

   d. It helps astronomers find new planets.

**2.** What information caused Pluto to be called a planet in the first place?

   **a.** Its gravitational pull was great enough.

   b. It was named after a Roman god.

   c. It had a moon called Charon.

   d. It was far out in space.

**3.** Work with a partner to discuss the events that occurred around 1950 and in 1978. What caused these events? Cite text evidence.

Sample answer: In the paragraph under "A Dwarf Planet," it says that

around 1950, a scientist named Gerard Kuiper studied Pluto with a

high-powered telescope. In 1978, other scientists discovered one of

Pluto's moons. They named it Charon. Both of these events occurred

because scientists decided to study Pluto.

## Guided Practice

### Comprehension Check

**Answer Explanations:**

**1.** Students should understand that Choice B, *It pulls objects to the ground*, is the effect of Earth's gravity, described in paragraph 7.

**2.** Choice A, *Its gravitational pull was great enough*, was the reason Pluto was called a planet, as described in paragraph 7.

**3.** Students should identify the dates 1950 and 1978 in paragraph 10. Both of these events occurred due to scientists' desire to study Pluto and our solar system.

### Reciprocal Teaching

Put students in groups of four, and assign each a role: summarizer, questioner, clarifier, and predictor. Students should then reread the selection on pages 240–241.

After they have completed the selection, the Summarizer will review what events were described on these pages. The Questioner will ask two or three questions about the topic that the selection has not yet answered. The Clarifier will attempt to answer the questions for the group. Finally, the Predictor will predict what information will be included in the next section of the text. Students should switch roles as they continue with the next section of the text.

## Foundational Skills Review: Digraph *ch*

Review the use of the digraph *ch* with students, reminding them that the two letters work together to make a single sound. Model how this digraph works in the word *search* that appears in the text. Challenge students to find other words in which this digraph appears. Students will likely point out the word *Charon*, the name of Pluto's moon. Explain that the name, which comes from ancient Greek, is pronounced KA-ren. In this case, the *ch* has a different pronunciation.

Additional phonics activities can be found in the *Foundational Skills Handbook* at the end of this guide.

# Describing Text Structures

## Independent Practice

### Recap Reading Selection

Continue filling in the time line with students. Also, ask students to summarize what gravity is and how Pluto was named.

### Read and Apply

Have students read the selection independently as you circulate. If you notice students struggling, you can provide support with the suggestions that follow.

### CITE EVIDENCE

**A** Help students find the sentence in paragraph 14 that describes some people's reasoning. Guide students to see that the first sentence of this paragraph shows that some people disagree with calling Pluto a dwarf planet; the next sentence tells why they disagree.

**B** Prompt students to look for time-related clue words that indicate a sequence. You may wish to add these final events to the time line you have been creating. Finally, discuss the mnemonic of the planets' names with students. You may wish to have students look at the illustration of the planets on page 240 as you do so. If students are still confused about why the mnemonic must change, have a student cover up Pluto in the picture.

---

**WORDS TO KNOW**
asteroid
dwarf planet
mnemonic

**CITE EVIDENCE**

**A** Underline the text that describes why some people think Pluto should still be called a planet.

**B** Draw a box around words in the first and last sentence in paragraph 16 that point to a sequence of events. Why was a new mnemonic needed?

12   In 2006, astronomers came up with new measurements for what makes something a planet. They said a planet had to have a certain level of gravity. Pluto did not meet that measurement. Its gravity was not strong enough to pull **asteroids** close or push them away.

13   Instead, Pluto became known as a **dwarf planet**, which is smaller than a regular planet. There are at least two other dwarf planets, Ceres and Eris. In fact, there might be many, many more.

14   Many people question the new classification. After all, Pluto does orbit the sun like the planets of the solar system. Yet size seems to matter the most, and Pluto is simply too small. Plus, it travels around the sun in a strange way. Also, sometimes Pluto passes in and out of Neptune's orbit. No other planets cross orbits with another planet.

#### Pluto Remains a Puzzle

15   Today, Pluto remains a puzzle for many people. Some think it should still be considered a planet. Others consider it to be only a dwarf planet. Still others believe it is somewhere in between. Will Pluto ever be a planet again? Its history shows that anything can happen. After all, 20 years ago, almost no one would have thought that the solar system would *lose* a planet.

**242**   Unit 11 ■ Reading Informational Text: Integration of Knowledge and Ideas

---

## Words to Know

**General Academic Vocabulary**
**mnemonic** (*noun*): a phrase or trick to help one remember something

**Domain-Specific Vocabulary**
**asteroid** (*noun*): a rocky space object
**dwarf planet** (*noun*): a very small planet

**Working with Word Meaning** Help students extend their understanding of these words by giving them examples of mnemonics. Challenge students to work in pairs to come up with their own mnemonic for the names of the planets and share it with the class.

---

## INTEGRATION OF KNOWLEDGE AND IDEAS

**Independent Practice**

### A Way to Remember

16 After 2006, we looked at Pluto in a new way. We also came up with a new **mnemonic** (nih-MAH-nik). A mnemonic is a phrase that helps you remember something. A mnemonic for the solar system used to be "My Very Educated Mother Just Served Us Nine Pies." The first letter of each word represents a planet. So "My" stood for Mercury, and so on. Now, many students use "My Very Educated Mother Just Served Us Noodles."

**Comprehension Check**  (MORE ONLINE) **sadlierconnect.com**

1. What happened in 2006 that changed Pluto to a dwarf planet?

   a. Scientists discovered Neptune.

   b. Scientists decided Ceres and Eris were dwarf planets.

   c. Scientists used new measurements to classify planets.

   d. Pluto failed to orbit the sun.

2. The author seems to suggest that because of its unpredictable past, Pluto could one day

   a. change in size.

   b. be named a planet again.

   c. change places with Neptune.

   d. drop out of the solar system.

3. Explain the decision astronomers made about Pluto in 2006. What was the cause of this decision? What was the effect?

   Sample answer: In 2006, astronomers decided to call Pluto a dwarf planet.

   They did this because they believed a planet had to have a certain level of

   gravity, which Pluto didn't have. People disagreed about this decision.

Unit 11 ■ Reading Informational Text: Integration of Knowledge and Ideas  **243**

## Independent Practice

**Comprehension Check**

### Answer Explanations:

1. Students should be able to use information in paragraph 12 to see that choice C, *Scientists used new measurements to classify planets*, is correct.

2. The discussion in paragraph 15 should lead students to choice B, *be named a planet again*.

3. Pluto was classified as a dwarf planet in 2006. The cause of this decision was a new definition of the word *planet*, and it led to disagreement and a changed view of the solar system.

## Critical Comprehension

Use the following questions to help students think more deeply about the text. Students should be prepared to support their answers with evidence from the text.

- *Why has the number of planets in our solar system changed over the years?* (New planets were discovered, and a new definition of the word *planet* has been determined.)

- *Based on this article, do you think Pluto should be called a planet?* (Answers will vary.)

**Assess and Respond**

**If** students have difficulty answering the Comprehension Check questions,

**Then** have them tell you where they had the most difficulty—reading the text, finding information, or understanding questions. Provide assistance according to the responses.

## Support English Language Learners

Help English language learners pronounce the word *mnemonic*. Point out that the pronunciation of this unusual word appears in parentheses directly after the word where it appears in paragraph 16 on page 243. Say the word aloud several times, and have students repeat after you. Explain that this parenthetical information is intended to help readers pronounce the word it follows and is not meant to be read separately. If time allows, discuss other words in which a letter is not pronounced, such as the words *climb* and *pneumonia*. Remind students that these kinds of words do appear in English, and their pronunciations simply have to be memorized.

## Guided Instruction

### OBJECTIVE
**Compare and contrast two texts on the same topic.**

### Genre: Editorial
Explain to students that an editorial is an article written to share an opinion or promote an idea.

### Set the Purpose
Help students set the purpose for reading by saying *The previous text, "Pluto: Planet or Not?" provided information about Pluto. Now we're going to compare it to another article that expresses an opinion about whether Pluto should be called a planet.*

### Model and Teach
Read the selection as students follow along in their books.

### CITE EVIDENCE

**A** *The key details are important information about a topic. I'll look for paragraphs that tell me a lot about Pluto.*

*Which paragraphs do this?* (paragraphs 2 and 3)

**B** *I'll look for scientific details about Pluto that were not in the previous article.*

*Do these details make Pluto seem like a planet?* (Yes. It orbits the sun like other planets do.)

---

## COMPARING AND CONTRASTING TEXTS
### Guided Instruction

**WORDS TO KNOW**
category
ellipsis
interior

> To **compare**, you look at how two or more things are alike. To **contrast**, you look at how they are different.

**CITE EVIDENCE**

**A** To **compare** or **contrast** two pieces on the same topic, it is necessary to find the **key details** in each. Box the paragraphs that give key details that describe Pluto.

**B** When comparing, see how details in the pieces are similar; when contrasting, see how they are different. Underline details about Pluto that did not appear in "Pluto: Planet or Not?" Do these details support the idea that Pluto is a planet?

## Pluto Is Our Planet!
(Genre: Editorial)

1    We used to have nine planets: Mercury, Venus, Earth, Mars, Jupiter, Saturn, Uranus, Neptune, and Pluto. Pluto was discovered in 1930 and was a planet until 2006. Then scientists decided that Pluto was only a "dwarf" planet. It does not make sense to add this other **category** of planet. Pluto and the other dwarf planets are planets, too!

2    Pluto is very, very far away from the sun. It is in the Kuiper Belt, an area in space that is full of icy, rocky objects. Pluto is very small. It is only about two-thirds the size of Earth's moon. However, it has at least five moons. One, named Charon, is half as big as Pluto. The other moons are very small.

3    Pluto has a rocky core surrounded by ice. It takes 248 years for Pluto to go around the sun. It moves in an **ellipsis**, so sometimes it is nearer to the sun than at other times. When it comes close to the sun, the ice on its surface melts and an atmosphere forms. When it moves farther away, the ice freezes again and the atmosphere disappears.

---

## Words to Know

**General Academic Vocabulary**
**category** (*noun*): a group of objects that are alike
**interior** (*noun*): the inside of an object

**Domain-Specific Vocabulary**
**ellipsis** (*noun*): an oval shape

**Working with Word Meaning** Help students understand the meanings of these words by having them write a paragraph that includes all three words.

## INTEGRATION OF KNOWLEDGE AND IDEAS

4   Pluto is not the only dwarf planet. (Another) dwarf planet is named Eris. This little world is very similar to Pluto. It, (too,) has a rocky middle and icy outer surface. It is (also) about the same size. Eris is even farther from the sun than Pluto. Its orbit around the sun takes 557 years and moves Eris beyond the Kuiper Belt. It only has one known moon.

5   Ceres is yet another dwarf planet. It is in the asteroid belt between Mars and Jupiter. Ceres is only about the size of Texas, but it is more like a planet than an asteroid. It is rocky and nearly round, and it has a lot of water. Its **interior** is in layers like a planet. Astronomers at first called Ceres a planet, too. They then called it an asteroid before deciding it was a dwarf planet.

### Comprehension Check

Compare the details given here about Pluto to those given in "Pluto: Planet or Not?" Which are the same? Which are different? Cite text evidence.

Kuiper Belt

Uranus

Saturn

Jupiter

Neptune          Pluto

Eris

Outer
Solar System

Unit 11 ■ Reading Informational Text: Integration of Knowledge and Ideas   245

### Guided Instruction

**CITE EVIDENCE**

C  Look for clue words like *another*, *both*, and *too* that show comparison. Circle the comparison words in paragraph 4.

D  Underline details that show how the dwarf planets Eris and Ceres are similar to Pluto. Were Eris and Ceres described in "Pluto: Planet or Not?"

---

### Support English Language Learners

Help students understand the technical details explained in paragraphs 2 and 3 on page 244. Encourage them to read slowly, making sure they understand each sentence before they move on. It may help for students to illustrate each detail they read about Pluto, especially the elliptical shape of Pluto's orbit and the way its atmosphere forms and then disappears.

---

### CITE EVIDENCE

C  *I'll look for those clue words in paragraph 4.*

*What are these words comparing?* (Pluto and the dwarf planet Eris)

D  *I'll use the clue words I just circled and look for others to help me find the details about other dwarf planets.*

*How are these dwarf planets similar? Were Eris and Ceres discussed in "Pluto: Planet or Not?"* (Eris and Pluto are similar in size and have rocky cores with icy surfaces. They were mentioned but not described.)

### Comprehension Check

**Sample Answer:** These details are a scientific description of Pluto instead of the history of its discovery. Both texts describe Pluto as a small planetlike object that is very far away. This editorial says Pluto has a rocky core surrounded by ice, an atmosphere, and at least five moons.

**Answer Explanation:** Encourage students to refer back to the article "Pluto: Planet or Not?" Students should see that the focus of the two articles is different, but that both contain similar details about Pluto.

## Listening and Viewing Skills

Have students study the image on page 245 while you reread paragraphs 4–5. *Locate Pluto and Eris. What shape is Eris's orbit? Where would Ceres appear in the image?* (Eris has an elliptical orbit. Ceres would appear within Jupiter's orbit.)

## Review: Describing Text Structures

Have students use their knowledge of text structures to determine the cause of Pluto having an atmosphere only some of the time.

# Comparing and Contrasting Texts

## Guided Practice

### Recap Reading Selection

Place students in groups of three. One student should describe Pluto, one Eris, and one Ceres. Encourage students to refer to or create a picture of the solar system and identify where each dwarf planet is located.

### Read and Practice

Have partners take turns reading the selection as you circulate to provide support. Model comparing and contrasting with Cite Evidence callout A. For callout B, circulate and provide partners with scaffolding as needed. You might use the following suggestions to help students who are having difficulty.

### CITE EVIDENCE

**A** Remind students that contrast clue words include *but*, *unlike*, *instead*, *on the other hand*, *in contrast*, and *on the contrary*. These words let readers know that a description of differences will follow. Students should be able to locate the contrast clue words *On the other hand* at the beginning of paragraph 8.

**B** Help students find the information in paragraph 7 that shows that Pluto and Mercury are similar in size. The similar size of Mercury and Pluto was not described in "Pluto: Planet or Not?"

## COMPARING AND CONTRASTING TEXTS

### Guided Practice

**WORDS TO KNOW**
diameter
judging

**CITE EVIDENCE**

**A** Underline the clue words that show a contrast is being made in paragraph 8.

**B** Circle the name of the planet that is close in size to Pluto. Did the other article discuss the similar size of this planet and Pluto?

**Pluto Is Our Planet!** *continued*

6  Pluto and the other dwarf planets *are* different in some ways. But the dwarf planets are not different enough to be in their own group. In fact, in many ways the dwarf planets are more similar to the interior planets, Mercury, Venus, Earth, and Mars, than these planets are to the outer planets of our solar system.

7  The name *dwarf planet* makes it seem as if these objects are simply too small to be planets. But this is not true. They are small, but the planet Mercury has a **diameter** similar to that of Earth's moon. Pluto is much more similar in size to Mercury than Mercury is to any of the outer planets. Mercury and Venus have no moons. Earth has one, and Mars has only two. These interior planets are small and have only a few moons, just like Pluto.

8  On the other hand, the outer planets, Jupiter, Saturn, Uranus, and Neptune, are all much bigger than Earth. Jupiter is more than ten times bigger, Saturn nine times, and Neptune and Uranus almost four times bigger. All have many moons. Neptune has the fewest with 13. Saturn has at least 53! **Judging** simply by size, it seems that Earth and the inner planets are much more similar to each other and the dwarf planets. Maybe the outer planets should be called "giant planets"!

## Words to Know

**General Academic Vocabulary**
**judging** (*noun*): forming a conclusion or making a decision

**Domain-Specific Vocabulary**
**diameter** (*noun*): the distance through the middle of a planet or space object

**Working with Word Meaning** Help students become more familiar with these vocabulary words by having them use each one in a sentence of their own.

# INTEGRATION OF KNOWLEDGE AND IDEAS
**Guided Practice**

9    Pluto and the other dwarf planets are not big enough to clear asteroids out of their orbits. Instead, they are surrounded by other objects. This is the main difference scientists use to call them "dwarf planets." This difference is not nearly as important as the similarities between Pluto and the planets.

**Comprehension Check**    MORE ONLINE **sadlierconnect.com**

1. What does "Pluto: Planet or Not?" say about dwarf planets that this article does not?

   a. There is only one, Pluto.

   b. There might be many, many more.

   c. There are only two, Eris and Ceres.

   d. There are some as big as Mercury.

2. Contrast this article so far to the first one, "Pluto: Planet or Not?" How are they different?

   a. The first is an opinion piece; this one is nonfiction.

   b. The first is fiction; this one is nonfiction.

   c. They are not different; both are opinion pieces.

   d. The first is nonfiction; this one is an opinion piece.

3. What key point is the author making in this section? Compare and contrast how this point is discussed here and in "Pluto: Planet or Not?"

   Sample answer: The author points out that Pluto is more similar in size and

   number of moons to Earth and the interior planets than those planets are

   to the giant planets. In "Pluto: Planet or Not?" the author does not discuss

   Pluto's moons or the the differences between the inner and outer planets.

Unit 11 ■ Reading Informational Text: Integration of Knowledge and Ideas    **247**

## Guided Practice

**Comprehension Check**

**Answer Explanations:**

1. Students will need time to refer back to "Pluto: Planet or Not?" They should see that choice B, *There might be many, many more*, is correct.

2. "Pluto: Planet or Not?" tells about Pluto but does not state an opinion; "Pluto Is Our Planet!" is an editorial with a clearly stated opinion. Therefore, students should recognize that choice D, *The first is nonfiction; this one is an opinion piece,* is the correct answer.

3. Guide students to see that this section of the editorial shows how Pluto shares similarities with the inner planets, and that Pluto and all the inner planets are very different from the outer planets. These issues are not discussed in the other article.

## Turn and Talk

Place students in pairs, and ask them to discuss this question: *What categories of planets do we have in our solar system? What size are the planets in each group?* Then ask volunteers to share their ideas with the class.

## Discussion Skills

Remind students to apply their own thinking to what others say during a discussion. Tell them to think about whether they agree or disagree with what is said and then add their own comments—with reasons. Students' active participation helps to develop a true discussion instead of just one in which each participant states his or her opinion.

Help students apply their own ideas and reasoning by using these prompts:

• *I mostly agree with what you say, but I think… because ….*

• *I have to disagree with you because….*

## Independent Practice

### Recap Reading Selection

Lead students to make three lists: one describing features of the inner planets, one describing features of the outer planets, and one describing features of dwarf planets. Ask students to summarize the differences among these planets.

### Read and Apply

Have students read the selection independently as you circulate. If you notice students struggling, you can provide support with the suggestions that follow.

### CITE EVIDENCE

**A** Remind students that in the previous section you discussed the clue words that signal contrast. Remind them of the clue words that signal comparison: *although*, *also*, *too*, *however*, *similarly*, *likewise*, *as well*, and *both*. Guide them to search for these words in the text.

**B** Help students see that in the callout the word *versus* tells them to look for contrasts between the outer and inner planets. Remind them to look for contrast signal words (*different*) that will show the differences between the two categories.

---

**WORDS TO KNOW**
**core**
**tilted**

**CITE EVIDENCE**

**A** Circle the clue words that signal comparison and contrast on this page.

**B** Underline the details that describe the qualities of the outer versus the inner planets. Did the other article also cover these details?

10   Pluto is not that different from Earth in how it is formed. Earth and the inner planets Mercury and Mars are mostly made up of rock. Their surfaces are surrounded by an atmosphere, although Mercury has only a very thin one. Pluto also has an atmosphere some of the time. It and the other dwarf planets are rocky, too.

11   However, the outer giants are different. They are not made up mostly of rock. Jupiter has a small, rocky **core** deep inside the planet, but most of it is made of gases like hydrogen and helium. Saturn is very similar to Jupiter, which is made of hydrogen and helium. Spaceships could not land on these planets! Uranus and Neptune are ice giants. Both have thick atmospheres as well. Both are **tilted** strangely to the side and are very, very cold.

12   It is clear that planets have a lot of differences. It is also clear that Pluto is more similar to Earth and the inner planets than the outer planets are. Saying that Pluto is not a planet makes little sense when it is compared to Earth, and Earth to Jupiter or Saturn.

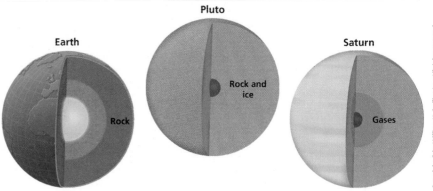

Earth — Rock
Pluto — Rock and ice
Saturn — Gases

---

## Words to Know

**General Academic Vocabulary**
**tilted** (*adjective*): at an angle, aslant

**Domain-Specific Vocabulary**
**core** (*noun*): the center of a planet or space object, often surrounded by a surface or atmosphere

**Working with Word Meaning**  Help students become more familiar with these words by having them give an example and nonexample for each.

# INTEGRATION OF KNOWLEDGE AND IDEAS

13 Pluto deserves to be a planet. It is small, far away, and very cold, but it is still part of our solar system. Our solar system has room for planets as different as Mercury and Jupiter. It has room for Ceres, Eris, and especially for Pluto, too!

**Comprehension Check**      (MORE ONLINE) sadlierconnect.com

1. What does this article tell us about Uranus and Neptune that "Pluto: Planet or Not?" does not?

   a. They have rocky cores.

   b. They were discovered 65 years apart.

   c. They are ice giants.

   d. They are similar to Jupiter.

2. What does the author of "Pluto: Planet or Not?" tell us about Pluto that this opinion article does not?

   a. how Pluto was formed

   b. how Pluto first became a planet

   c. why Pluto was named a dwarf planet

   d. why Pluto should be a regular planet again

3. What key point is the author making in this section? Compare and contrast how this point is discussed here and in "Pluto: Planet or Not?"

   Sample answer: The author points out that Pluto is similar to Earth and

   the interior planets. They are all unlike the gas and ice giant outer

   planets. The article "Pluto: Planet or Not?" does not compare Pluto

   directly to other planets in the solar system.

**Comprehension Check**

**Answer Explanations:**

1. Students may need time to refer back to "Pluto: Planet or Not?" in order to determine that choice C, *They are ice giants*, is the correct answer.

2. Students may need time to refer back to "Pluto: Planet or Not?" to see that choice B, *how Pluto first became a planet*, is the correct answer.

3. Guide students to see that this section compares the composition of Pluto and the inner planets, which is similar, and contrasts it to that of the outer planets. Students may need to refer back to "Pluto: Planet or Not?" to see that it does not discuss this issue.

## Critical Comprehension

Use the following questions to help students think more deeply about the text. Students should be prepared to support their answers with evidence from the text.

- *What types of information did each article give? What was the effect on the reader of the information they gave?* (The first article addressed the history of Pluto's discovery; the second addressed its scientific qualities.)

- *Now that you have read this editorial, do you think Pluto should be a planet? Why? Did your opinion change from the last discussion? Why?* (Answers will vary.)

**Assess and Respond**

**If** students have trouble answering the questions in the Comprehension Check,

**Then** ask them comprehension questions about pages 248–249 to determine whether they understood what they read. If they did not, you may wish to form a reading group to support them.

## Speaking and Listening: Presentation

Have students create a presentation on a way that people have extended their understanding of the solar system. After gathering information, students should take turns presenting to the class. Presenters should:

- state their topic, choose words for effect, and present appropriate facts.
- use formal language suitable for an academic presentation.
- speak clearly and answer questions in complete sentences.
- provide engaging visuals to enhance their presentation.

Listeners should listen attentively and ask questions.

## OBJECTIVES

- **Use illustrations and words to understand the concepts and events in a text.**
- **Understand the use of cause/effect and sequence in a text.**
- **Compare and contrast two texts on the same topic.**

## Genre: Explanatory Text

Explain to students that an explanatory text explains something to readers. Point out the similarities between the words *explanatory* and *explain*. Tell students that the title of an explanatory text often tells readers what the text will explain. Ask them to read the essay title and answer the question *What will this text explain?*

## Path Options

You may want to do a close reading with students; if so, use the supports provided on these pages. Or, you may wish to have students read the text independently and apply the skills learned in this unit. In either case, students should read the text more than once to facilitate understanding and to be able to answer the Comprehension Check questions correctly.

---

### CLOSE READING

# Why the Solar System Moves
(Genre: Explanatory Text)

1    Long ago, people thought the sun moved around Earth. The sun rose in the east and set in the west, so they thought it must be moving. They also saw that the sun was not the only object in the sky that moved. Most stars were still, but some moved. The ancient astronomers called these "wanderers," or "planets." They thought these planets moved around Earth, which was still, or unmoving.

2    In the early 1500s, however, the astronomer Nicolaus Copernicus began to suspect that Earth moved around the sun. It took a long time for this new idea to be accepted. The astronomer Galileo was even arrested for believing it! Slowly, however, more people began to understand this different idea of the universe.

3    Today, we know that Earth and the other seven planets move around the sun. Each moves in its own orbit. One trip, or revolution, around the sun can take anywhere from 88 days for Mercury to 165 years for Neptune. Also, everything in our solar system is spinning. The sun and all the planets rotate. There are different reasons for each of these movements, however. Everything has been spinning from the beginning of our galaxy, but the planets move around the sun because of gravity.

**Hot, spinning gases and dust formed the sun.**

**250**    **Unit 11** ■ Reading Informational Text: Integration of Knowledge and Ideas

---

## Peer Support: Turn and Talk

Ask students to stop after each paragraph. With a partner, students can take turns summarizing what has been discussed in each paragraph. Encourage students to use techniques, such as marking essential concepts and vocabulary with highlighters and writing notes and explanations in the margins of their text as they read, in order to increase understanding and engagement with the text.

# INTEGRATION OF KNOWLEDGE AND IDEAS

4    Billions of years ago, our solar system was only a spinning cloud of dust and gas. Our galaxy is full of these clouds, which are called nebulas. Something made the nebula become thicker in the center. This change started a chain reaction. The dense center pulled more and more dust into it. Then, the cloud collapsed on itself and began to spin faster and faster. This momentum is like an ice skater moving more quickly as she pulls in her arms while spinning. The nebula flattened out into a spinning disc. The temperature became hotter and hotter. Finally, atoms of different gases reacted together in violent explosions. At this point, our sun was born.

5    The planets and other objects in our solar system were made when dust and gases swirled together. The same energy that spun the ancient cloud that became our solar system keeps everything in our solar system spinning to this day. The sun, planets, moons, and other objects in our solar system are always on the move.

6    These objects keep spinning because there is nothing in space to make them slow down or stop. Earth spins once per day. Mars spins at about the same rate. Mercury and Venus spin slowly. The giant, outer planets spin much more quickly. Even the sun spins. Some people think that Earth's moon does not rotate because the same side always faces Earth. In fact, the moon does spin, but it spins as it moves around our planet, so we only see one side of it.

**Unit 11** ■ Reading Informational Text: Integration of Knowledge and Ideas    **251**

## Support First Reading

Circulate to check students' understanding. As needed, use the following comprehension and strategy check-ins to support basic understanding of the selection as students read.

### Check-in Questions

- *Describe what happened when the solar system was formed.* (A nebula became thicker in the center and spun around until it exploded and formed the sun. Dust and gases swirled together to make the planets and other objects.)

- *What parts of the solar system spin and why?* (Everything in the solar system spins because of the spinning nebula that formed it.)

## Review: Connecting Visual Information and Text

Have students examine the images on pages 250–251. Ask them to use the text to describe what is happening in each of the illustrations. (The first illustration shows a spinning nebula; the second shows the cloud collapsing on itself; the third shows the nebula collapsing into a spinning disc; the fourth shows the explosion that forms the sun.)

## Differentiate Instruction

The scientific concepts in this text may be difficult for some students to grasp. Help them understand the text by using images or animations to illustrate the birth of the solar system and its movements. You may also choose to have students act out the text by using props that stand for the space objects, or even by representing these objects themselves. Students may each represent a step in a sequence, or one may be a cause and others the effects.

**Check-in Question**

• *In paragraph 8, what does the ball in the analogy stand for? What does it do?* (The ball stands for Earth. It constantly falls in space and thus rotates around another space object.)

## Review: Describing Text Structures

Have students use the information in paragraph 7 to answer this question: *What is the cause of Earth moving around the sun? Is this the same cause that makes the moon orbit Earth?* (gravity)

## Review: Comparing and Contrasting Texts

Have students review paragraphs 7 and 8. Each describes why Earth moves around the sun in a different way. Ask students to consider how each paragraph describes this physical phenomenon. *Which description helps them understand the reasons better? Why?*

**CLOSE READING**

All of the planets in our solar system orbit the sun.

7    Earth moves around the sun for a completely different reason than it rotates, or spins. The huge sun keeps the planets circling around it by gravity. Without the sun, Earth would use its spinning energy from its formation to zoom off into space. As Earth tries to move forward, the gravity of the sun pulls it in. As a result, Earth moves in a circle around the sun. The same thing happens with the other planets moving around the sun. Gravity is also the reason that moons orbit their planets!

8    Here is how one scientist described it: "Imagine that a very powerful robot was standing on top of a tall mountain holding a ball. The robot throws the ball. If you threw a ball, it would fall back to the ground. But this robot is so strong and throws the ball so far, it moves past the curve of Earth before it starts to fall. So there's nothing it can hit! It just keeps falling. However, it can't ever hit the ground because the ground curves away in front of it. At last the ball goes all around Earth, and the robot catches it again. This is how Earth moves around the sun. It is always falling in, but since there's nowhere to fall, it just keeps going."

252    Unit 11 ■ Reading Informational Text: Integration of Knowledge and Ideas

### Strategic Reading

Encourage students to read strategically by making a mental image of the text as they read. Advise students to read slowly, taking the text one paragraph at a time, and then carefully visualizing what is being described. If students are having trouble picturing the text in their heads, encourage them to use illustrations or a model of the solar system to help them make their mental image.

# INTEGRATION OF KNOWLEDGE AND IDEAS

9    Of course, a giant robot didn't throw Earth around the sun! But the original energy from our planet's creation acts as the "robot" that tossed Earth forward and keeps it moving around the sun.

10    Humans have come a long way. They once looked up at the sun and believed that it moved around Earth. Today, we have telescopes and powerful instruments. These instruments let astronomers look into the sky and work out details about how the universe works. These details also show how connected our world still is to the ancient past. Every new thing we learn brings our planet's beginnings a little closer.

11    The beginning of our solar system happened so long ago that it is hard to even imagine it. Yet the forces that created our system are still with us. The spin of our planet, which gives us day and night, is the same spin that created Earth in the first place. The planets move overhead, and our moon circles us because of those ancient forces. The movement of Earth around the sun that gives us the seasons of the year is directly tied to the creation of that same planet and star.

## Comprehension Check

**1.** Reread paragraph 4. Which statement describes the first step in the birth of the sun?

   **a.** The cloud collapsed on itself.

   **b.** The nebula flattened out into a spinning disc.

   **c.** The nebula becomes thick at its center.

   **d.** Next, it started to spin faster and faster.

**2.** According to the text, what is the direct cause that created the sun?

   **a.** gravity from nebulas

   **b.** powerful robots spinning around

   **c.** Earth's motion left over from its creation

   **d.** atoms of different gases reacting and exploding

Unit 11 ■ Reading Informational Text: Integration of Knowledge and Ideas    **253**

## Research to Build Knowledge

Ask students to choose a planet (other than Pluto, which this unit has covered extensively) or other object in our solar system (such as a moon or comet) to research. Students should explain the history of how people discovered this object, what it is like, what part it plays in our solar system, and whether it could be seen with a simple telescope as described in the first text. Students may work in pairs and create a visual to present their findings to the class.

## Multiple Readings for Critical Comprehension

Have students reread this selection and pose questions that focus on critical comprehension. Remind them to annotate text.

- *What would Earth be like if it did not spin or move around the sun?* (There would be no day or night, and no seasons.)

- *How have humans' ideas about the solar system changed over the years? Why?* (People have accepted that Earth and other planets move around the sun and have learned how the solar system was formed.)

## Self-Select Text

As preparation for Connect Across Texts, have students select one of the four selections in this unit and reread it independently. Students can access full PDF versions of the selections at **sadlierconnect.com**.

## Comprehension Check

Begin scoring students' understanding of unit skills and texts from Comprehension Check on this page through Connect Across Texts on page 255. Use students' total scores to determine their readiness for the Unit 11 Review on page 257.

## Multiple-Choice Questions: *1 point each*

**1.** Students should be able to use the text of paragraph 4 to see that choice C, *The nebula becomes thick at its center*, is correct.

**2.** Students should be able to use the final sentences of paragraph 4 to see that choice D, *atoms of different gases reacting and exploding*, is the correct answer.

## Short-Answer Questions: 2 points each

### Item 3 Rubric

| | |
|---|---|
| 2 | Students are able to correctly identify gravity as the cause that makes the planets orbit the sun, as the planets fall towards the sun and spin around it. |
| 1 | Students are able to correctly identify gravity as the cause of the planets orbiting the sun but do not include how it has this effect. |
| 0 | Students cannot correctly identify gravity as a cause of the planets orbiting the sun. |

### Item 4 Rubric

| | |
|---|---|
| 2 | Students correctly contrast the two paragraphs and explain why one better helps them understand. |
| 1 | Students include some of the differences between the two paragraphs and explain why one better helps them understand. |
| 0 | Students do not contrast the two paragraphs. |

## Theme Wrap-Up

Lead students in a group discussion on the theme of the solar system. Discuss how people have learned about the solar system and how the ideas about it have changed over the years.

---

3. Use the information in paragraph 7 and the accompanying illustration to explain why Earth and other planets orbit the sun.

Sample answer: Students should explain in their own words that the sun's

gravity pulls Earth and other planets toward it, keeping them in a

regular orbit.

_____

_____

_____

_____

_____

_____

4. Compare and contrast the way information is presented in paragraphs 7 and 8. Which way better helped you understand why Earth orbits the sun? Why?

Sample answer: Students should describe how paragraph 7 gives this

information in a straightforward way. Paragraph 8 uses a story example to

explain the same information.

_____

_____

_____

_____

_____

_____

### Digital Connection: Exploring Online Sources

Let students know that a trustworthy website in which to find information on the solar system is **solarsystem.nasa.gov**. Encourage students to use the website to find the latest information on all of the planets and other space objects that circle our sun, as well as images, facts, and figures. Students can also explore NASA's plans for future missions to explore our solar system and the technology that makes our explorations possible.

# CONNECT ACROSS TEXTS

## Compare and Contrast Texts

In this unit, you read about whether Pluto should be considered a planet and why the solar system moves. Think about what you learned from these texts and compare and contrast them using the T-chart below. List key details and important points from the texts to show the similarities and differences between them. Be prepared to discuss your ideas with your class.

| Similarities | Differences |
|---|---|
| **Pluto: Planet or Not? and Pluto Is Our Planet!** | **Pluto: Planet or Not?** |
| how Pluto became a dwarf planet | discovery of Pluto asks whether Pluto should be a planet |
| size, gravity, and orbit of Pluto | **Pluto is Our Planet!** |
| other dwarf planets | more details of Pluto characteristics |
| | compares Pluto's size, moons, structure, atmosphere to other planets |
| | argues should be a planet again |

## Return to the Essential Question

How can authors use text structure to connect ideas and information?

In small groups or as a class, discuss the Essential Question. Think about what you have learned about text illustrations, text structures, and comparing and contrasting texts. Use evidence from the four unit texts to answer the question.

Unit 11 ■ Reading Informational Text: Integration of Knowledge and Ideas **255**

## Connect Across Texts: *4 points* Review Reading Selections

Place students in groups of four. Each student should create a summary of one of the four texts. Then work with the class to summarize each of the texts together.

## Compare and Contrast Texts

Review the directions on page 255 with students. Instruct students to fill in the chart with information about the two texts they are comparing.

### Rubric

| | |
|---|---|
| **4** | Student has identified multiple similarities and differences between the two texts. |
| **3** | Student has identified some of the similarities and differences between the two texts. |
| **2** | Student has identified one similarity or difference between the two texts. |
| **1** | Student has identified some similarities OR differences between the two texts. |
| **0** | Student has not identified the similarities and differences between the two texts. |

## Support Essential Question Discussion

Have students reread the Essential Question. Challenge them to finish this sentence: *I understand the ideas and information authors want to share when…*

Encourage students to think about the skills covered in this unit as they answer.

## Assess and Respond (pages 253–255)

| If | Then |
|---|---|
| Students scored 0–4 points, they are **Developing** their understanding of unit skills… | Provide students with reading support and more intensive modeling of skills. |
| Students scored 5–7 points, they are **Improving** their understanding of unit skills… | Use students' scores to target areas that are weak, and review those specific skills. |
| Students scored 8–10 points, they are **Proficient** in their understanding of unit skills… | Have these students move on. They are ready for the formal assessment. |

## OBJECTIVE

**Understand shades of meaning in words that describe states of mind or degrees of certainty.**

## Guided Instruction

Review the Guided Instruction section on page 256 with students. Go over the words and their definitions in the chart. Help the class write example sentences using the word *think* and each of its synonyms in the chart.

## Guided Practice

If students are having trouble, encourage them to try filling in the definitions from the chart into the sentence in place of the word and see which one makes the best sense.

## Independent Practice

If students are having trouble, suggest that they try randomly plugging the boldfaced words into the blanks and then reading aloud the sentences to hear how they sound. If they are still not sure, they can again apply the strategy of replacing the word with its definition until they can match the words *suspect*, *wonder*, and *believe* to the correct sentences.

## Apply to Reading

Have students work in pairs to write a paragraph summarizing the changing ideas humans have held about Pluto or about the movement of the sun around Earth, using three of the words from the chart correctly.

# LANGUAGE

## Shades of Meaning

**Guided Instruction** Sometimes words have similar meanings, but they do not mean exactly the same thing. Instead, words have different shades of meaning—like different shades of blue in a box of crayons. Each word describes the same thing in a slightly different way. Compare the synonyms for the word *think* in the chart.

**Guided Practice** Refer to the chart. Answer *yes* or *no* to show whether or not there is evidence for each statement below.

<u>yes</u> **1.** We know that Earth and the other planets move around the sun.

<u>no</u> **2.** Ancient people looked at the sun and believed it moved around Earth.

<u>yes</u> **3.** Copernicus suspected that Earth moved around the sun.

| suspect | think based on clues or evidence |
|---------|----------------------------------|
| wonder | think about without evidence |
| believe | accept without evidence |
| know; understand | accept based on evidence |

**Independent Practice** Pick the correct synonym to complete each sentence below.

    **suspect**        **wonder**        **believe**

**1.** Children might ___believe___ that the sun moves around Earth.

**2.** As scientists gathered evidence, they began to ___suspect___ that Pluto was not a planet.

**3.** Ancient people would ___wonder___ why stars seemed to move.

## Support English Language Learners

Students who are learning English are less likely to have an intuitive sense of the shades of meaning of the words listed in the chart on this page. Help these students become more familiar with these words by providing several sample sentences for each word and encouraging students to write their own sentences with each word. You may wish to use these prompts:

**1.** *The clues the detective found led her to* **suspect** _____.

**2.** *The child shook his birthday present and* **wondered** _____.

**3.** *She had never been to California, but she* **believed** _____.

**4.** *After she read the book, she* **knew** _____.

## UNIT 11 REVIEW

Read the following passage, which includes illustrations and text features. Then answer the questions on pages 257 and 258.

# Comets

(Genre: Scientific Text)

### Comets

1    People once believed that comets were signs of something important about to happen. Today, we know that they are huge balls of frozen gases, like giant, dirty snowballs. As comets near the sun, they heat up. <u>Because</u> the comet gets warmer, some of the ice melts and a long tail blows out behind the comet. Astronomer Gerard Kuiper first suspected in 1951 that many comets come from a field of objects beyond Neptune. These comets orbit Earth at a great distance.

### The Tale of a Tail

2    The tail of a comet is an amazing thing! It shines like a sword in the sky. No wonder ancient people thought it was an omen. At right, you can see how a comet's tail forms.

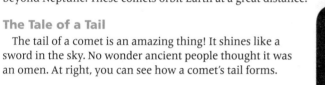

**Fill in the circle of the correct answer choice.**

**1.** What word in sentence 1 of paragraph 1 shows you that people had no evidence that comets were omens?

- ● believed
- ○ signs
- ○ about
- ○ know

**2.** Which word or phrase could best replace the word *know* in sentence 2 of paragraph 1?

- ○ suspect
- ○ believe
- ● have evidence to show us
- ○ do not have evidence to show us

Unit 11 ■ Reading Informational Text: Integration of Knowledge and Ideas    **257**

---

## Unit Summary

At this point, students have had instruction and practice in reading informational text, with a focus on learning about the solar system. Students have learned how to connect visual information and text, to describe text structures, and to compare and contrast texts on the same topic. Students have completed an independent close reading of a text, practiced working with concepts across texts, and examined how shades of meanings contribute to their understanding of words. They should be well prepared for the review session.

### Introduce the Review

Explain to students that they will read a new passage that is related to the unit's theme and the selections they have already read. Instruct students to read the passage carefully and then answer the questions on pages 257 and 258.

### Answer Explanations

Scoring: Items 1–6 on pages 257–258 are worth 1 point each. See the rubrics on the next page for guidance scoring the short-answer questions on page 258.

**1.** Students should understand that the word *believed* shows that people had no evidence.

**2.** Students should use what they learned from the chart on page 256 to understand that the phrase *have evidence to show us* would best replace the word *know*.

---

## Self-Assessment: Progress Check

Have students revisit the Progress Check on page 229 and respond to the questions again. Ask them to compare their Before and After responses.

You may wish to have students rate their answers on a scale of 0–2 rather than simply checking (or not checking) the box. Instruct them to write a 0 if they feel they do not understand a given skill at all, a 1 if they feel they have some understanding, and a 2 if they feel they have a solid grasp of the skill.

## Answer Explanations

**3.** *Cause and effect* is the connection between these two sentences.

**4.** Students should refer back to the texts to see that "Why the Solar System Moves" also has an image of a comet.

**5.** The word *because* in sentence 4 should be underlined.

**6.** The text *some of the ice melts* in sentence 4 should be circled, as well as the center image.

### Item 7 Rubric

| | |
|---|---|
| 2 | Answer includes that a comet looks like a ball of ice with no tail. |
| 1 | Answer includes that a comet looks like a ball of ice or that it has no tail. |
| 0 | Answer does not mention a ball of ice or a tail. |

### Item 8 Rubric

| | |
|---|---|
| 2 | Answer includes heat from the sun. |
| 1 | Answer does not mention heat from the sun but offers another explanation. |
| 0 | Answer does not include heat from the sun or another explanation. |

### Item 9 Rubric

| | |
|---|---|
| 2 | Answer includes: "Comets" tells what a comet is and how it forms; "Tale" describes a comet's tail. |
| 1 | Answer includes most important point(s) from one text. |
| 0 | Answer does not include the main point(s) of either text. |

### Item 10 Rubric

| | |
|---|---|
| 2 | Answer explains text and makes connection to illustration. |
| 1 | Answer explains text or makes connection to illustration. |
| 0 | Answer does not explain text or make a connection to illustration. |

## UNIT 11 REVIEW

**3.** What is the connection between sentences 3 and 4 in paragraph 1?

- ○ none
- ● cause and effect
- ○ steps in a sequence
- ○ comparison

**4.** Which other text in this unit has an image of a comet?

- ○ "How to Make a Telescope"
- ○ "Pluto: Planet or Not?"
- ○ "Pluto Is Our Planet!"
- ● "Why the Solar System Moves"

**5.** Underline the cause-and-effect clue word that connects sentences 3 and 4 in paragraph 1.

**6.** Circle the text and the image that describe the first step in the formation of a comet's tail.

**7.** What does a comet look like before it enters our solar system?

It just looks like a ball of ice. It has no tail.

**8.** According to the illustration, what causes the comet's tail to form?

heat from the sun

**9.** What are the most important points in "Comets" and "The Tale of a Tail"?

Sample answer: "Comets" describes what a comet is and how it forms. "The Tale of a Tail" describes how a comet's tail looks.

**10.** In your own words, explain the sequence of events described in the text and shown in the illustrations.

Sample answer: First, the comet nears the sun, then it heats up and starts to melt, and finally the tail forms behind it.

## Analyze Student Scores

| | |
|---|---|
| **11–14 pts Strong** | Student has a good grasp of the skills and concepts taught in this unit. Point out any mistakes the student has made, and explain the correct answers if necessary. |
| **7–10 pts Progressing** | Student is struggling with some skills or concepts. Identify the specific skills that are problematic to target a review of instruction. |
| **0–6 pts Emerging** | Student is having serious problems understanding the skills and concepts taught in this unit. Student may need to redo the work with a higher level of support. |

## Performance Task Overview

The Performance Tasks in *Progress English Language Arts* are designed to determine a student's ability to closely read and understand a complex text, locate textual evidence to support analysis of the text, and create an extended response that shows deep comprehension of the text. Writing prompts in each part of the Performance Task address requirements for creating opinion pieces, informative texts, and narratives. Each Performance Task has three main parts: a Literary Analysis Task, a Narrative Writing Task, and a Research Simulation Task.

Each Performance Task requires students to read multiple thematically related texts—literature, a nonfiction narrative, and a research-based informational text—and to respond to two types of assessment items:

• **Selected response items** require students to choose the correct answer from a number of options. Selected response items are divided into two parts: Part A requires students to answer a question related to the content or language of the text; Part B requires students to identify textual evidence that supports the answer to Part A.

• **Constructed response items** require students to create a brief written response—a literary analysis, a narrative, or an informational text—in response to a prompt.

You can help your students by introducing the overall topic of the Performance Task, orienting students to the requirements of each part of the task, and communicating helpful reminders that will enable students to approach each part successfully. Once students have completed each part, go over the items and correct responses with them, especially focusing on the connection between textual evidence and acceptable responses.

In **Performance Task 2,** students will read and respond to three texts relating to community.

- *The Summer of Sunflowers* (realistic fiction)
- *One Park for All to Enjoy* (nonfictional narrative)
- *Composting* (informational text)

Specific information about how these texts are used with each section of **Performance Task 2** is shown in the chart at the right.

---

**ONLINE Digital Resources**

Go to **sadlierconnect.com** to download the following resources for **Performance Task 2**:

**Texts:**
- *The Summer of Sunflowers*
- *One Park for All to Enjoy*
- *Composting*

**Answer Keys and Rubrics:**
- Literary Analysis Task
- Narrative Writing Task
- Research Simulation Task

---

## RECOMMENDED PACING

Administer the entire Performance Task over a three-day period. Students should complete one part per day, accompanied by instructional support and review.

| Performance Task 2 |
|---|
| **PART 1: LITERARY ANALYSIS** *(30 minutes)* |
| **TASK** Students will respond to questions that require careful analysis of a literary text and then write a brief literary analysis text. |
| **SELECTION** *The Summer of Sunflowers* |
| **PART 2: NARRATIVE WRITING** *(30 minutes)* |
| **TASK** Students will respond to questions that require careful analysis of a nonfictional narrative text and then synthesize information from two texts to respond to a prompt. |
| **SELECTION(S)** *One Park for All to Enjoy* and *The Summer of Sunflowers* |
| **PART 3: RESEARCH SIMULATION** *(30 minutes)* |
| **TASK** Students will respond to questions that require careful analysis of two texts and then respond to a writing prompt that requires them to synthesize information from the two texts. |
| **SELECTION(S)** *Composting* and *One Park for All to Enjoy* |

## PERFORMANCE TASK 2

There are three parts to this performance task. Your teacher will provide you with copies of three selections.

- *The Summer of Sunflowers*  Genre: Realistic Fiction
- *One Park for All to Enjoy*  Genre: Nonfictional Narrative
- *Composting*  Genre: Informational Text

**Part 1:** Literary Analysis

☐ Read *The Summer of Sunflowers* carefully. Take notes that will help you understand the passage.

☐ Answer Items 1–3 on pages 260–261.

☐ Then read the prompt for Item 4 and write a paragraph on your own paper. You may want to make some notes on scratch paper first.

**Part 2:** Narrative Writing

☐ Read *One Park for All to Enjoy* carefully. Take notes that will help you understand the passage.

☐ Answer Items 1–2 on page 262.

☐ Review *The Summer of Sunflowers*. You will use both passages in this task.

☐ Then read the prompt for Item 3 and write an essay on your own paper. You may want to make some notes on scratch paper first.

**Part 3:** Research Simulation

☐ Read *Composting* carefully. Take notes that will help you understand the passage.

☐ Answer Items 1–3 on pages 263–264.

☐ Review *One Park for All to Enjoy*. You will use both passages in this task.

☐ Then read the prompt for Item 4 and write an essay on your own paper. You may want to make some notes on scratch paper first.

## Test-Taking Tips

**Selected response items:** Remind students to . . .

- read each question closely and follow the directions carefully.

- read every answer choice carefully before deciding on an answer.

- use a pencil so that a wrong answer can be corrected.

**Constructed response items:** Remind students to . . .

- focus on a clear main idea.

- be well-organized and stay on topic.

- provide details from the passage to support their responses.

- use clear language and include linking words to connect ideas.

- follow rules of formal writing (spelling, punctuation, capitalization, and grammar).

## Administration Procedure

### STEP 1  Introduce the Task

Tell students that this Performance Task may cover any of the skills they have learned and practiced in Units 1–11 of *Progress English Language Arts*.

Explain that students will read three texts. After each reading, they will answer questions and then write about what they read. Familiarize students with the types of items they will see:

- Selected response items have two parts. Part A asks students to answer a question about the reading selection; Part B asks them to identify textual evidence—details from the selection—that point to the correct answer.

- Constructed response items are writing prompts based on one or more of the reading selections. Students should use textual evidence from the selections to support their responses to these items. They can make notes before writing.

**\* Repeat Steps 2–4 for each part of the Performance Task.**

### STEP 2  Reading

Tell students that they will read a text about community resources and citizens' responsibility to help maintain them. Remind them that they should read the text closely and that they can take notes about key ideas and details as they read. Have students read the text(s) for that part.

### STEP 3  Selected Response

Have students complete the selected response items.

### STEP 4  Constructed Response

Read the writing prompt, and make sure students understand the directions. Explain: *Your task is to write a paragraph. You may use your notes. Also, you may go back to the text(s) to find ideas and details you want to use in your paragraph.* Answer any questions. Then have students respond to the writing prompt.

### STEP 5  Check the Task

Go over the selected response items so students understand why each answer is correct; help them identify the textual evidence that supports each item. Review the writing prompt and discuss what an effective response should include.

## Part 1: Literary Analysis Task

**Selection:** *The Summer of Sunflowers* [ONLINE]

**Genre:** Realistic fiction

**Core Task:** Students will read a literary text and respond to three selected response items. Then students will write a literary analysis of the text.

**Text Summary:** In this story, a young girl's father gives her part of the family's plot in a community garden so that she can grow her own sunflowers. He carefully mentors her through the process, helping her to overcome problems all along the way. The resulting bumper crop of flowers is a thrill!

**Score Points:** Up to **9 points** total

- Selected response items: Up to 6 points (1 point for each part of three 2-part items)
- Constructed response item: Up to 3 points for one item

**Depth of Knowledge Levels:**

| **Item 1:** | **Item 2:** | **Item 3:** | **Item 4:** |
|---|---|---|---|
| Level 1 | Level 2 | Level 2 | Level 3 |

[ONLINE] Download the reading selection and the Answer Key and Rubric.

**Selected Response Items:** When students have completed the items, go over the correct answers with them. Help them locate the evidence in the text that supports each answer.

**Constructed Response Items:** While reading the prompt, have students circle the most important words that explain what they must do to respond to the prompt.

**Analyzing the Constructed Response:** When students have finished writing, present the rubric's key elements to students and discuss their importance. Ask volunteers to share how they could improve the answer by paying attention to the elements the rubric outlines for an excellent answer.

**How this task contributes to reading and writing grounded in evidence from literary text:** In order to complete the task, students 1. analyze and select information from a realistic fiction selection; 2. answer questions about a character in the selection and identify the evidence the author presents as support; 3. write a descriptive paragraph about the character; 4. organize ideas by stating and maintaining a focus; 5. develop a topic, including citing supportive evidence and details; 6. effectively organize ideas, appropriate transitions, and a relevant conclusion; 7. follow conventions and rules of grammar, usage, and mechanics.

---

### Part 1 Literary Analysis

Read all parts of the question before responding. Circle the correct answer to Items 1–3. Use your own paper to respond to Item 4.

**Item 1**

**Part A** In *The Summer of Sunflowers*, why was the narrator most upset?

a. Some sunflower seeds were taken by animals.
b. Some sunflower plants were added to the compost pile.
c. Some sunflower flowers were broken off the stem.
d. Some sunflower plants were taken by other gardeners.

**Part B** Which sentence from the story supports the answer to Part A?

a. "Who is doing this?" I cried to Daddy.
b. "Sunflowers!" I shouted.
c. "At least the plants will do some good there," I said to myself.
d. When my plants started coming up, there were two or three crowded together in every spot!

**Item 2**

**Part A** Read this exchange between the girl and her father.
"Do cats like sunflowers?" I asked.
"Yes," he answered shortly.
Which sentence is true about this brief conversation?

a. The father is angry with the daughter for asking so many questions.
b. The father is too upset at the situation to say very much.
c. The father is angry at the situation and thinking about how to fix it.
d. The daughter was just thinking aloud and didn't expect such a quick response.

---

**Part B** Which pair of words from the story are most helpful in understanding the conversation in Part A?

a. overjoyed, pretty
b. snapped, cried
c. carefully, glaring
d. stopped, flourished

**Item 3**

**Part A** What does the word *overabundance* mean in this sentence from *The Summer of Sunflowers*?
They are the only ones in the garden, but I have an *overabundance*.

a. an incredibly strong support
b. an extremely large quantity
c. a very beautiful vision
d. a feeling of great joy

**Part B** Which sentence from the story best helps the reader understand the meaning of *overabundance*?

a. "In fact, I had so many sunflowers that I put a sign up on the community garden gate."
b. "So Daddy decided I should have the whole back row, along the fence."
c. "And like my sunflowers, I grew up this summer."
d. "The big, bright, yellow flowers were so pretty."

**Item 4**

How would you describe the girl's father in *The Summer of Sunflowers*? Decide three character traits that he has. Write a one-paragraph description of him that includes these traits. Use details from the story to explain why you think he has them. See online rubric for scoring.

# NARRATIVE WRITING

## Part 2 Narrative Writing

Read all parts of the question before responding. Circle the correct answer to Items 1–2. Use your own paper to respond to Item 3.

**Item 1**

**Part A**   Which sentence best describes the author?
a. The author is like a friend who appreciates your opinions.
b. The author thinks everyone should love Brook Run Park.
**c.** The author is a good "tour guide" for Brook Run Park.
d. The author knows what you enjoy about Brook Run Park.

**Part B**   Which sentence supports the answer to Part A?
**a.** "Our first stop is the Children's Adventure Garden."
b. ". . . Brook Run Park truly offers something for everyone."
c. "Children, teenagers, and adults were all involved . . ."
d. "To look at it now, you would never guess . . ."

**Item 2**

**Part A**   What does *residents* mean in this sentence from the text?
Park developers wanted . . . a place . . . for Dunwoody *residents*.
a. people who are very much alike
b. people who use things again and again
**c.** people who live in a certain place
d. people who design and build parks

**Part B**   Which phrase best helps readers understand *residents*?
a. "Park developers wanted to create"
**b.** "many people who reside in Dunwoody"
c. "Recycling is encouraged."
d. "you would like Brook Run to resemble"

**Item 3**

Write a new first paragraph for *The Summer of Sunflowers*, in which you describe the setting as if it were Dunwoody Community Garden. Use details from the text. Describe the setting from the girl's point of view. See online rubric for scoring.

## Part 2: Narrative Writing Task

**Selections:** *One Park for All to Enjoy* and *The Summer of Sunflowers*   **ONLINE**

**Genres:** Nonfictional narrative and realistic fiction

**Core Task:** Students will read a nonfictional narrative text and respond to two selected response items. Then they will use what they learned from the text to write a new opening paragraph for the story they read in Part 1.

**Text Summary:** Readers learn about the history and layout of Brook Run Park in Dunwoody, Georgia, as they read the story of its development since 1998. The children's garden, dog park, skate park, and community garden are all described by the narrator, who serves as a tour guide.

**Score Points:** Up to **7 points** total

- Selected response items: Up to 4 points (1 point for each part of two 2-part items)
- Constructed response item: Up to 3 points for one item

**Depth of Knowledge Levels:**

| Item 1: | Item 2: | Item 3: |
|---|---|---|
| Level 3 | Level 2 | Level 3 |

**ONLINE**   Download the reading selections and the Answer Key and Rubric.

**Selected Response Items:** Remind students to carefully read each of the answer options in Part B of each item. Only one will make sense as support for the Part A answer.

**Constructed Response Items:** To make sure students understand the writing prompt, have them answer specific questions that you ask about it, such as *What are you going to write about? Where will you find details to support what you write?*

**Analyzing the Constructed Response:** Have student volunteers share their responses. Discuss key elements of the scoring rubric and ask students to make one significant change to improve their response.

**How this task contributes to reading and writing grounded in evidence from informational text:**
Students 1. analyze and select information from a nonfictional narrative selection; 2. answer questions about the selection and identify evidence the author presents as support; 3. write a new opening paragraph for a story, using ideas and facts from the nonfiction selection; 4. organize appropriate setting details to develop the opening paragraph of the story; 5. effectively organize ideas, using appropriate transitions; 6. follow conventions and rules of grammar, usage, and mechanics.

## Test-Taking Tips

Remind students to . . .

- read the directions carefully.
- determine clearly what is being asked.
- read the entire question and all of the choices.
- pay close attention to words that will help you identify the answer, e.g., *in paragraph 2.*
- narrow down possible answers by getting rid of incorrect choices.
- answer all parts of the question and use text evidence.
- review your responses after you are done to check for errors.
- plan what you want to say before you begin writing.
- write as neatly and legibly as possible.

## Part 3: Research Simulation Task

**Selections:** *Composting* and *One Park for All to Enjoy* ( ONLINE )

**Genres:** Informational text and nonfictional narrative

**Core Task:** Students will read an informational text and respond to three selected response items, two of which require them to compare the text with the nonfictional narrative from Part 2. Then students will write an essay that requires them to synthesize information from the two texts.

**Text Summary:** The article *Composting* describes composting and explains how it works.

**Score Points:** Up to **9 points** total

- Selected response items: Up to 6 points (1 point for each part of three 2-part items)
- Constructed response item: Up to 3 points for one item

**Depth of Knowledge Levels:**

| **Item 1:** | **Item 2:** | **Item 3:** | **Item 4:** |
| Level 2 | Level 2 | Level 2 | Level 3 |

( ONLINE ) Download the reading selections and the Answer Key and Rubric.

**Selected Response Items:** Tell students that one way to tell which Part B answer is correct is to locate each choice in the text and check the words and sentences around it. This will help them understand what each choice does and does not mean.

**Constructed Response Items:** Remind students that they should combine information from both texts in their response to the writing prompt.

**Analyzing the Constructed Response:** Discuss key elements of the scoring rubric with students. Have students underline the beliefs and supporting details.

**How this task contributes to reading and writing grounded in evidence from informational texts:**
Students 1. analyze and select information from informational selections; 2. answer questions about a selection and identify the evidence the author presents as support; 3. write a paragraph identifying and supporting the two authors' beliefs about composting; 4. organize ideas by stating and maintaining a focus; 5. develop a topic, including citing supportive evidence and details, and elaboration consistent with the source selections; 6. effectively organize ideas, use transitions, and include a conclusion; 7. follow conventions and rules of grammar, usage, and mechanics.

---

### Part 3 Research Simulation

Read all parts of the question before responding. Circle the correct answer to Items 1–3. Use your own paper to respond to Item 4.

**Item 1**

**Part A**  What is the best way to describe how the information in *Composting* is organized?
a. sequence
b. comparison and contrast
c. opinion supported by fact
d. cause and effect *(circled)*

**Part B**  Which phrase from the text supports the answer to Part A?
a. "However, inside the compost pile"
b. "you would be correct"
c. "Because landfills are filling up so quickly" *(circled)*
d. "Your compost is now ready"

**Item 2**

**Part A**  Both *One Park for All to Enjoy* and *Composting* include guidance about how to compost. As you compare and contrast these directions, which statement is true?
a. *Composting* has information that anyone can use, but *One Park* includes some things that only Dunwoody gardeners would do. *(circled)*
b. Both sets of directions help readers understand how waste is turned into compost.
c. Only *Composting* points out how the process is good for the environment.
d. The same specific examples of green and brown wastes are given in both texts.

---

### RESEARCH SIMULATION

**Part B**  Which details from the texts support the answer to Part A?
a. Add brown waste on top. *(One Park)*
   brown stuff such as leaves and pine needles *(Composting)*
b. Place the scraps inside the cans found at the center of the wire cages. *(One Park)*
   great compost is made of two basic things *(Composting)* *(circled)*
c. the more good is done for the environment *(One Park)*
   Composting is a great way to recycle *(Composting)*
d. The directions are easy to follow. *(One Park)*
   Worms are very helpful in composting piles. *(Composting)*

**Item 3**

**Part A**  Read this sentence from *Composting*.
Have you ever ***wondered*** how you can change garbage into treasure?
Think about how ***wondered*** fits in with words that describe degrees of certainty. Choose the group that ***wondered*** fits best.
a. wondered, believed, knew *(circled)*
b. wondered, felt, smelled
c. wondered, asked, said
d. wondered, read, wrote

**Part B**  Which words from the text support the answer to Part A?
a. You will know it is done *(circled)*
b. If you said "COMPOSTING,"
c. "Yuck!" you say?
d. when the dirt is crumbly and dark and smells earthy

**Item 4**

You have read two texts that give information about composting. What two similar beliefs about composting do the authors of the texts have? (Hint: Think about *how* to compost and *why*.) Write a paragraph presenting these two beliefs. Include details from each text that support these beliefs. See online rubric for scoring.

---

## The Foundational Skills Handbook:
**What should students know about phonics, word recognition, and fluency?**

In the *Foundational Skills Handbook*, students will learn about two categories of fundamental skills that they must master in order to become fluent readers who comprehend what they read: vocabulary and word recognition, and fluency.

These skills are not ends in themselves; instead, they provide important foundations for students so that they will be able to comprehend texts across a wide range of genres and disciplines. These skills will apply to all of the kinds of reading students will do this year.

## How to Use the Handbook

The handbook may be used at the beginning of the school year to introduce students to the foundational skills or give them opportunities for review. It may also be used to supplement instruction throughout the year, proving particularly helpful when used with vocabulary-oriented Language lessons in Reading and Writing units. Once students have mastered these skills, the handbook may be used as a student reference.

### Foundational Skills Overview

| Unit | Skills Taught |
|------|---------------|
| 2 | Irregularly spelled words |
| 6 | Affixes; Suffixes/base word instruction |
| 7 | Affixes/base word instruction |
| 8 | Using spelling patterns (syllable patterns, meaningful words parts) in writing words |
| 9 | Using root words to understand unknown words |

## Guided Instruction

By understanding the meaning of a base word and its prefix or suffix, students can work out the meanings of new words. Emphasize that a base word is a complete word that can stand on its own. A prefix is added to the beginning of a base word, and a suffix is added to the end of a base word. So, in the word *untie, tie* is the base word, and *un-* is the prefix.

## Guided Practice

Using the words below, work with students to find the base word, its prefix, and the word's meaning. Point out that each prefix on page 267 adds an extra syllable to a word. Students can look for the syllable break at the beginning of the word to identify the prefix.

- reread, rewrite, return

- unsafe, uncover, unfair

- pretest, preplan, preschool

## Independent Practice

Have students choose one base word for each prefix, *re-, un-,* and *pre-* and write a sentence using the word correctly.

### Strategic Reading

Students can also use context clues to determine prefix meanings. Give the following example and help students find the clue words that tell what the italicized word means:

The dog seems *unfriendly* because he growls at everyone. (the word *growls* tells us the dog is *not* friendly.)

### Challenge Assignment

Challenge students to choose two different words from each set of prefix examples and write two new sentences. The first sentence should use the word with a prefix. The second sentence should use the base word. Have students explain the difference in meaning of their sentence pairs.

---

### Base Words

A **base word** is a complete word. It makes sense as a word on its own. Many words are formed by adding a prefix or suffix to a base word. Recognizing the base word in words that have these word parts can help you read the words.

> Our new puppy is so **playful**.

The base word in *playful* is *play*. The suffix *-ful* has been added to *play* to form the word *playful*.

Look at the words in the More Words column. Notice that many words can be formed from the base word *play*.

| Base Word | More Words |
|-----------|------------|
| play | play**ing** |
|  | play**er** |
|  | **re**play |

Read each sentence. Circle the base word in the underlined word. Then write two new words with the same base word. Add a different prefix or suffix to form each word.

1. We pre**heat** the oven before we bake the bread.

   reheat          heated          Answers will vary.

2. My math **teach**er lives down the street.

   teaching          teaches          Answers will vary.

3. Our new neighbor was very **help**ful after the storm.

   helpless          helper          Answers will vary.

Choose one of the new words to write a sentence of your own.

4. _____ Answers will vary.

---

### Prefixes

A **prefix** is a word part that is added to the beginning of a base word. A base word is a complete word. It makes sense as a word on its own. Adding a prefix creates a new word by adding to the meaning of a base word. One way to read unknown words is to look for a prefix.

> I **reread** my report to fix any mistakes.

The prefix in *reread* is *re-*. It comes at the beginning of the base word *read*. The prefix *re-* means "again." To reread a report means to read the report again.

| Prefix | Meaning | Word | Meaning |
|--------|---------|------|---------|
| re- | "again" | **re**pack | "pack again" |
| un- | "not" or "opposite of" | **un**kind | "not kind" |
| pre- | "before" | **pre**wash | "wash before" |

Underline the prefix in each group of words. Then write the meaning of each word.

1. unlock — opposite of lock

   unhappy — not happy

   untie — opposite of tie

2. rebuild — build again

   refill — fill again

   repaint — paint again

3. premix — mix before

   prepay — pay before

   preview — view before

In each sentence, underline the word with a prefix. Then take turns reading the sentences with a partner.

4. My aunt was unable to go to our school play.

5. I recycle bottles so they can be used again.

6. Preheat the oven before you bake the muffins.

7. Please restate your answer.

8. My little brother was unaware that I had borrowed one of his toys.

9. We took a pretest in school today so that we would know what to study.

## PHONICS AND WORD RECOGNITION

### Suffixes

A **suffix** is a word part that is added to the end of a base word. A suffix creates a new word by adding to the meaning of a base word. One way to read unknown words is to look for a suffix.

*Someday I want to be a science **teacher**.*

The suffix in teacher is *-er*. It comes at the end of the base word *teach*. The suffix *-er* means "person who." A science teacher is a person who teaches science.

| Suffix | Meaning | Word | Meaning |
|---|---|---|---|
| *-ful* | "full of" | play*ful* | "full of play" |
| *-ly* | "in a certain way" | safe*ly* | "in a safe way" |
| *-er* | "person who" | sing*er* | "a person who sings" |

Underline the suffix in each group of words. Then write the meaning of each word.

1. farm<u>er</u>    A person who farms
   build<u>er</u>    A person who builds
   climb<u>er</u>    A person who climbs

2. cheerf<u>ul</u>    Full of cheer
   helpf<u>ul</u>    Full of help
   harmf<u>ul</u>    Full of harm

3. bright<u>ly</u>    In a bright way
   quick<u>ly</u>    In a quick way
   strong<u>ly</u>    In a strong way

In each sentence, underline the word with a suffix. Then take turns reading the sentences with a partner.

4. Please be <u>careful</u> when you use scissors.

5. The <u>painter</u> used two colors to paint the kitchen.

6. We tiptoe into the room <u>quietly</u>.

7. The girl <u>proudly</u> crossed the finish line.

8. I was <u>joyful</u> because we were going to have a picnic.

9. The <u>catcher</u> caught the ball without even looking!

268    Foundational Skills Handbook

## FOUNDATIONAL SKILLS

### Latin Suffixes

The word parts *-able*, *-ment*, and *-ion* are also suffixes. Recognizing them in unknown words can help you read the words. These suffixes came from the Latin language.

Look at the words in the chart. Notice how separating the base word and Latin suffix makes it easier to read the words.

| Word | Base Word | Suffix |
|---|---|---|
| agreeable | agree | -able |
| measurement | measure | -ment |
| correction | correct | -ion |

Look at each group of words. Circle the suffix in each word. Then read the words.

1. state(ment)    pay(ment)    improve(ment)
2. direct(ion)    elect(ion)    inspect(ion)
3. wash(able)    break(able)    bend(able)

In each sentence, underline the word with a suffix. Then take turns reading the sentences with a partner.

4. We spent an <u>enjoyable</u> day at the park.

5. The <u>excitement</u> of the day made me tired.

6. Look at our <u>collection</u> of rocks.

7. We watch the dolphins in <u>amazement</u>.

8. The computer is a great <u>invention</u>.

9. My quick <u>movement</u> may scare the cat.

10. Large print is more <u>readable</u> than small print.

### Guided Instruction

Point out that sometimes a suffix will usually change a word's part of speech. For example, *-ful* can change a noun to an adjective, and *-ly* can change an adjective to an adverb.

Explain using the Latin suffix examples:

*-able* means "able to." It turns a verb into an adjective. Example: *comfort + able = comfortable*, or "able to give comfort."

*-ment* means "action or result." It turns a verb into a noun. Example: *argue + ment = argument*, or "the action of arguing."

*-ion* means "the act of or the state of." It also turns a verb into a noun. Example: *invent + ion = invention*, or "the act of inventing."

### Guided Practice

Work with students to find the base word, its suffix, and the meaning of each word:

- *believable, acceptable, likable*
- *government, placement, treatment*
- *celebration, completion, action*

### Independent Practice

Have students choose one word for each suffix, *-ful, -ly, -er, -able ,-ment,* and *-ion,* and write a sentence using the word.

#### Support English Language Learners

**Cognates/False Cognates** Words with the same etymology and similar meanings in two languages are called *cognates*. Many English words that end in *-tion* correspond to Spanish words that end in the suffix *-ción*, such as *celebration/celebración*. Students should be aware of false cognates, or words that look related but are not. For example: *decepción* means *disappointment,* not *deception*. Point out that the suffixes *-ment* in English and *-mente* in Spanish are not cognates. In Spanish, *-mente* is added to adjectives to make adverbs, acting as *-ly* does in English: *clearly/claramente*.

#### Challenge Assignment

Challenge students to choose two different words from each set of suffix examples and write two new sentences.

## Guided Instruction

**Vowel-Consonant-Vowel (VCV) Words** A consonant between two vowels tends to go with the second vowel (open syllable that ends in a vowel: *bro*-ken). The exception is when the first vowel is accented and short (closed syllable that ends in a consonant: *wag*-on). Read aloud the examples (*open, habit, below, cabin*), emphasizing the short or long vowel sound that is stressed. Have the class repeat each word after you.

**Vowel-Consonant-Consonant-Vowel (VCCV) Words** Read aloud the examples (*signal, husband, blossom*), emphasizing the stress on the first syllable. Have the class repeat each word after you.

## Guided Practice

Work with students on more examples to find the syllable breaks and pronunciation.

- VCV: *ever, event, nature*
- VCCV: *happen, mirror, happen*

## Independent Practice

Have students write the vowel-consonant letters for syllable breaks in these words: *after, bacon, closet, cover, helmet, metal, muffin, napkin, problem.*

## Grouping Options

Give students an opportunity to help and learn from peers by creating pairs with different levels of speaking ability. Have the more proficient partner read aloud the following words, saying each word with a brief pause between syllables: *assure, begin, commit, compete, moment, native, paper.* Have the partner listen closely and then repeat back each word twice. Then have the students change roles.

### Challenge Assignment

Challenge students to divide each set of VCV and VCCV words into syllables using hyphens.

- VCV: *vanish, natural, educate*
- VCCV: *respect, pretty, picnic*

---

### Multisyllable Words: VCV

Sometimes a word has one consonant between two vowels. To figure out the word, divide it into syllables before the consonant and pronounce the first syllable with a long vowel sound. If you do not recognize the word, divide the word after the consonant and pronounce the first syllable with a short vowel sound.

| open | habit | below | cabin |
|------|-------|-------|-------|
| **o-pen** | **hab-it** | **be-low** | **cab-in** |

Write each word, dividing it into syllables with a hyphen. The first one has been done for you.

1. over    o-ver
2. idea    i-dea
3. clever    clev-er
4. reward    re-ward
5. visit    vis-it
6. river    riv-er
7. hero    he-ro
8. began    be-gan
9. beyond    be-yond
10. decide    de-cide

Choose the best word from the list above to complete each sentence. Then read this paragraph about a girl who rescues a cat.

As Gina ___began___ to take a bite of her fish sandwich, she heard cries outside. She looked out the window and saw that a cat was in her neighbor's tree ___beyond___ its owner's reach. Gina had an ___idea___. She went ___over___ to her neighbor's yard. Hoping the cat would ___decide___ to climb down to eat the sandwich, Gina put it on the ground. The cat came down! "Thank you for being such a ___clever___ girl," the cat's owner said to Gina. "I will give you a ___reward___." Gina shook her head and said, "Feeling like a ___hero___ is enough for me!"

---

### Multisyllable Words: VCCV

A **syllable** is a word part with one vowel sound. Multisyllable words are words with more than one syllable. When you see an unknown word, divide it into syllables. Doing this will help you figure out the word. If a word has two consonants between two vowels, you can usually divide it between the consonants.

| signal | husband | blossom |
|--------|---------|---------|
| **sig-nal** | **hus-band** | **blos-som** |

Write each word, dividing it into syllables with a hyphen. The first one has been done for you.

1. insect    in-sect
2. coffee    cof-fee
3. sudden    sud-den
4. practice    prac-tice
5. welcome    wel-come
6. rescue    res-cue
7. invite    in-vite
8. doctor    doc-tor

Choose the best word from the list above to complete each sentence. Take turns reading the sentences with a partner.

9. Do you plan to ___invite___ all of your cousins to your birthday party?
10. The ride's ___sudden___ starts and stops made it very thrilling.
11. All team members who miss ___practice___ will not be allowed to play.
12. I am going to the ___doctor___ today for my yearly checkup.
13. Any ___insect___ that crawled into the spider's web was trapped.
14. The other students gave Raquel a warm ___welcome___ on her first day.
15. My mother has a cup of ___coffee___ with her breakfast every morning.
16. The Coast Guard's bold ___rescue___ of the ship's passengers was on the news.

## PHONICS AND WORD RECOGNITION

### Multisyllable Words: *-le*

Sometimes a word ends in a consonant followed by *-le*. The *-le* and the consonant before it form a syllable. Recognizing this syllable can help you read words ending in a consonant followed by *-le*.

| puzzle | table | candle |
|--------|-------|--------|
| puz-**zle** | ta-**ble** | can-**dle** |

Write each word, dividing it into syllables with a hyphen. The first one has been done for you.

1. sparkle    spar-kle     6. battle    bat-tle
2. bubble    bub-ble     7. simple    sim-ple
3. purple    pur-ple     8. dangle    dan-gle
4. circle    cir-cle     9. needle    nee-dle
5. tumble    tum-ble     10. gentle    gen-tle

Choose the best word from the list above to complete each sentence. Take turns reading the sentences with a partner.

11. To make the color _____purple_____, mix red and blue.
12. "Jack and Jill" is a rhyme about children who _____tumble_____ down a hill.
13. Tamika liked _____simple_____ clothes more than fancy dresses.
14. Before you can sew, you'll have to thread the _____needle_____.
15. The children chased the _____bubble_____ so they could pop it.
16. My mother likes to _____dangle_____ her feet in the pool, but I jump right in.
17. The glitter made the poster _____sparkle_____.
18. Please be _____gentle_____ with the baby so he doesn't get hurt.

## FOUNDATIONAL SKILLS

### Reading Irregularly Spelled Words

Words such as *said*, *enough*, and *beautiful* are words that you come across often when you read. These words have irregular spellings. They do not follow common spelling patterns. This makes the words hard to read.

Recognizing irregularly spelled words can help you read them quickly. Try looking for parts of words that have the same spelling. Sometimes these parts have the same pronunciation.

In each column, underline the part of each irregularly spelled word that has the same spelling. The first one has been done for you.

| 1. crumb | 2. could | 3. another | 4. rough |
|----------|----------|------------|----------|
| numb | would | mother | tough |
| thumb | should | other | enough |

Read the paragraph. Search for words from the list above. Write these words on the lines below.

When my brothers were little, they loved playing pranks. Every year on the day before April Fools' Day, they _____would_____ come up with a prank. As if that wasn't bad _____enough_____, they would always try to get me to go along with them. Even though saying *no* was _____tough_____, I always did. Here are some of my favorites. Buy some cream-filled cookies and take the cream filling out. Then put toothpaste between the cookies instead. Be careful not to leave a single _____crumb_____ in the bathroom, or your family will know that something is up! Here's _____another_____ one. One year my brothers made a cake out of sponges. They covered the sponges with frosting and sprinkles. Then they told our _____mother_____ it was a special cake. She tried, but she _____could_____ not cut it. I have to admit, our family had a lot of fun on April Fools' Day.

## Guided Instruction

One common pattern in multisyllable words is a word ending that consists of a consonant followed by the letters *-le,* such as *jungle* and *candle.* Point out to students that the *e* at the end is silent, and that the final consonant, combined with *-le,* forms a syllable: *rum-ble.*

## Guided Practice

Work with students on more examples of multisyllable words that end with a consonant followed by *-le.* Have them find the syllable breaks and practice the pronunciation by chorally repeating each word after you: *able, double, eagle, fable, people.*

Then have students sort the following words into groups that share each of these word parts: *-umb, -ould, -other, -ough.* Ask volunteers to pronounce each word: *brother, cough, couldn't, dumb, smother.*

## Independent Practice

Have students write the consonant followed by *-le* for syllable breaks in these words: *beagle, couple, cycle, needle.* Then have students write a complete sentence using each of these words: *thumb, could, mother, enough.*

## Peer Collaboration

Have students work in pairs so that peers can support each other in responding to the Independent Practice. Ask students to share their answers with a partner and make changes to their answers based on the discussion with their partner. Finally, ask pairs to report their answers to the whole group.

### Challenge Assignment

Have students divide each of these words into syllables with a hyphen. Then ask volunteers to say each word aloud: *article, bicycle, divisible, favorable, horrible, likable, popsicle, recycle, terrible.*

## Reading "Aloud" to Yourself

Discuss that when students read silently, they should imagine "hearing" their own voice speaking the words they are reading. This helps them sound out words and syllables, read in phrases, and "hear" how characters sound.

## Fluency Skills

1. **Attend to punctuation** with inflection rising near the end of questions, getting stronger with exclamation points, and pausing slightly at commas and more fully at periods.

2. **Read in phrases** with appropriate pausing at phrase boundaries, including subject-verb divisions and conjunctions.

3. **Read with emotion** with the voice tone rising and falling appropriately.

4. **Reflect change in characters while reading dialogue** by using appropriate vocal tone to represent characters' emotions.

5. **Use context to self-correct or reread as necessary.**

## Differentiated Instruction

Support students as they prepare to read the passage aloud by suggesting that they mark up the "script" by underlining words and sentences that should be read with more emphasis.

## Speaking and Listening

**Audio recordings** Have student partners work together to make audio recordings that demonstrate their ability to read fluidly with appropriate expression. Partners can choose poems and/or short works to record.

### Partner Practice

Have partners use the Reading Checklist on page 274 as they take turns reading the story aloud to each other. Have each student read the story two or more times, each time incorporating partner feedback.

---

FLUENCY

**Practicing Fluency**

**Read the following retelling of an Aesop fable. Use the checklist below to help guide your reading.**

## The Fox and the Goat

One day Fox stumbled into a well and couldn't escape. Eventually along came Goat, thirsty and sweaty. As he longingly peered into the well, Fox sweetly surprised him. "Welcome, Goat!"

"Greetings, Fox! Is the water fresh?" called Goat.

"It's the purest you'll ever taste," replied Fox cheerfully. "There's plenty to share, so come join me!"

Without thinking, Goat plunged into the well and drank his fill.

"Now that we are refreshed, let's leave," Fox said.

Goat looked up, crying, "Oh, no! How will we climb out?"

"With my clever plan!" answered Fox. "Press your feet against the stones that line the well. I'll climb your back, hop out, and fetch help."

Goat agreed gladly. Fox scampered up Goat's back, bounced off his horns, and was free. Before disappearing, he scolded Goat. "Foolish animal! Don't you know to look before you leap?"

**Now read the story aloud to a partner. Use the checklist below and your understanding of the story to guide your reading.**

### Reading Checklist

- [ ] Does my voice go up if there is a question mark? Does it get stronger if there is an exclamation point? Do I pause for periods and commas?

- [ ] How should a character's thoughts or words affect how I read?

- [ ] How does the tone or mood of the story—suspenseful, scary, sad, happy—change the way I read? (Remember, the tone or mood can change more than once in a story.)

---

## Assessing Fluency Rate (Oral Reading Rate)

Time the student reading "The Fox and the Goat" aloud for 60 seconds while you follow along on your own copy. Slash through any words the student skips, mispronounces, or says incorrectly (word substitution or wrong order). If the student struggles for more than three seconds, say the word, slash it on your copy, and continue the student reading. When a student self-corrects, score the word as correct. Say "stop" after one minute and circle the last word read.

The word count for "The Fox and the Goat" is 141. If a student finishes the selection before 60 seconds pass, the student is above grade-level fluency norms. Determine words correct per minute and compare to the recommended grade-level fluency rates by using the chart below. (Fountas & Pinnell)

| Grade 3 First half of year | 100–120 WCPM | Grade 3 Second half of year | 120–140 WCPM |
|---|---|---|---|

### Calculating Words Correct per Minute (WCPM)

_____ − _____ = _____

| Total Words Read per Minute | Words Read Incorrectly | Words Correct per Minute |
|---|---|---|

---

Writing Handbook **275**

## The Writing Handbook: What are the steps in the writing process?

In the *Writing Handbook,* students will learn about the steps in the writing process. These steps apply to all of the kinds of writing students will do this year. This guide will help students move from their ideas to a finished piece of writing.

### How to Use the Handbook

The handbook may be used at the beginning of the school year to introduce students to the writing process. Once students are familiar with the writing process, it may be used as a student reference with any writing unit.

### Steps in the Writing Process

**Planning** Outline the big ideas and details based on responses to the questions: What is the writing type and purpose? Who is the audience?

**Drafting** Write the first version of the piece.

**Revising** Use a checklist to review ideas and voice; organization and coherence; and word choice.

**Editing** Review grammar and conventions such as spelling, punctuation, and capitalization.

**Producing, Publishing, and Presenting** Review the appearance of the writing. Prepare the final form. Present the writing to others.

| Unit | Genre |
|------|-------|
| 2 | Fictional Narrative |
| 4 | Informative/ Explanatory Text |
| 6 | Nonfictional Narrative |
| 8 | Opinion Piece |
| 10 | Research Report |

## Writing Process Overview

| Step in the Writing Process | Focus |
|------|-------|
| Planning | Central idea and details; outlining; planning the research |
| Drafting | Student model: "Types of Clouds" |
| Revising | Working with a partner; writing clearly |
| Editing | Correcting mistakes using proofreading symbols |
| Producing, Publishing, and Presenting | Sharing the writing |

## Step 1: Planning

**Assignment/Genre** Point out that the model outline on page 277 is for a genre, or type of text, called *informational text,* a type of nonfiction that is not narrative. Specifically, the model is for an informative/explanatory essay. Its purpose is to inform or explain.

**Brainstorming** Explain that one effective way to decide on a writing topic is to brainstorm with a partner or in a small group. This means that students will jot down all the ideas that come to mind. Have students review their list to choose which idea they think will work best as a topic.

**The Big Idea** Tell students that the most important thing about their topic is their "big idea"—the central idea of their writing. After they ask themselves questions about their topic, have students write a complete sentence that states their central idea.

**Supporting Details** Explain that all other sentences in their writing should support the central idea in their topic sentence. If a detail is interesting but not important to the central idea, discard it.

**Digital Integration: Research Tip** When conducting research online, students should always be supervised by an adult. Explain why students should use precise search words or phrases. For example, if a student wants to know what to feed a parrot, the search term *bird* would be far too broad. The search term *parrot* would be more focused but still too broad. The search term should be *parrot diet*.

**Support English Language Learners** Create heterogeneous pairings so that proficient students can help English language learners. Have these "writing buddies" state their big ideas. English language learners can often speak their thoughts better than they can write them. Allow their partners to assist them in writing and connecting these ideas in a logical order. English language learners may also benefit from hearing how their partners state their ideas and connect them to supporting details.

### Assignment: Planning

Have students identify a topic for an informational essay, preferably related to their science curriculum. Before outlining, students can use a graphic organizer to plan their writing. They may begin by writing their central idea in a circle with more connected circles for supporting details.

---

## WRITING HANDBOOK

This year, you will write fiction and nonfiction narratives. You will also write an informative/explanatory text, an opinion piece, and a research report. This handbook is your guide to writing. It takes you through the steps of the writing process. These steps help you move from ideas to a finished piece of writing. Once you know the steps, you can use them for any kind of writing.

### STEP 1 Planning

Let's say you are going to write an informative/explanatory essay for school about the four different types of clouds. Good writing begins with planning. To plan, begin by asking yourself some questions.

- **What** am I writing?

  In this assignment, you are writing a type of essay that provides information or explains something. It is nonfiction because it is about actual, or real, people, places, events, or ideas.

- **Why** am I writing? What is my **purpose**?

  Your purpose for writing is your reason for writing. For this assignment, your purpose is to inform. You will do this by explaining the four different kinds of clouds.

- **Who** is my audience? Who will read my writing?

  In this case, your audience is anybody who wants to learn about clouds.

> **RESEARCH TIP**
>
> When you research a topic, you gather information about it. You can use sources such as magazines, books, and online resources. You can even interview an expert. Be sure to take notes from the sources you use. Sort the information in the notes to help you organize your writing.

---

## WRITING HANDBOOK

Then, think of ideas and organize them. An outline is one way to plan.

- Begin with your **big idea**.

  For informational text, begin with your **topic**—the central idea of your writing. Ask yourself, "What facts do I know about my topic that I can use?"

  For fiction, you might begin with the problem in the story that requires a solution.

- Then add **details**.

  For informational text, add ideas and facts that support your topic. Often, finding the ideas and facts requires research.

Here's what an outline for your essay on clouds might look like.

For fiction, add characters, setting, and plot events to your outline.

**Types of Clouds**

I. Introduction
   Topic: Clouds come in many shapes and sizes, but scientists have identified four basic types.

II. Explanation
   Topic 1: Cumulus Clouds
   Facts:

   Topic 2: Stratus Clouds
   Facts:

   Topic 3: Cirrus Clouds
   Facts:

   Topic 4: Nimbus Clouds
   Facts:

III. Conclusion

### PLANNING TOGETHER

- A partner can help you to get your ideas flowing.
- You might brainstorm together. Let one idea lead to the next.

---

## WRITING HANDBOOK

### STEP 2 Drafting

When you draft, you do the actual writing of your essay. Many writers use a computer to write drafts. Follow your outline, but don't worry about making everything perfect. Just write and get your ideas down!

Here is a handwritten draft of an essay about the different kinds of clouds. This is a great start!

#### Types of Clouds

Clouds come in many, many shapes and sizes. However, scientists have identified four basic types. The types have Latin names: cumulus, stratus, cirrus, nimbus.

Cumulus means "heap." You usually see these puffy white clouds when the weather is fair. However, they can change quickly when hot air pushes them up. Then a thunderstorm might happen.

Stratus means "layer." These gray clouds are flat. They go across the sky. Light rain might fall from them.

Cirrus means "curl of hair." These thin, wispy clouds are high in the sky. They made of ice. You can watch them move, like streamers.

Nimbus means "rain." If these dark clouds are up overhead, you are probably experiencing rain or snow.

Now you know more about clouds. They are more than shapes in the sky.

278    Writing Handbook

## WRITING HANDBOOK

### STEP 3 Revising

During this step, you think about how to make your writing better. This step is about ideas, not about spelling and grammar. Focus on the items in the checklist below. Your goal is to check each item. Then make changes on your computer or on a handwritten copy. If you are using pencil and paper, make a fresh copy.

#### REVISING TOGETHER

- You can work with a partner during revising. Have your partner read your draft and use a checklist to give you feedback. Use your partner's feedback to improve your draft.
- Finally, read your revised draft aloud to yourself or to your partner. See if you want to make any more improvements.

#### REVISING CHECKLIST

**Ideas and Voice**
- ☐ Do all of my ideas support my topic?
- ☐ Have I developed my ideas by including enough details?
- ☐ Does my writer's voice sound interesting and believable?

**Organization and Coherence**
- ☐ Does each idea fit with those before and after it?
- ☐ Have I used clue words to help readers follow the sequence or order of my ideas?
- ☐ Have I used a variety of sentence types?

**Word Choice**
- ☐ Have I avoided using the same words over and over?
- ☐ Do my words bring my ideas to life?

Writing Handbook    279

## Step 2: Drafting

Encourage students to think about their draft as their sketch. It is not a finished drawing or painting but a trial run of their ideas in organized form. They can change and improve it in any way in the next step, Revising.

**Digital Integration** Since students can delete words as well as move words and sentences around, word processing on a computer can help them "leap into" writing more confidently. This allows them to focus on fluency of ideas, ordering of information, and connecting thoughts from sentence to sentence.

**Time Management/Milestones** To help students manage time, you may want to provide a series of short-term deadlines for the following milestones:

- Complete outline.
- Complete first draft.
- Revise the draft.
- Edit the revised draft.
- Create clean final copy of writing.
- Produce, publish, or present work.

**Differentiated Instruction** Review the draft of "Types of Clouds" on page 278. Be sure students understand that the text reflects the organization shown in the outline on page 277. Label the introduction as part 1; the supporting details as part 2; and the conclusion as part 3.

### Assignment: Drafting

After you conference on students' outlines, students are ready to draft. As they draft, you should continue to conference with individuals on drafts and revisions as the rest of the class continues their work. "Dropping in" on student writing will help keep students focused and on target. In addition, pairs can meet quietly to review their peer comments in a corner.

## Step 3: Revising

Tell students that although they can use the Revising Checklist to check their own work, it is helpful to have a partner respond to the questions. The revision stage is time to focus on big issues and overall organization.

**Peer Review** When you have students work together in pairs or small groups, make sure they are polite and respectful. They should use sticky notes for writing down suggestions. Explain that it is the writer's responsibility to use his or her partner's comments to revise.

## Step 3: Revising *continued*

### Peer Collaboration

Explain to students that as they make comments on their partner's writing, they should encourage and support their partner by asking questions such as:

- *What is another way to draw the reader in from the beginning?*
- *Can you think of other details to add?*
- *What is another word you could use to say that?*
- *How can the conclusion provide a better sense of closure?*

## Step 4: Editing

Have students use the Editing Checklist by responding to the sentences.

### Editing Tips

- Read the writing slowly to find mistakes.
- Don't edit for every type of mistake at once. Instead, read the writing four times, once for each heading on the checklist. Each reading should focus on the convention listed.
- Point a finger to one word at a time to check each word.
- Use a blank sheet of paper as you read to cover sentences you have not yet edited.
- Be careful your eyes do not skip from one big mistake to the next big mistake, missing small mistakes in between. Double check little words such as *it, of, or,* and *the.*
- Keep a list of your most common editing mistakes and edit for those on a separate reading.
- Have someone else read your work aloud to catch any mistakes.

**Digital Integration** If students are using a computer, encourage them to use a spellchecker, but make sure they understand that software will not find every mistake. Spellcheckers will not always catch words that are spelled correctly, but used incorrectly, such as *there, their,* and *they're.*

### Assignment: Revising and Editing

Organize students into pairs to review each other's informational essay revisions and offer constructive feedback. Make sure they focus on the big picture. Circulate to monitor the pairs and remind students not to argue, but to be helpful, positive, and polite.

---

Here is a draft with notes for revisions. To see the revised draft, turn to page 282.

> In my next draft, I want to draw in the reader with a stronger introduction.

### Types of Clouds

~When we look at the sky, it seems like there are a million~
Who hasn't stared at the sky and found clouds that look like people or animals? Clouds do come in many, many shapes and sizes. ~different types of beautiful clouds?~ However, scientists have identified four basic types. The types have Latin names: cumulus, stratus, cirrus, nimbus.

Cumulus means "heap." You usually see these puffy white clouds when the weather is fair. However, they can change quickly when hot air pushes them up. Then a thunderstorm might happen.

> I'm going to combine two sentences here to make my writing flow more smoothly.

Stratus means "layer." These gray clouds are flat, and they move across the sky. Light rain might fall from them.

Cirrus means "curl of hair." These thin, wispy clouds are high in the sky. They made of ice. You can watch them move, like streamers.

Nimbus means "rain." If these dark clouds are up overhead, you are probably experiencing rain or snow.
~So now when you study the clouds, you can call them by their~
~Now you know there are four basic types of clouds.~
Latin names. You can also make smart guesses about the
~Each one is different. They are more than just shapes in~
weather. Of course, you can still have fun finding faces or
~the sky.~
shapes in the clouds you see.

> My conclusion needs to have more information about the topic.

---

**STEP 4** Editing

This step is about making your writing correct. Now is the time to focus on grammar, punctuation, and spelling. Read your revised draft carefully. Sometimes it helps to read it aloud. Use the checklist to correct your writing on the computer or your handwritten draft.

### EDITING CHECKLIST

**Sentences**
- ☐ Every sentence is a complete sentence. I have corrected any sentence fragments or run-on sentences.

**Grammar**
- ☐ The subject and verb of every sentence agree.
- ☐ The verb tense stays the same throughout.
- ☐ Pronouns match the nouns they replace.

**Mechanics**
- ☐ Every sentence begins with a capital letter and ends with the correct punctuation mark.
- ☐ Commas, quotation marks, and other punctuation marks are used correctly, and no marks are missing.
- ☐ The title and all proper nouns are capitalized.
- ☐ Paragraphs are indented.

**Spelling**
- ☐ I have used a dictionary to check spellings I am unsure about.
- ☐ I have correctly used any homophones (words that sound the same, such as *their/there/they're*).

## WRITING HANDBOOK

### PROOFREADING MARKS

Always proofread and correct your own work. Seeing your own mistakes can be difficult, though. Asking a partner to check your work can help.

| ∧ | Add | ✐ | Take out | / | Small letter |
|---|-----|---|----------|---|--------------|
| ⊙ | Period | ≡ | Capital letter | ◯ | Spelling error |

#### Types of Clouds

Who hasn't stared at the sky and found clouds that look like people or animals? Clouds do come in many, many shapes and sizes. However, scientists have identified four basic types. The types have Latin names: cumulus, stratus, cirrus, nimbus.

Cumulus means "heap." you usually see these puffy white clouds when the weather is fair, but they can change quickly when hot air pushes them up. Then a thunderstorm might happen.

Stratus means "layer." These gray clouds are flat, and they (seam) to stretch across the sky. Light rain might fall from stratus clouds.

Cirrus means "curl of hair." These thin, wispy clouds are high in the sky. They made of ice. You can watch them move, like streamers⊙

Nimbus means "rain." If these dark clouds are up overhead, you are probably experiencing rain or snow.

So now when you study the clouds, you can call them by their Latin names. You can also make smart guesses about the weather. Of course, you can still have fun finding faces or shapes in the clouds you see.

282   Writing Handbook

---

## WRITING HANDBOOK

**STEP 5** Producing, Publishing, and Presenting

Now that you've worked so hard on your writing, it's time to share it with others! Think about how your writing looks. Is it neatly handwritten or typed and printed from the computer?

Would images add interest?
- photographs
- illustrations

Would text features make your ideas easier to understand?
- diagrams
- graphs
- charts
- maps

Think about the final form of your writing. Be sure the way you present your final version fits your purpose and audience.

**DIGITAL CONNECTION**
Technology makes it easy to present your writing to a bigger audience, especially on the Internet.

You might be asked to share your writing orally with others. Follow these rules to make your oral presentation effective.

- If you are changing a written essay into an oral presentation, make changes in words and in sentences that will help you talk to your audience. The language used for writing and speaking is not always the same.
- Use visuals as needed to support what you say.
- Speak clearly and loudly enough for everyone to hear.
- Speak slowly enough so that everyone can understand you.
- Make your gestures and facial expressions match your words.
- Change your voice at times, just as when you speak in real life.
- Be prepared to answer questions after your presentation.

**LISTENING TIP**
- Keep your eyes on the presenter, and focus your mind on the ideas.
- Make connections from what you hear to what you already know.
- Take notes. Include questions you want to ask.
- Try to picture the things that are described.

Writing Handbook   **283**

---

## Step 4: Editing *continued*

**Using Proofreading Marks** Explain that proofreading marks are symbols used to correct mistakes found in writing. Using the same symbol helps everyone understand the correction to be made.

Write these sentences with errors on the board. Call on volunteers to use the proofreading symbols.

- *The school is their, near miami.* (spelling, capital)
- *We going on a field trip Today.* (add, small letter)
- *We're leaving a a day later* (take out, period)

## Step 5: Producing, Publishing, and Presenting

**Running Class Presentations** Outline the structure of the session at the start by telling when and how long the presentations will be. You may want to use the checklist from Unit 2 to guide students on speaking/listening conduct.

**Evaluations** Use a form for evaluations that students review as they prepare to share their work. This form will also help to establish a focus for feedback.

**Digital Integration** Encourage students to think of ways to use social media before or after a presentation, especially if you have a classroom site. Students may share what they are planning to produce, and ask for feedback on one or two specific things they want help with.

**Speaking and Listening Presentation** Review rules for listening and giving feedback:

1. Listen actively to others with care and respect.

2. Ask questions after—not during—a presentation.

3. Focus on the content of the presentation.

4. Speak one at a time. No yelling or interrupting.

5. Be aware of word choice, tone, and gestures that could make the presenter feel criticized.

### Assignment: Digital Presentation

Encourage students to use digital technology to present and publish their work. They can publish in digital formats, such as a slide show, complete with music and video. Students could read their work aloud in a video conference to another class or make digital recordings of their readings. Tablet users can use apps to create eBooks. A group of students could work on a class eBook anthology of student writing.

# Glossary

## What should students know about using glossaries, dictionaries, and other reference materials to learn words?

## How to Use the Glossary

This glossary is a cumulative list of the boldfaced Words to Know from the reading selections. The definitions reflect the words' meanings as they are used in those selections. The glossary is intended as a quick reference for students. To find parts of speech, pronunciations, word origins, and alternative definitions, students should consult a print or online dictionary.

## Guided Instruction

Make sure students understand that a glossary is an alphabetical list of words with definitions that appears at the end of a book, usually a nonfiction book or textbook. Point out that the purpose of a glossary is to provide the spellings and definitions of key words used in the book. Help students understand the connection between this glossary and the Words to Know by directing them to open their books to page 12. Ask students to identify the first of the Words to Know—*condition*. Then have them search for the word in the glossary (page 284). Ask a volunteer to read aloud the word's definition. Repeat the process with another Word to Know from the same or a different page.

Then compare the glossary to a dictionary. Explain that dictionaries include pronunciations, parts of speech, word origins, and all the meanings of the word. Show students a dictionary entry for the word *condition* and have them compare and contrast it to the glossary entry.

Encourage students to create a word log as they read the selections in the Student Book. Have them write each word and its meaning after checking the glossary. Encourage them to then consult a print or online dictionary for more information, such as the word's pronunciation, its various parts of speech, and additional meanings.

---

## GLOSSARY

### A

**abnormal** strange; weird

**absorb** to take in something; suck up

**adapted** changed to fit a new situation

**admiring** looking at something with enjoyment

**anew** again

**applaud** clap

**approaching** coming closer

**assign** give; appoint

**asteroid** space object made of rock

**astronomer** a person who studies the stars and planets

**atmosphere** the layer of air that surrounds Earth

### B

**bait** food used to catch an animal

**barrier** wall or other structure that blocks off something

**biology** way an animal's body works

**bloodshot** red

**bond** connection; attachment

**bragging** boasting; being conceited

### C

**cactus** a plant with thick stems and sharp thorns

**calculation** the use of math or logic to figure something out

**category** group, class

**cave-in** collapse of a mine tunnel

**Centaur** a mythical creature that is half human, half horse

**centimeter** a small unit of measurement

**chamber** room

**civilization** society; culture

**classification** the placing of similar objects in groups; organization

**cloning** using science to make a copy of a living thing

**comet** an icy object in space that sometimes forms a tail

**commotion** loud noise

**condense** shrink; come together

**condition** the state something or someone is in; situation

**conserving** saving; using less of something

**constellation** a group of stars that seems to make a picture

**constructed** built

**contaminated** dirty or unhealthy

**continent** giant landmass such as North America, Asia, or Australia

**core** center

**crater** hole; hollow

**crew** team; staff

**culture** a group's way of life and beliefs

---

## GLOSSARY

### D

**dangerous** something that can be harmful

**debris** broken pieces; trash

**demonstration** example; showing

**despair** hopelessness; sadness

**destroy** knock down; wreck

**devastating** causing terrible harm

**diameter** the distance across a circle or sphere

**digestive system** system in the body that processes food

**disaster** terrible event

**DNA** genes

**dominated** ruled over; controlled

**dwarf planet** a space object smaller than a planet and bigger than an asteroid

### E

**ellipsis** an oval shape

**embarrassed** made self-conscious

**endangered** rare; in danger of vanishing

**enormous** huge

**environment** nature; surrounding area

**evaluate** examine and make a decision

**evidence** proof; facts

**excavate** dig up

**excess** extra

**exhibit** display; show

**expedition** a group of explorers

**expert** skilled and knowledgeable

**exploration** discovery

**expression** look on someone's face

**extinct** when a species of plant or animal is no longer alive

### F

**focused** paying attention to; concentrated

### G

**gravitational pull** the pull of an object's gravity on another object

**gravity** the pull each object has on another object; larger objects have stronger gravity

**grief** great sadness; heartache

### H

**hammock** a sling bed, often made of net

**hatchling** baby bird

**healthy** well and strong

**hinge** attachment that allows something, such as a door, to bend or open

## GLOSSARY

**I**

**imperiously** bossily, commandingly
**instructor** teacher
**interfere** get in the way
**interior** inner, inside
**intervened** stepped in to take action
**invention** coming up with new ideas
**investigate** look into something
**invisible** when something can't be seen
**irrigation** watering
**isolated** alone

**J**

**judging** making a decision

**L**

**labor** work
**lay claim** assert a right to or ownership of something
**levee** a ridge or wall along a river to stop flooding
**log book** notebook that contains a list or record of activities

**M**

**mammoth** extinct hairy elephant
**massive** huge
**mature** grown-up; adult
**mnemonic** a clue to help you remember something
**mobility** ability to move around

**mummy** a dried body wrapped in bandages
**murmur** whisper; hum of voices

**N**

**nonprofit organization** a business with the goal of helping people, not making money

**O**

**observation** noticing things
**offering** gift given to a god to ask for his or her blessing
**onlooker** person watching
**orbit** path around the sun
**orientation** knowing where you are and how to go
**original** beginning, first
**outdrilled** drilled better than
**outrage** great anger
**outskirts** edges, borders, limits

**P**

**prairie** grassy plains
**precious** valuable, often also hard to find
**precise** careful, detailed
**predict** guess what will happen next
**prehistoric** happening before written history; ancient
**preserved** kept carefully; protected

## GLOSSARY

**proportion** true importance or size; to blow something out of proportion is to make it a bigger deal than it is
**prospect** possibility; idea
**proteins** important, tiny parts of plants and animals

**R**

**react** respond; act
**reflecting telescope** an instrument that uses mirrors to look at faraway objects
**refracting telescope** an instrument that uses lenses to look at faraway objects
**review** look over again
**royal** belonging to a king or queen
**ruins** old, fallen-down buildings and towns

**S**

**sandbar** a ridge of sand in a river or lake
**sarcophagus** a kind of coffin
**separated** taken away from each other
**severe** strong; terrible
**skeleton** bone structure inside an animal's body
**snowmelt** water from melting snow
**solar system** the system of the sun and the planets and other orbiting objects
**specialist** an expert in a certain field
**spirit** attitude; quality; essence
**spotlight** attention; time on stage
**stealthy** quiet and sneaky

**steam-powered** run by steam instead of electricity or human power
**strum** to run a hand over strings on a musical instrument
**sulked** pouted; got in a bad mood
**suspense** anxious waiting
**swooped** flew suddenly; pounced
**system** arrangement, organization

**T**

**theory** idea about how or why something happened
**tilted** slightly turned
**tombs** graves; places where people are buried
**tradition** custom; something that has been done the same way for generations
**treasure** value greatly; find very important

**U**

**ultimate** greatest; best possible
**universe** everything that exists in space
**university** college

**V**

**vapor** mist; haze
**vein** line of mineral through rock

**W**

**wildfire** fire that burns wild land
**wildlife** wild animals

## Guided Practice

Extend the comparison between this glossary and dictionaries by having students participate in a word scavenger hunt. Place students in teams of three. Then randomly assign each team three words from the glossary (pages 284–287). Tell teammates to divide up the words and complete the following tasks:

• Locate the word and its specific meaning in the glossary.

• Use a dictionary to find the word's part(s) of speech, origins, and at least one alternative meaning.

• Record one or two interesting additional facts about the word, such as original meaning(s), multiple meanings, spelling peculiarities, and so on.

Assign bonus points to the team that provides the most information about its words accurately. As a class, discuss each team's findings.

## Independent Practice

Have students meet in small homogeneous groups to conduct informal spelling bees. One student in each group should begin by choosing a word from the glossary and saying it aloud. Another teammate then volunteers to spell it. If that student spells the word correctly, he or she then gets to select the next word for another teammate to spell. Each teammate should have an opportunity to choose and spell a word. Misspelled words should be added to students' word logs. Each group should have access to a print or online dictionary to aid with pronunciations.

# INDEX